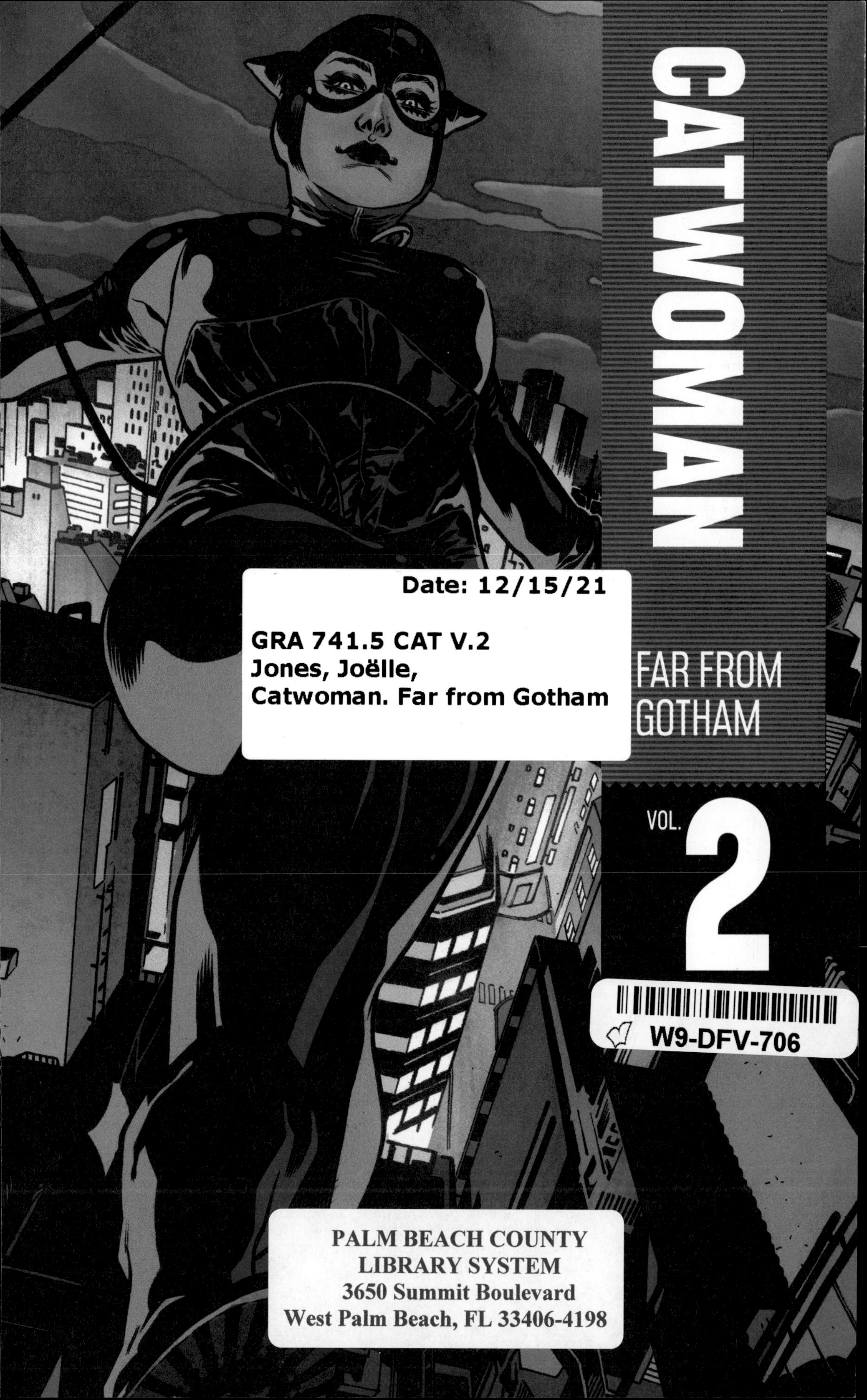
CATWOMAN
FAR FROM GOTHAM
VOL. 2

# CATWOMAN
## FAR FROM GOTHAM

writers
**JOËLLE JONES
RAM V**

artists
**FERNANDO BLANCO
ELENA CASAGRANDE
JOHN TIMMS
SCOTT GODLEWSKI
HUGO PETRUS
JOËLLE JONES
LE BEAU UNDERWOOD**

colorists
**JOHN KALISZ
JOHN TIMMS
JORDIE BELLAIRE
LAURA ALLRED**

letterers
**SAIDA TEMOFONTE
JOSH REED**

collection cover artists
**JOËLLE JONES & LAURA ALLRED**

SUPERMAN created by JERRY SIEGEL and JOE SHUSTER
By special arrangement with the Jerry Siegel family

VOL.
# 2

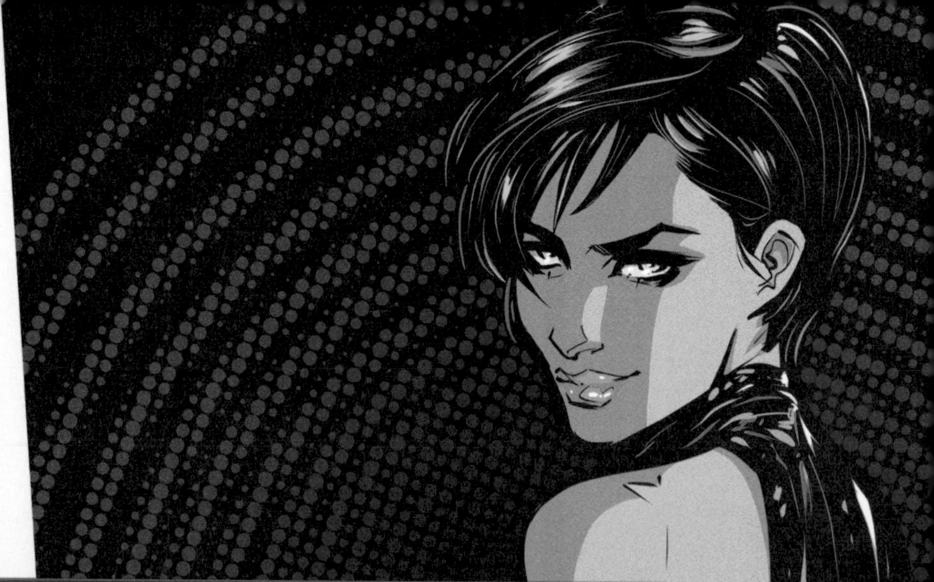

**JAMIE S. RICH** Editor – Original Series
**BRITTANY HOLZHERR**
**HARVEY RICHARDS** Associate Editors – Original Series
**JEB WOODARD** Group Editor – Collected Editions
**ROBIN WILDMAN** Editor – Collected Edition
**STEVE COOK** Design Director – Books
**MONIQUE NARBONETA** Publication Design
**ERIN VANOVER** Publication Production

**BOB HARRAS** Senior VP – Editor-in-Chief, DC Comics
**PAT McCALLUM** Executive Editor, DC Comics

**DAN DiDIO** Publisher
**JIM LEE** Publisher & Chief Creative Officer
**BOBBIE CHASE** VP – New Publishing Initiatives & Talent Development
**DON FALLETTI** VP – Manufacturing Operations & Workflow Management
**LAWRENCE GANEM** VP – Talent Services
**ALISON GILL** Senior VP – Manufacturing & Operations
**HANK KANALZ** Senior VP – Publishing Strategy & Support Services
**DAN MIRON** VP – Publishing Operations
**NICK J. NAPOLITANO** VP – Manufacturing Administration & Design
**NANCY SPEARS** VP – Sales
**MICHELE R. WELLS** VP & Executive Editor, Young Reader

CATWOMAN VOL. 2: FAR FROM GOTHAM



DC Comics, 2900 West Alameda Ave., Burbank, CA 91505
Printed by LSC Communications, Owensville, MO, USA. 8/2/19. First Printing.
ISBN: 978-1-4012-9477-9

Library of Congress Cataloging-in-Publication Data is available.

PEFC Certified
This product is from sustainably managed forests and controlled sources
PEFC/29-31-337
www.pefc.org

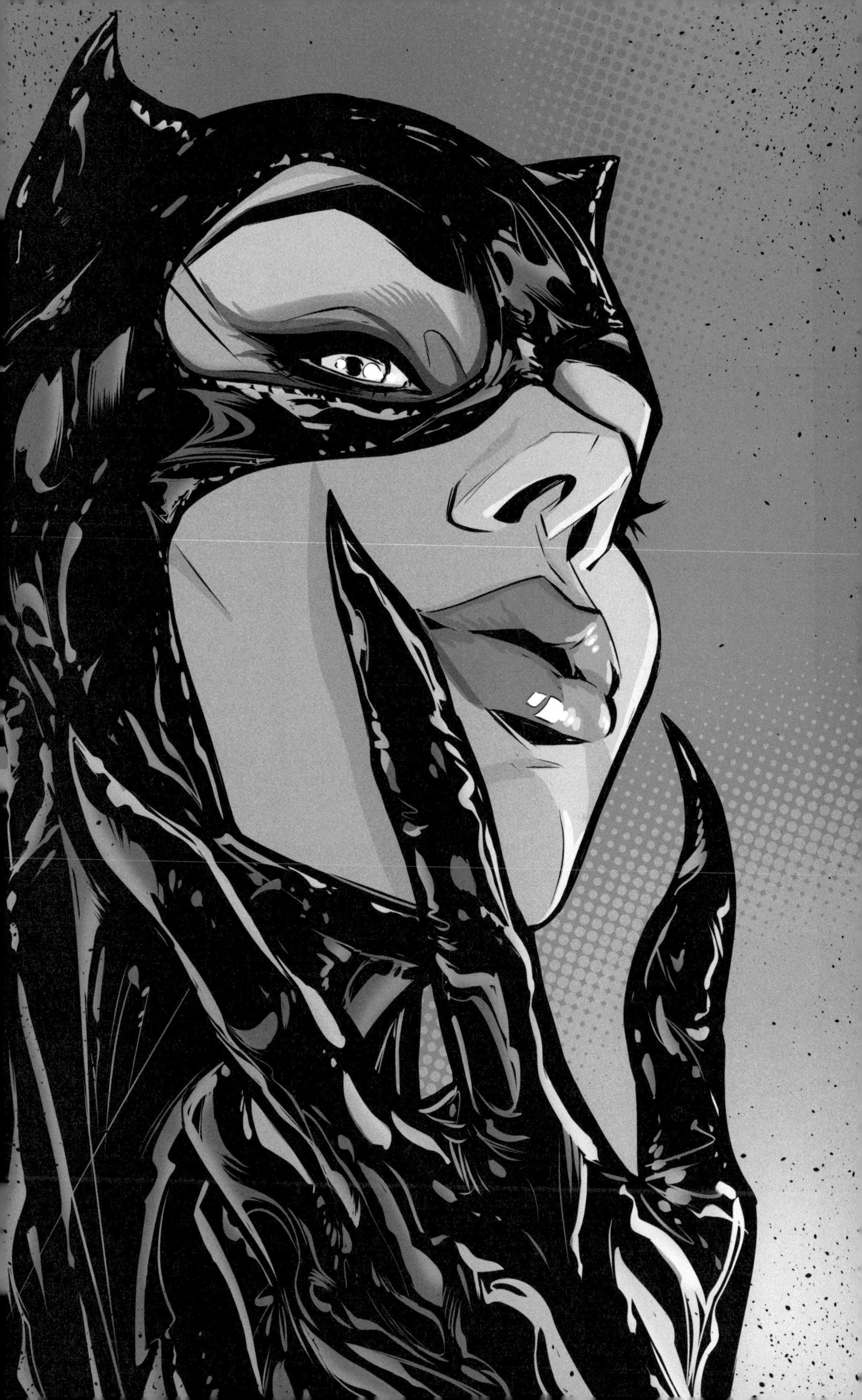

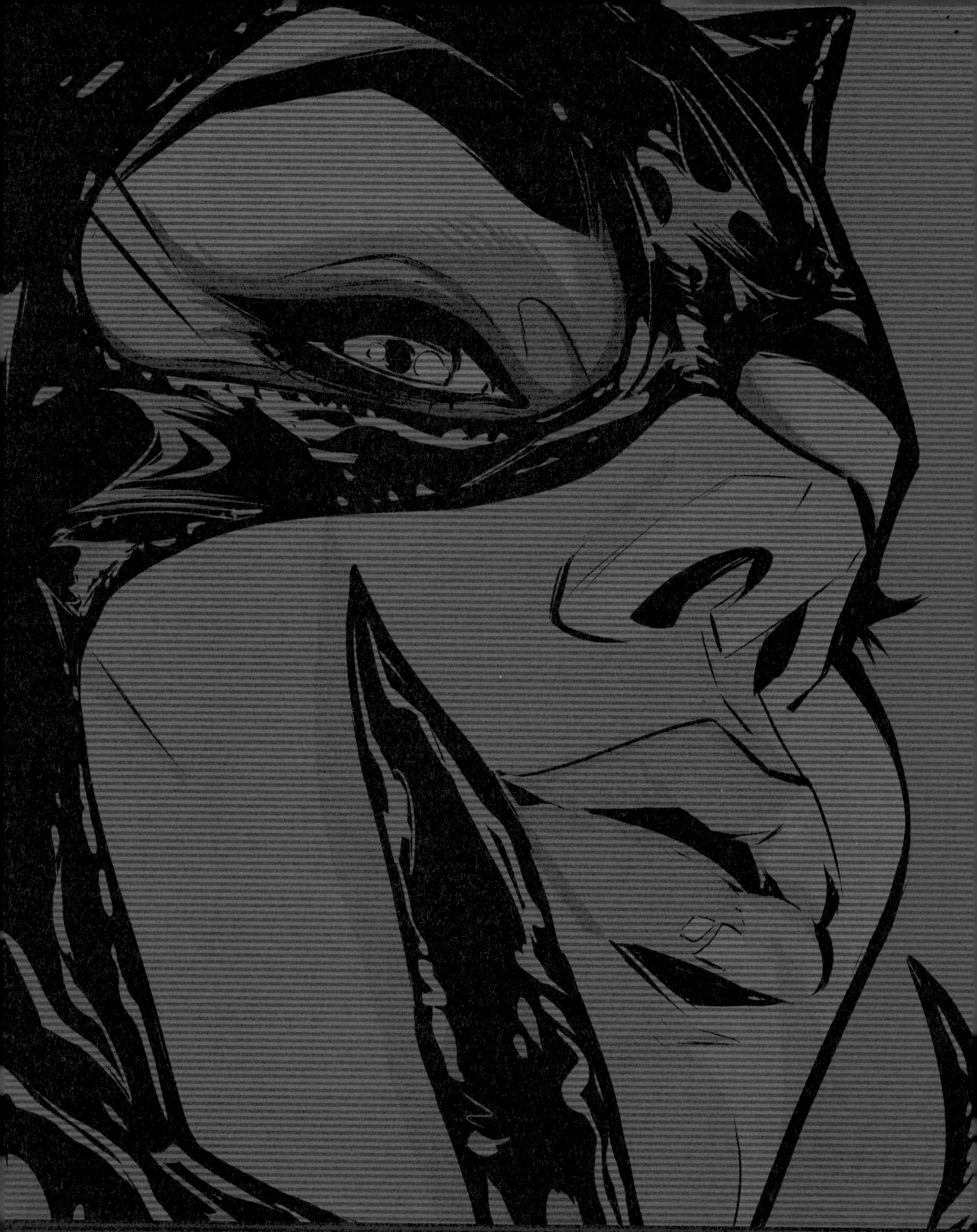

# CATWOMAN
#7

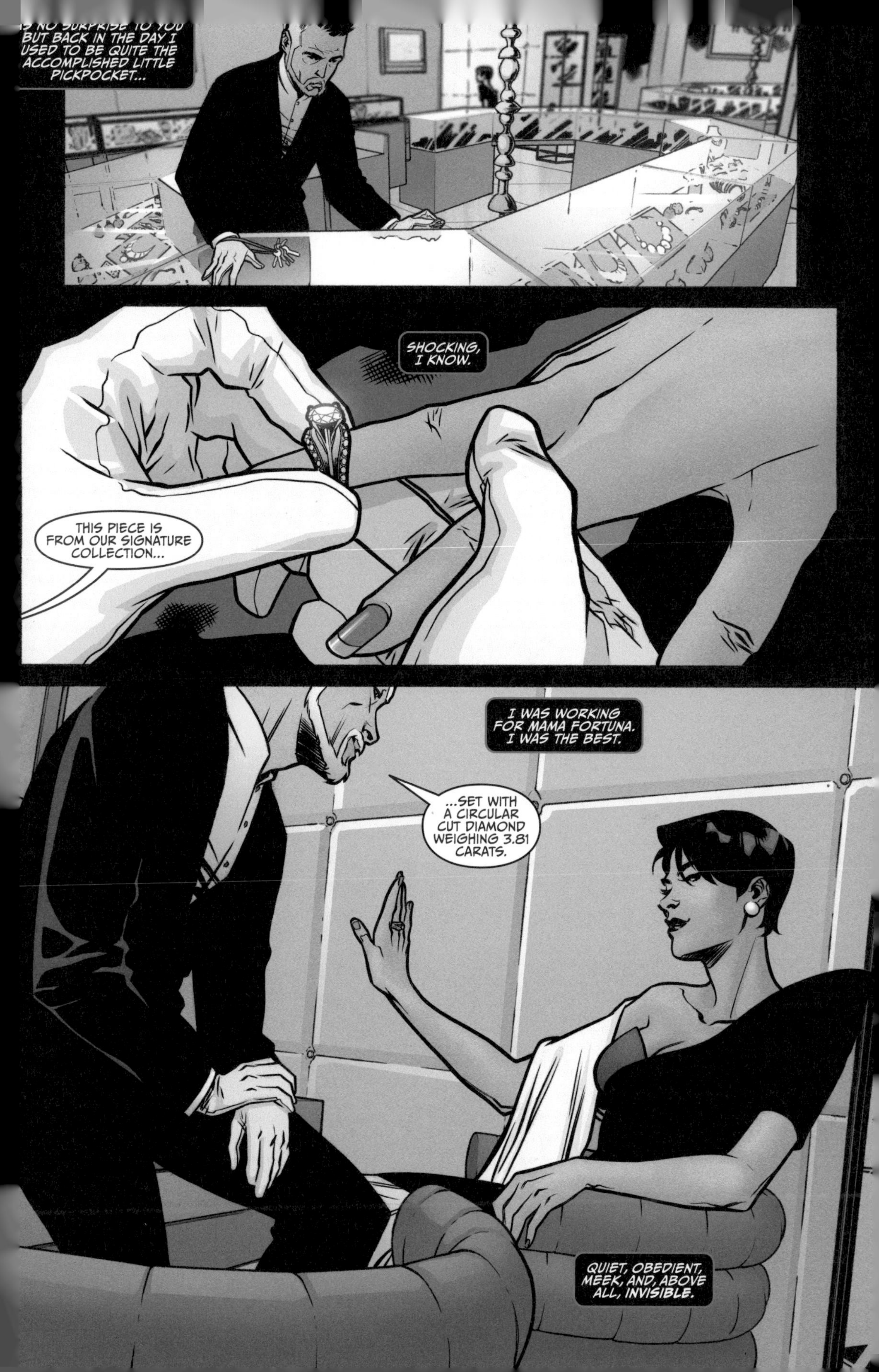
NO SURPRISE TO YOU BUT BACK IN THE DAY I USED TO BE QUITE THE ACCOMPLISHED LITTLE PICKPOCKET...
SHOCKING, I KNOW.
THIS PIECE IS FROM OUR SIGNATURE COLLECTION...
I WAS WORKING FOR MAMA FORTUNA. I WAS THE BEST.
...SET WITH A CIRCULAR CUT DIAMOND WEIGHING 3.81 CARATS.
QUIET, OBEDIENT, MEEK, AND, ABOVE ALL, INVISIBLE.

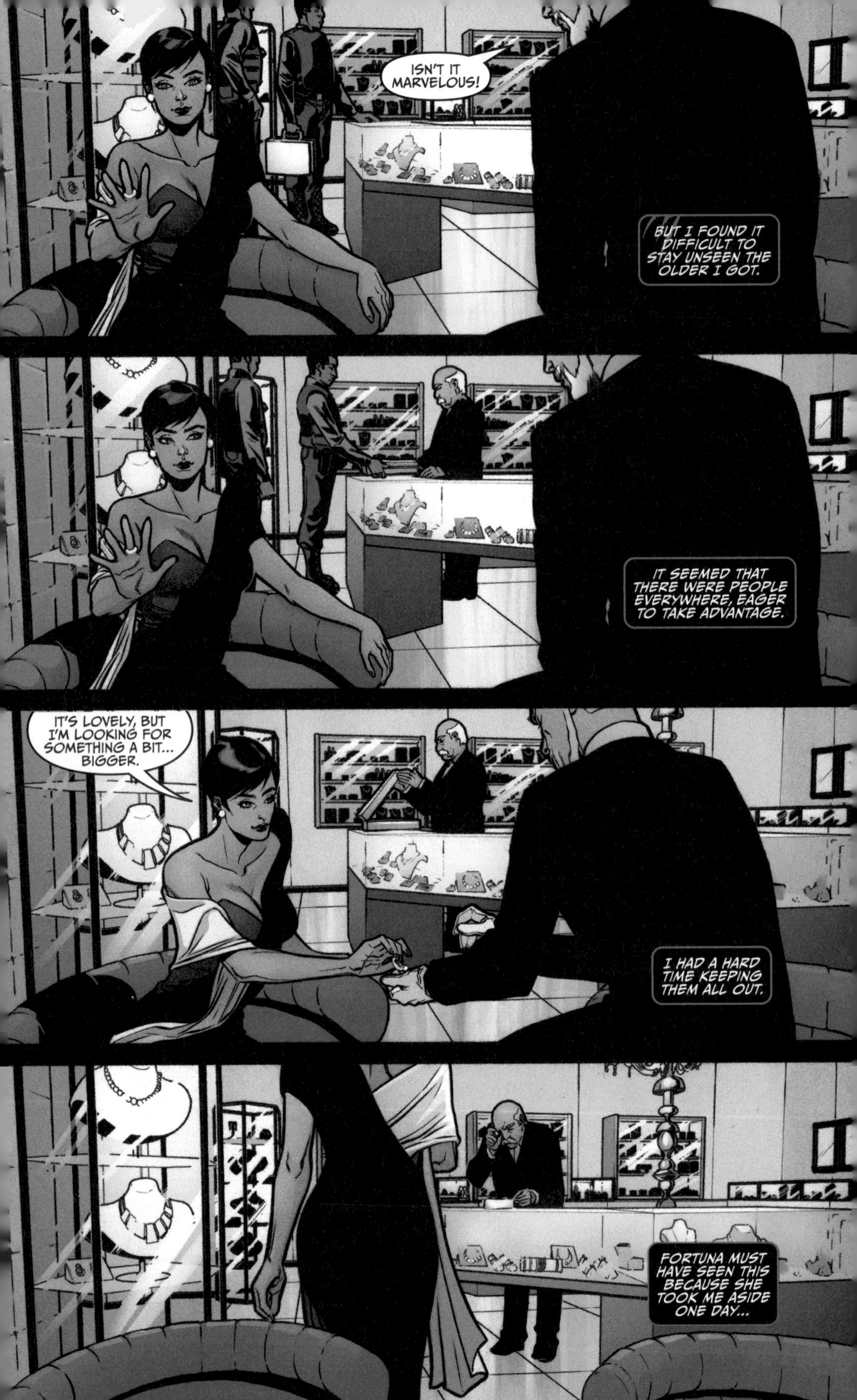
ISN'T IT MARVELOUS!
BUT I FOUND IT DIFFICULT TO STAY UNSEEN THE OLDER I GOT.
IT SEEMED THAT THERE WERE PEOPLE EVERYWHERE, EAGER TO TAKE ADVANTAGE.
IT'S LOVELY, BUT I'M LOOKING FOR SOMETHING A BIT... BIGGER.
I HAD A HARD TIME KEEPING THEM ALL OUT.
FORTUNA MUST HAVE SEEN THIS BECAUSE SHE TOOK ME ASIDE ONE DAY...

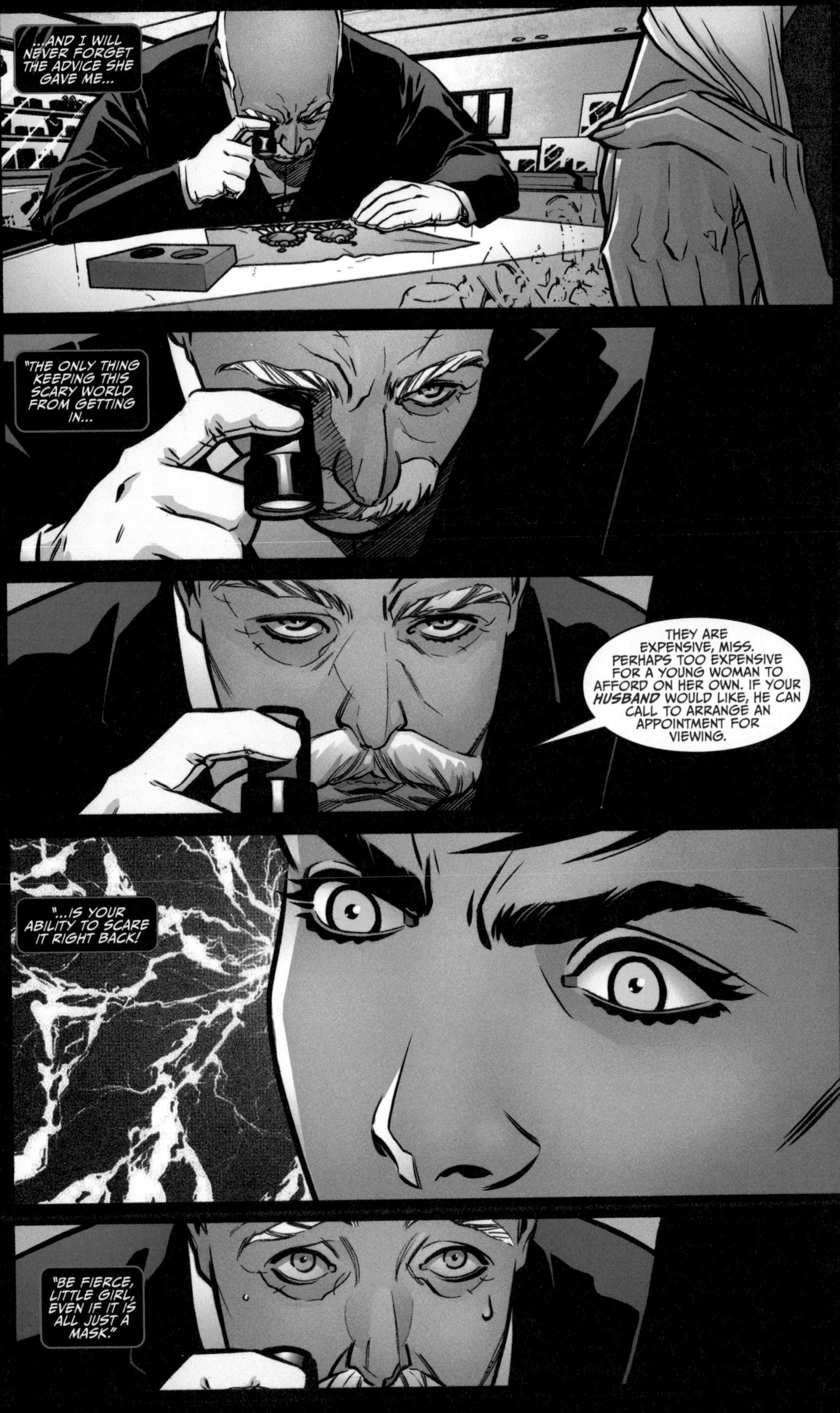
...AND I WILL NEVER FORGET THE ADVICE SHE GAVE ME...
"THE ONLY THING KEEPING THIS SCARY WORLD FROM GETTING IN...
THEY ARE EXPENSIVE, MISS. PERHAPS TOO EXPENSIVE FOR A YOUNG WOMAN TO AFFORD ON HER OWN. IF YOUR HUSBAND WOULD LIKE, HE CAN CALL TO ARRANGE AN APPOINTMENT FOR VIEWING.
"...IS YOUR ABILITY TO SCARE IT RIGHT BACK!
"BE FIERCE, LITTLE GIRL, EVEN IF IT IS ALL JUST A MASK."

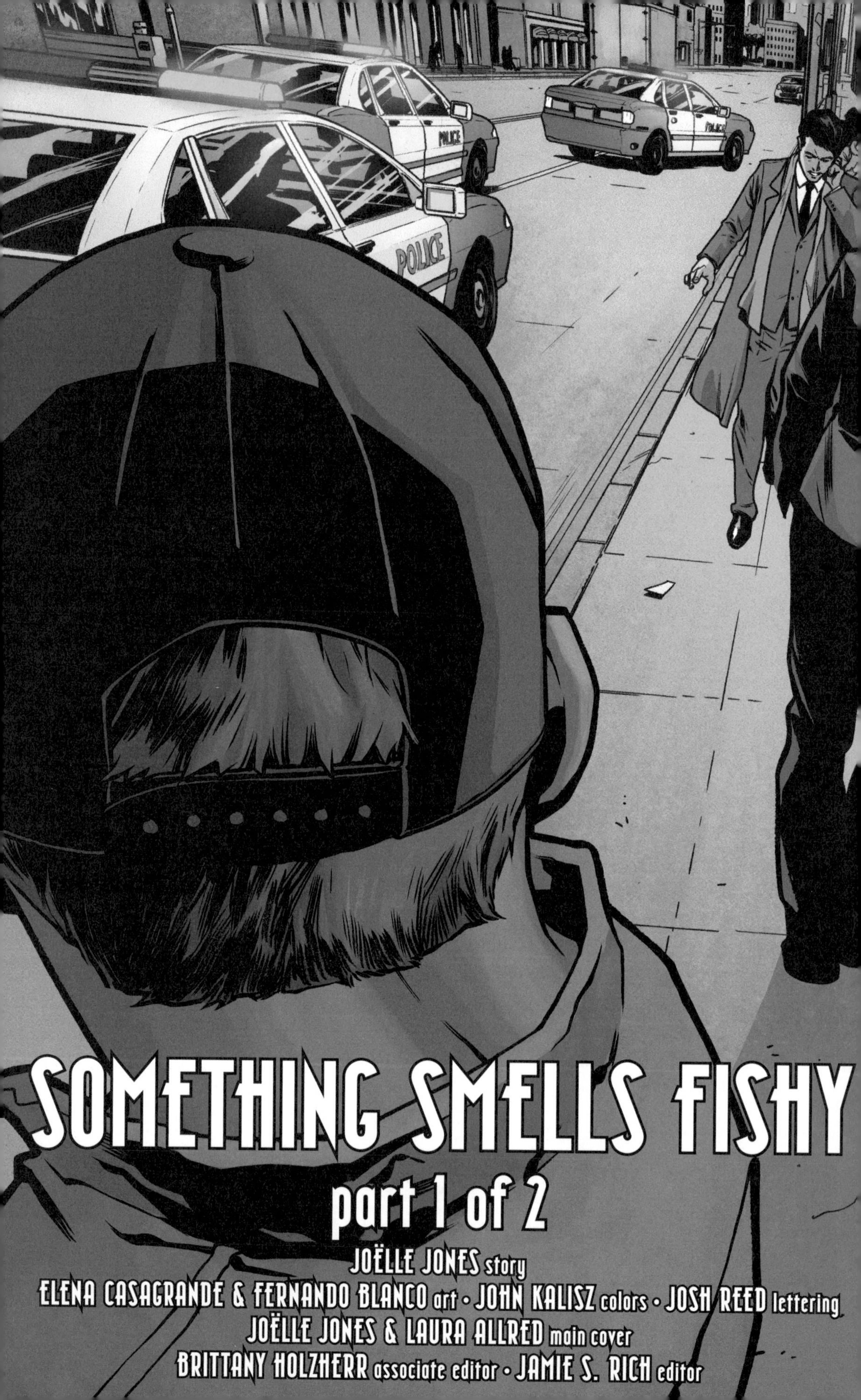
POLICE
POLICE
POLICE
SOMETHING SMELLS FISHY
part 1 of 2
JOËLLE JONES story
ELENA CASAGRANDE & FERNANDO BLANCO art • JOHN KALISZ colors • JOSH REED lettering
JOËLLE JONES & LAURA ALLRED main cover
BRITTANY HOLZHERR associate editor • JAMIE S. RICH editor

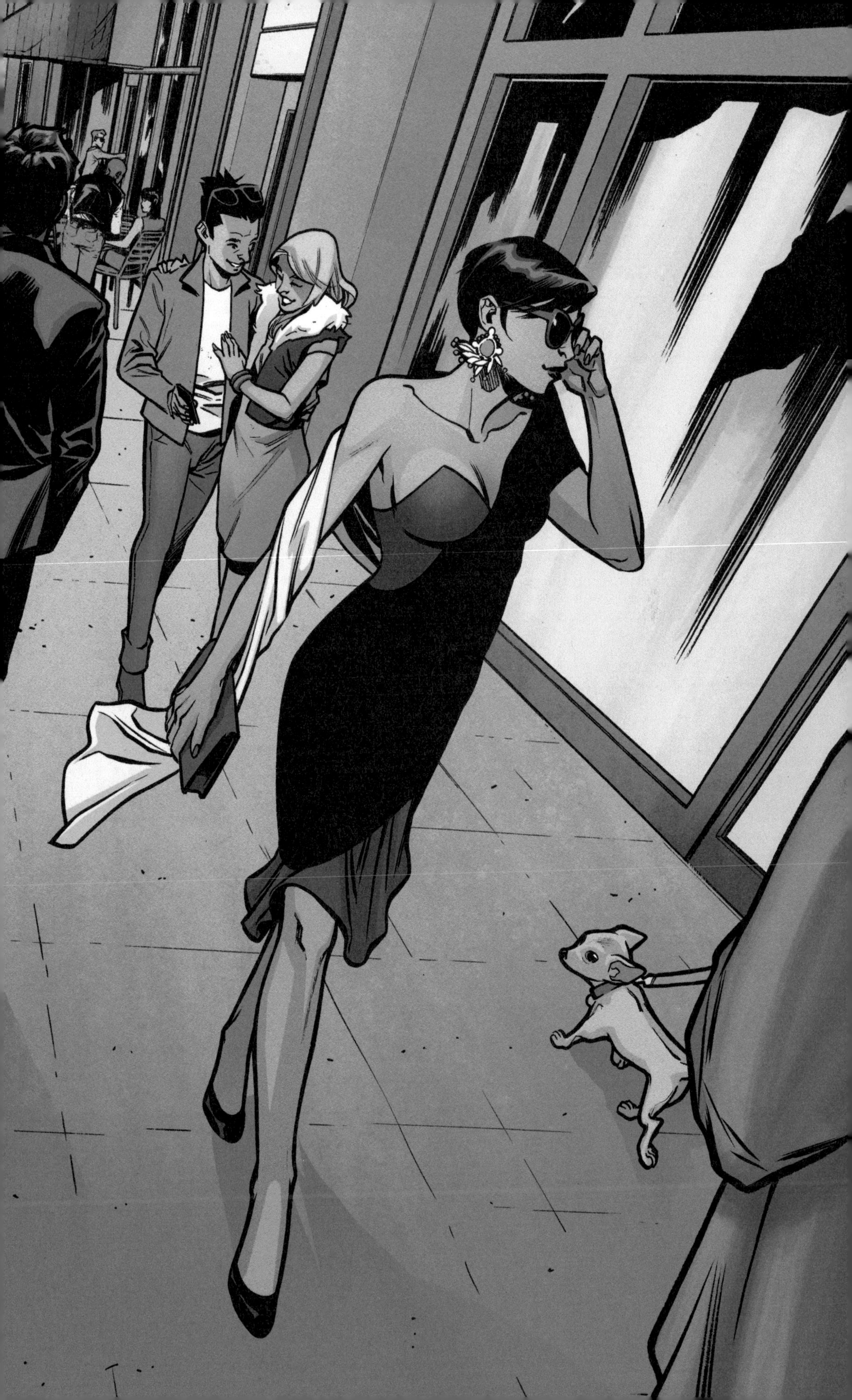

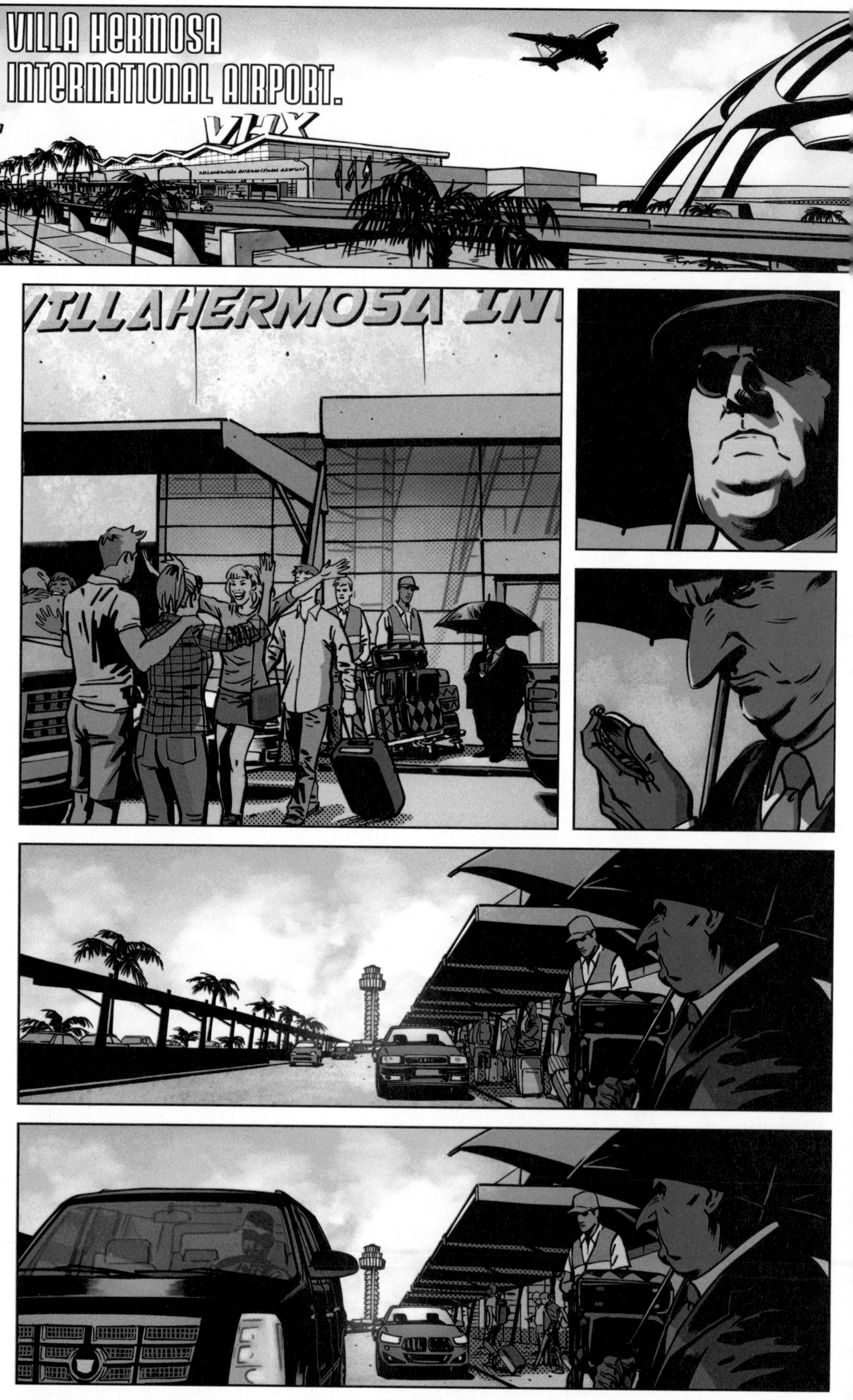
VILLA HERMOSA
INTERNATIONAL AIRPORT.
VHX
VILLAHERMOSA

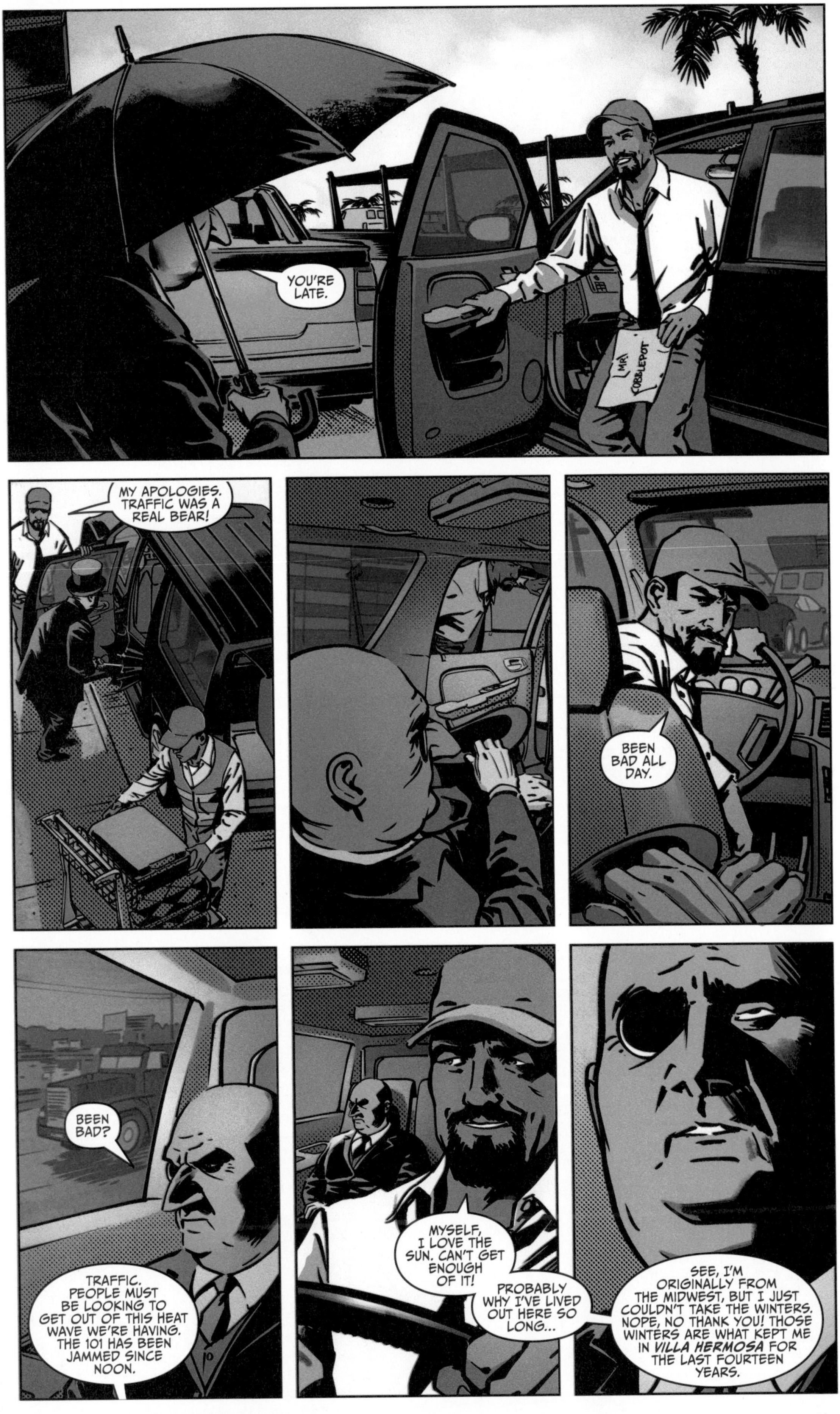
YOU'RE LATE.
MR. COBBLEPOT
MY APOLOGIES. TRAFFIC WAS A REAL BEAR!
BEEN BAD ALL DAY.
BEEN BAD?
TRAFFIC. PEOPLE MUST BE LOOKING TO GET OUT OF THIS HEAT WAVE WE'RE HAVING. THE 101 HAS BEEN JAMMED SINCE NOON.
MYSELF, I LOVE THE SUN. CAN'T GET ENOUGH OF IT!
PROBABLY WHY I'VE LIVED OUT HERE SO LONG...
SEE, I'M ORIGINALLY FROM THE MIDWEST, BUT I JUST COULDN'T TAKE THE WINTERS. NOPE, NO THANK YOU! THOSE WINTERS ARE WHAT KEPT ME IN *VILLA HERMOSA* FOR THE LAST FOURTEEN YEARS.

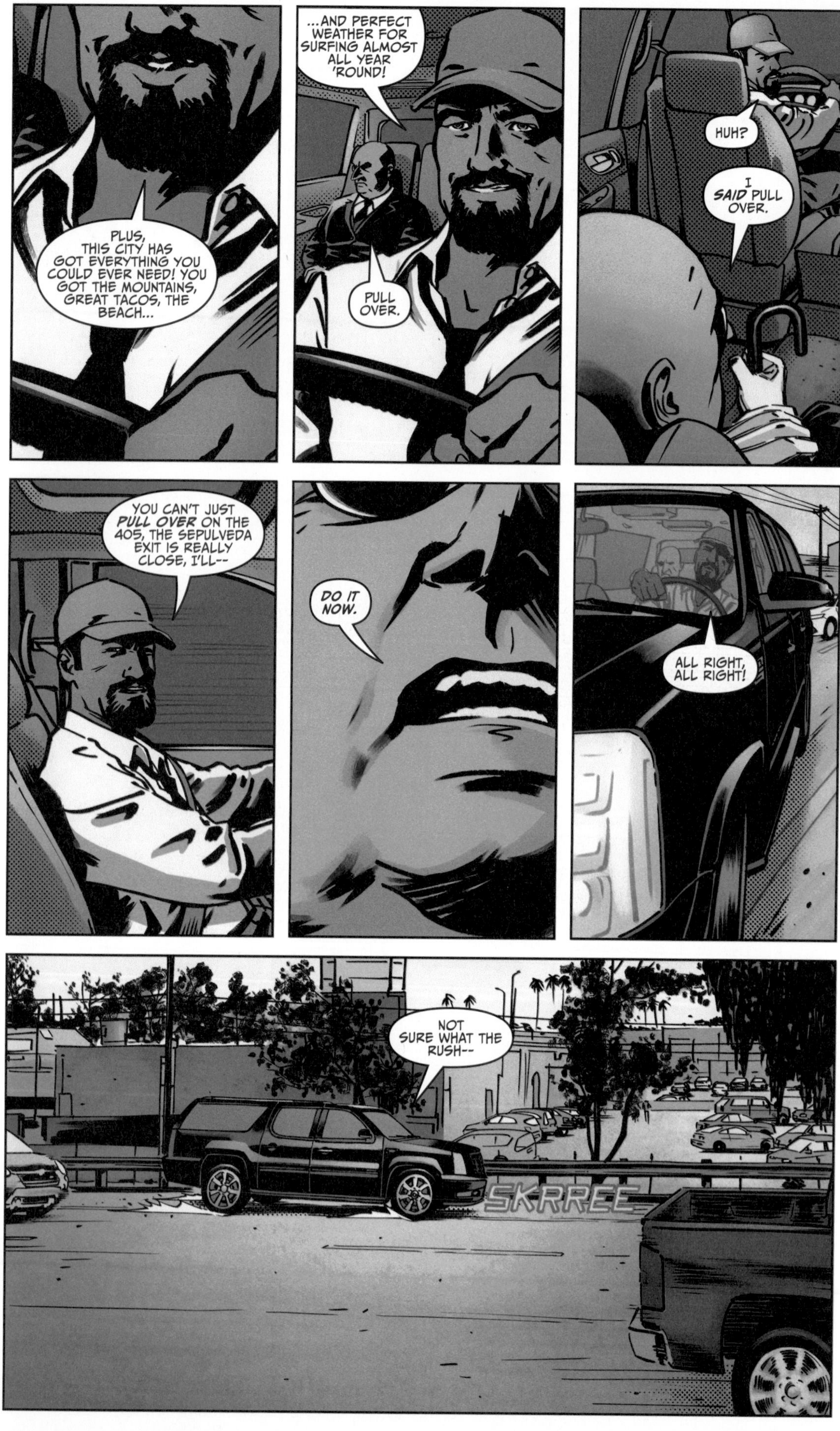
PLUS, THIS CITY HAS GOT EVERYTHING YOU COULD EVER NEED! YOU GOT THE MOUNTAINS, GREAT TACOS, THE BEACH...
...AND PERFECT WEATHER FOR SURFING ALMOST ALL YEAR 'ROUND!
PULL OVER.
HUH?
I SAID PULL OVER.
YOU CAN'T JUST PULL OVER ON THE 405, THE SEPULVEDA EXIT IS REALLY CLOSE, I'LL--
DO IT NOW.
ALL RIGHT, ALL RIGHT!
NOT SURE WHAT THE RUSH--
SKRREE

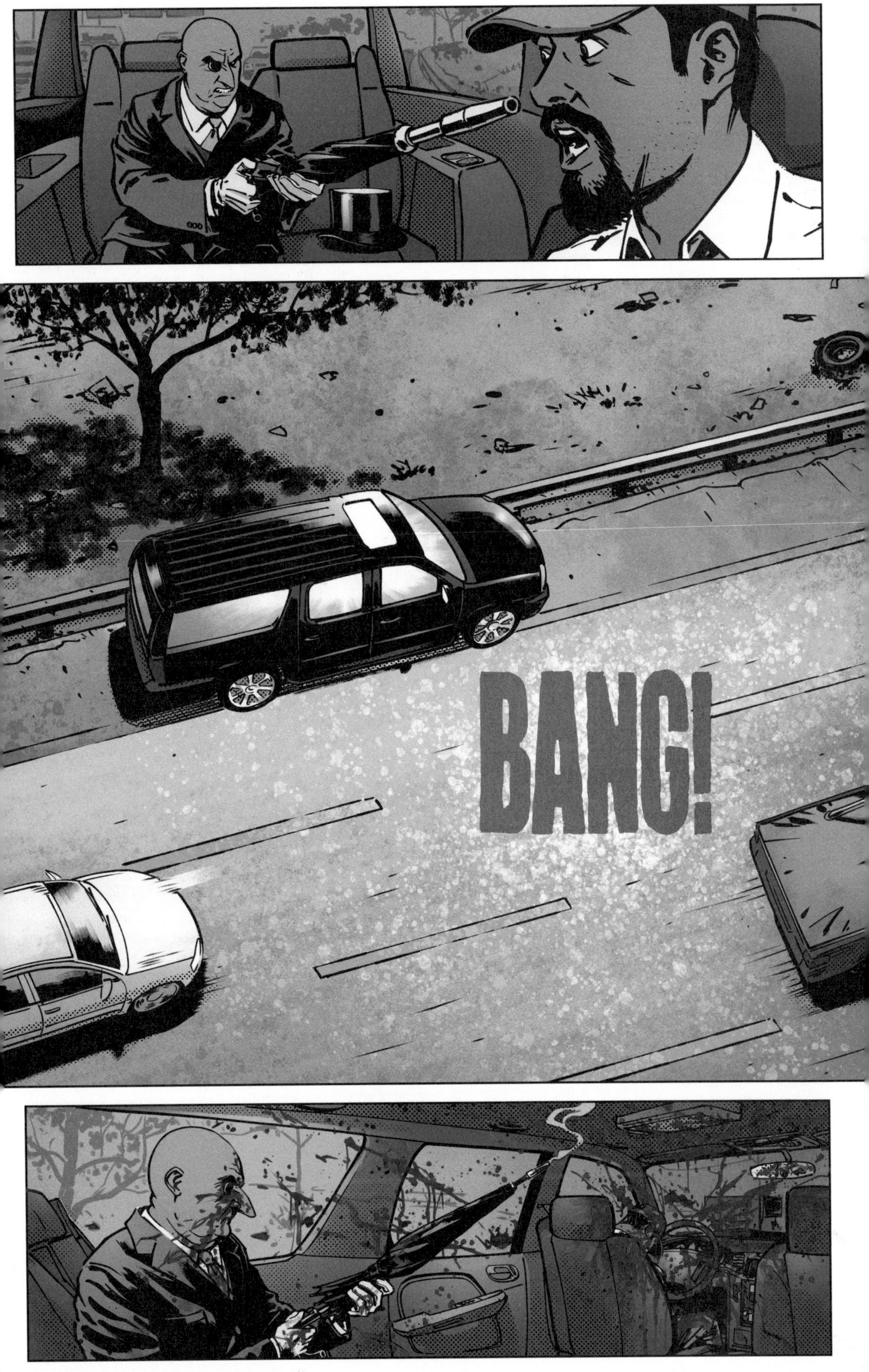
BANG!

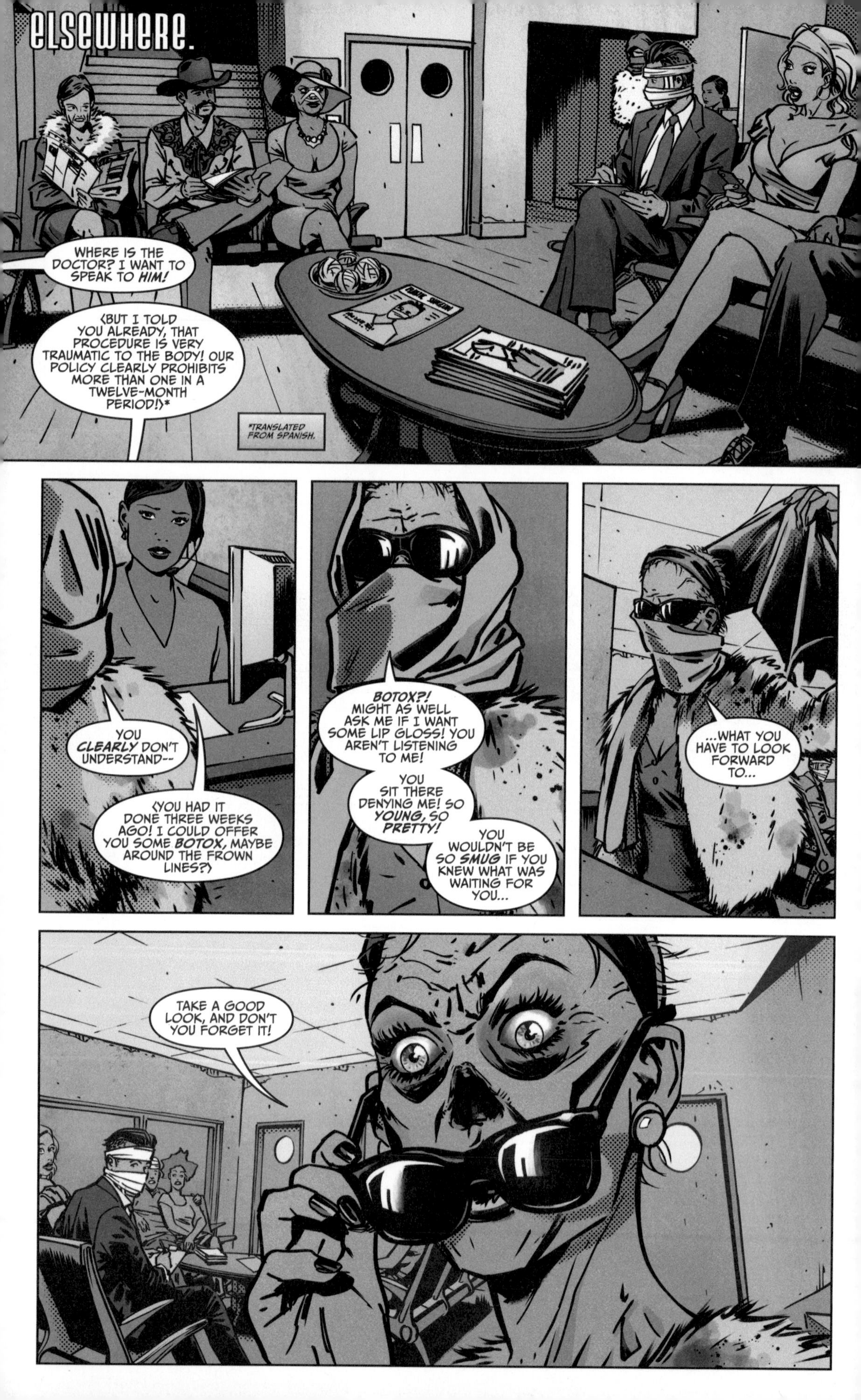
ELSEWHERE.
WHERE IS THE DOCTOR? I WANT TO SPEAK TO *HIM!*
‹BUT I TOLD YOU ALREADY, THAT PROCEDURE IS VERY TRAUMATIC TO THE BODY! OUR POLICY CLEARLY PROHIBITS MORE THAN ONE IN A TWELVE-MONTH PERIOD!›*
*TRANSLATED FROM SPANISH.
YOU *CLEARLY* DON'T UNDERSTAND--
‹YOU HAD IT DONE THREE WEEKS AGO! I COULD OFFER YOU SOME *BOTOX*, MAYBE AROUND THE FROWN LINES?›
*BOTOX?!* MIGHT AS WELL ASK ME IF I WANT SOME LIP GLOSS! YOU AREN'T LISTENING TO ME!
YOU SIT THERE DENYING ME! SO *YOUNG*, SO *PRETTY!*
YOU WOULDN'T BE SO *SMUG* IF YOU KNEW WHAT WAS WAITING FOR YOU...
...WHAT YOU HAVE TO LOOK FORWARD TO...
TAKE A GOOD LOOK, AND DON'T YOU FORGET IT!

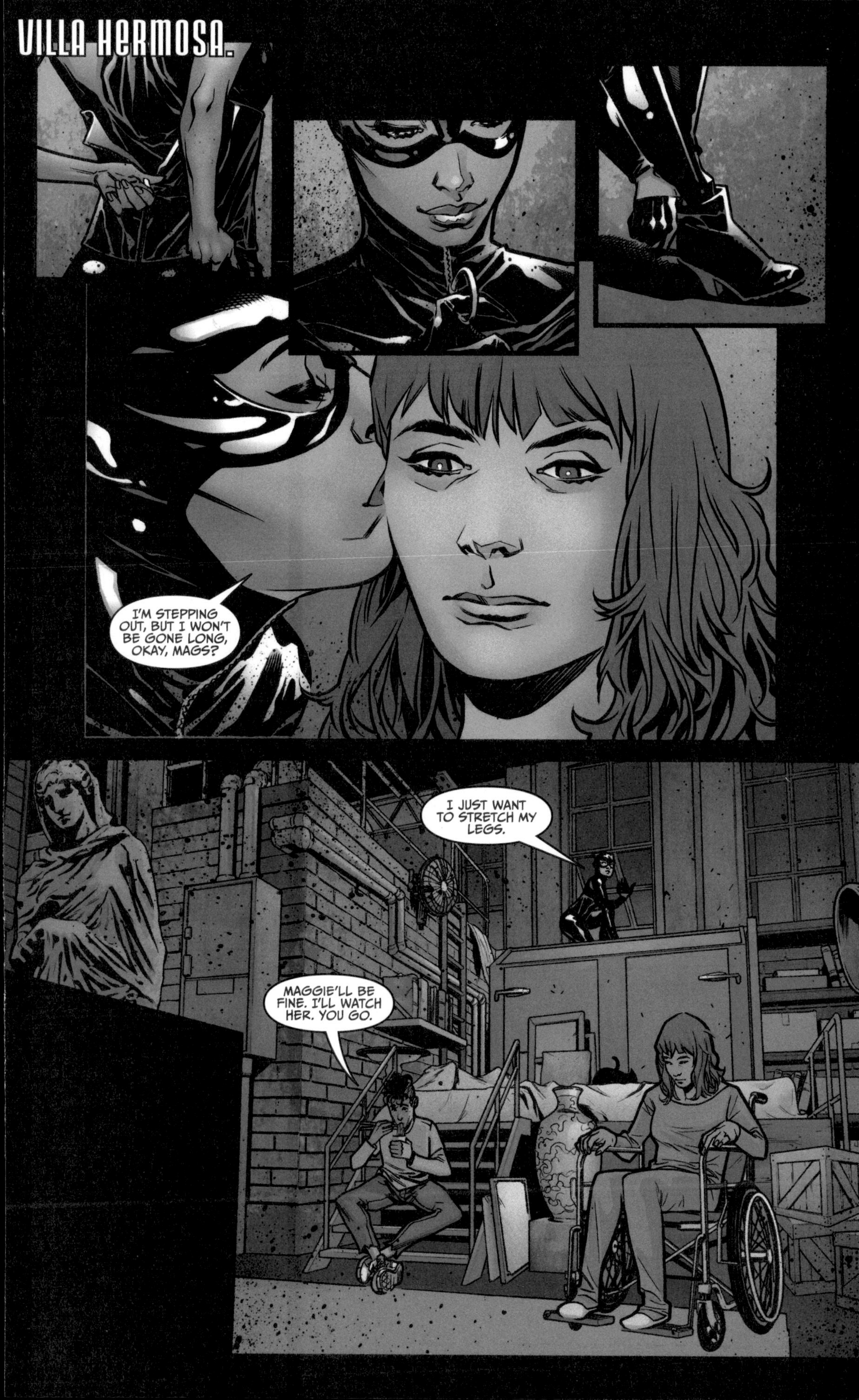
VILLA HERMOSA.
I'M STEPPING OUT, BUT I WON'T BE GONE LONG, OKAY, MAGS?
I JUST WANT TO STRETCH MY LEGS.
MAGGIE'LL BE FINE. I'LL WATCH HER. YOU GO.

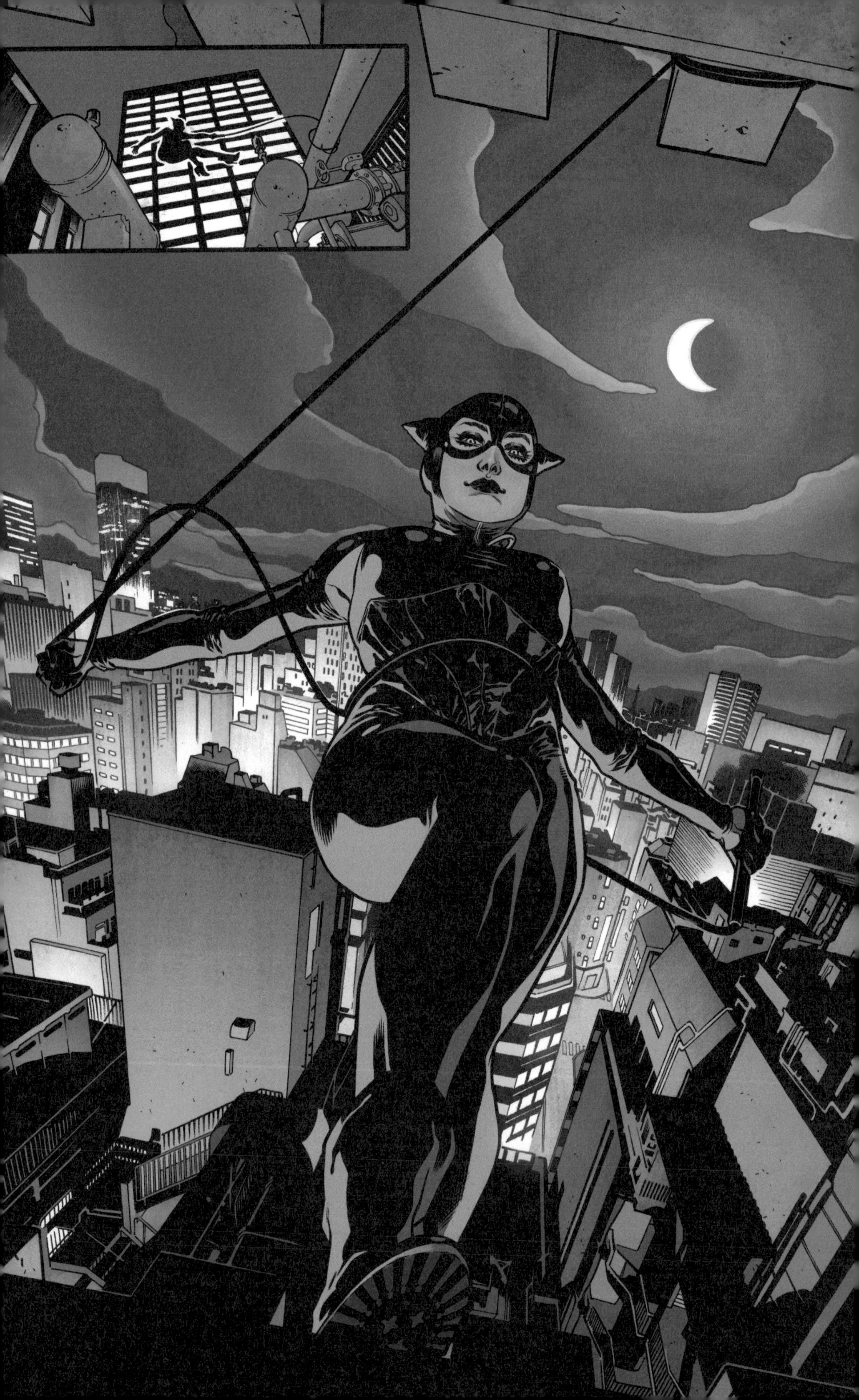

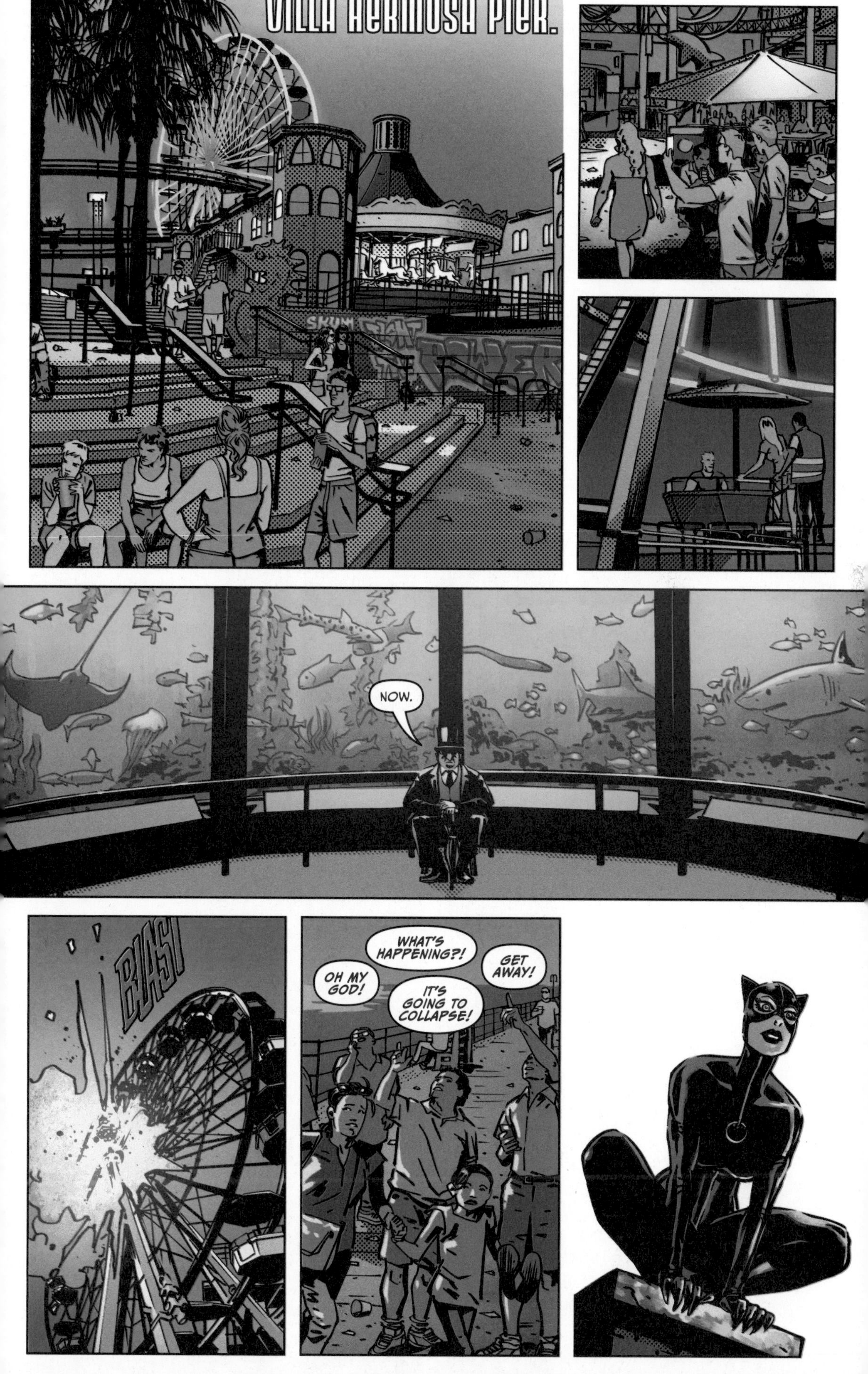
VILLA HERMOSA PIER.
SKUM
NOW.
BLAST
WHAT'S HAPPENING?!
OH MY GOD!
IT'S GOING TO COLLAPSE!
GET AWAY!

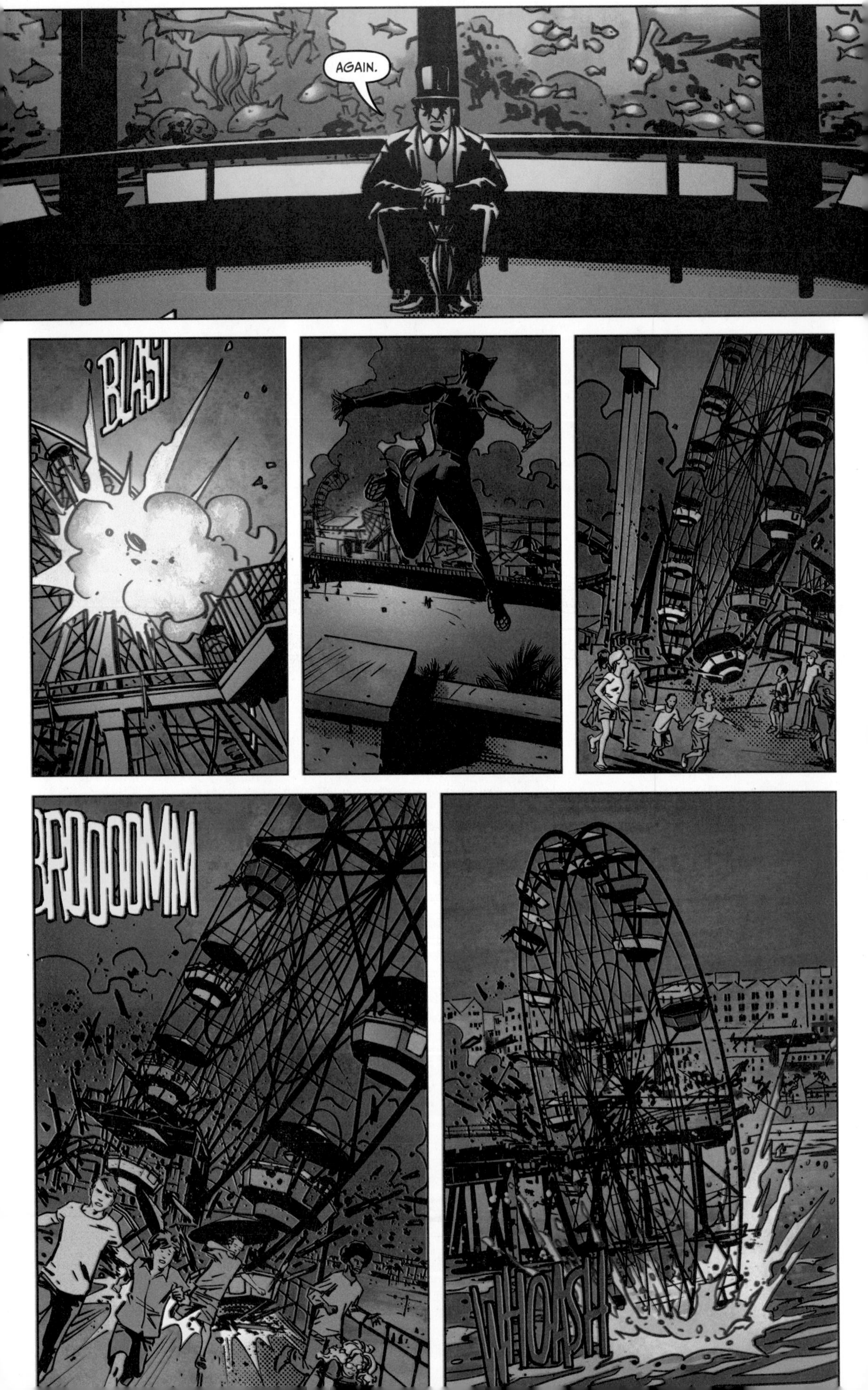
AGAIN.
BLAST
BRDOOOMM
WHOASH

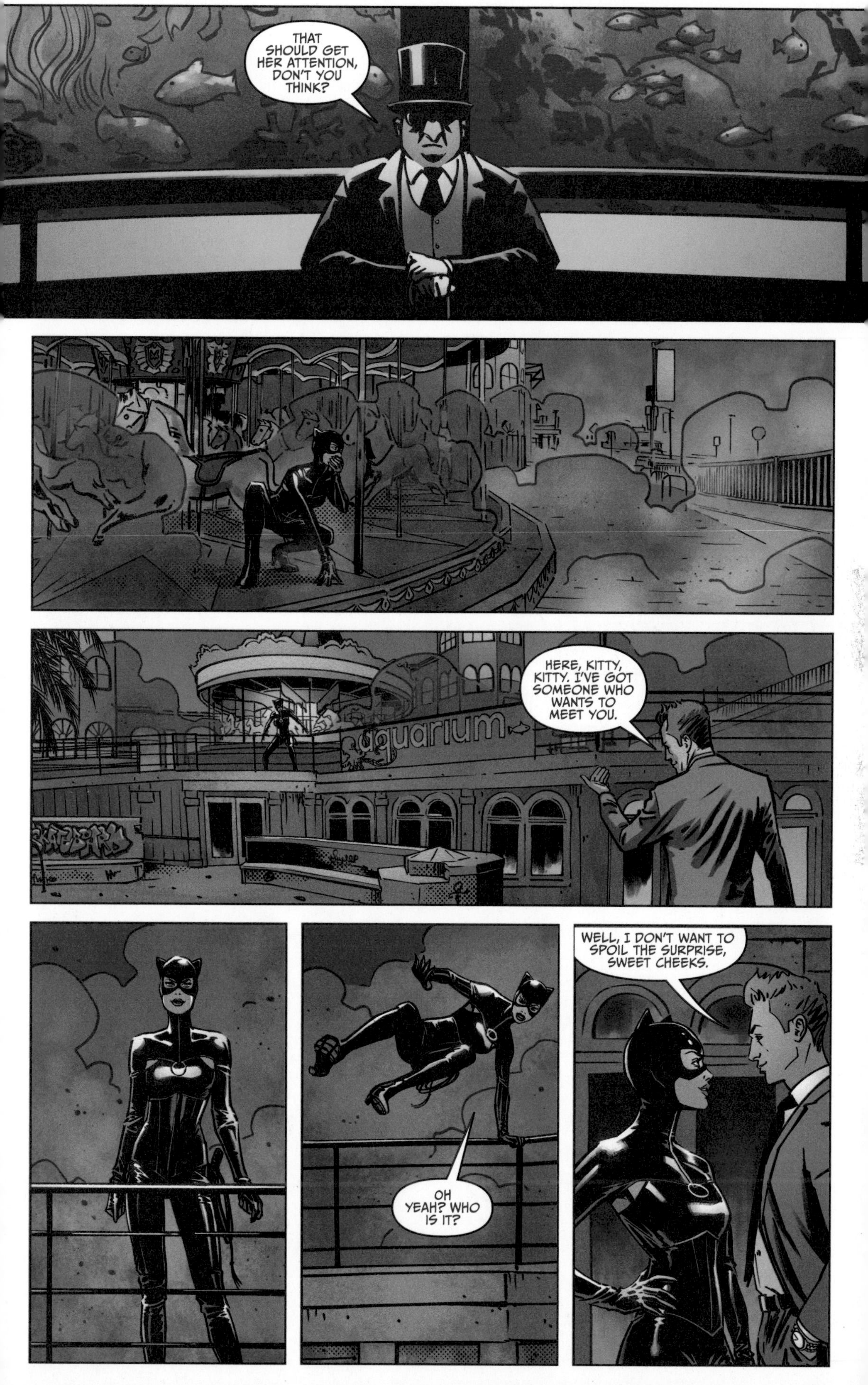
THAT SHOULD GET HER ATTENTION, DON'T YOU THINK?
aquarium
HERE, KITTY, KITTY. I'VE GOT SOMEONE WHO WANTS TO MEET YOU.
OH YEAH? WHO IS IT?
WELL, I DON'T WANT TO SPOIL THE SURPRISE, SWEET CHEEKS.

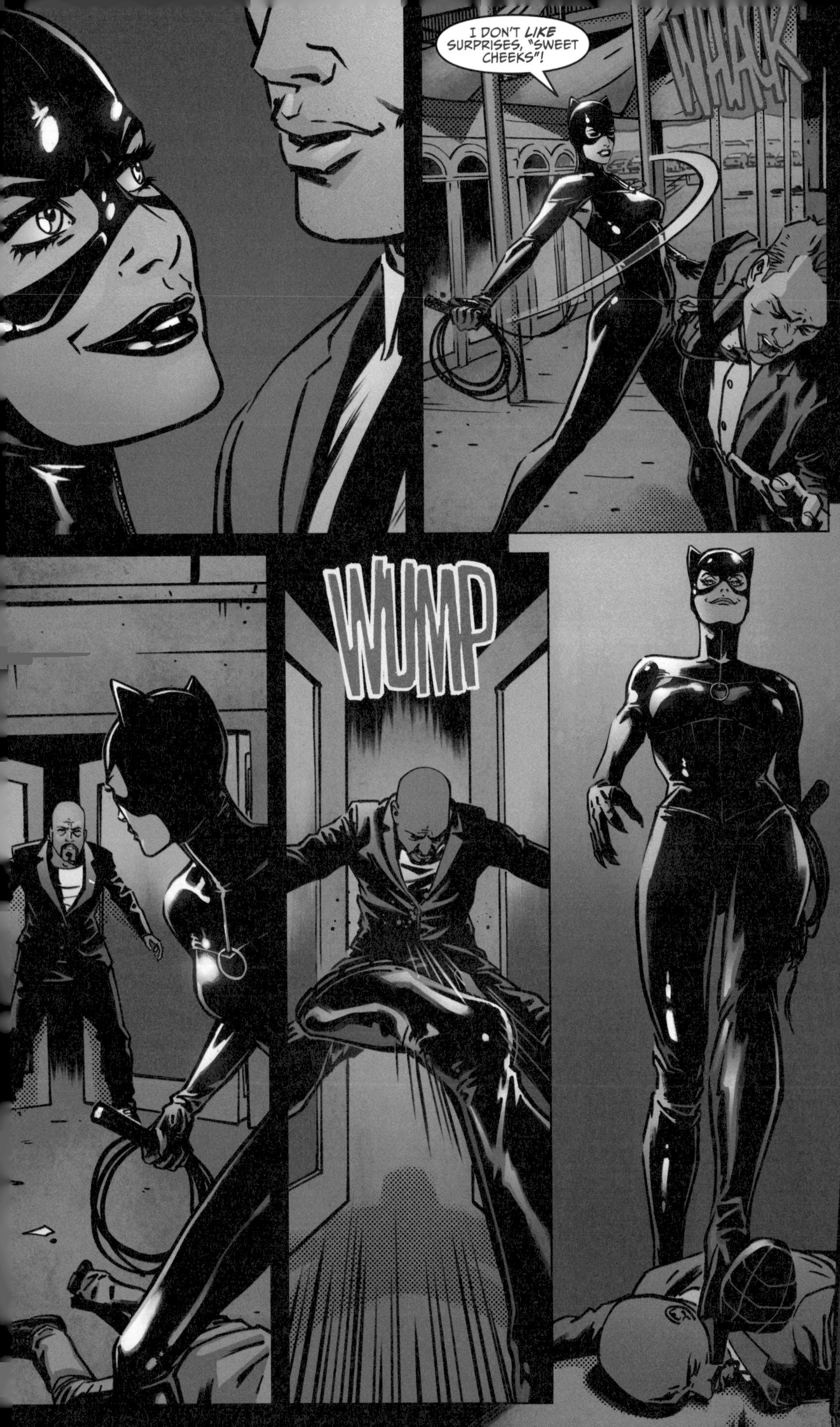
I DON'T LIKE SURPRISES, "SWEET CHEEKS"!
WHAAK
WUMP

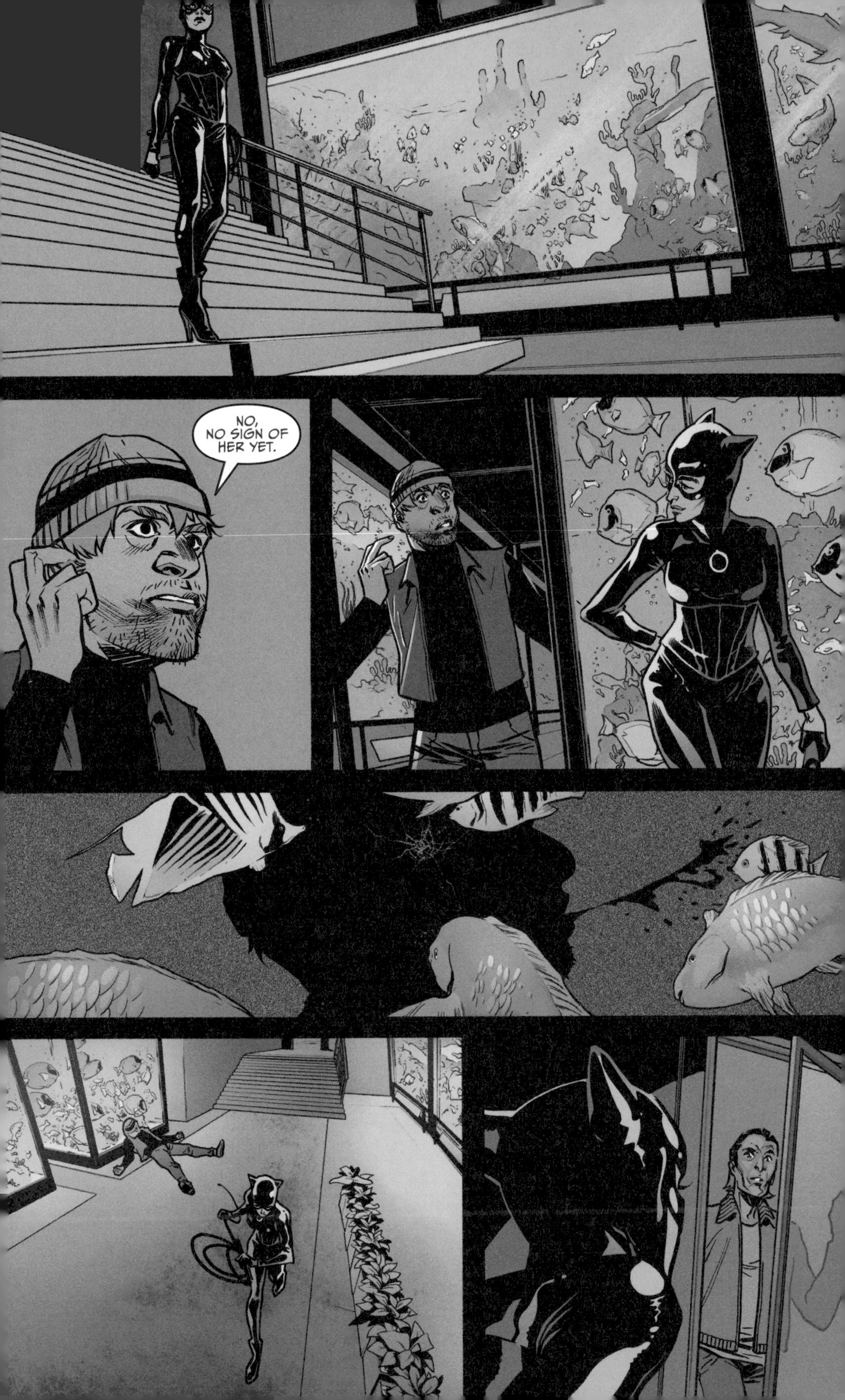
NO, NO SIGN OF HER YET.

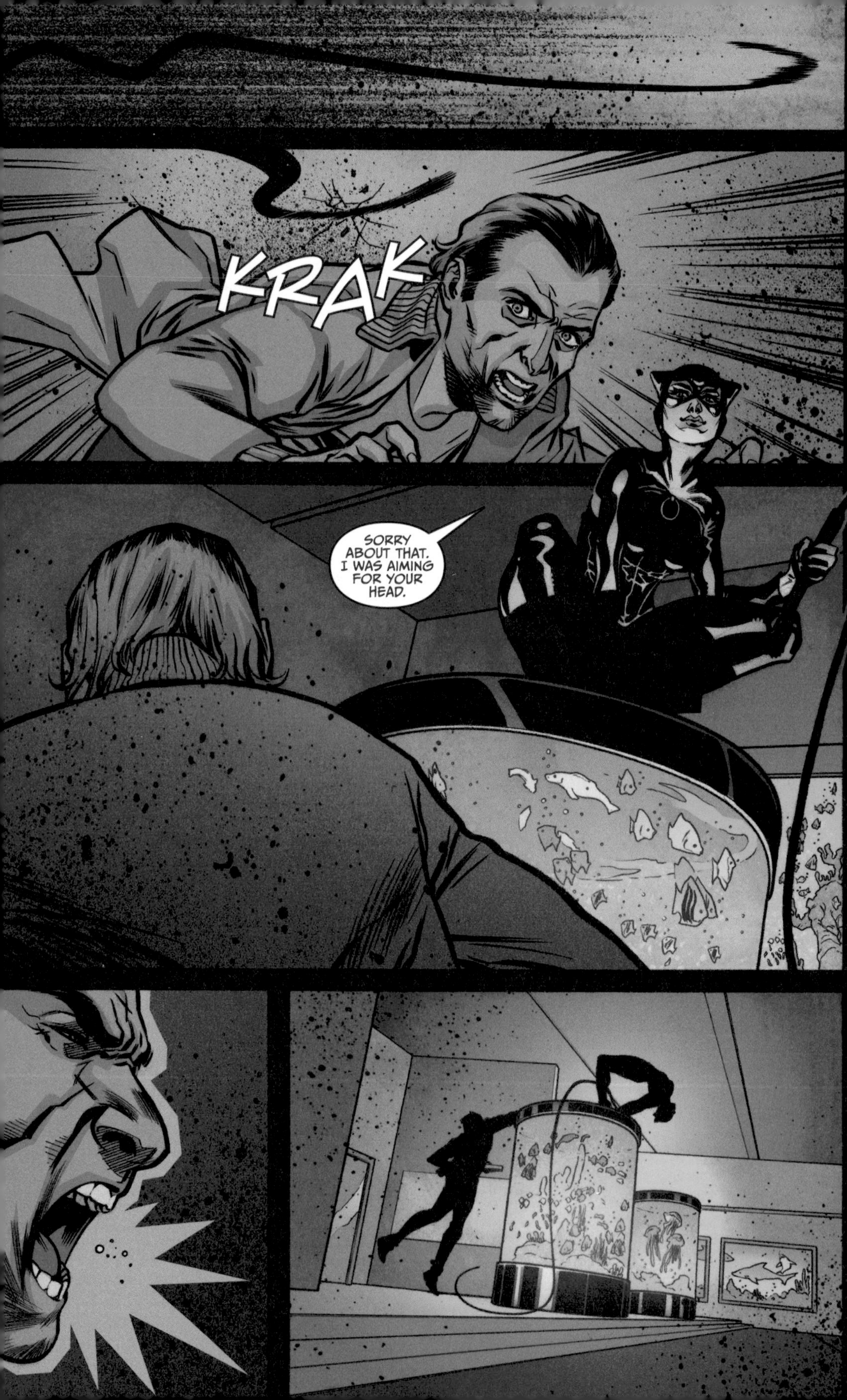
KRAK
SORRY ABOUT THAT. I WAS AIMING FOR YOUR HEAD.

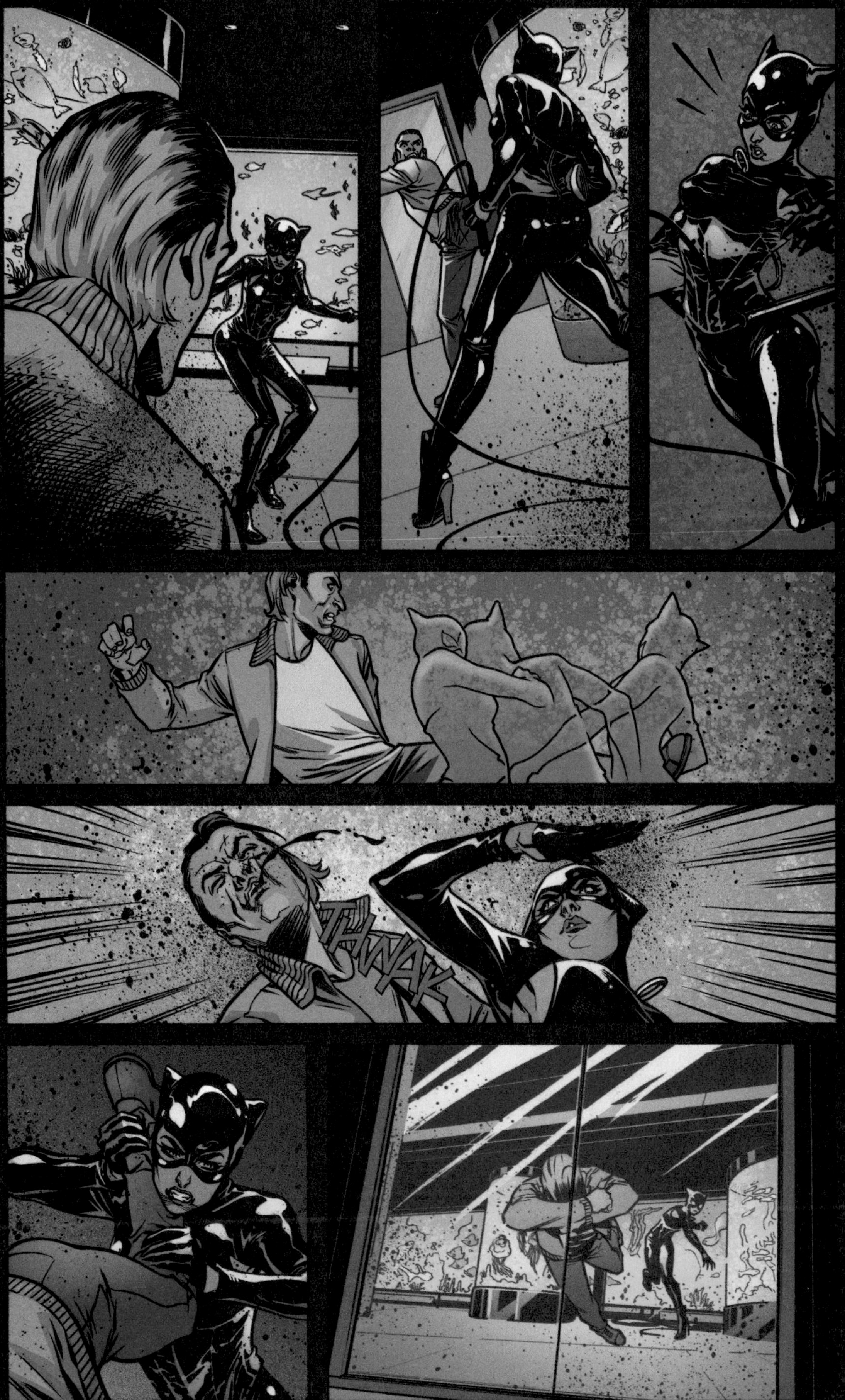
THWAK

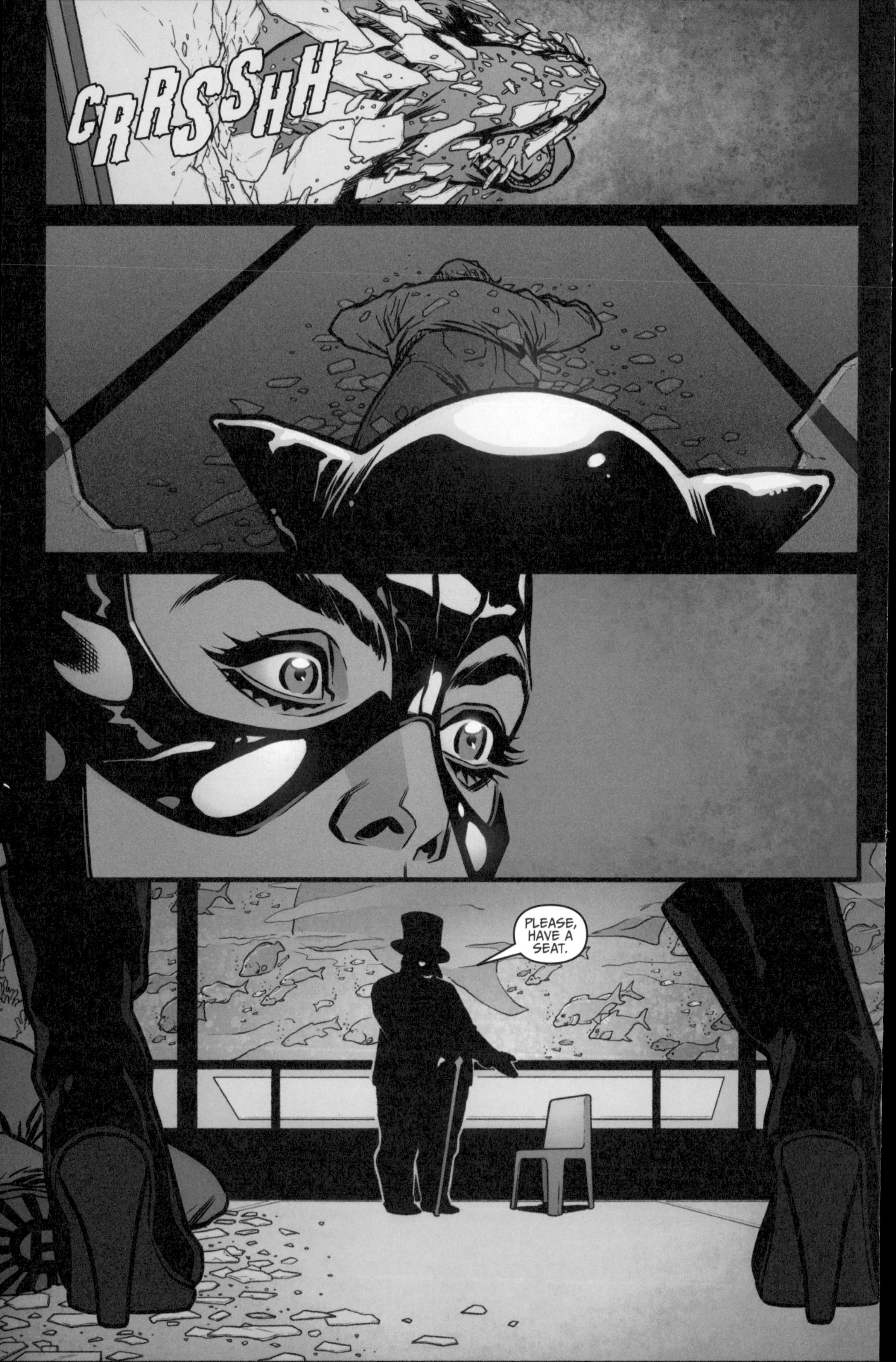
CRRSSHH
PLEASE, HAVE A SEAT.

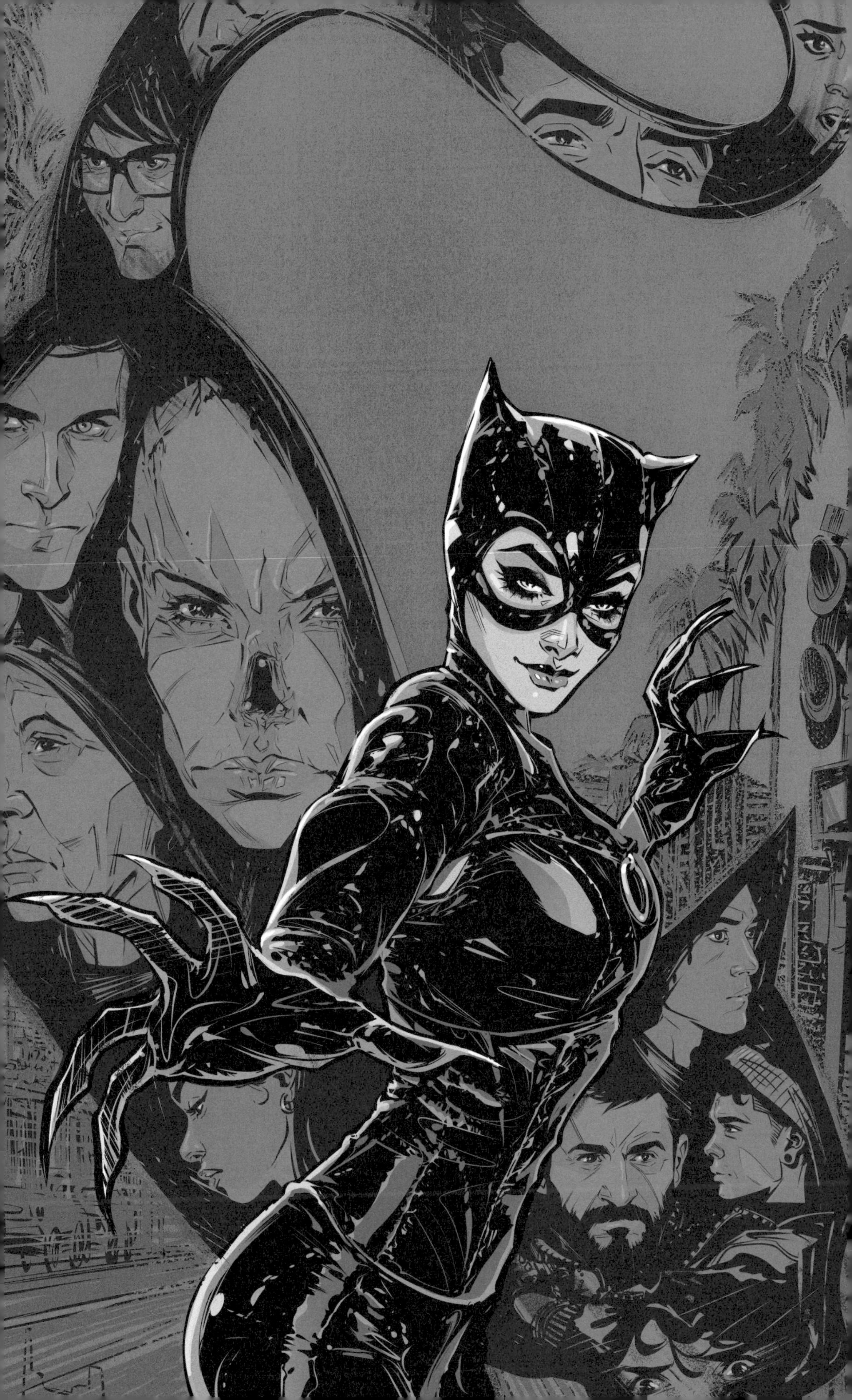

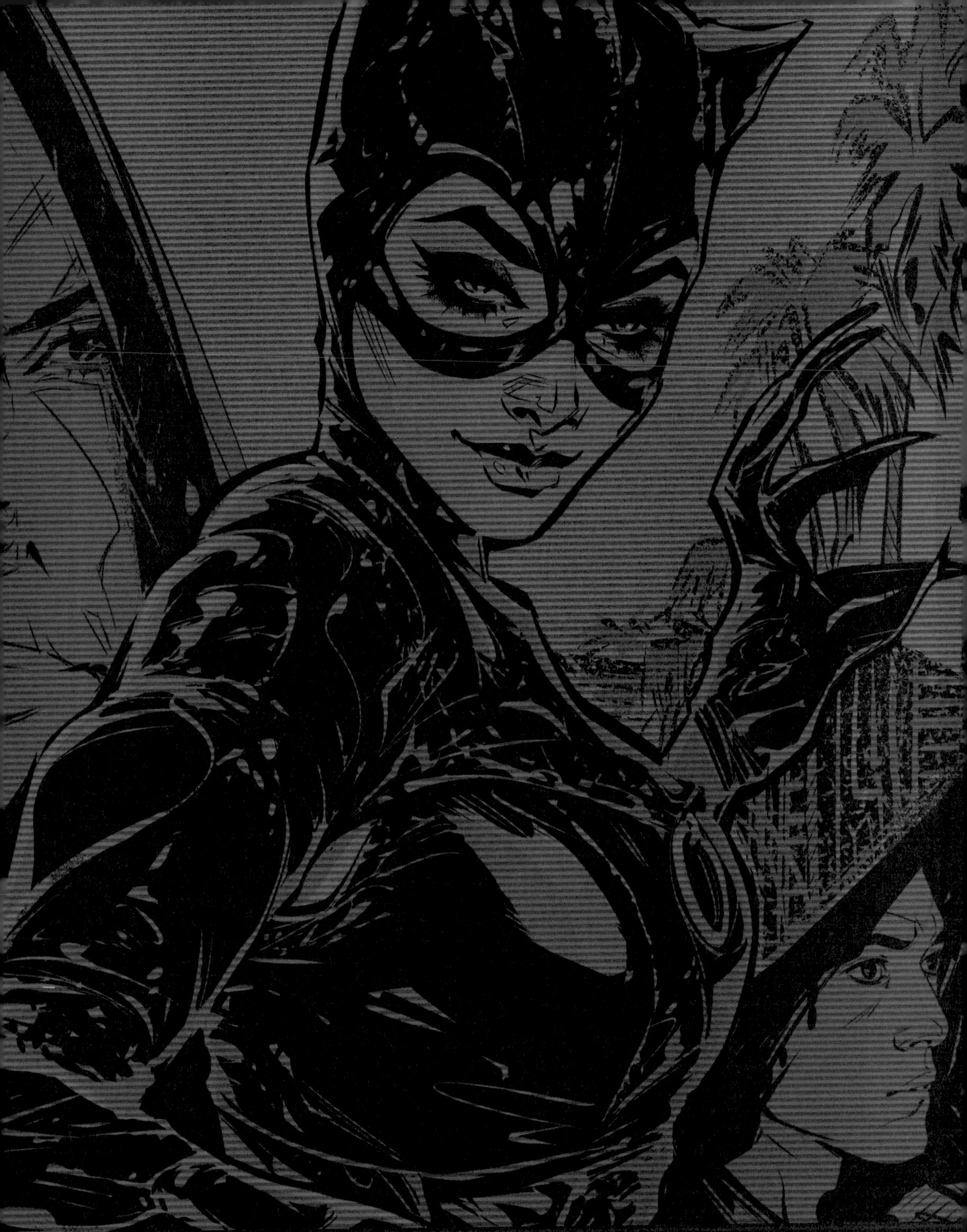

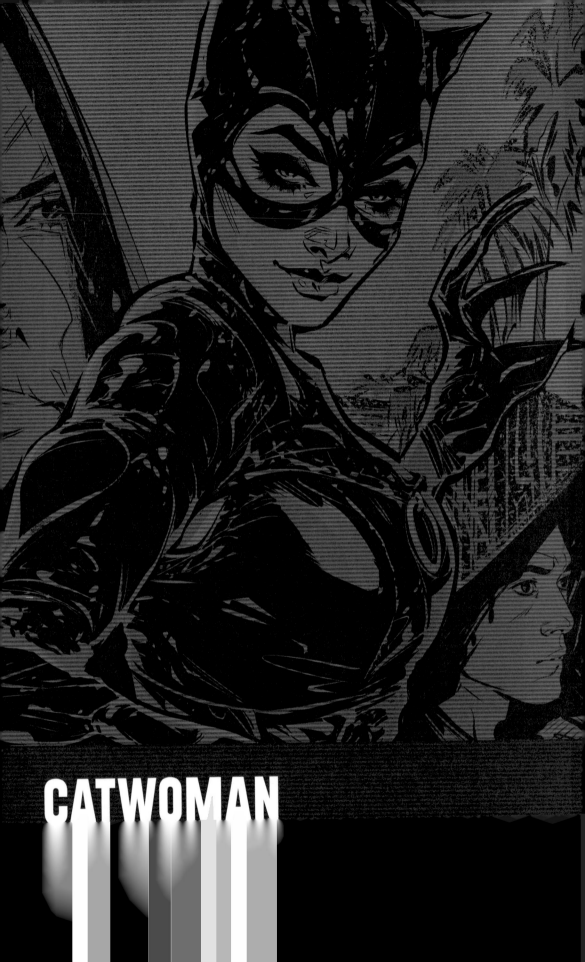

# CATWOMAN

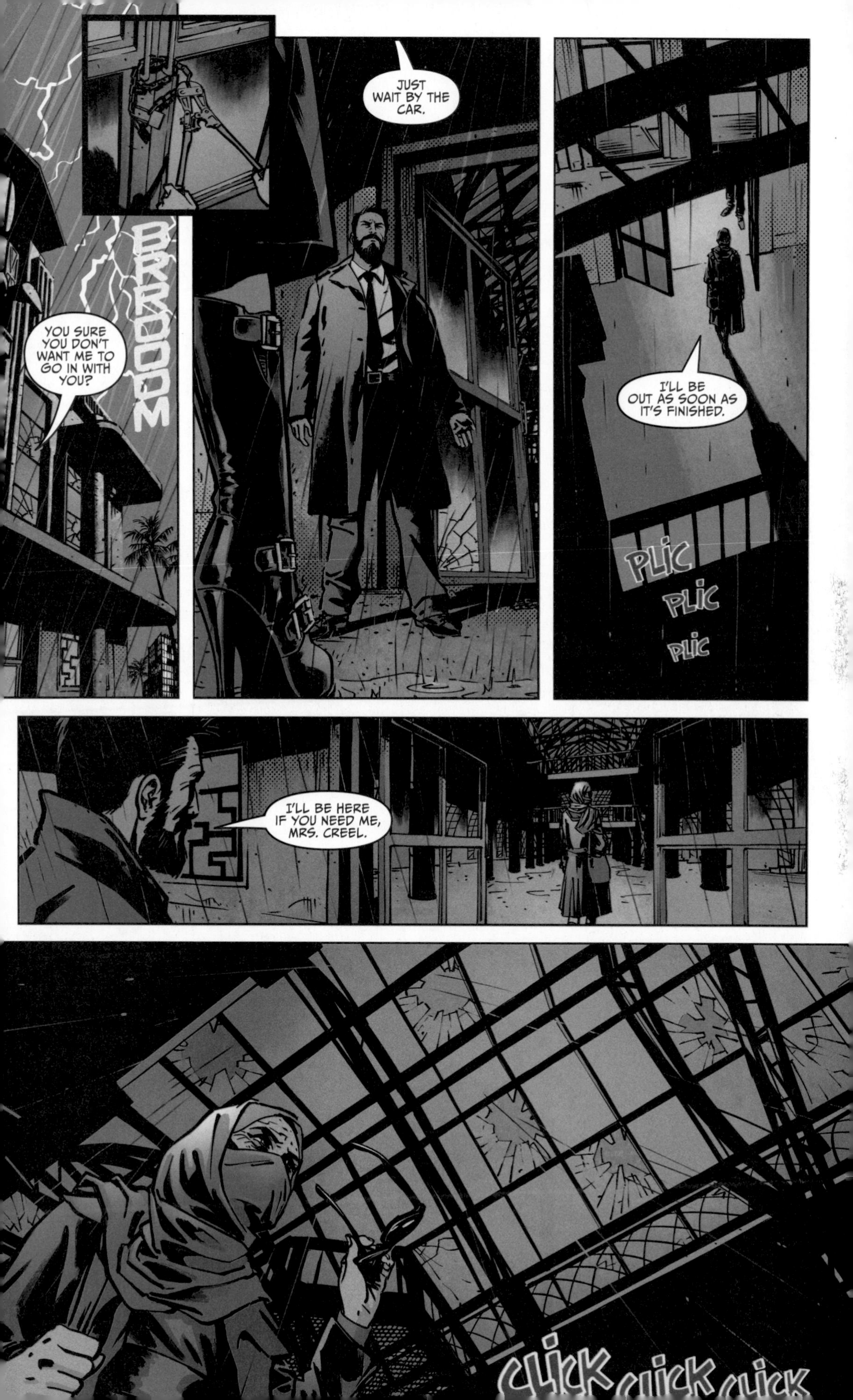
BRRROOOM
YOU SURE YOU DON'T WANT ME TO GO IN WITH YOU?
JUST WAIT BY THE CAR.
I'LL BE OUT AS SOON AS IT'S FINISHED.
PLIC
PLIC
PLIC
I'LL BE HERE IF YOU NEED ME, MRS. CREEL.
CLICK CLICK CLICK

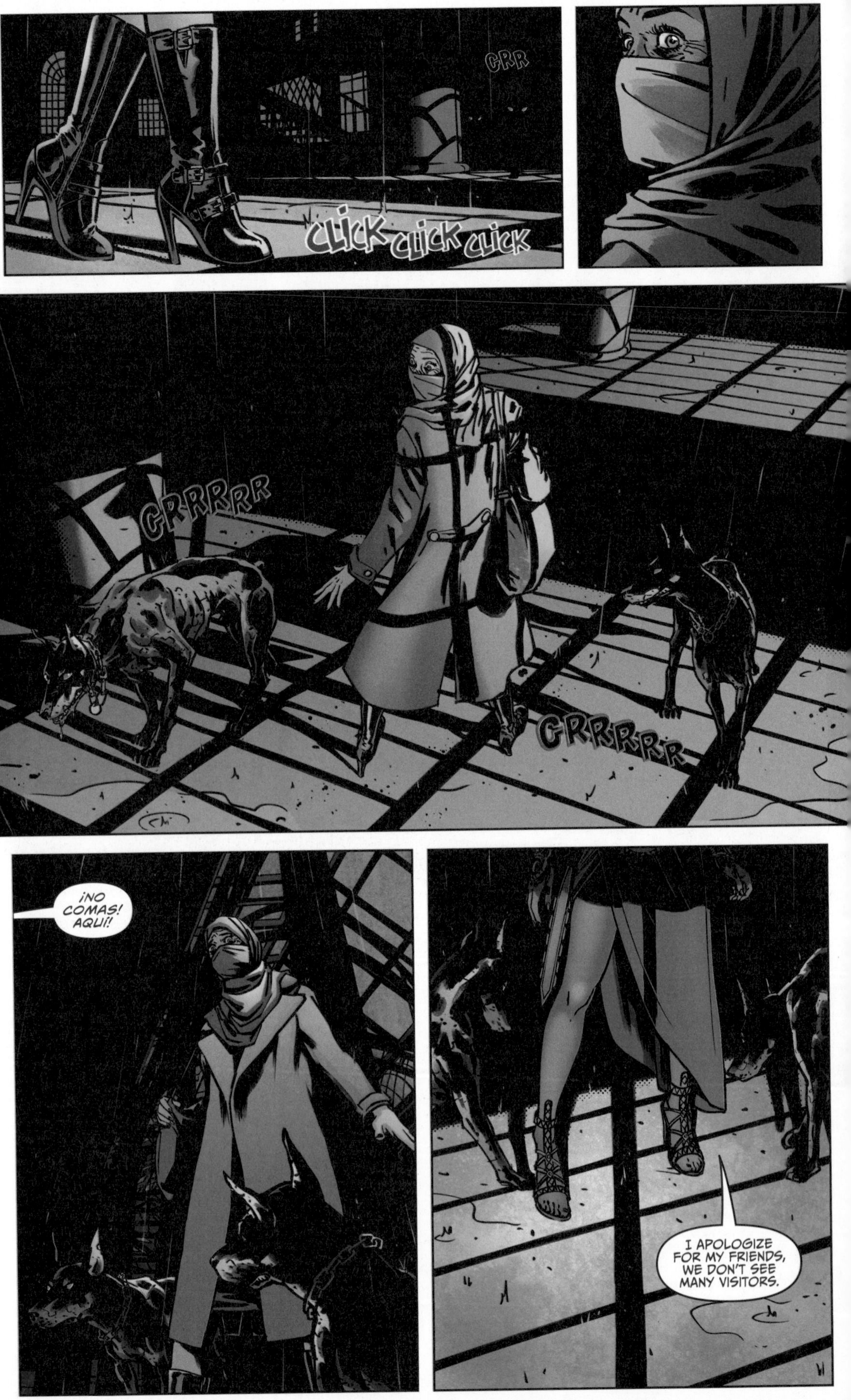
CRR
CLICK CLICK CLICK
GRRRRR
GRRRRRR
¡NO COMAS! AQUÍ!
I APOLOGIZE FOR MY FRIENDS, WE DON'T SEE MANY VISITORS.

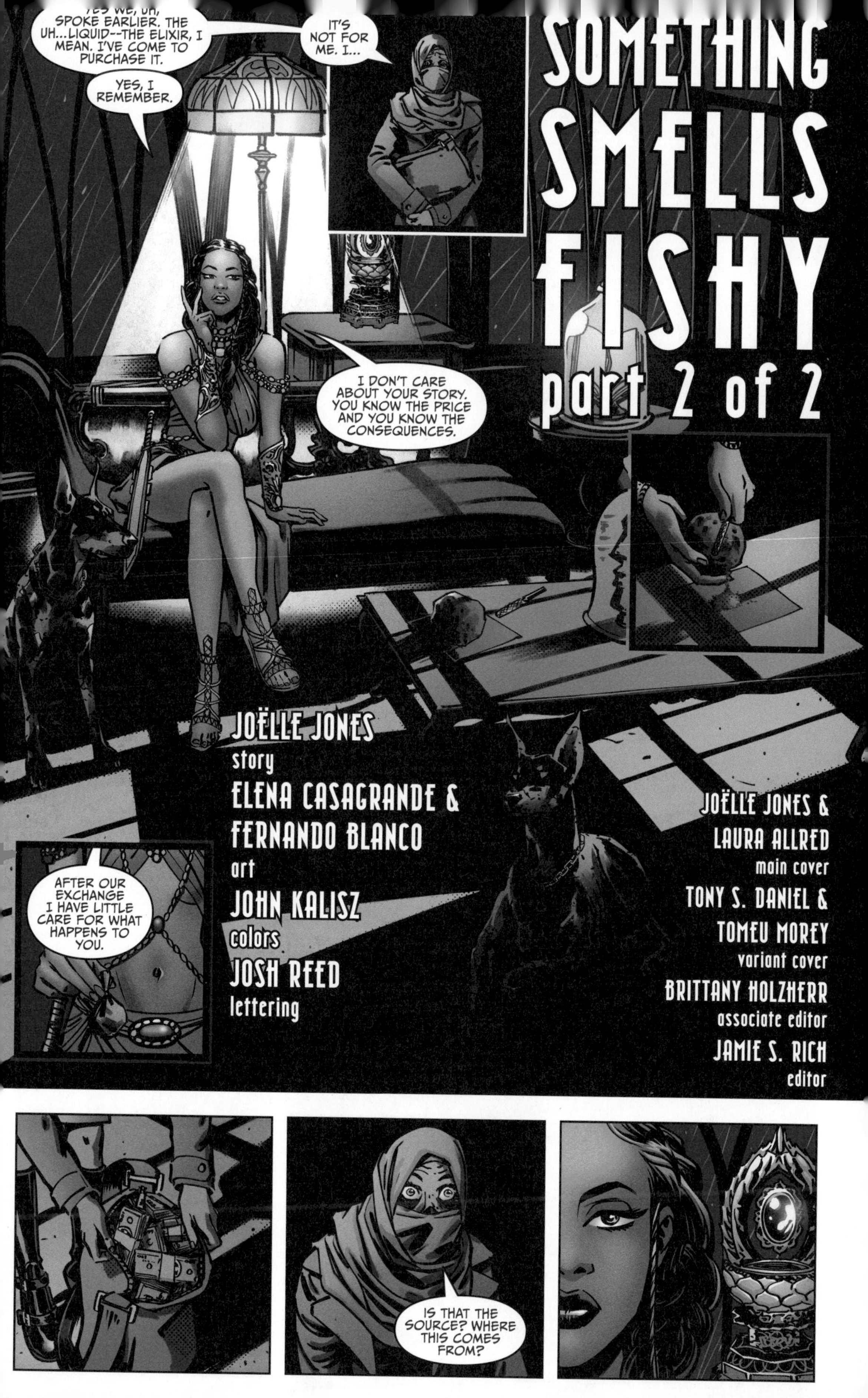
SPOKE EARLIER. THE UH...LIQUID--THE ELIXIR, I MEAN. I'VE COME TO PURCHASE IT.
YES, I REMEMBER.
IT'S NOT FOR ME. I...
SOMETHING SMELLS FISHY
part 2 of 2
I DON'T CARE ABOUT YOUR STORY. YOU KNOW THE PRICE AND YOU KNOW THE CONSEQUENCES.
JOËLLE JONES
story
ELENA CASAGRANDE & FERNANDO BLANCO
art
JOHN KALISZ
colors
JOSH REED
lettering
JOËLLE JONES & LAURA ALLRED
main cover
TONY S. DANIEL & TOMEU MOREY
variant cover
BRITTANY HOLZHERR
associate editor
JAMIE S. RICH
editor
AFTER OUR EXCHANGE I HAVE LITTLE CARE FOR WHAT HAPPENS TO YOU.
IS THAT THE SOURCE? WHERE THIS COMES FROM?

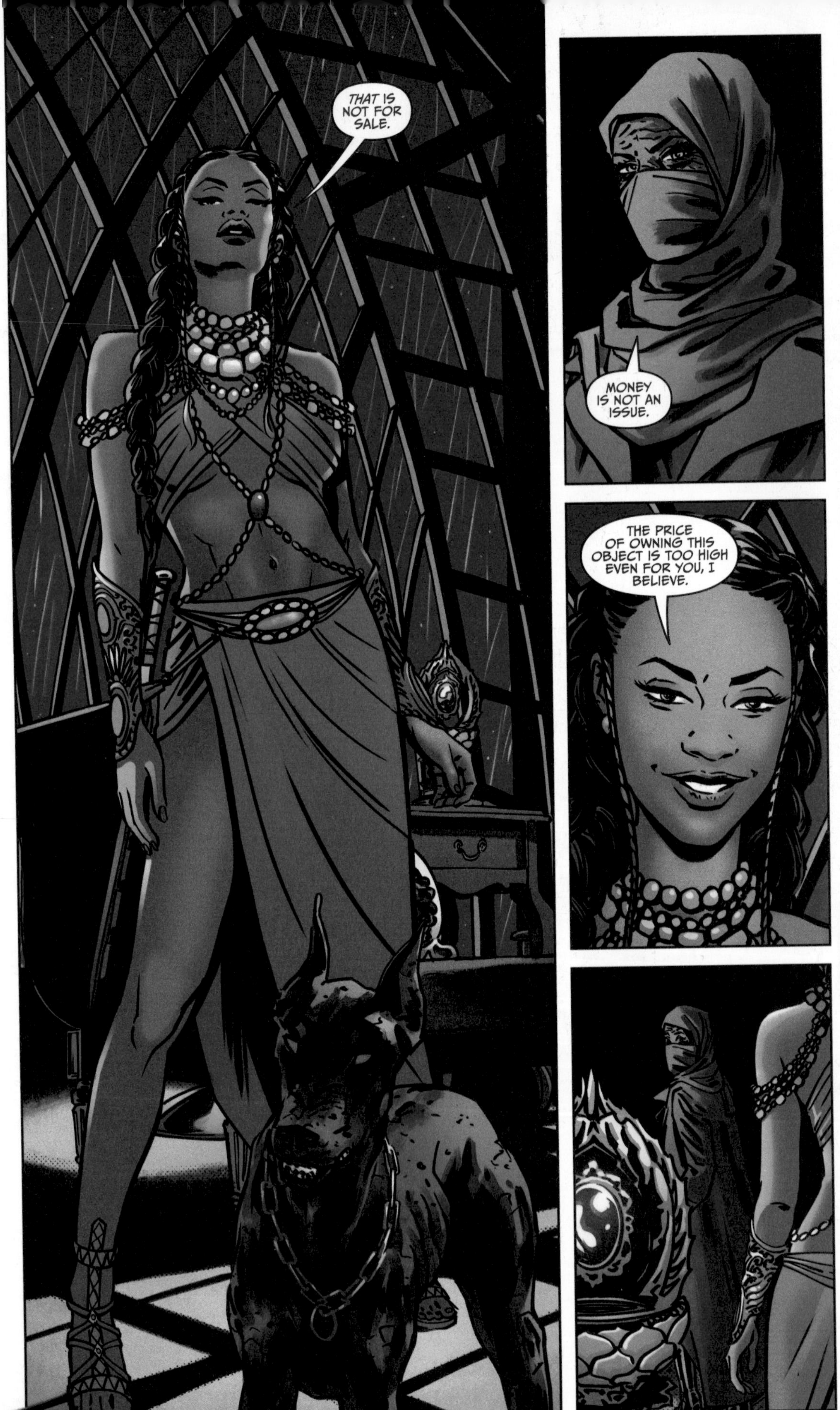
THAT IS NOT FOR SALE.
MONEY IS NOT AN ISSUE.
THE PRICE OF OWNING THIS OBJECT IS TOO HIGH EVEN FOR YOU, I BELIEVE.

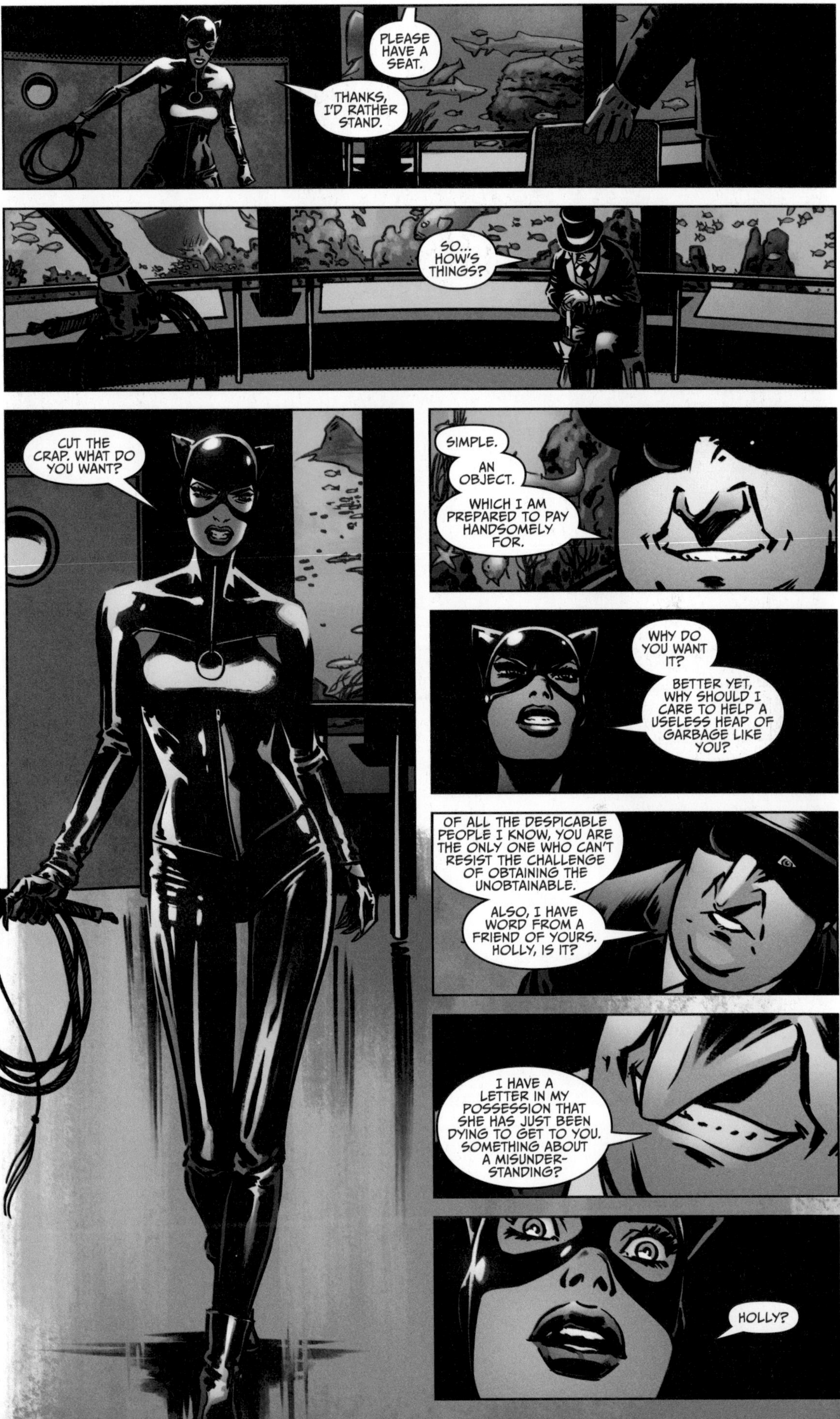
PLEASE HAVE A SEAT.
THANKS, I'D RATHER STAND.
SO... HOW'S THINGS?
CUT THE CRAP. WHAT DO YOU WANT?
SIMPLE.
AN OBJECT.
WHICH I AM PREPARED TO PAY HANDSOMELY FOR.
WHY DO YOU WANT IT?
BETTER YET, WHY SHOULD I CARE TO HELP A USELESS HEAP OF GARBAGE LIKE YOU?
OF ALL THE DESPICABLE PEOPLE I KNOW, YOU ARE THE ONLY ONE WHO CAN'T RESIST THE CHALLENGE OF OBTAINING THE UNOBTAINABLE.
ALSO, I HAVE WORD FROM A FRIEND OF YOURS. HOLLY, IS IT?
I HAVE A LETTER IN MY POSSESSION THAT SHE HAS JUST BEEN DYING TO GET TO YOU. SOMETHING ABOUT A MISUNDER-STANDING?
HOLLY?

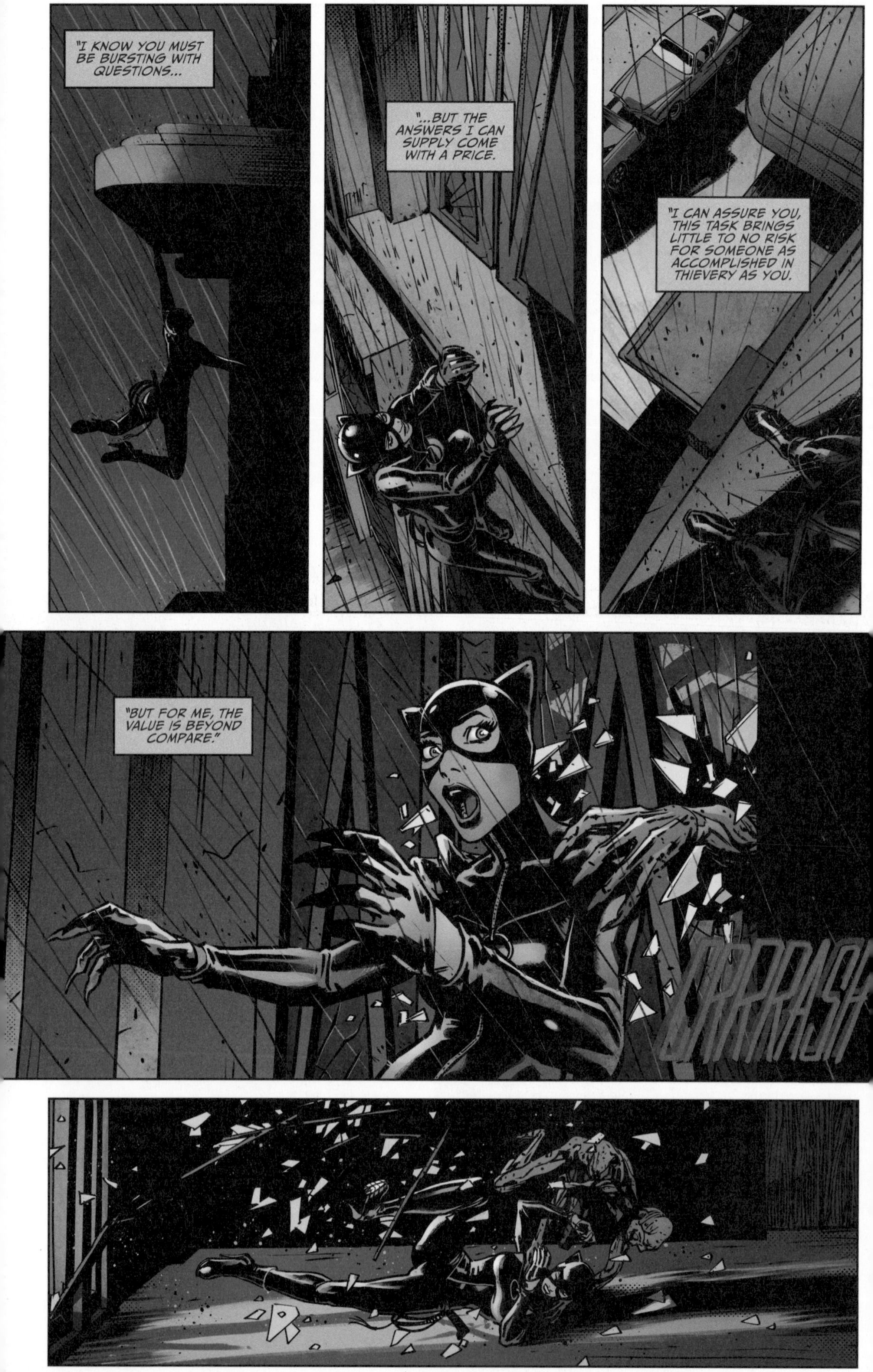
"I KNOW YOU MUST BE BURSTING WITH QUESTIONS...
"...BUT THE ANSWERS I CAN SUPPLY COME WITH A PRICE.
"I CAN ASSURE YOU, THIS TASK BRINGS LITTLE TO NO RISK FOR SOMEONE AS ACCOMPLISHED IN THIEVERY AS YOU.
"BUT FOR ME, THE VALUE IS BEYOND COMPARE."
CRRRASH

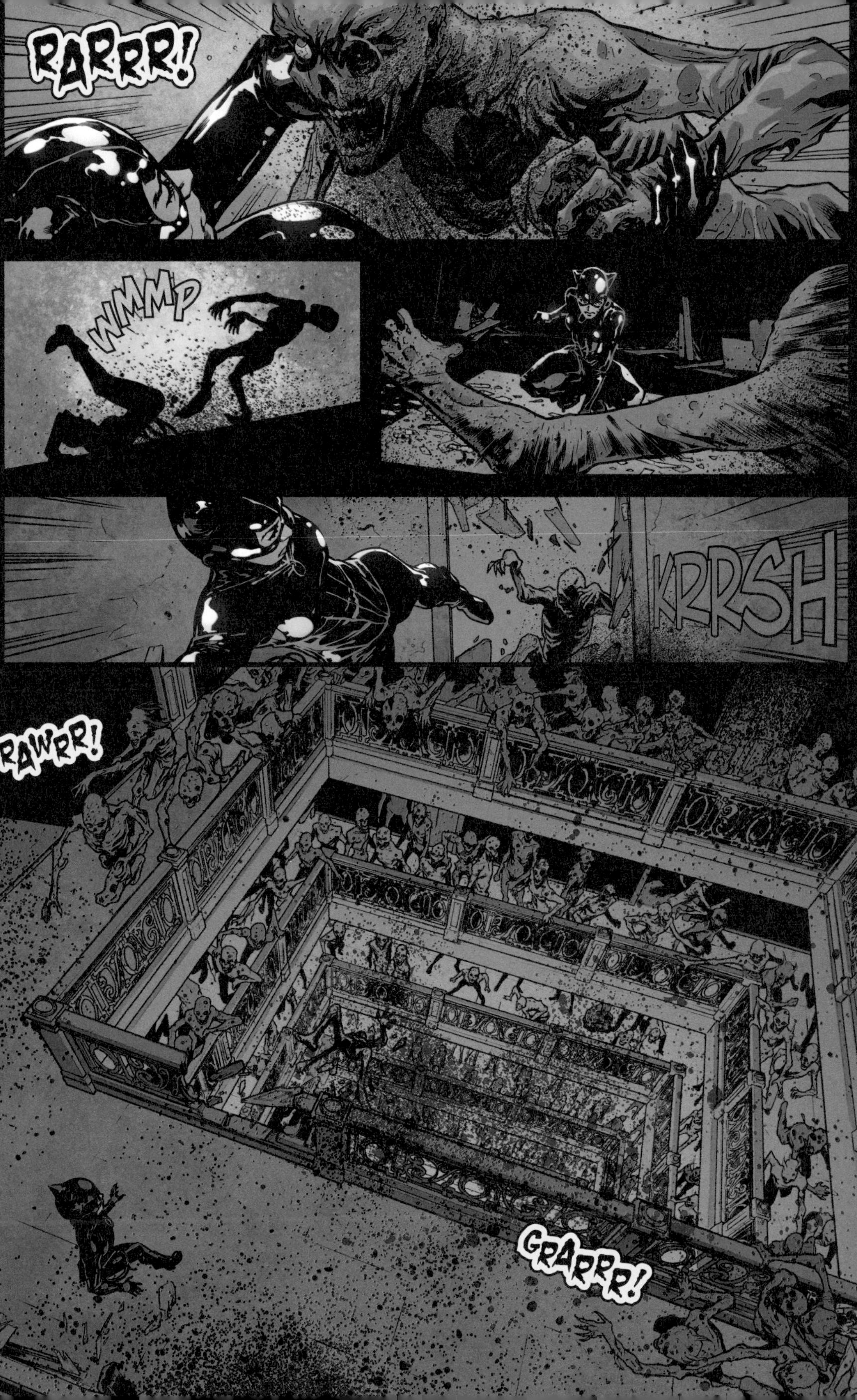
RARRR!
WMMMP
KRRSH
RAWRR!
GRARRR!

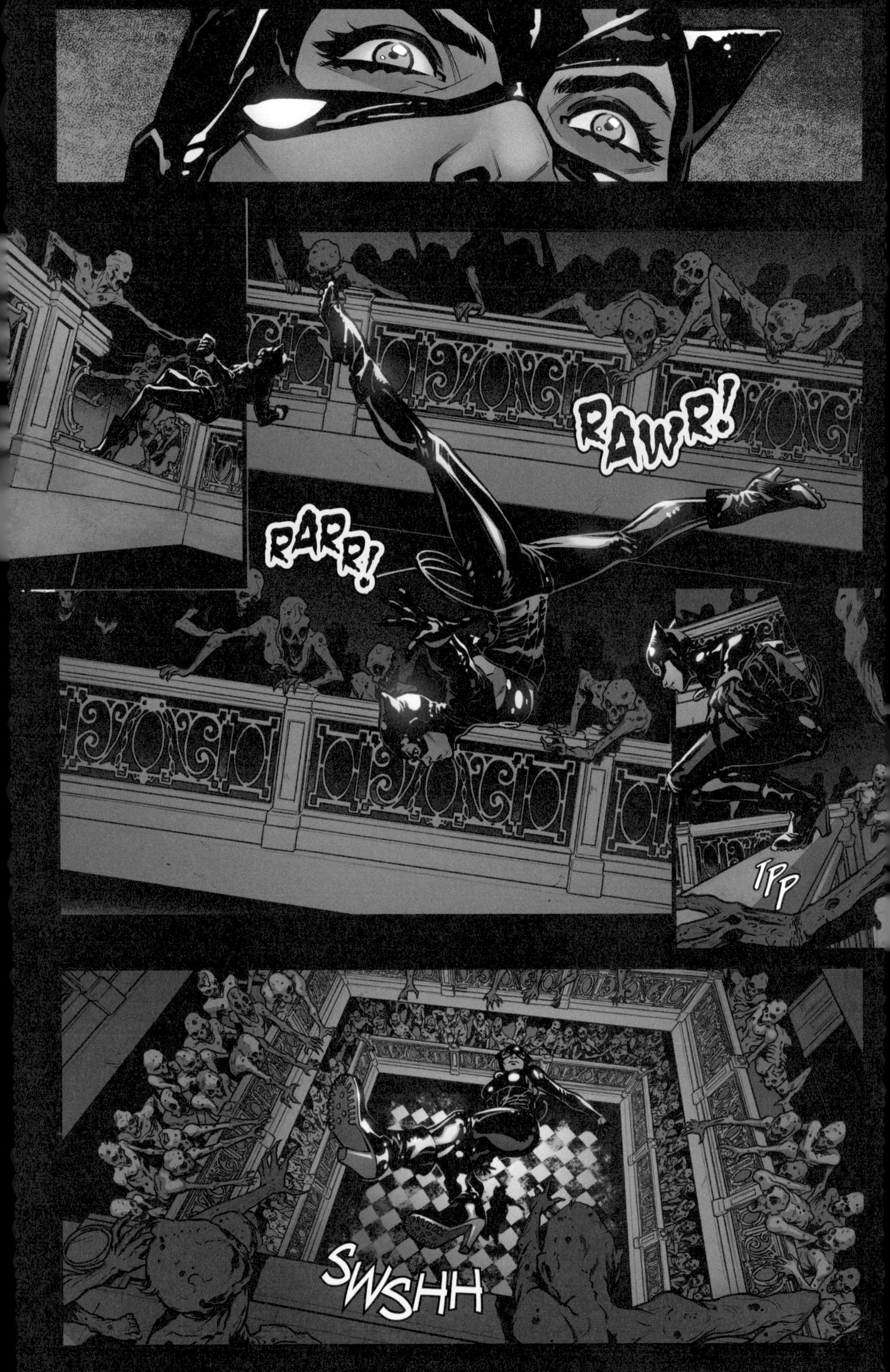
RAWR!
RARR!
TPP
SWSHH

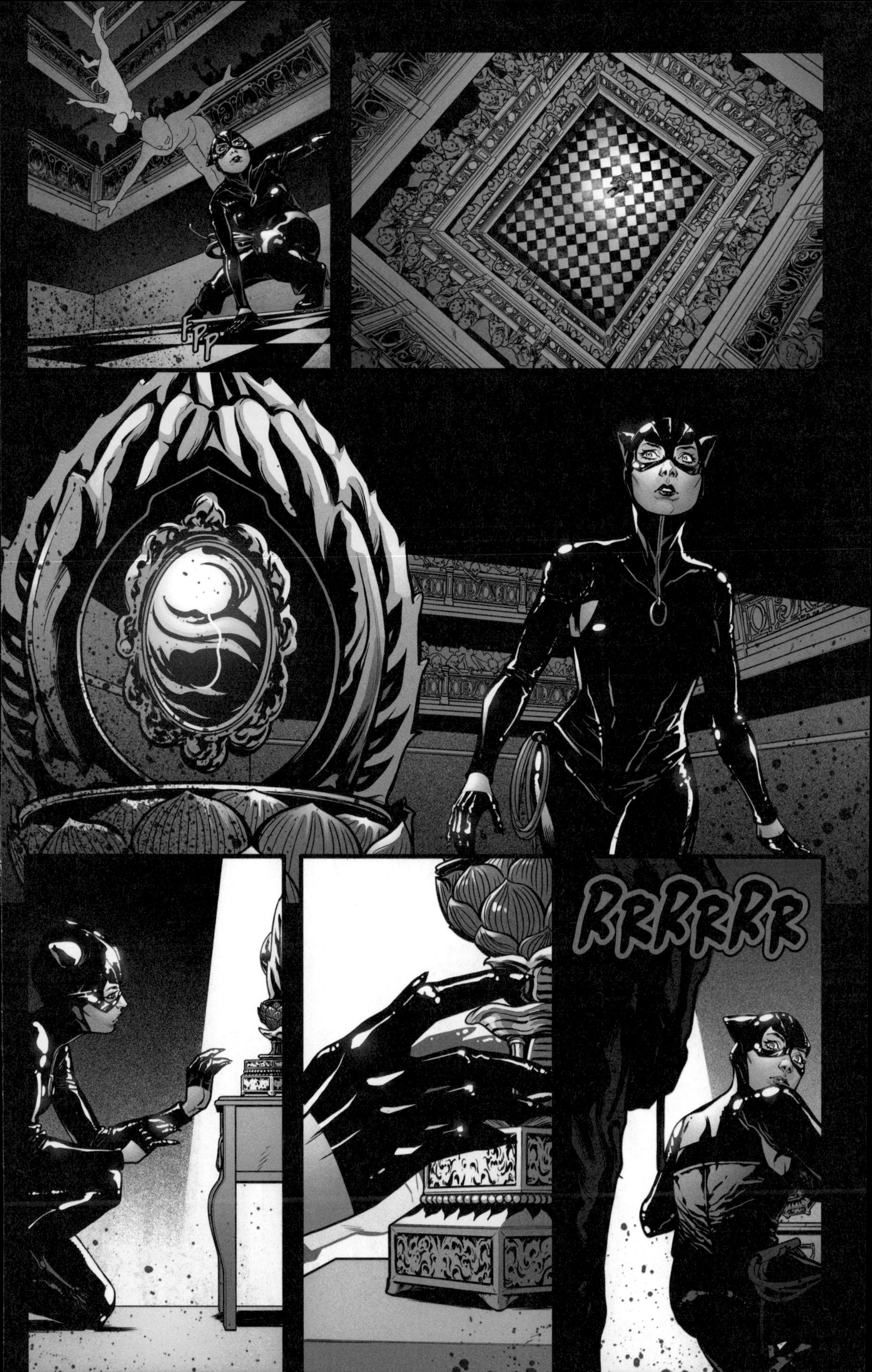
FPP
RRRRRR

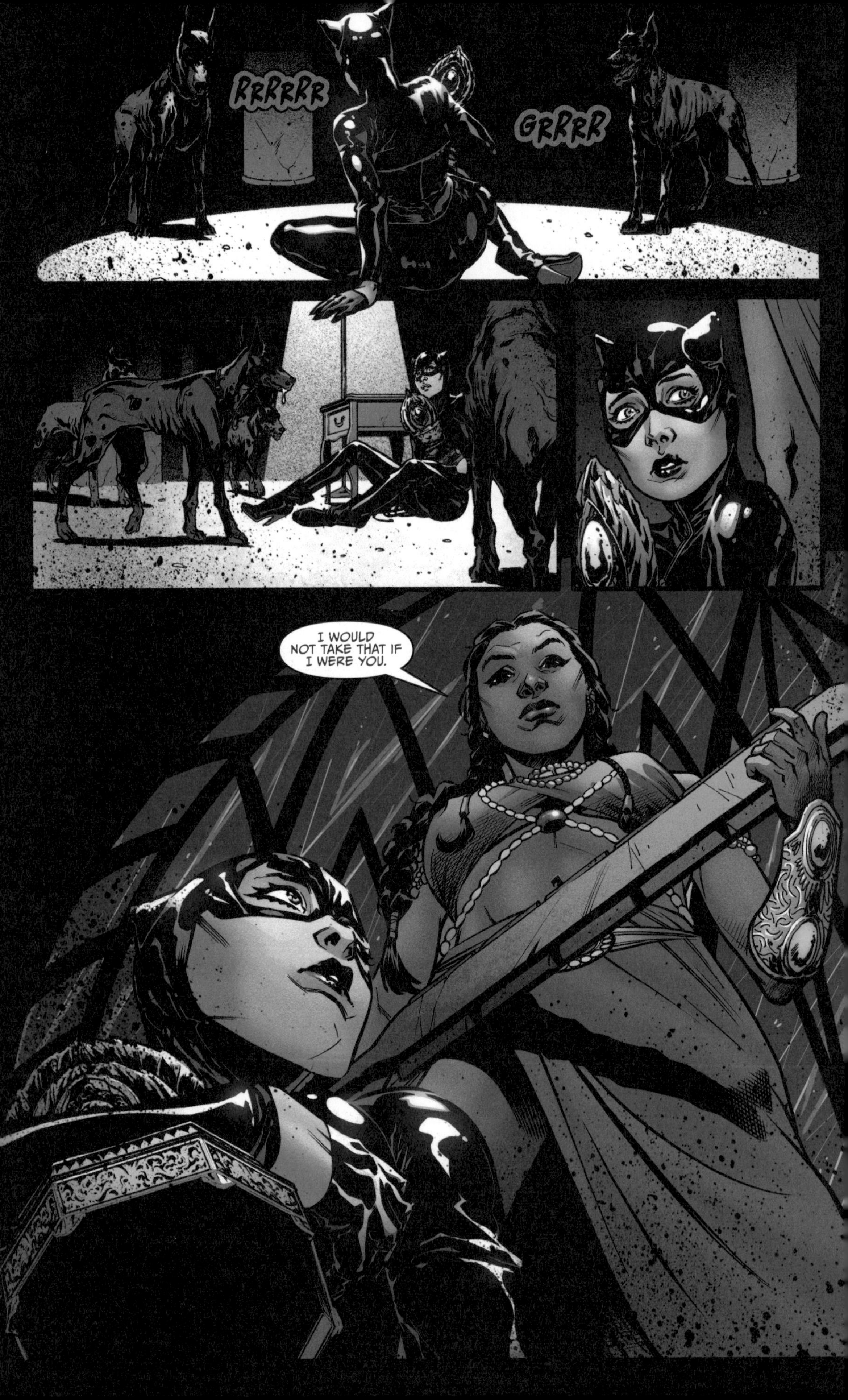
RRRRRR
GRRRR
I WOULD NOT TAKE THAT IF I WERE YOU.

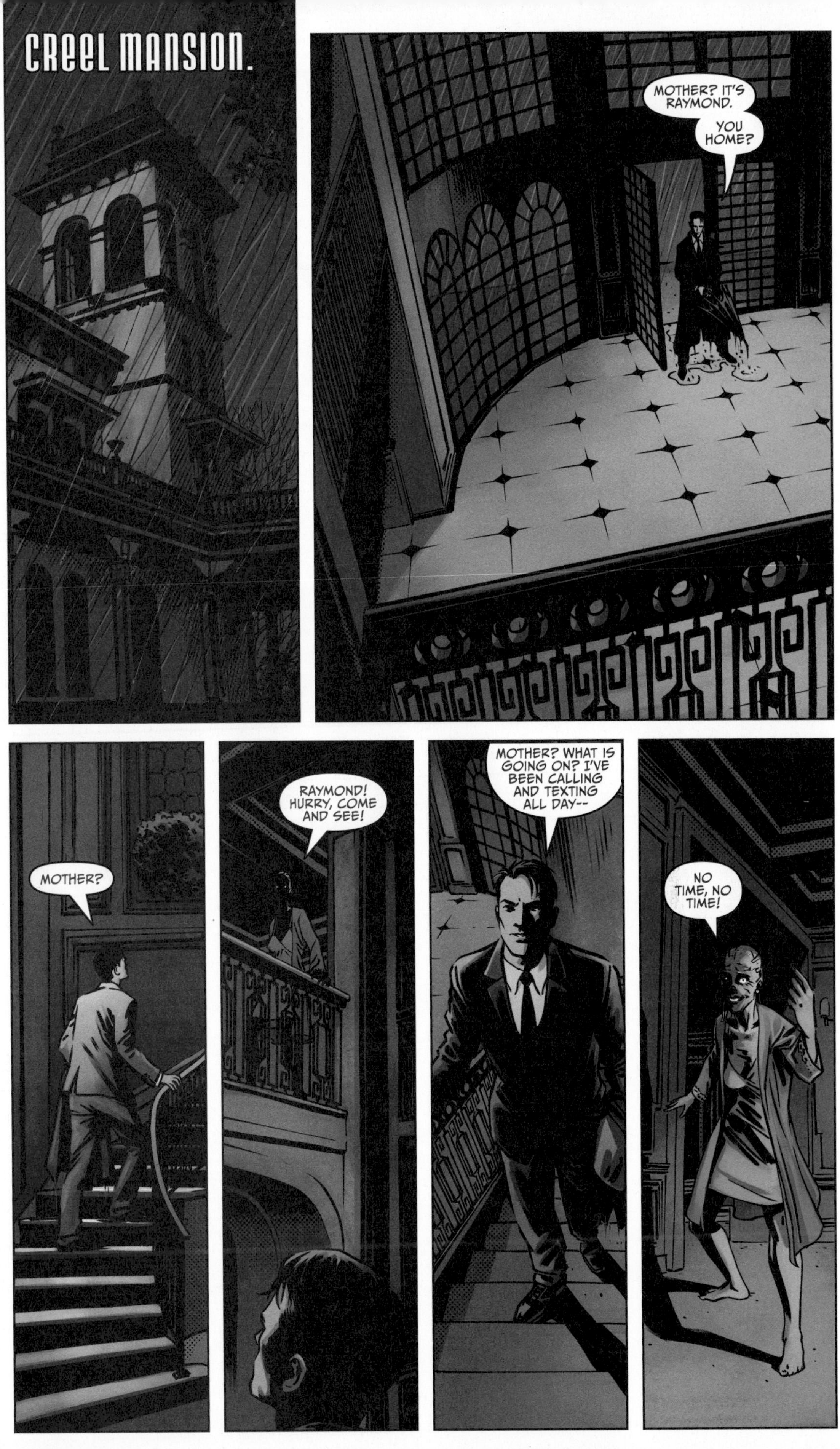
CREEL MANSION.
MOTHER? IT'S RAYMOND.
YOU HOME?
MOTHER?
RAYMOND! HURRY, COME AND SEE!
MOTHER? WHAT IS GOING ON? I'VE BEEN CALLING AND TEXTING ALL DAY--
NO TIME, NO TIME!

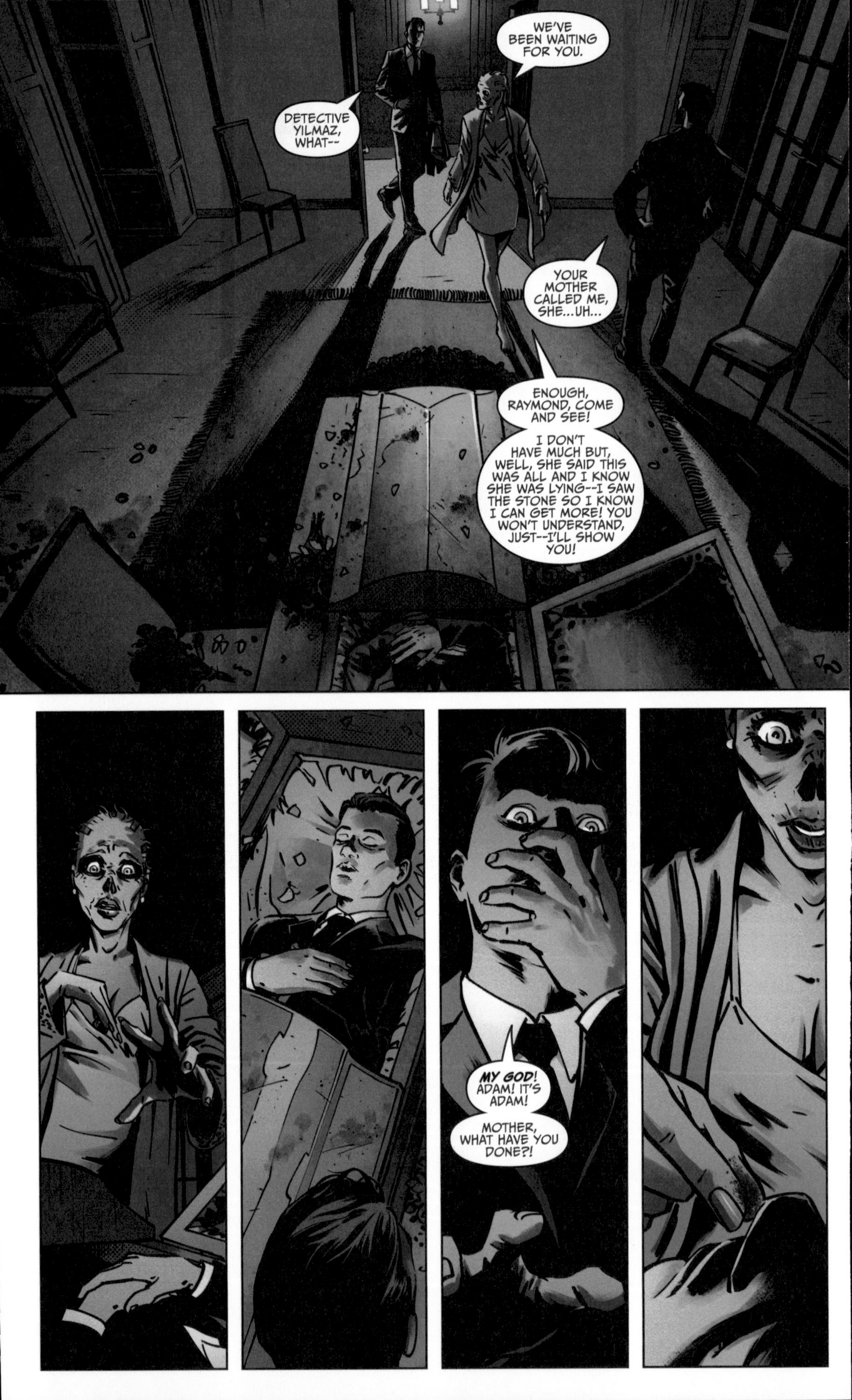

DETECTIVE YILMAZ, WHAT--
WE'VE BEEN WAITING FOR YOU.
YOUR MOTHER CALLED ME, SHE...UH...
ENOUGH, RAYMOND, COME AND SEE!
I DON'T HAVE MUCH BUT, WELL, SHE SAID THIS WAS ALL AND I KNOW SHE WAS LYING--I SAW THE STONE SO I KNOW I CAN GET MORE! YOU WON'T UNDERSTAND, JUST--I'LL SHOW YOU!
MY GOD! ADAM! IT'S ADAM!
MOTHER, WHAT HAVE YOU DONE?!

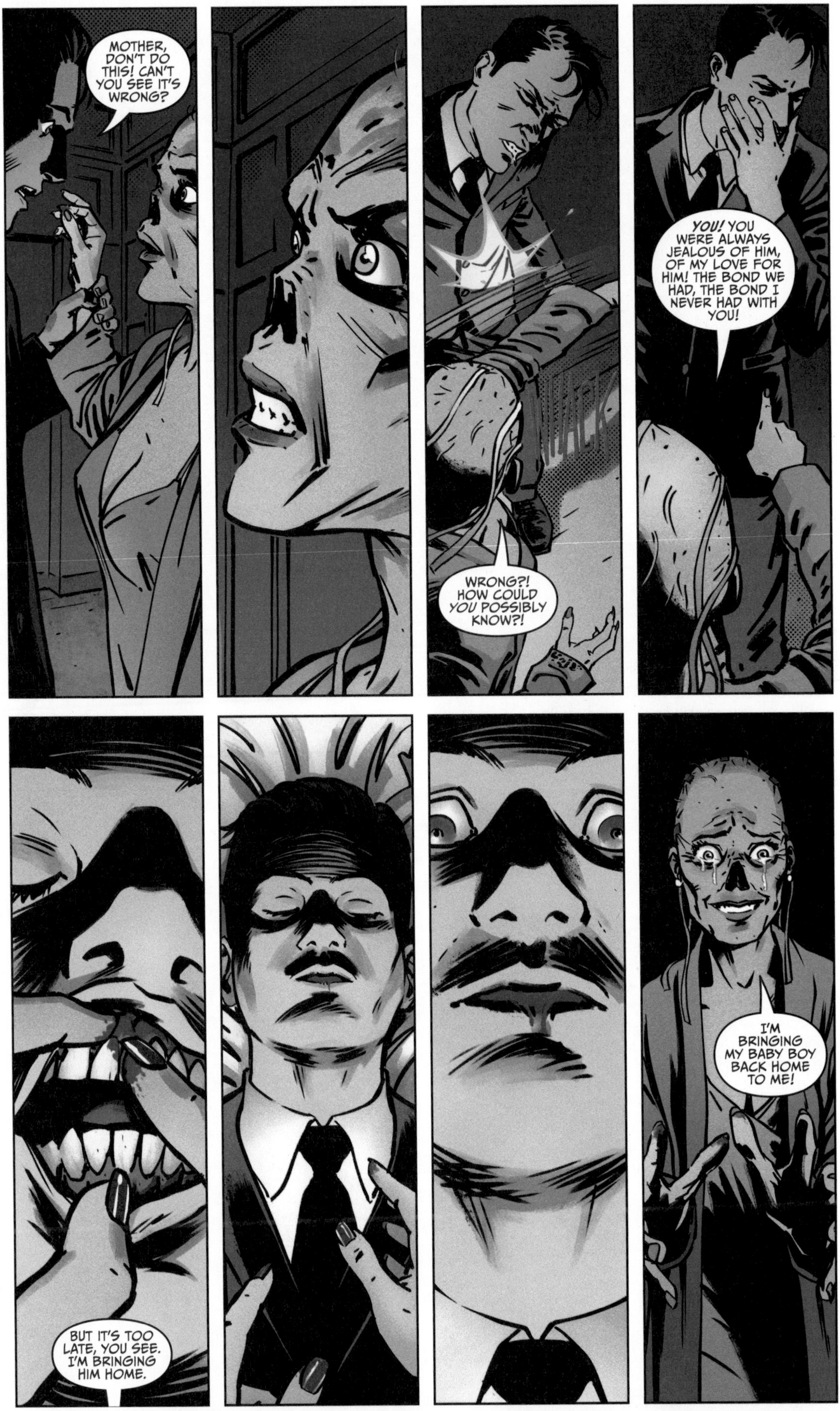
MOTHER, DON'T DO THIS! CAN'T YOU SEE IT'S WRONG?
WHACK
WRONG?! HOW COULD *YOU* POSSIBLY KNOW?!
*YOU!* YOU WERE ALWAYS JEALOUS OF HIM, OF MY LOVE FOR HIM! THE BOND WE HAD, THE BOND I NEVER HAD WITH YOU!
BUT IT'S TOO LATE, YOU SEE. I'M BRINGING HIM HOME.
I'M BRINGING MY BABY BOY BACK HOME TO ME!

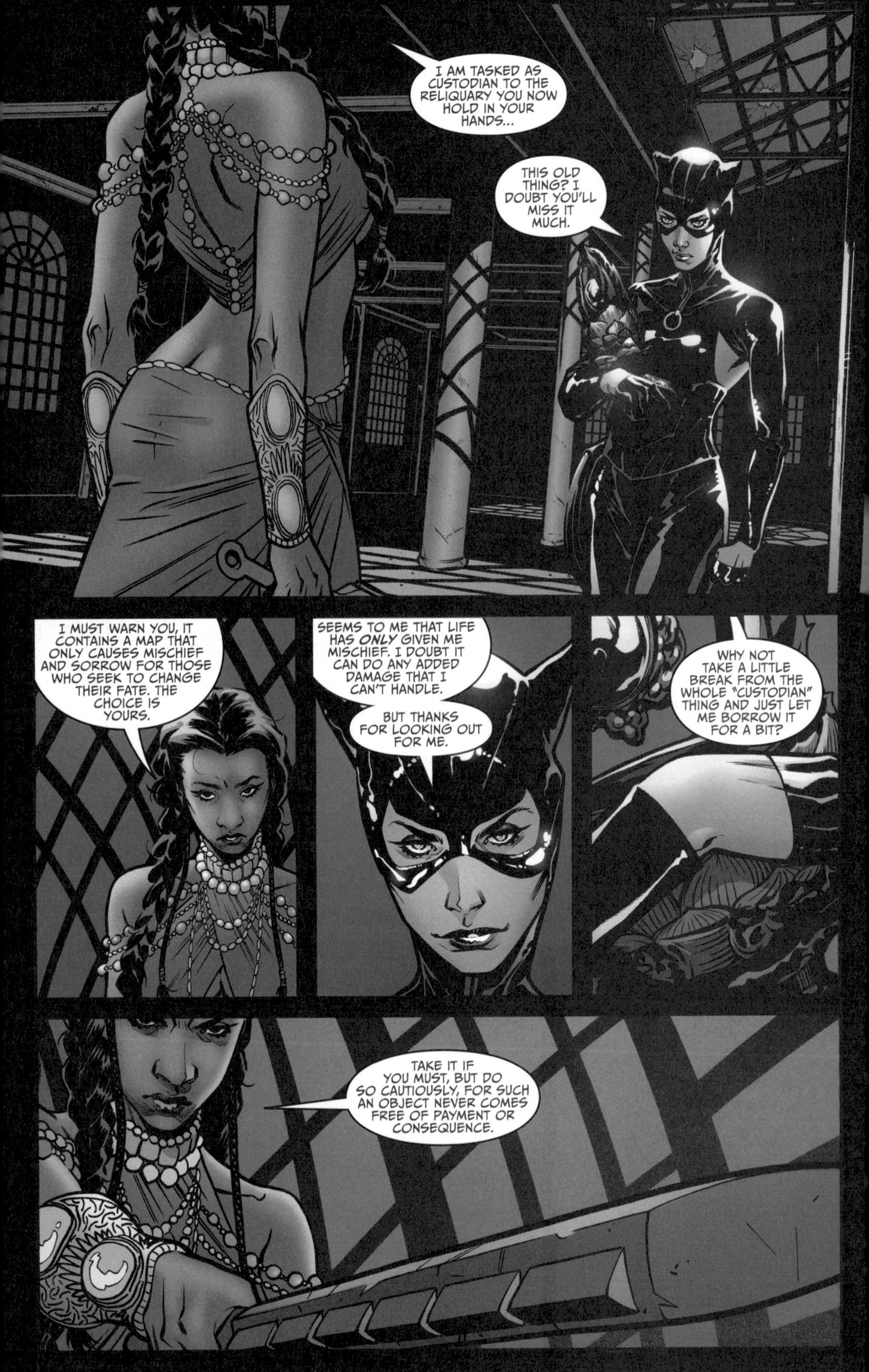
I AM TASKED AS CUSTODIAN TO THE RELIQUARY YOU NOW HOLD IN YOUR HANDS...
THIS OLD THING? I DOUBT YOU'LL MISS IT MUCH.
I MUST WARN YOU, IT CONTAINS A MAP THAT ONLY CAUSES MISCHIEF AND SORROW FOR THOSE WHO SEEK TO CHANGE THEIR FATE. THE CHOICE IS YOURS.
SEEMS TO ME THAT LIFE HAS *ONLY* GIVEN ME MISCHIEF. I DOUBT IT CAN DO ANY ADDED DAMAGE THAT I CAN'T HANDLE.
BUT THANKS FOR LOOKING OUT FOR ME.
WHY NOT TAKE A LITTLE BREAK FROM THE WHOLE "CUSTODIAN" THING AND JUST LET ME BORROW IT FOR A BIT?
TAKE IT IF YOU MUST, BUT DO SO CAUTIOUSLY, FOR SUCH AN OBJECT NEVER COMES FREE OF PAYMENT OR CONSEQUENCE.

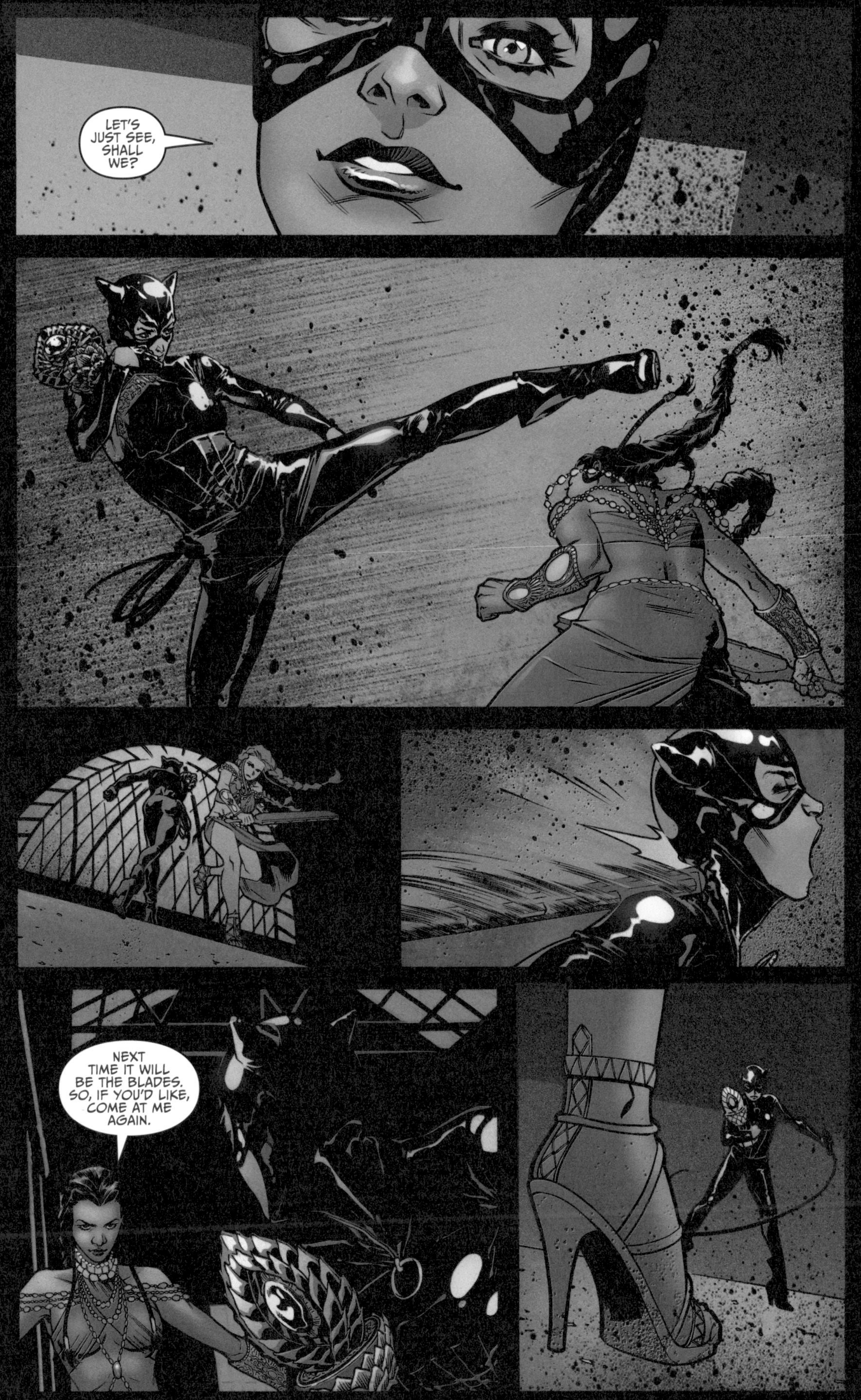
LET'S JUST SEE, SHALL WE?
NEXT TIME IT WILL BE THE BLADES. SO, IF YOU'D LIKE, COME AT ME AGAIN.

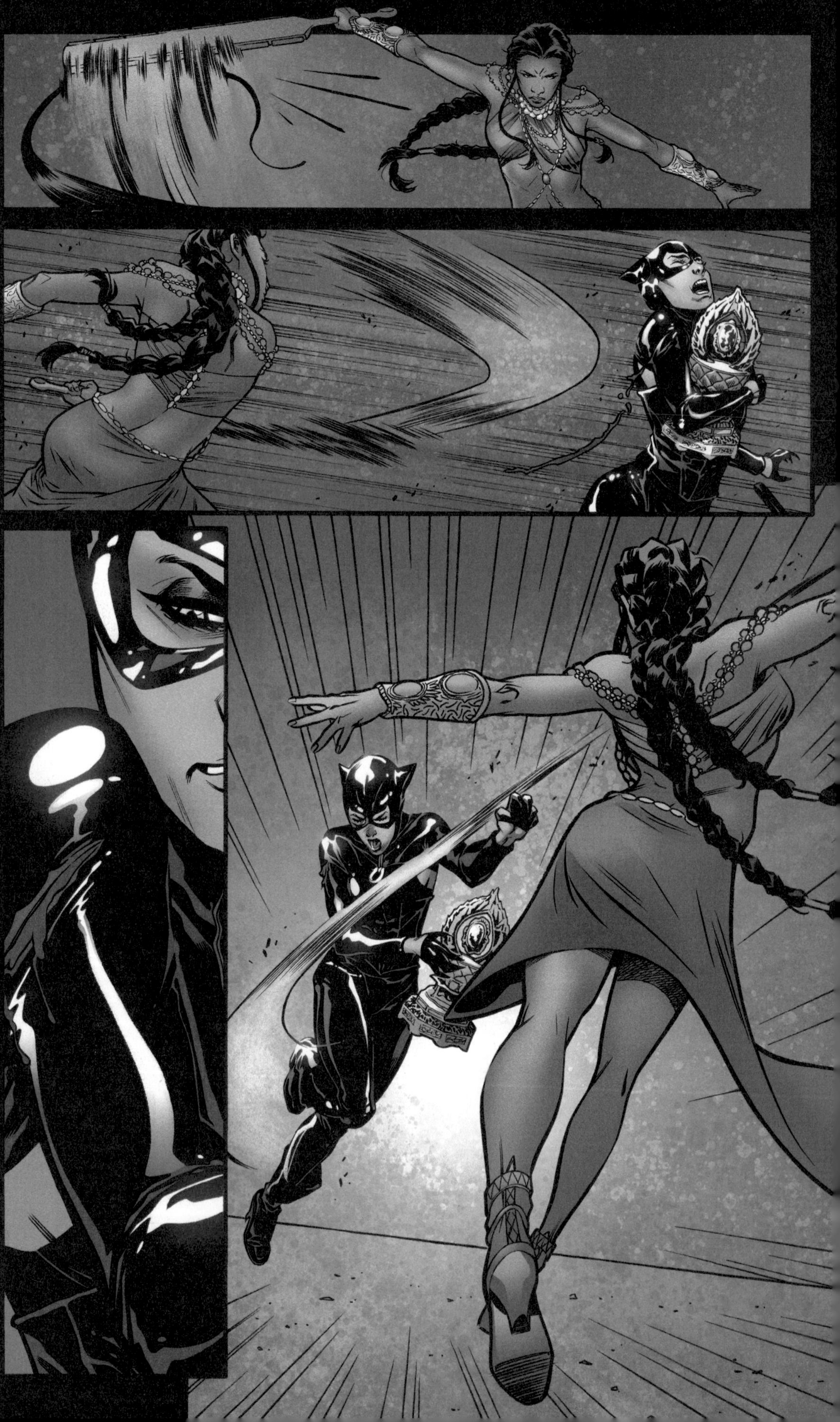

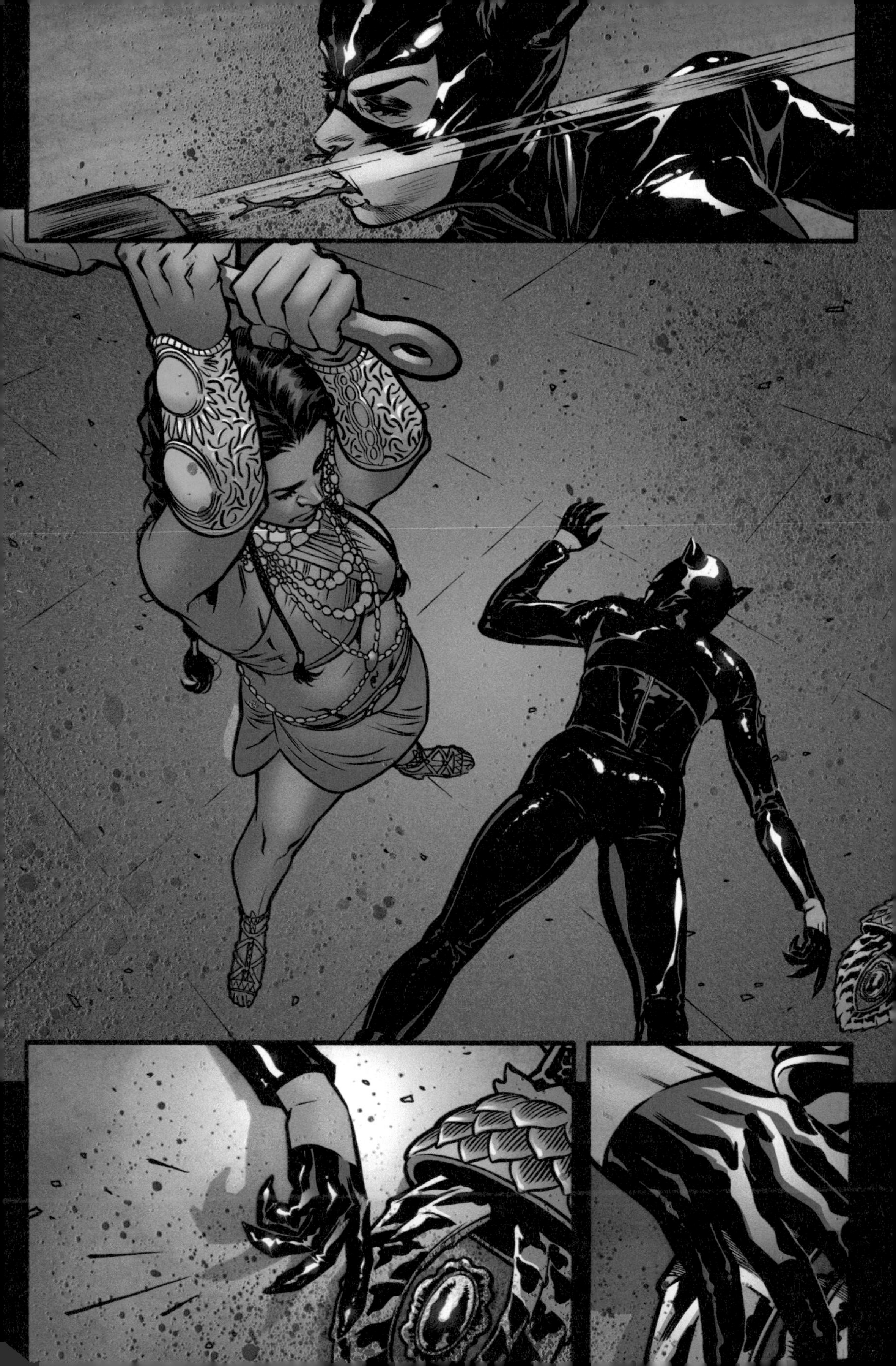

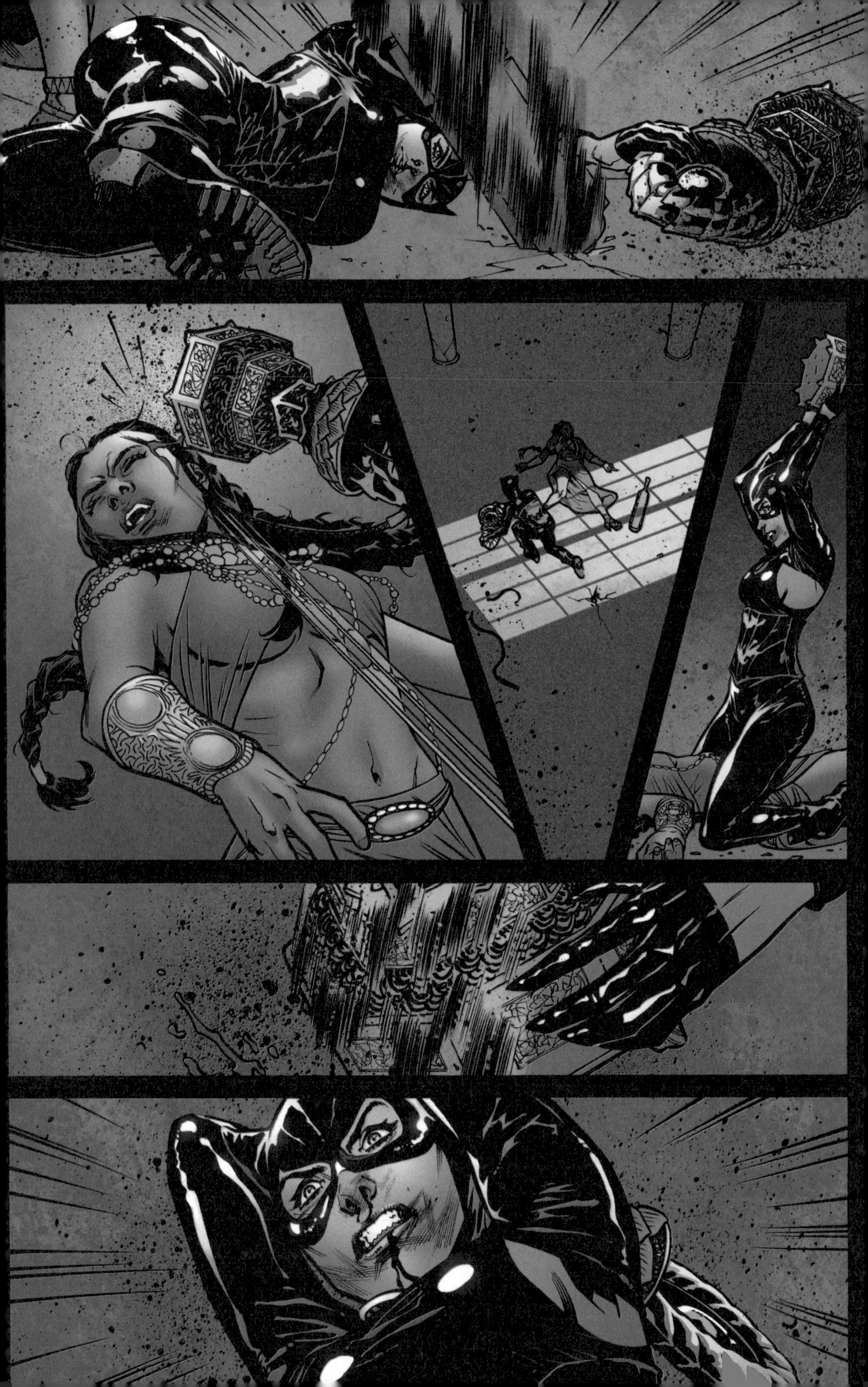

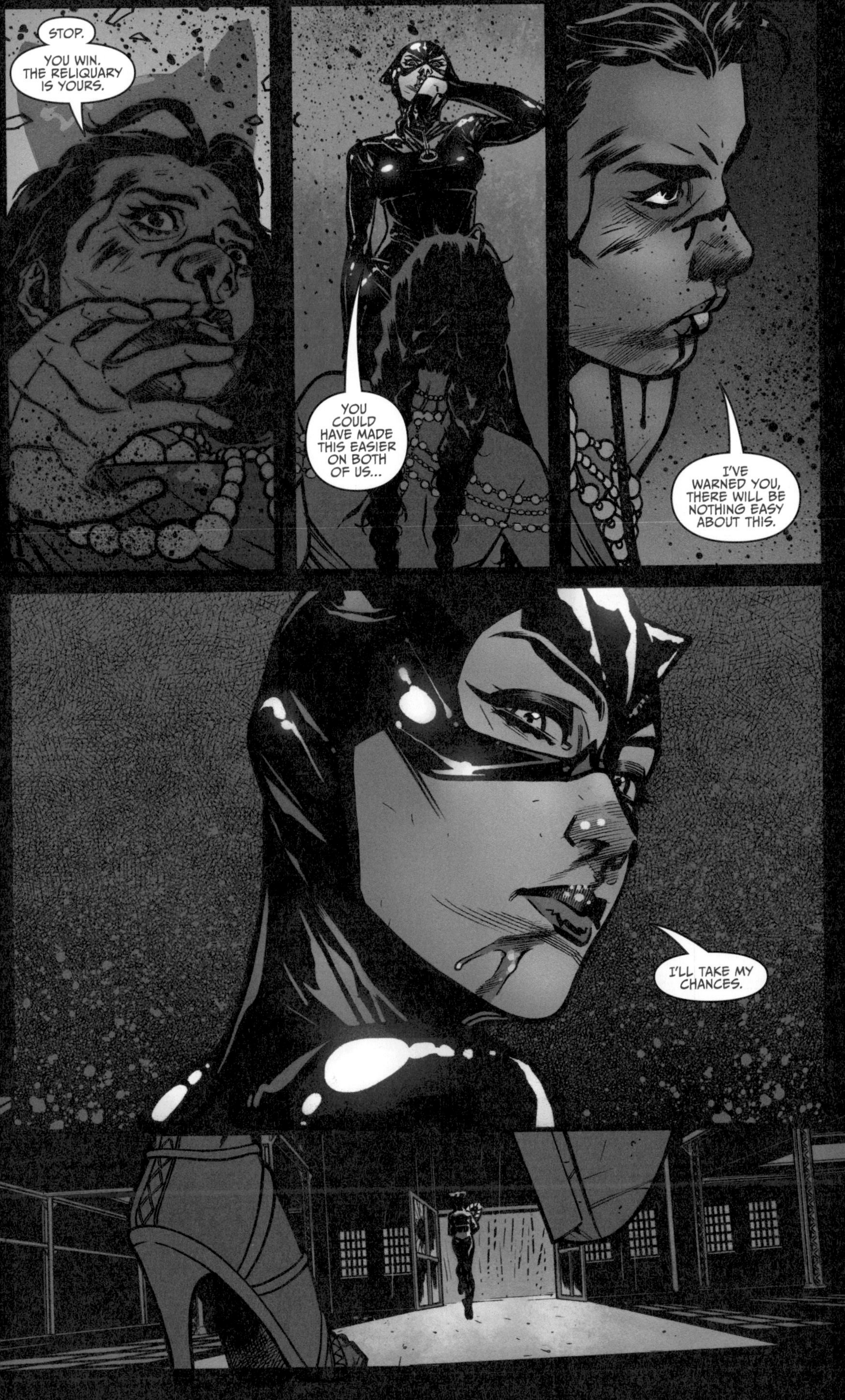
STOP.
YOU WIN. THE RELIQUARY IS YOURS.
YOU COULD HAVE MADE THIS EASIER ON BOTH OF US...
I'VE WARNED YOU, THERE WILL BE NOTHING EASY ABOUT THIS.
I'LL TAKE MY CHANCES.

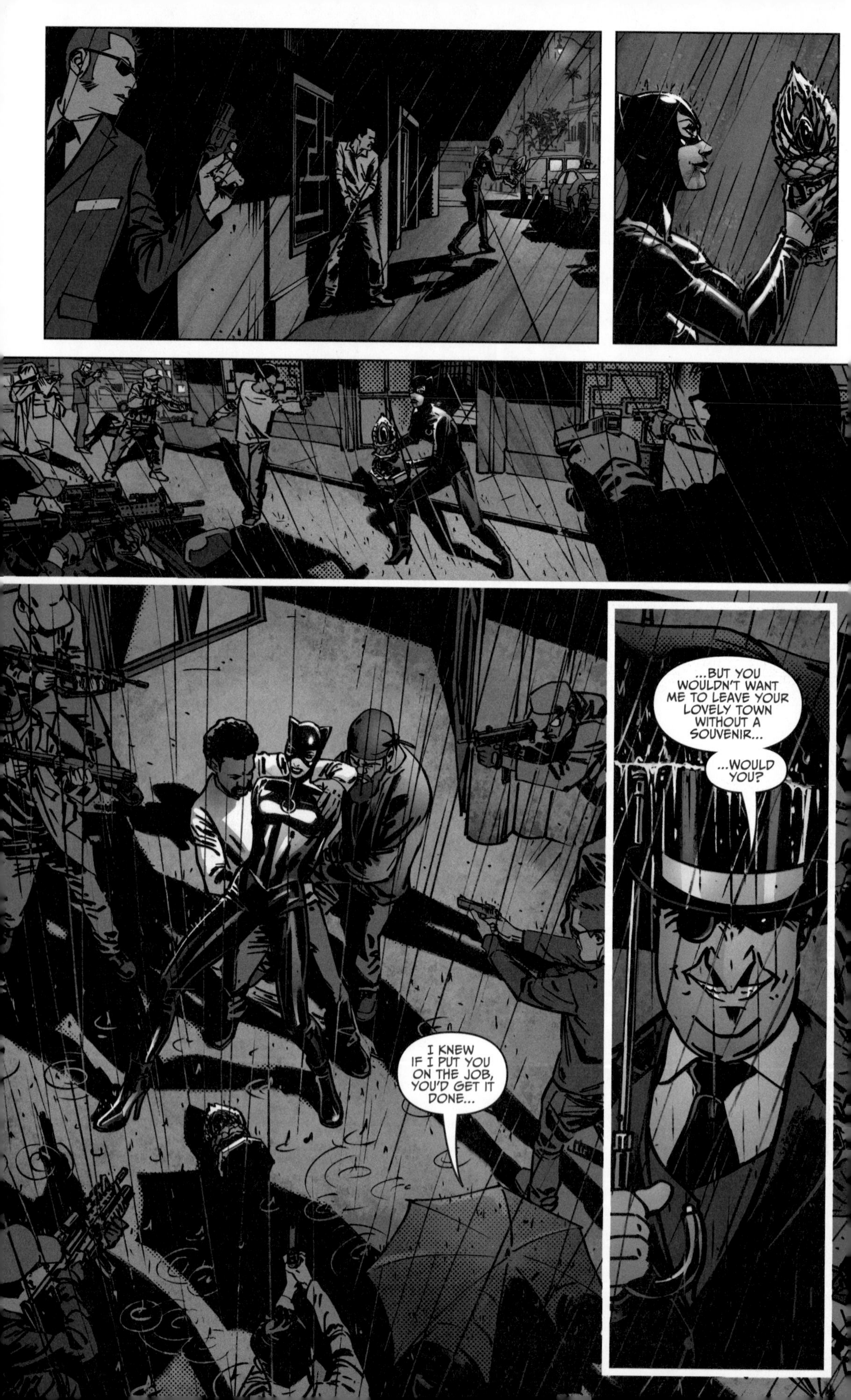
I KNEW IF I PUT YOU ON THE JOB, YOU'D GET IT DONE...
...BUT YOU WOULDN'T WANT ME TO LEAVE YOUR LOVELY TOWN WITHOUT A SOUVENIR...
...WOULD YOU?

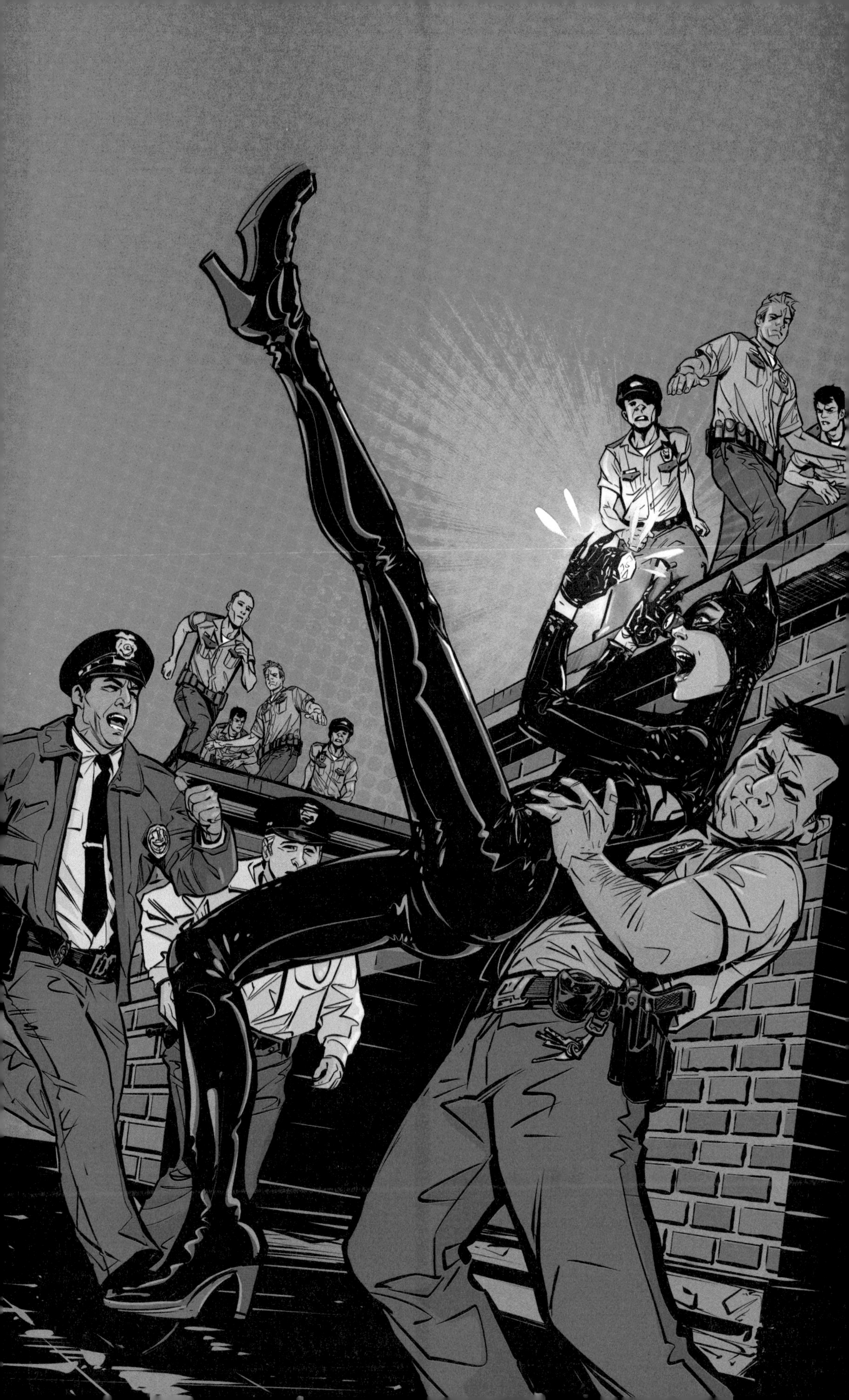

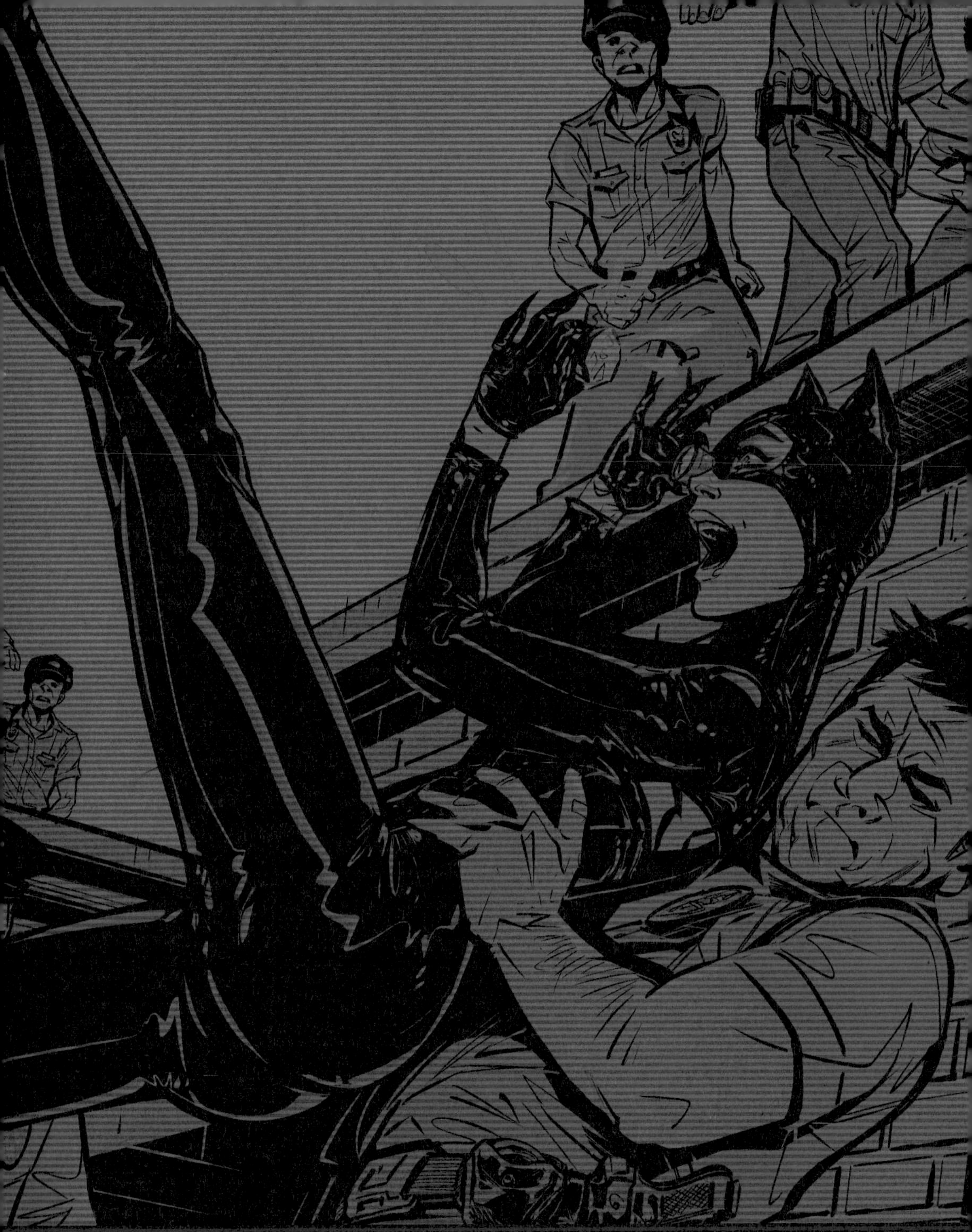

# CATWOMAN

"SO TODAY HAS BASICALLY BEEN A $%&#SHOW. IF YOU'RE CONFUSED ABOUT WHAT'S HAPPENING, DON'T WORRY, I GOT YOU.

"I'LL EXPLAIN BUT TIME IS TICKIN' AWAY SO YOU'RE JUST GOING TO HAVE TO DO YOUR BEST AND TRY TO KEEP UP."

33 / 35

SELINA! ANYTIME YOU FEEL LIKE RESCUING ME FROM THE BACK OF A SPEEDING ARMORED TRUCK WOULD BE GREAT!

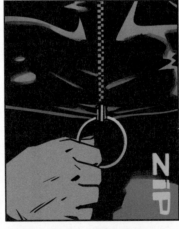

ZIP

YEAH, YEAH, HOLD YOUR HORSES.

VVRRRROOM

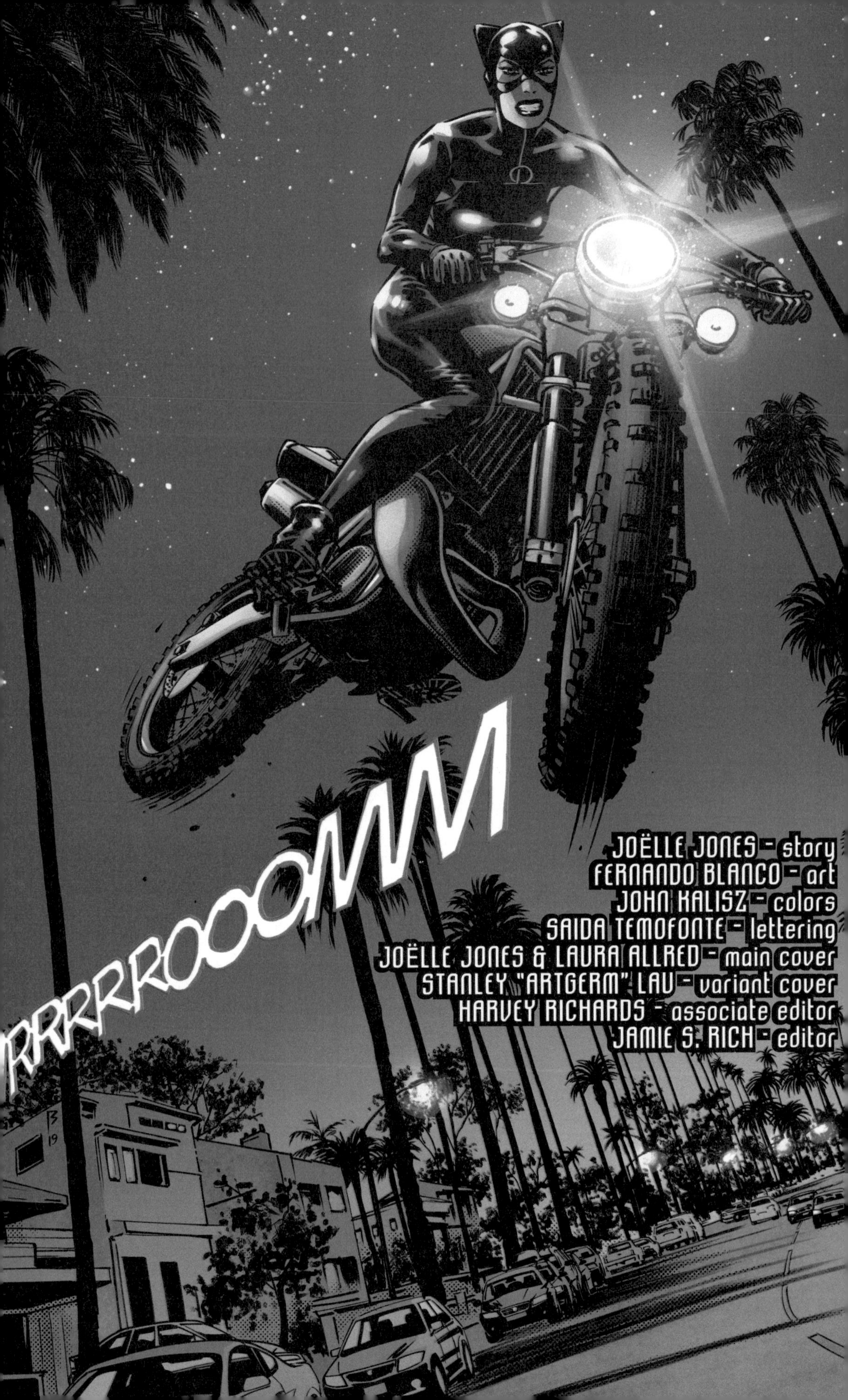
RRRRROOOOMM
JOËLLE JONES - story
FERNANDO BLANCO - art
JOHN KALISZ - colors
SAIDA TEMOFONTE - lettering
JOËLLE JONES & LAURA ALLRED - main cover
STANLEY "ARTGERM" LAU - variant cover
HARVEY RICHARDS - associate editor
JAMIE S. RICH - editor

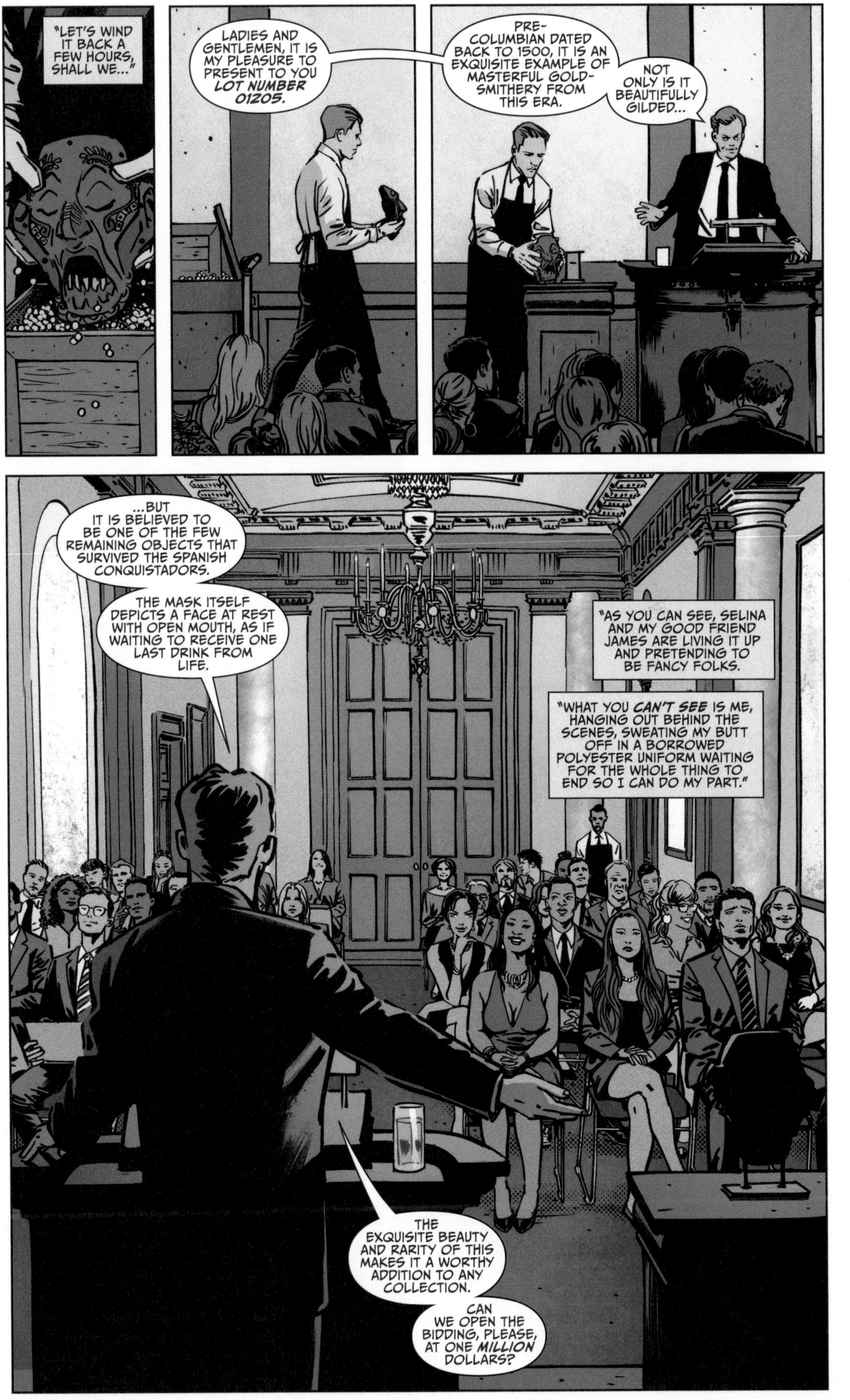
"LET'S WIND IT BACK A FEW HOURS, SHALL WE..."
LADIES AND GENTLEMEN, IT IS MY PLEASURE TO PRESENT TO YOU LOT NUMBER 01205.
PRE-COLUMBIAN DATED BACK TO 1500, IT IS AN EXQUISITE EXAMPLE OF MASTERFUL GOLD-SMITHERY FROM THIS ERA.
NOT ONLY IS IT BEAUTIFULLY GILDED...
...BUT IT IS BELIEVED TO BE ONE OF THE FEW REMAINING OBJECTS THAT SURVIVED THE SPANISH CONQUISTADORS.
THE MASK ITSELF DEPICTS A FACE AT REST WITH OPEN MOUTH, AS IF WAITING TO RECEIVE ONE LAST DRINK FROM LIFE.
"AS YOU CAN SEE, SELINA AND MY GOOD FRIEND JAMES ARE LIVING IT UP AND PRETENDING TO BE FANCY FOLKS.
"WHAT YOU CAN'T SEE IS ME, HANGING OUT BEHIND THE SCENES, SWEATING MY BUTT OFF IN A BORROWED POLYESTER UNIFORM WAITING FOR THE WHOLE THING TO END SO I CAN DO MY PART."
THE EXQUISITE BEAUTY AND RARITY OF THIS MAKES IT A WORTHY ADDITION TO ANY COLLECTION.
CAN WE OPEN THE BIDDING, PLEASE, AT ONE MILLION DOLLARS?

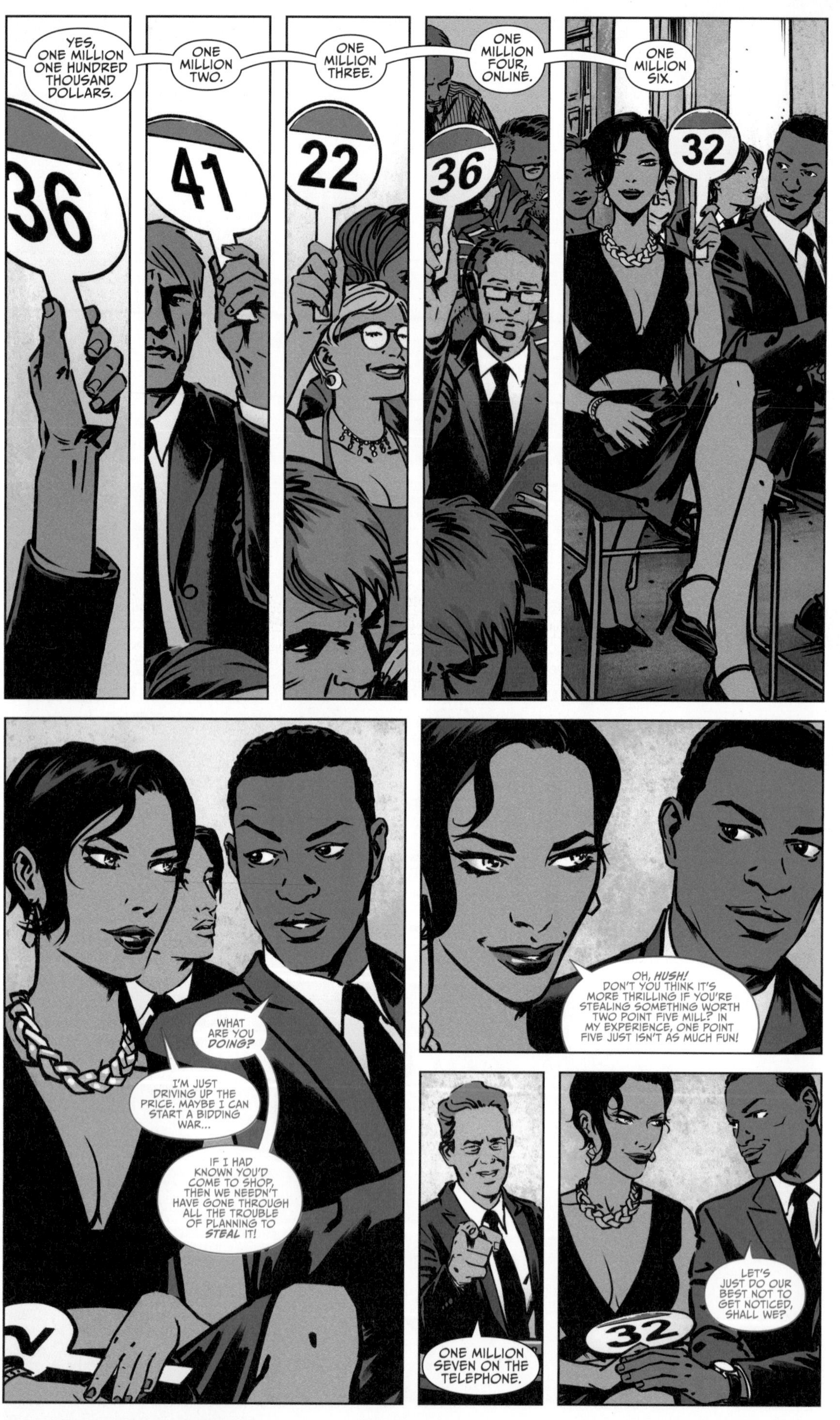
YES, ONE MILLION ONE HUNDRED THOUSAND DOLLARS.
ONE MILLION TWO.
ONE MILLION THREE.
ONE MILLION FOUR, ONLINE.
ONE MILLION SIX.
36
41
22
36
32
WHAT ARE YOU *DOING?*
I'M JUST DRIVING UP THE PRICE. MAYBE I CAN START A BIDDING WAR...
IF I HAD KNOWN YOU'D COME TO SHOP, THEN WE NEEDN'T HAVE GONE THROUGH ALL THE TROUBLE OF PLANNING TO *STEAL* IT!
OH, *HUSH!* DON'T YOU THINK IT'S MORE THRILLING IF YOU'RE STEALING SOMETHING WORTH TWO POINT FIVE MILL? IN MY EXPERIENCE, ONE POINT FIVE JUST ISN'T AS MUCH FUN!
ONE MILLION SEVEN ON THE TELEPHONE.
32
LET'S JUST DO OUR BEST NOT TO GET NOTICED, SHALL WE?

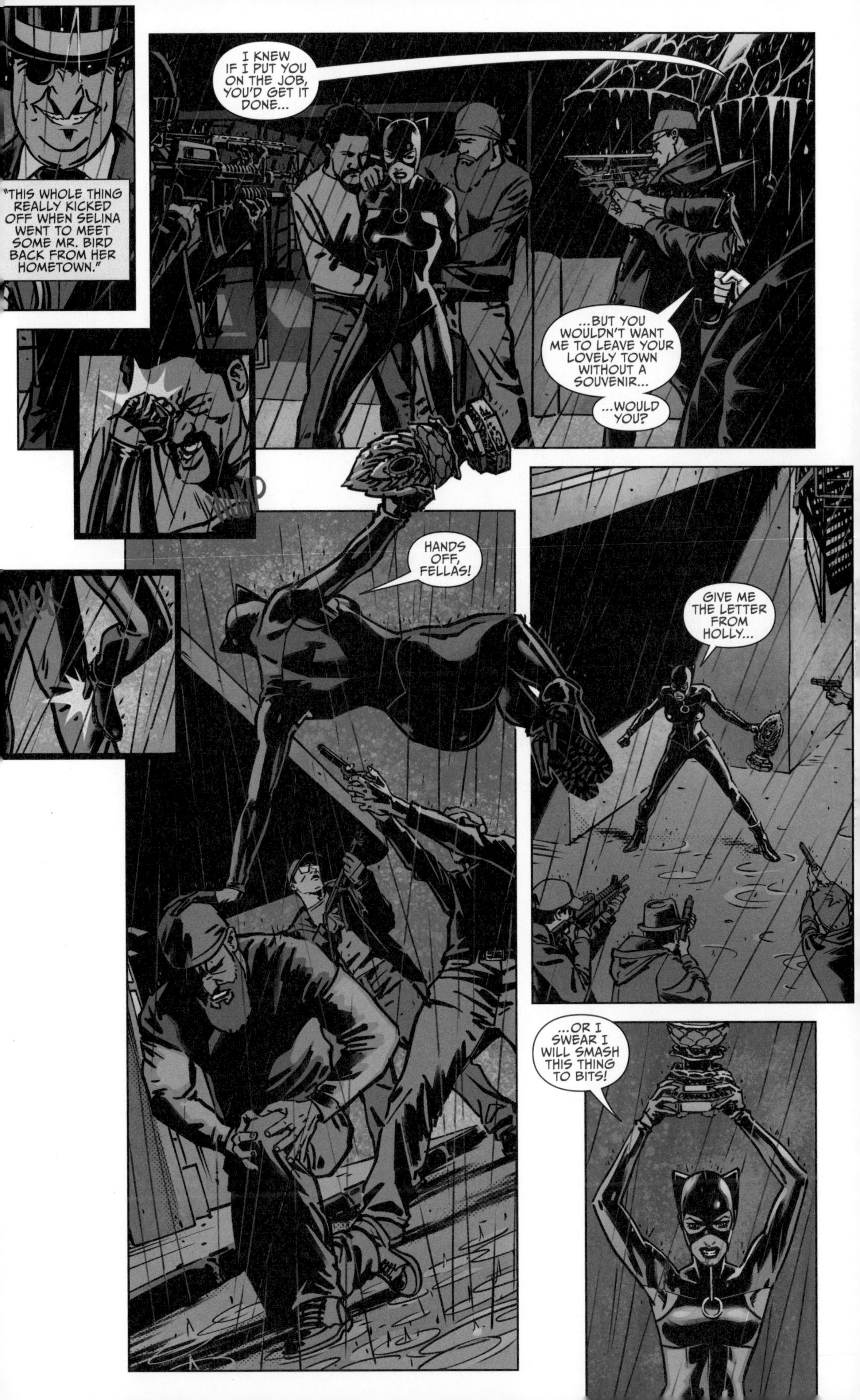
"THIS WHOLE THING REALLY KICKED OFF WHEN SELINA WENT TO MEET SOME MR. BIRD BACK FROM HER HOMETOWN."
I KNEW IF I PUT YOU ON THE JOB, YOU'D GET IT DONE...
...BUT YOU WOULDN'T WANT ME TO LEAVE YOUR LOVELY TOWN WITHOUT A SOUVENIR...
...WOULD YOU?
HANDS OFF, FELLAS!
GIVE ME THE LETTER FROM HOLLY...
...OR I SWEAR I WILL SMASH THIS THING TO BITS!

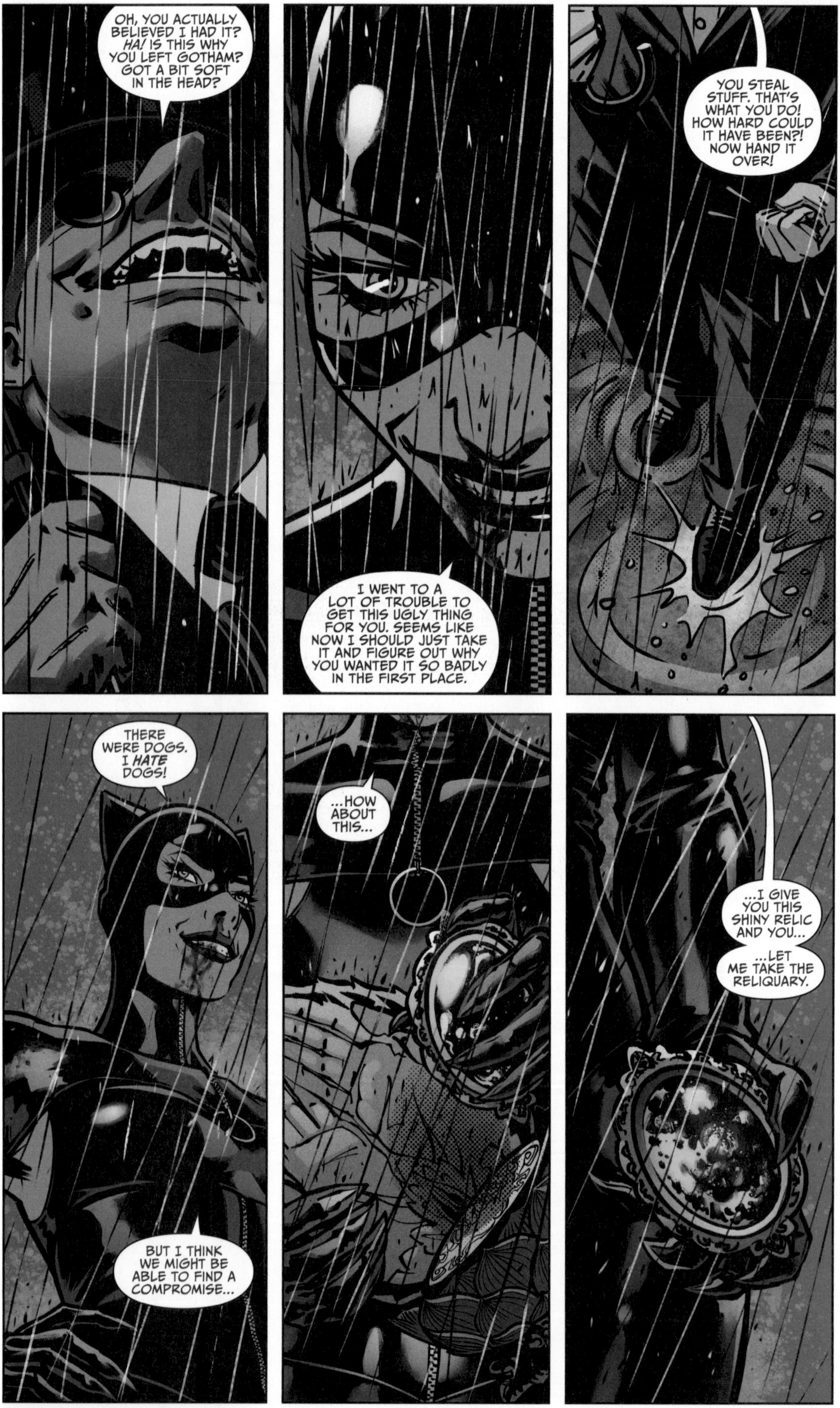
OH, YOU ACTUALLY BELIEVED I HAD IT? HA! IS THIS WHY YOU LEFT GOTHAM? GOT A BIT SOFT IN THE HEAD?
I WENT TO A LOT OF TROUBLE TO GET THIS UGLY THING FOR YOU. SEEMS LIKE NOW I SHOULD JUST TAKE IT AND FIGURE OUT WHY YOU WANTED IT SO BADLY IN THE FIRST PLACE.
YOU STEAL STUFF. THAT'S WHAT YOU DO! HOW HARD COULD IT HAVE BEEN?! NOW HAND IT OVER!
THERE WERE DOGS. I HATE DOGS!
BUT I THINK WE MIGHT BE ABLE TO FIND A COMPROMISE...
...HOW ABOUT THIS...
...I GIVE YOU THIS SHINY RELIC AND YOU...
...LET ME TAKE THE RELIQUARY.

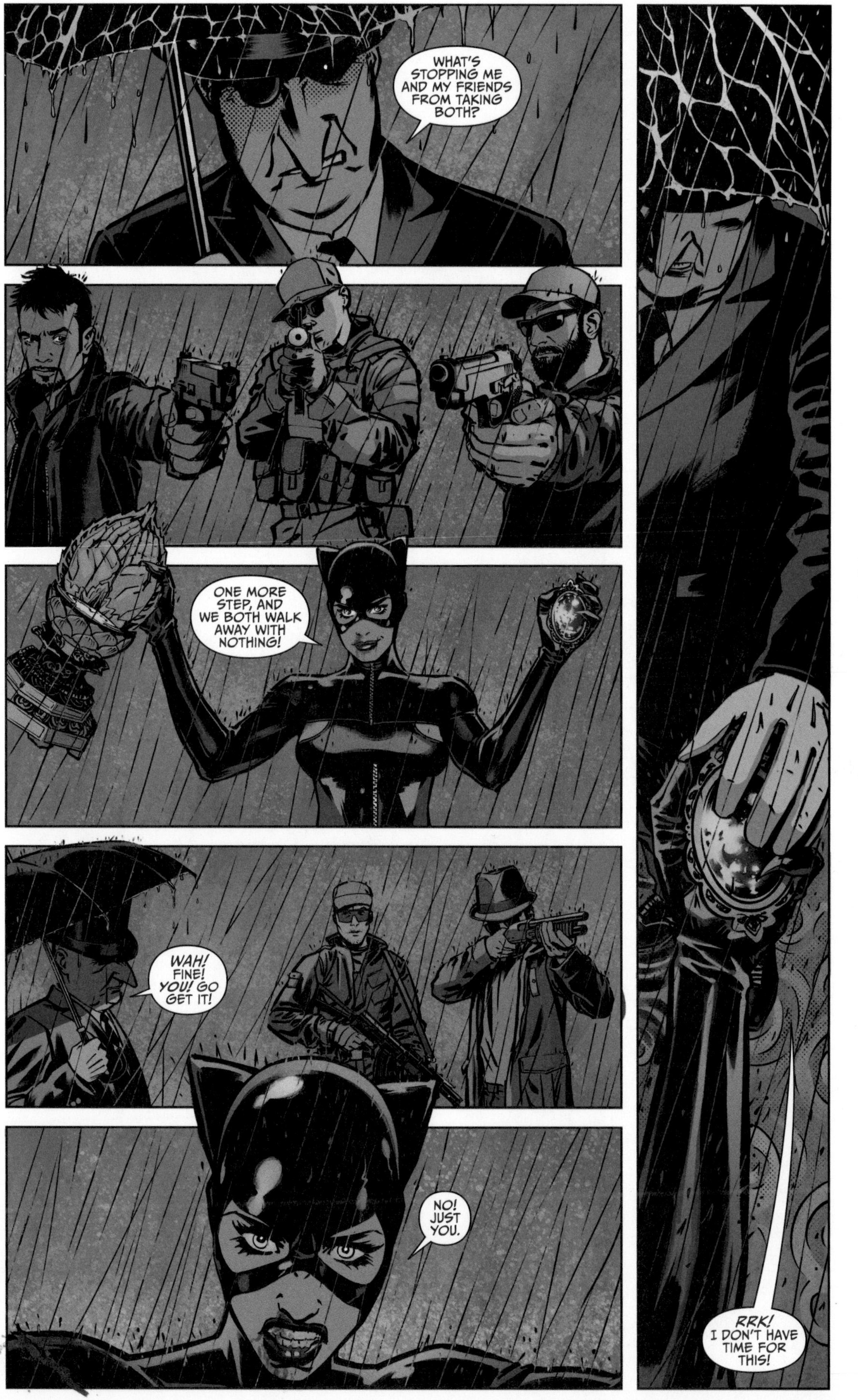
WHAT'S STOPPING ME AND MY FRIENDS FROM TAKING BOTH?
ONE MORE STEP, AND WE BOTH WALK AWAY WITH NOTHING!
WAH! FINE! YOU! GO GET IT!
NO! JUST YOU.
RRK! I DON'T HAVE TIME FOR THIS!

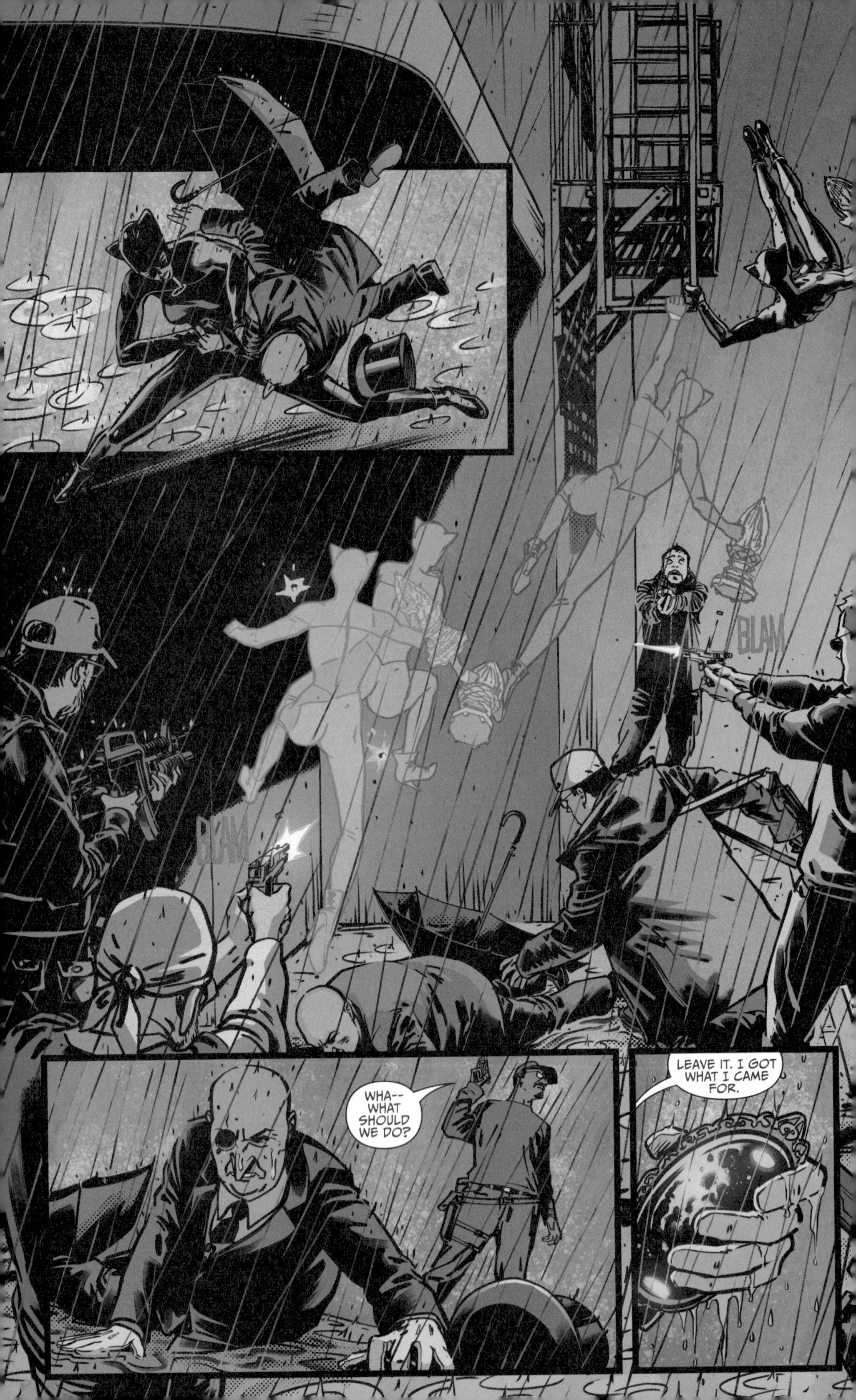
BLAM
BLAM
WHA-- WHAT SHOULD WE DO?
LEAVE IT. I GOT WHAT I CAME FOR.

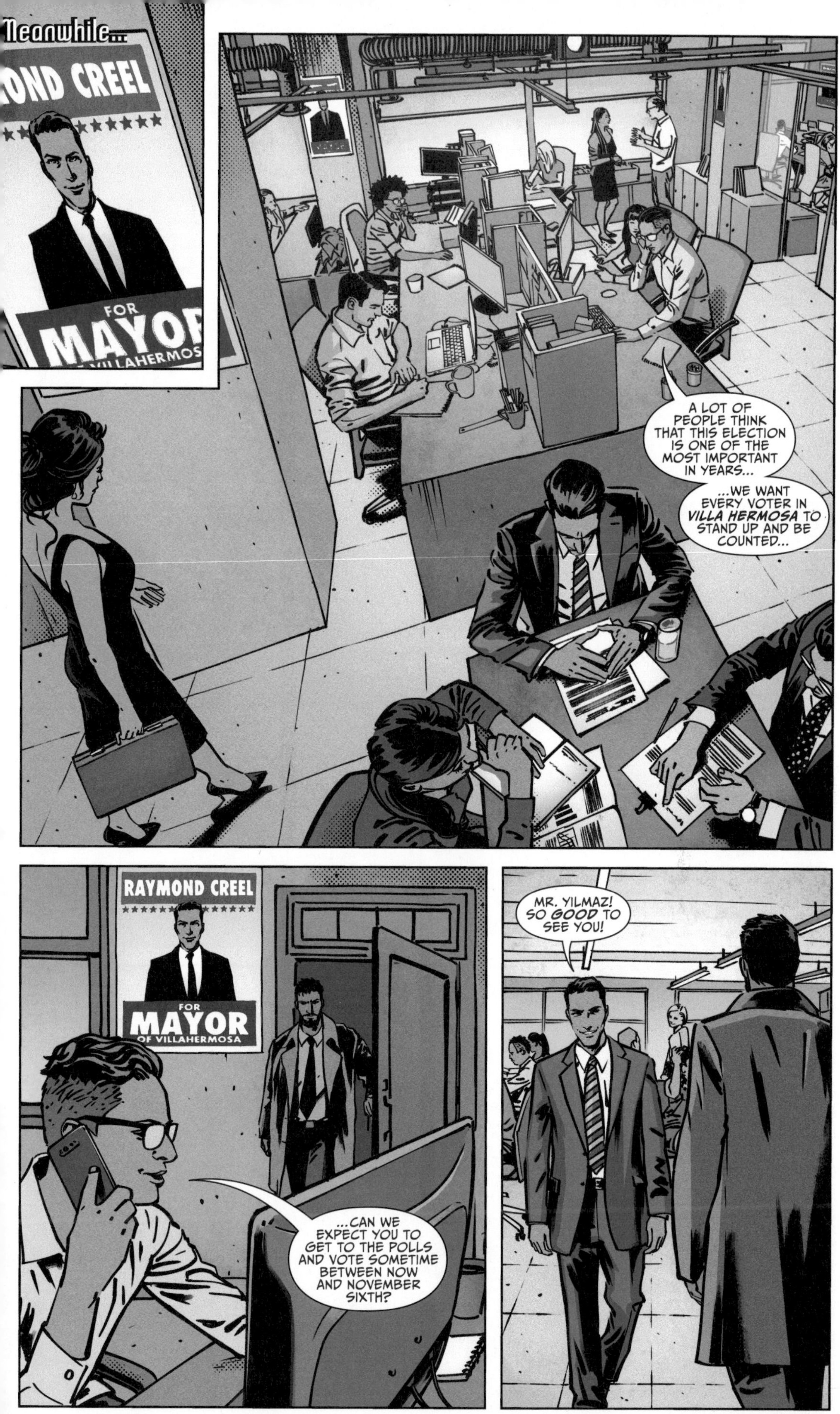
Meanwhile...
OND CREEL
FOR
MAYOR
OF VILLAHERMOSA
A LOT OF PEOPLE THINK THAT THIS ELECTION IS ONE OF THE MOST IMPORTANT IN YEARS...
...WE WANT EVERY VOTER IN VILLA HERMOSA TO STAND UP AND BE COUNTED...
RAYMOND CREEL
FOR
MAYOR
OF VILLAHERMOSA
...CAN WE EXPECT YOU TO GET TO THE POLLS AND VOTE SOMETIME BETWEEN NOW AND NOVEMBER SIXTH?
MR. YILMAZ! SO GOOD TO SEE YOU!

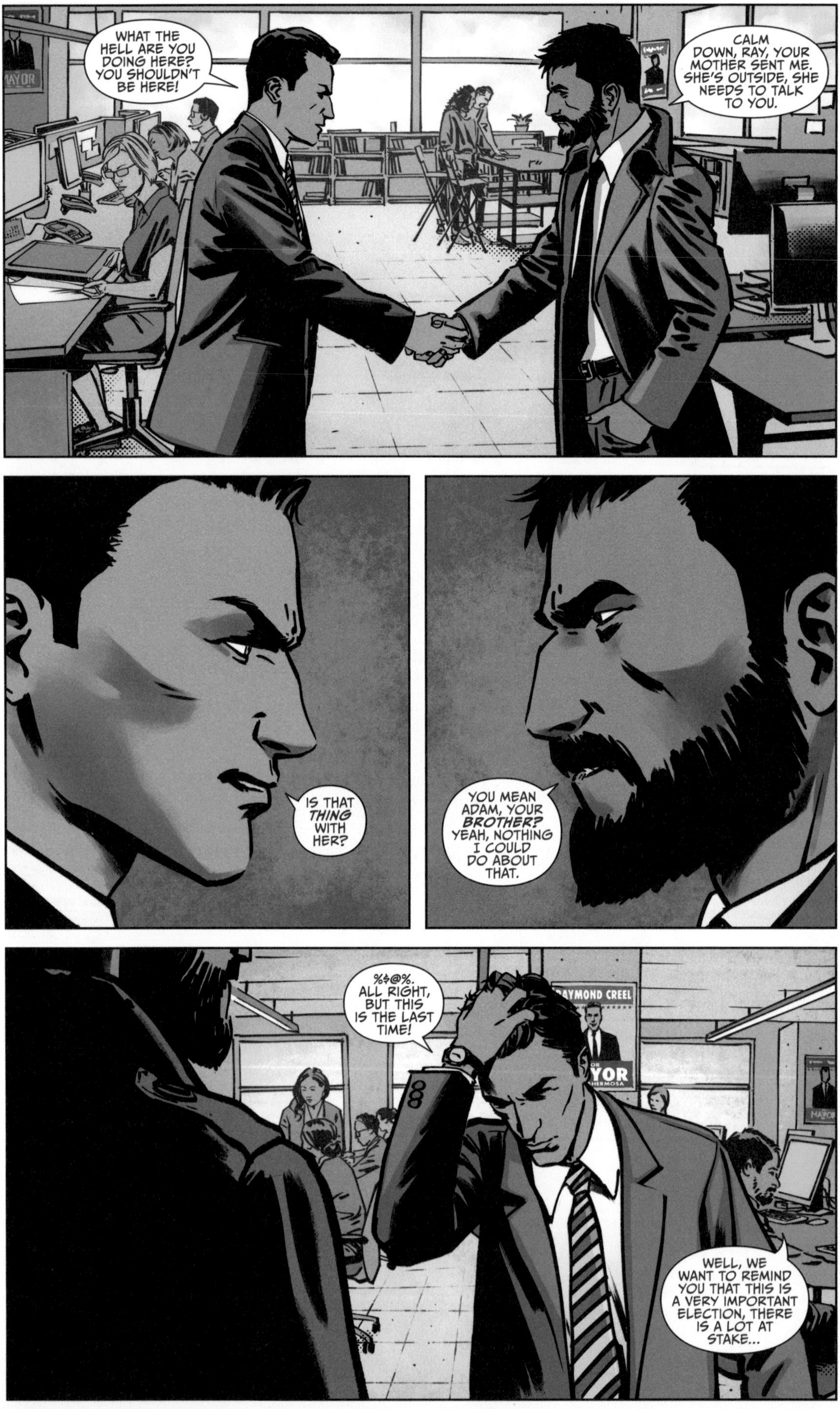
WHAT THE HELL ARE YOU DOING HERE? YOU SHOULDN'T BE HERE!
CALM DOWN, RAY, YOUR MOTHER SENT ME. SHE'S OUTSIDE, SHE NEEDS TO TALK TO YOU.
IS THAT *THING* WITH HER?
YOU MEAN ADAM, YOUR ***BROTHER?*** YEAH, NOTHING I COULD DO ABOUT THAT.
RAYMOND CREEL
%$@%. ALL RIGHT, BUT THIS IS THE LAST TIME!
WELL, WE WANT TO REMIND YOU THAT THIS IS A VERY IMPORTANT ELECTION, THERE IS A LOT AT STAKE...

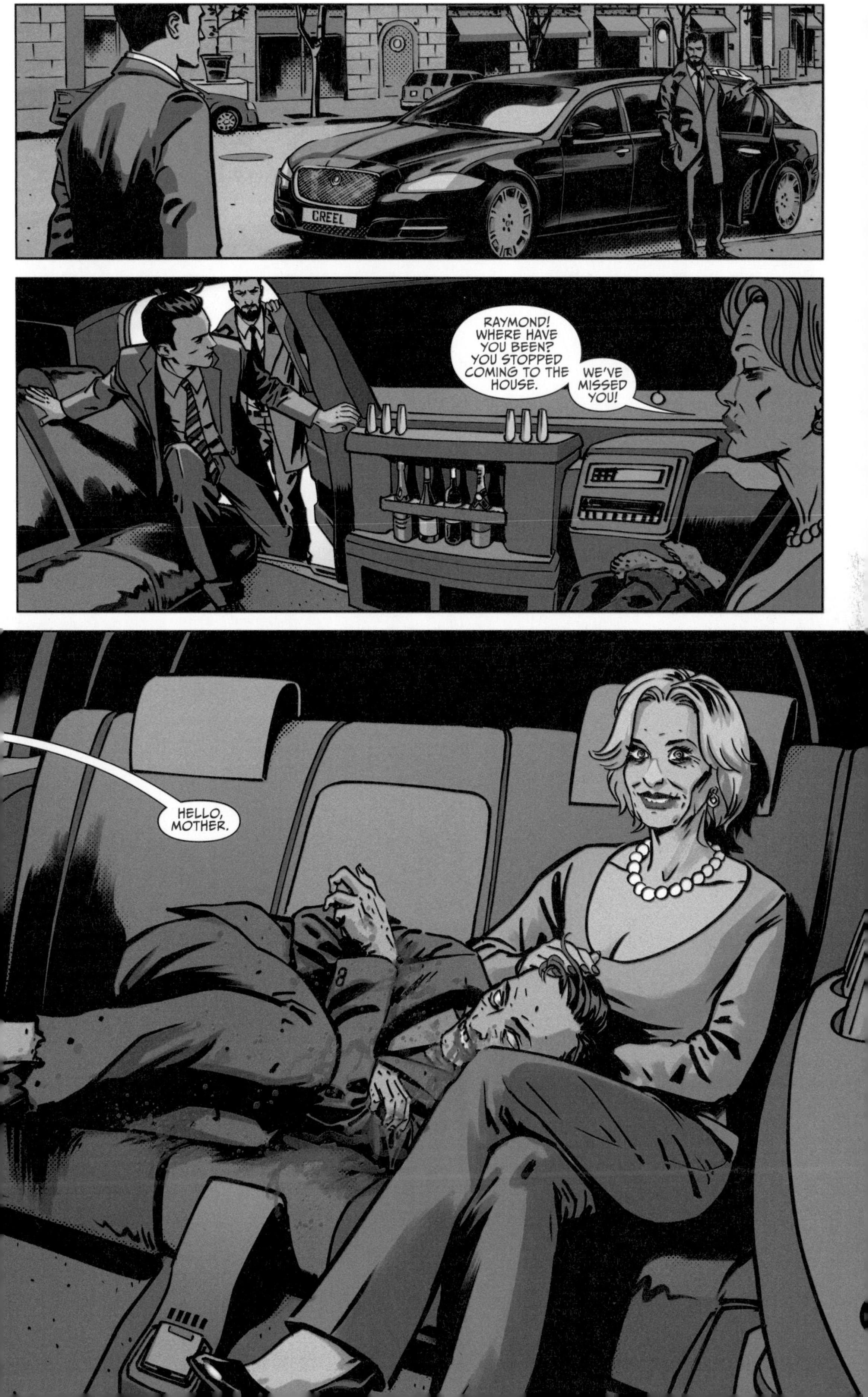
CREEL
RAYMOND! WHERE HAVE YOU BEEN? YOU STOPPED COMING TO THE HOUSE.
WE'VE MISSED YOU!
HELLO, MOTHER.

"SO, A FEW DAYS AFTER BIRD MAN, SELINA BROUGHT ME IN. GOOD THING, TOO-- SHE DOESN'T KNOW THIS TOWN OR ITS PEOPLE LIKE I DO. TURNS OUT THE 'RELIQUARY' WAS THE REAL DEAL."

YEAH, SO IT'S READY?

GREAT, BUT I'M BRINGING A FRIEND THIS TIME.

NO! THE ONE I TOLD YOU ABOUT.

COME ON NOW, JUST ONE BITE...

...FOR ME?

OPEN YOUR MOUTH.

THROUGH THE TEETH AND OVER THE GUMS...

...WATCH OUT STOMACH, HERE IT COMES...

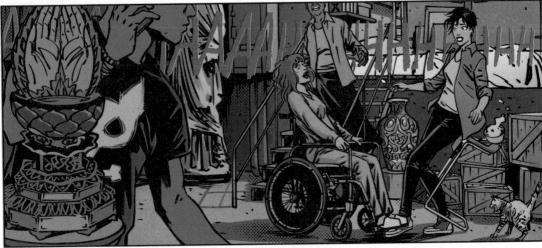

AAAAHHH

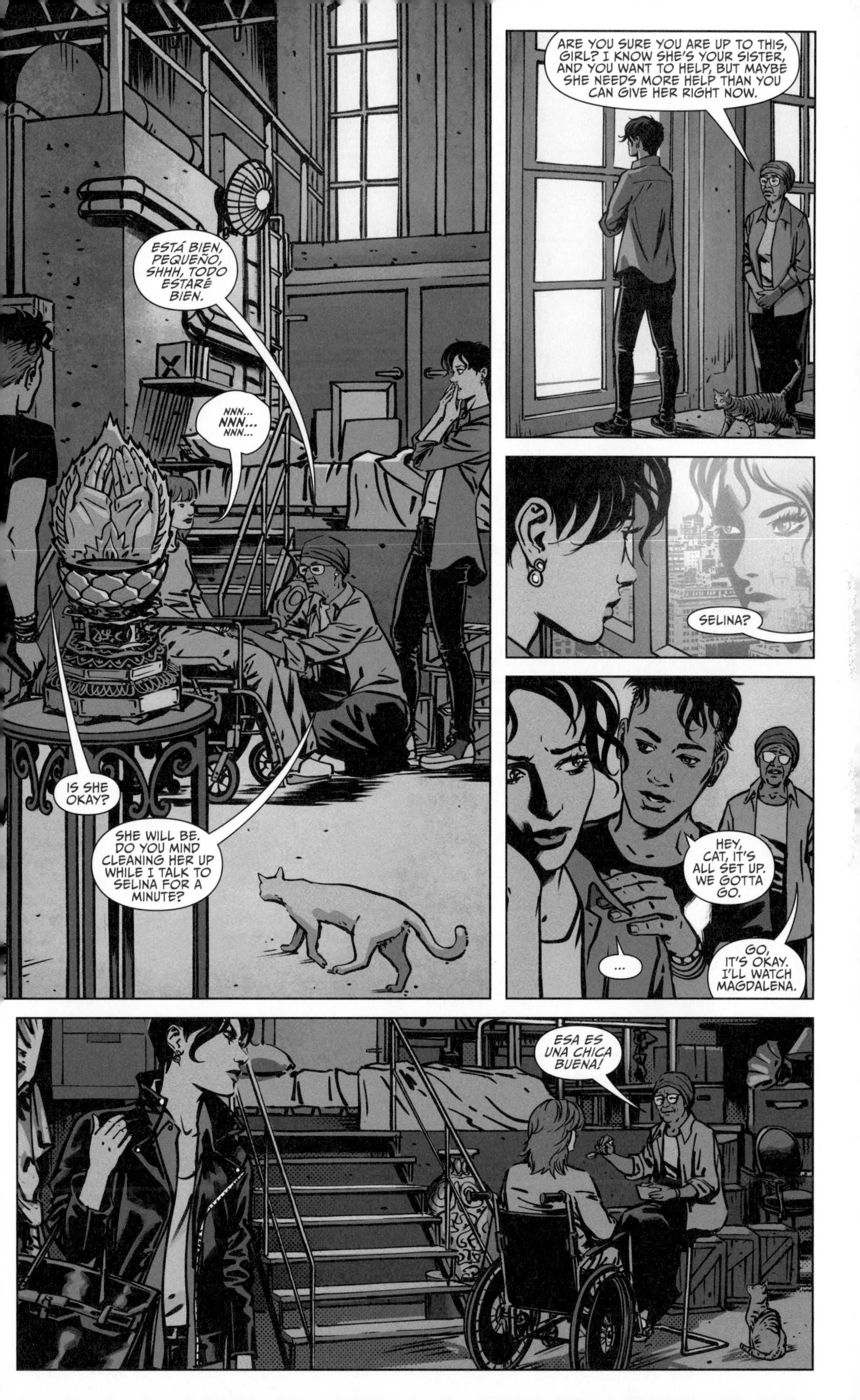
ESTÁ BIEN, PEQUEÑO, SHHH, TODO ESTARÉ BIEN.
NNN... NNN... NNN...
IS SHE OKAY?
SHE WILL BE. DO YOU MIND CLEANING HER UP WHILE I TALK TO SELINA FOR A MINUTE?
ARE YOU SURE YOU ARE UP TO THIS, GIRL? I KNOW SHE'S YOUR SISTER, AND YOU WANT TO HELP, BUT MAYBE SHE NEEDS MORE HELP THAN YOU CAN GIVE HER RIGHT NOW.
SELINA?
HEY, CAT, IT'S ALL SET UP. WE GOTTA GO.
...
GO, IT'S OKAY. I'LL WATCH MAGDALENA.
ESA ES UNA CHICA BUENA!

"SEEMS LIKE WE'RE RUNNING OUT OF TIME FOR ME TO SAY EVERYTHING I WANT TO SAY, SO I'LL SAVE THE NITTY-GRITTY DETAILS FOR NEXT TIME..."

"...BUT WHAT YOU NEED TO KNOW NOW..."

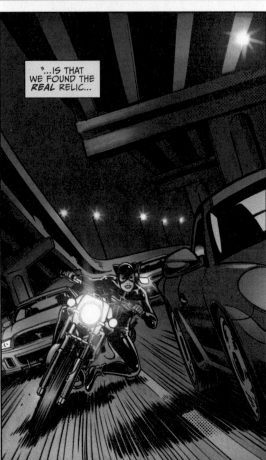

"...IS THAT WE FOUND THE *REAL* RELIC..."

"...THAT WAS MADE TO FIT *OUR* RELIQUARY!"

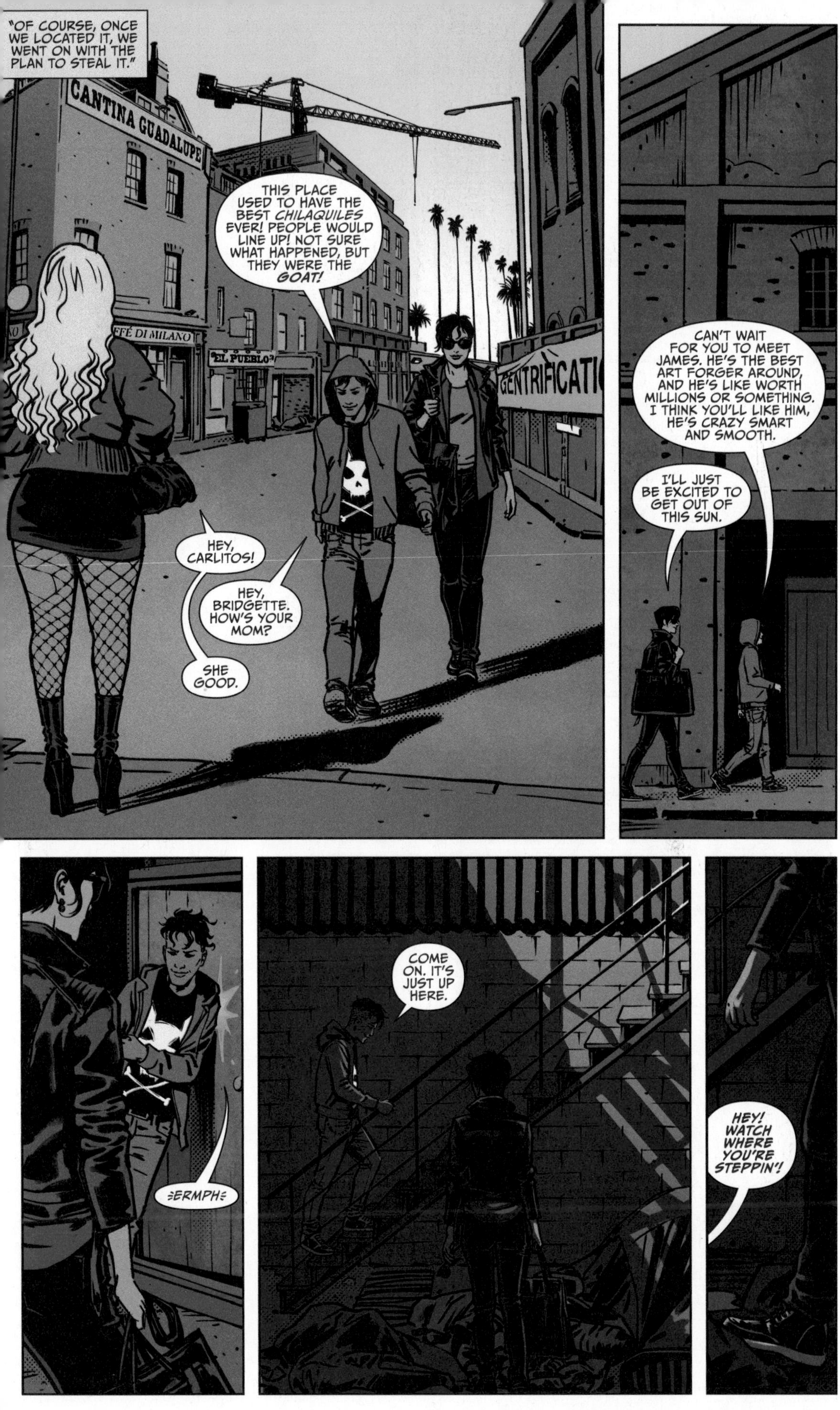

"OF COURSE, ONCE WE LOCATED IT, WE WENT ON WITH THE PLAN TO STEAL IT."
CANTINA GUADALUPE
FFÉ DI MILANO
EL PUEBLO
GENTRIFICATI
THIS PLACE USED TO HAVE THE BEST *CHILAQUILES* EVER! PEOPLE WOULD LINE UP! NOT SURE WHAT HAPPENED, BUT THEY WERE THE *GOAT!*
HEY, CARLITOS!
HEY, BRIDGETTE. HOW'S YOUR MOM?
SHE GOOD.
CAN'T WAIT FOR YOU TO MEET JAMES. HE'S THE BEST ART FORGER AROUND, AND HE'S LIKE WORTH MILLIONS OR SOMETHING. I THINK YOU'LL LIKE HIM, HE'S CRAZY SMART AND SMOOTH.
I'LL JUST BE EXCITED TO GET OUT OF THIS SUN.
ERMPH
COME ON. IT'S JUST UP HERE.
HEY! WATCH WHERE YOU'RE STEPPIN'!

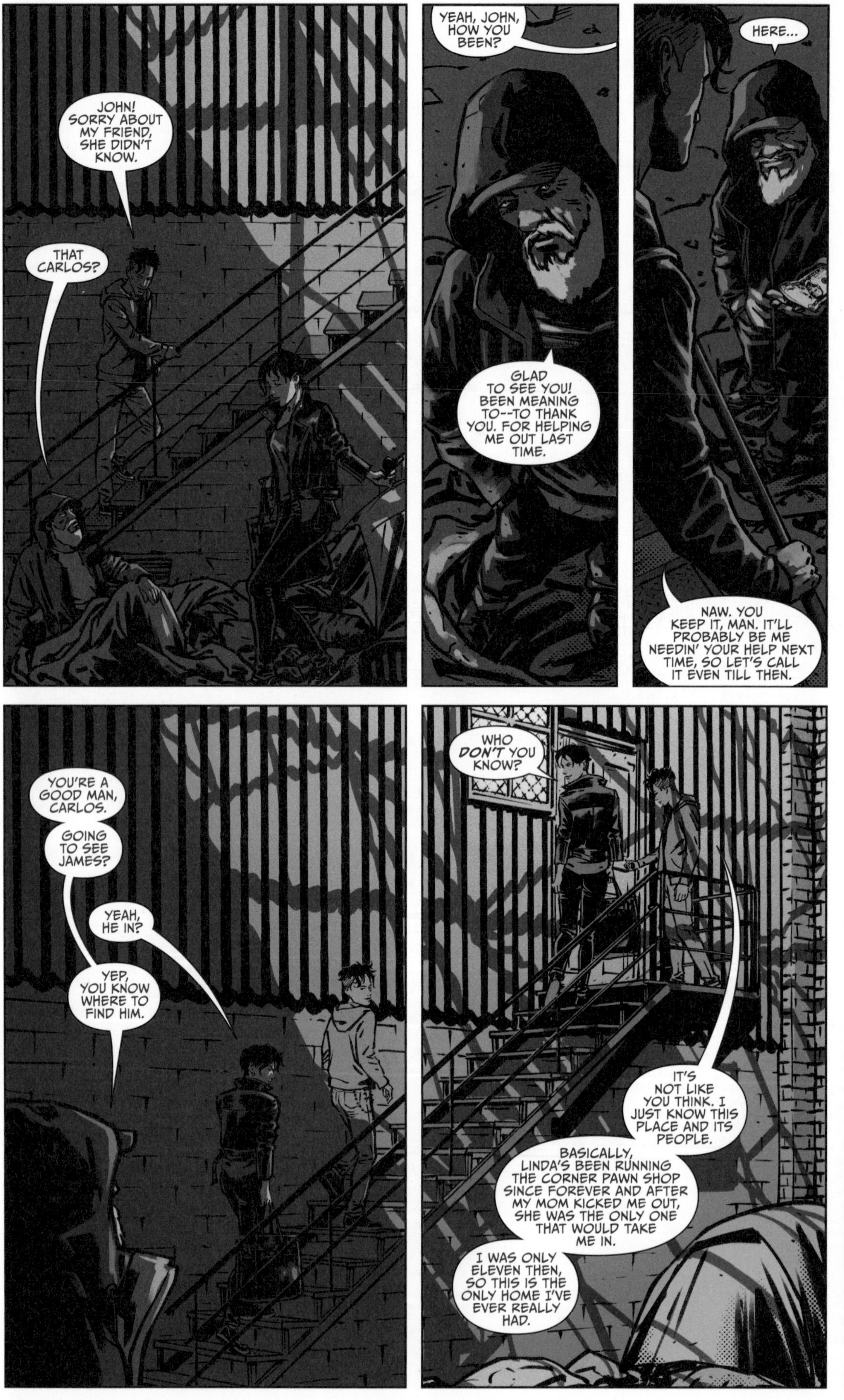
JOHN! SORRY ABOUT MY FRIEND, SHE DIDN'T KNOW.
THAT CARLOS?
YEAH, JOHN, HOW YOU BEEN?
GLAD TO SEE YOU! BEEN MEANING TO--TO THANK YOU. FOR HELPING ME OUT LAST TIME.
HERE...
NAW. YOU KEEP IT, MAN. IT'LL PROBABLY BE ME NEEDIN' YOUR HELP NEXT TIME, SO LET'S CALL IT EVEN TILL THEN.
YOU'RE A GOOD MAN, CARLOS.
GOING TO SEE JAMES?
YEAH, HE IN?
YEP, YOU KNOW WHERE TO FIND HIM.
WHO DON'T YOU KNOW?
IT'S NOT LIKE YOU THINK. I JUST KNOW THIS PLACE AND ITS PEOPLE.
BASICALLY, LINDA'S BEEN RUNNING THE CORNER PAWN SHOP SINCE FOREVER AND AFTER MY MOM KICKED ME OUT, SHE WAS THE ONLY ONE THAT WOULD TAKE ME IN.
I WAS ONLY ELEVEN THEN, SO THIS IS THE ONLY HOME I'VE EVER REALLY HAD.

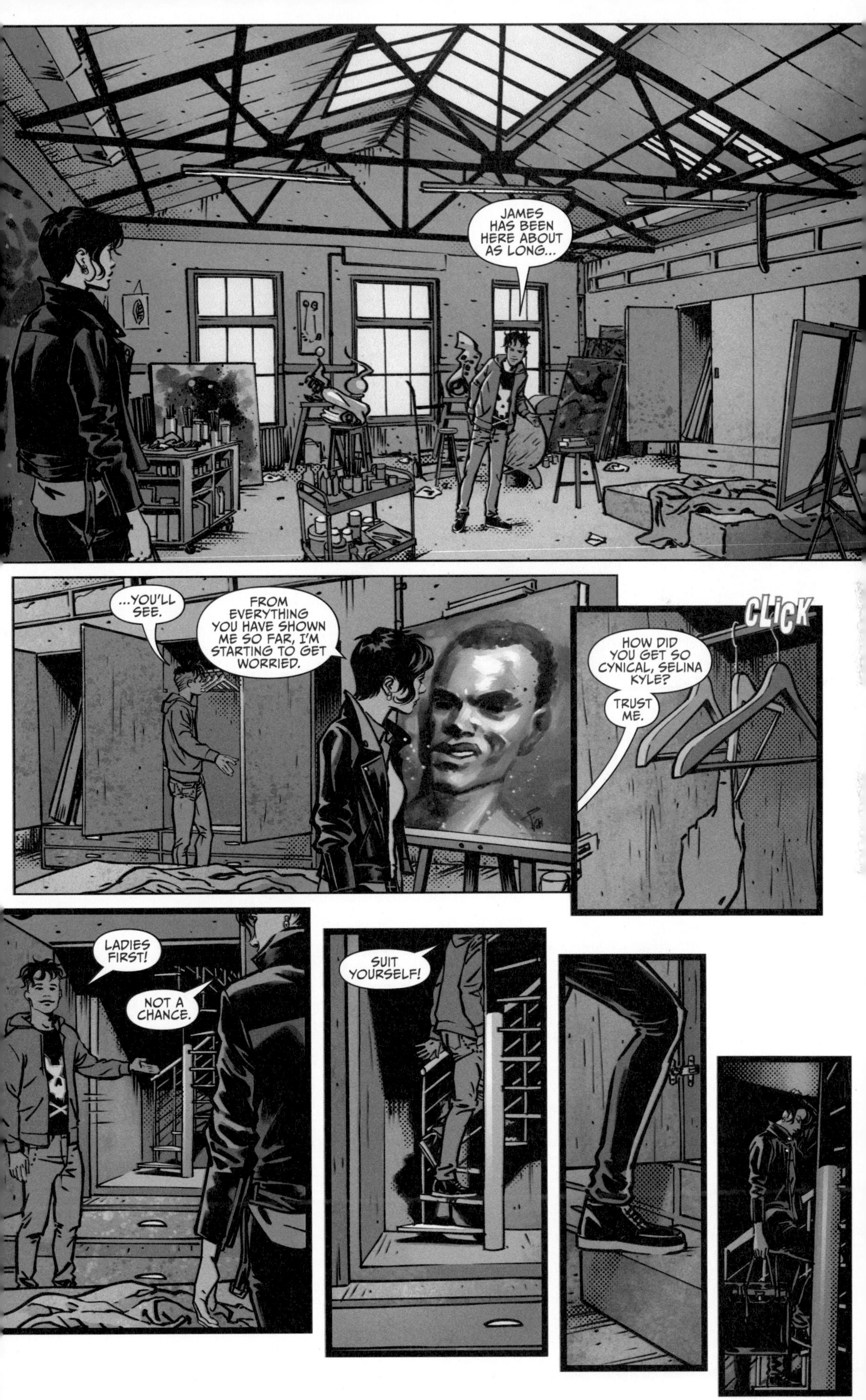
JAMES HAS BEEN HERE ABOUT AS LONG...
...YOU'LL SEE.
FROM EVERYTHING YOU HAVE SHOWN ME SO FAR, I'M STARTING TO GET WORRIED.
CLICK
HOW DID YOU GET SO CYNICAL, SELINA KYLE?
TRUST ME.
LADIES FIRST!
NOT A CHANCE.
SUIT YOURSELF!

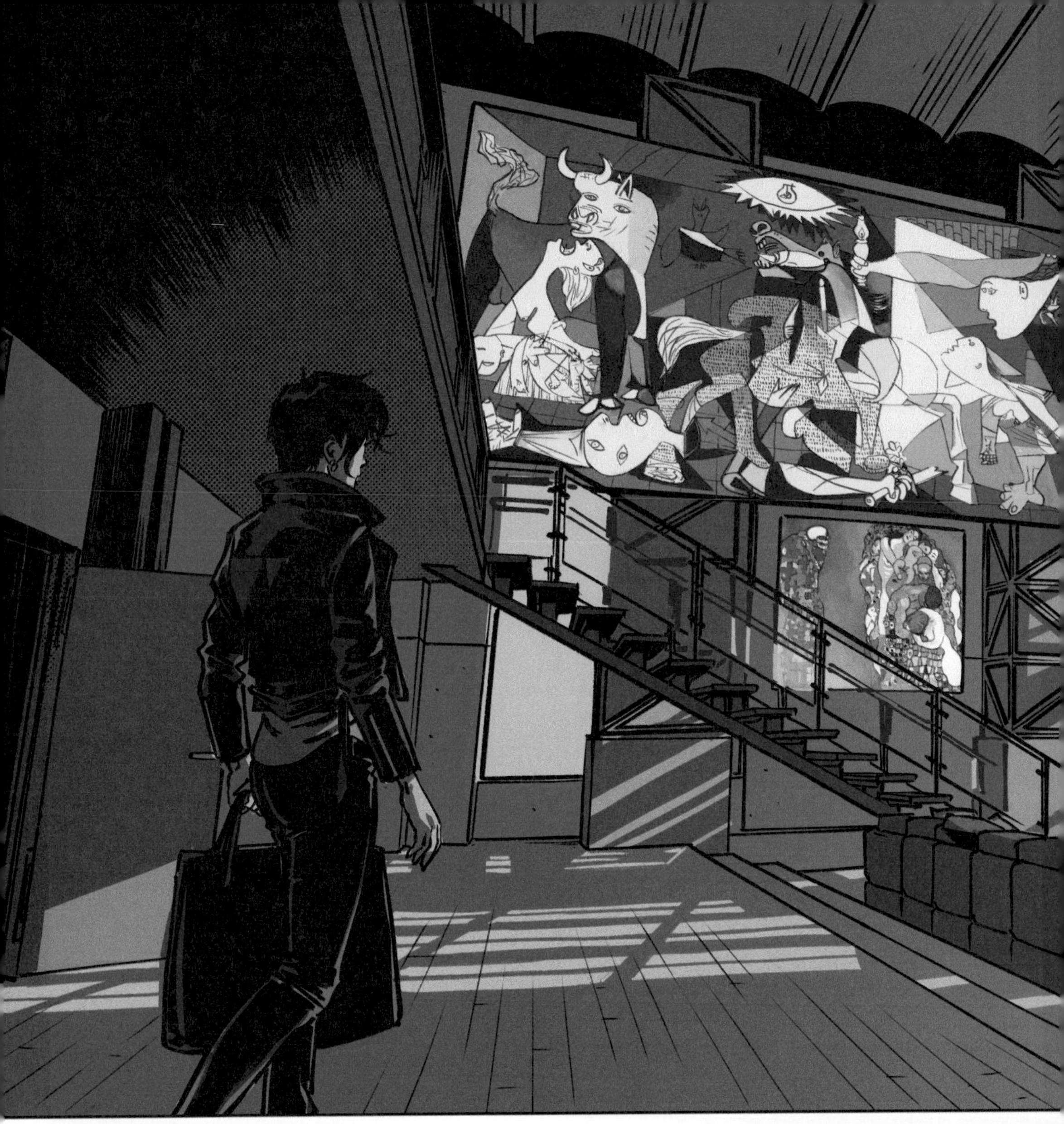

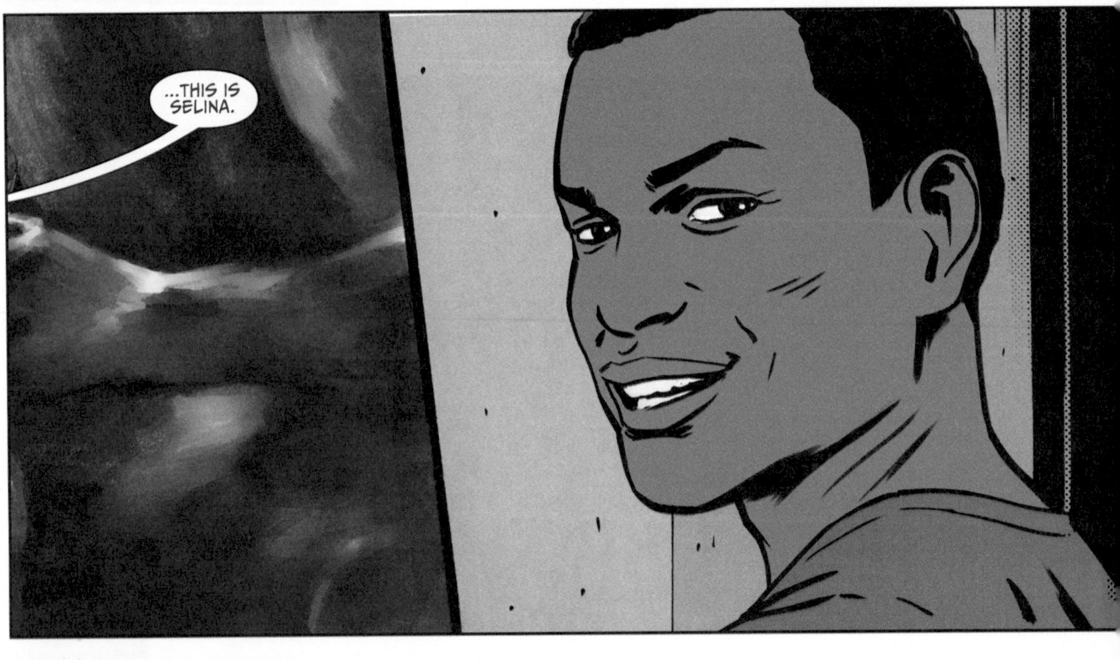
...THIS IS SELINA.

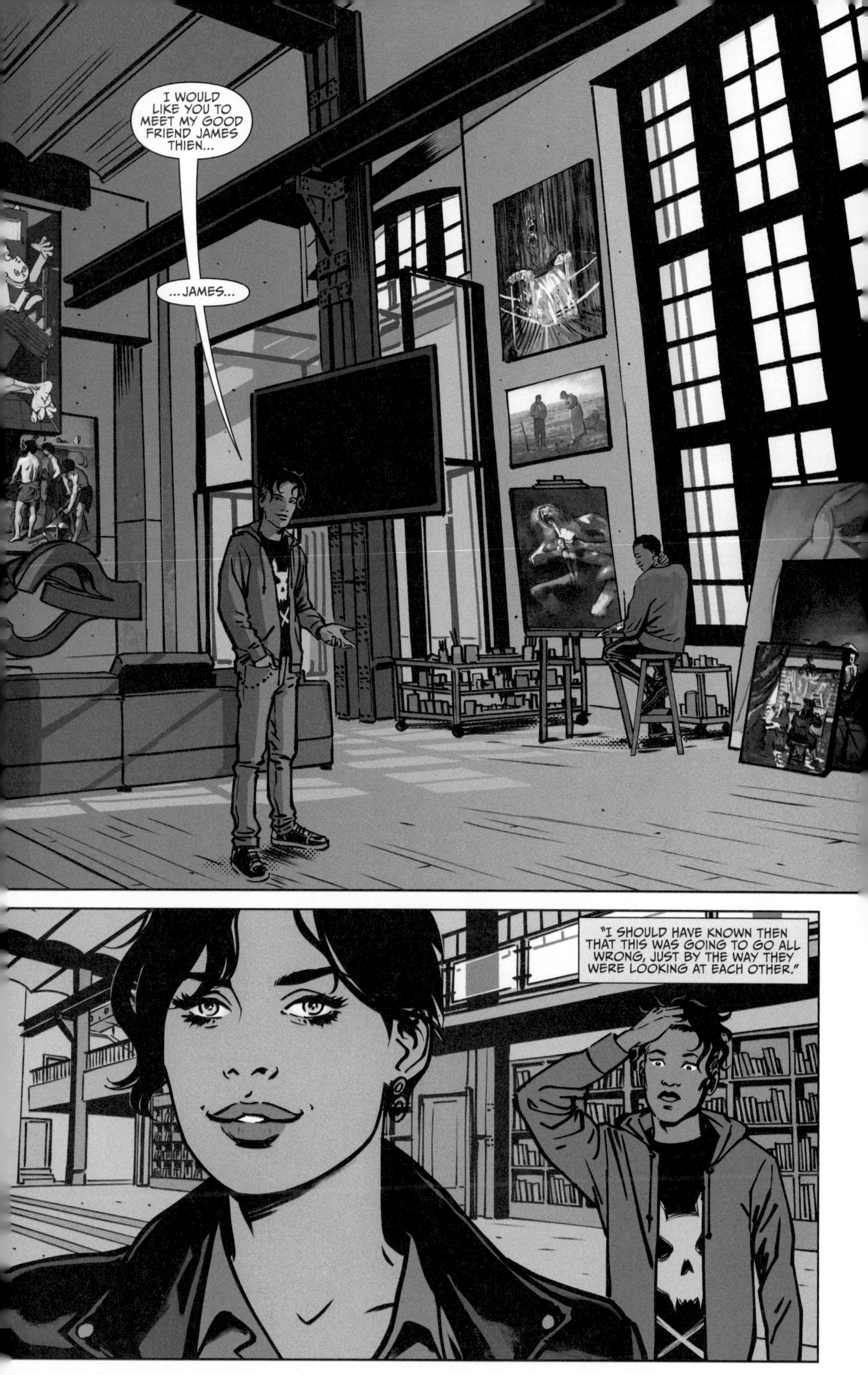
I WOULD LIKE YOU TO MEET MY GOOD FRIEND JAMES THIEN...
...JAMES...
"I SHOULD HAVE KNOWN THEN THAT THIS WAS GOING TO GO ALL WRONG, JUST BY THE WAY THEY WERE LOOKING AT EACH OTHER."

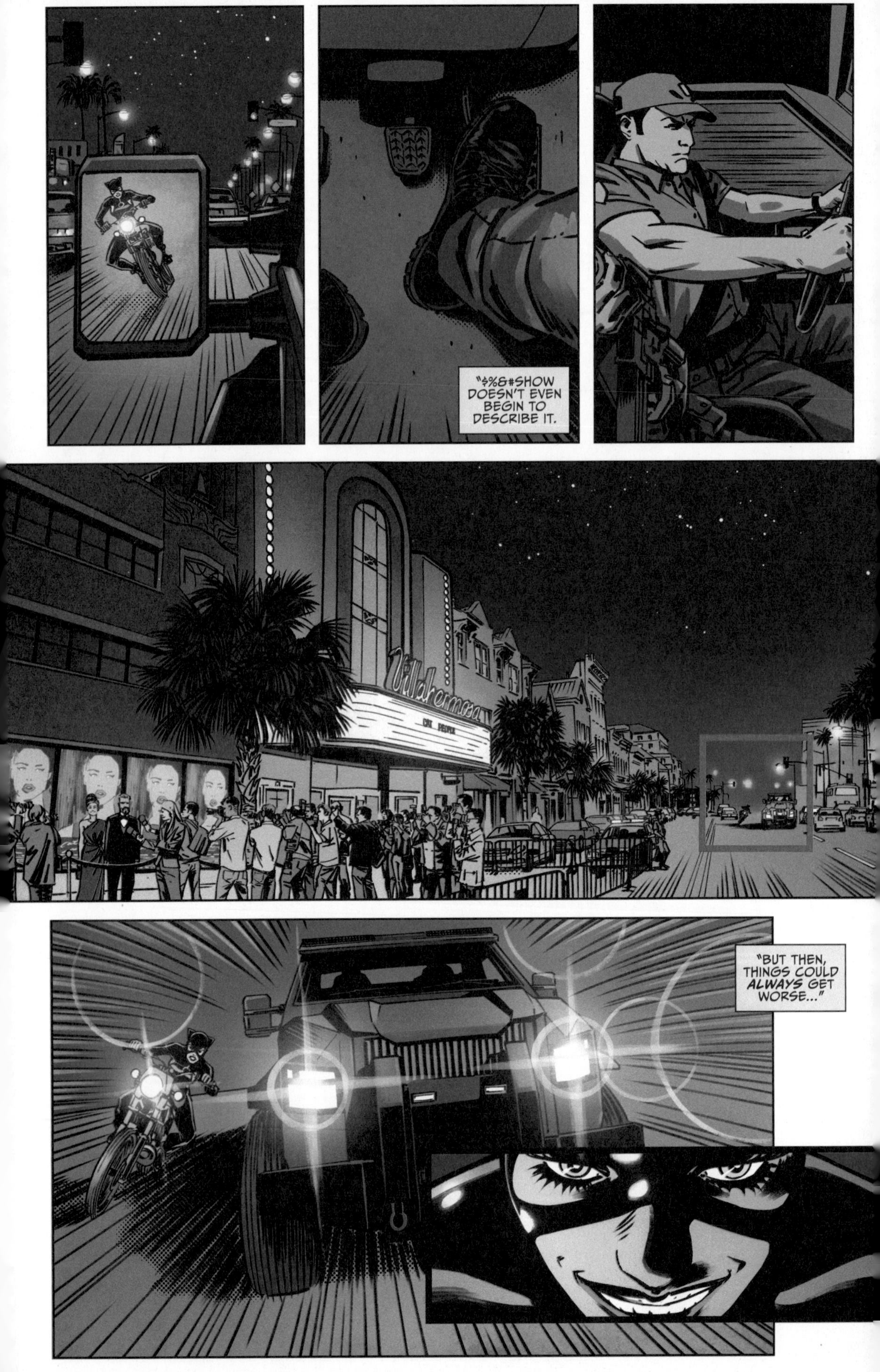
"$%&#SHOW DOESN'T EVEN BEGIN TO DESCRIBE IT.
"BUT THEN, THINGS COULD ALWAYS GET WORSE..."

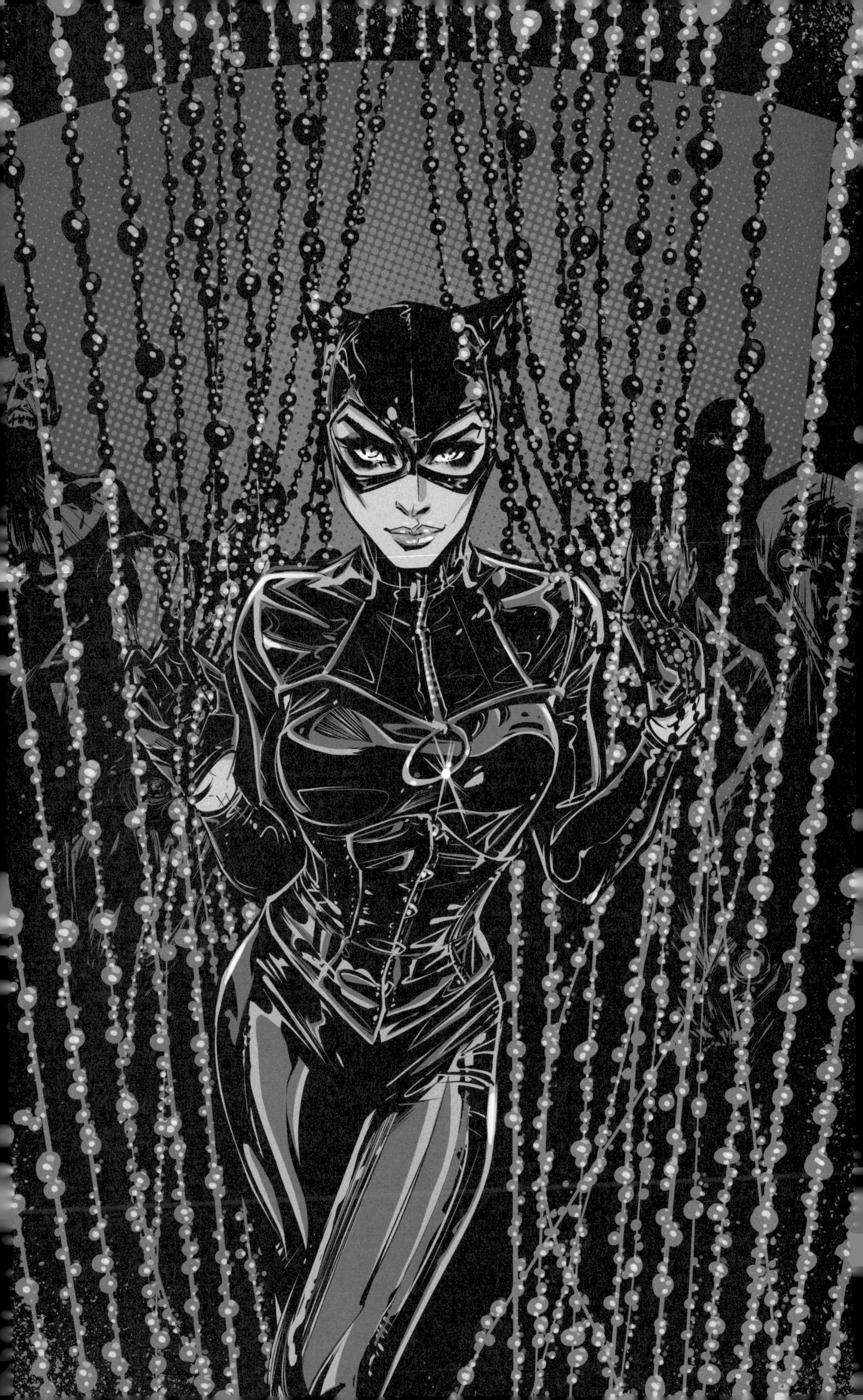

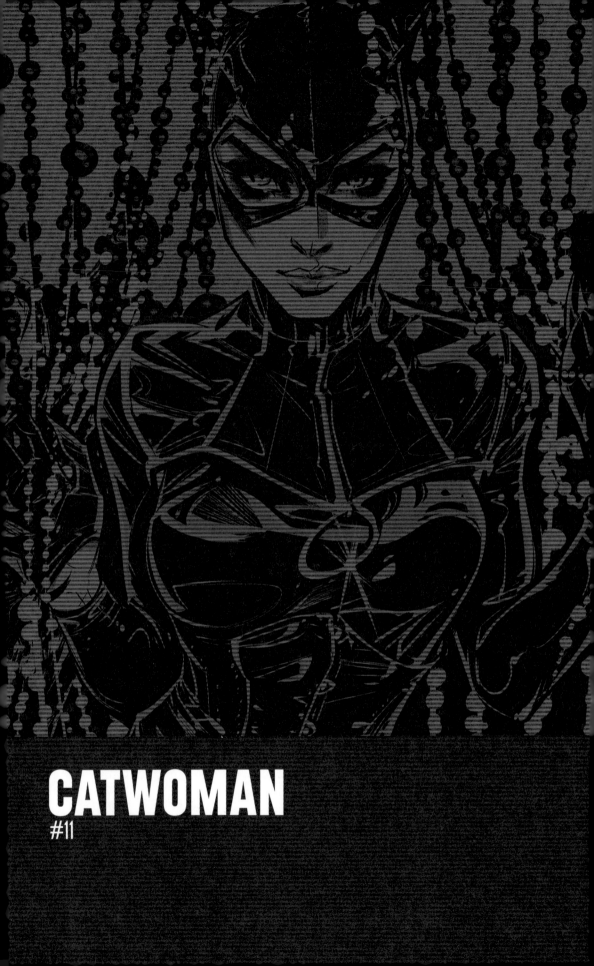

# CATWOMAN
#11

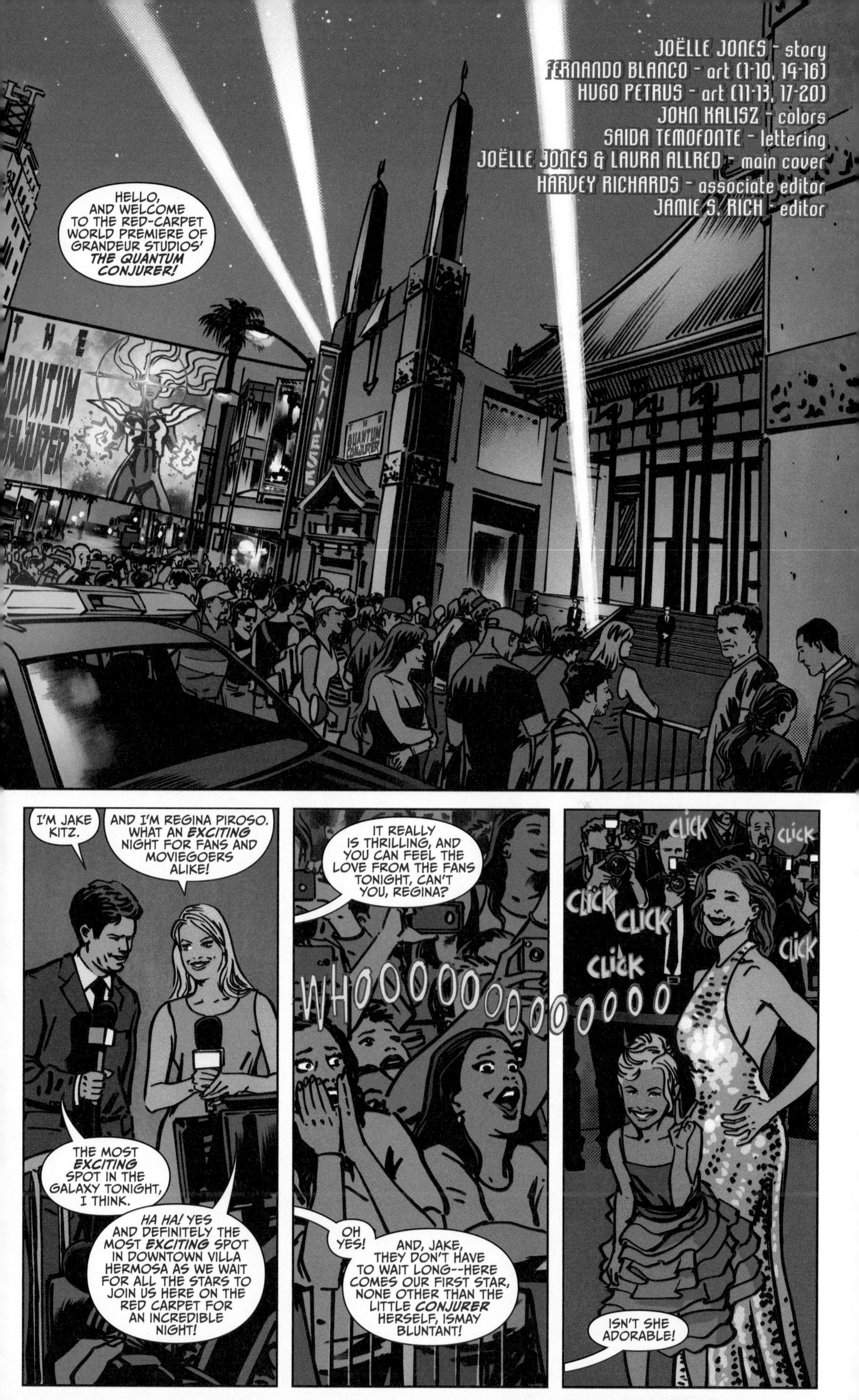
JOËLLE JONES - story
FERNANDO BLANCO - art (1-10, 14-16)
HUGO PETRUS - art (11-13, 17-20)
JOHN KALISZ - colors
SAIDA TEMOFONTE - lettering
JOËLLE JONES & LAURA ALLRED - main cover
HARVEY RICHARDS - associate editor
JAMIE S. RICH - editor
HELLO, AND WELCOME TO THE RED-CARPET WORLD PREMIERE OF GRANDEUR STUDIOS' *THE QUANTUM CONJURER!*
THE QUANTUM CONJURER
CHINESE
THE QUANTUM CONJURER
I'M JAKE KITZ.
AND I'M REGINA PIROSO. WHAT AN *EXCITING* NIGHT FOR FANS AND MOVIEGOERS ALIKE!
THE MOST *EXCITING* SPOT IN THE GALAXY TONIGHT, I THINK.
*HA HA!* YES AND DEFINITELY THE MOST *EXCITING* SPOT IN DOWNTOWN VILLA HERMOSA AS WE WAIT FOR ALL THE STARS TO JOIN US HERE ON THE RED CARPET FOR AN INCREDIBLE NIGHT!
IT REALLY IS THRILLING, AND YOU CAN FEEL THE LOVE FROM THE FANS TONIGHT, CAN'T YOU, REGINA?
WHOOOOOOOOOOOOOOO
OH YES!
AND, JAKE, THEY DON'T HAVE TO WAIT LONG--HERE COMES OUR FIRST STAR, NONE OTHER THAN THE LITTLE *CONJURER* HERSELF, ISMAY BLUNTANT!
CLICK
CLICK
CLICK
CLICK
CLICK
CLICK
ISN'T SHE ADORABLE!

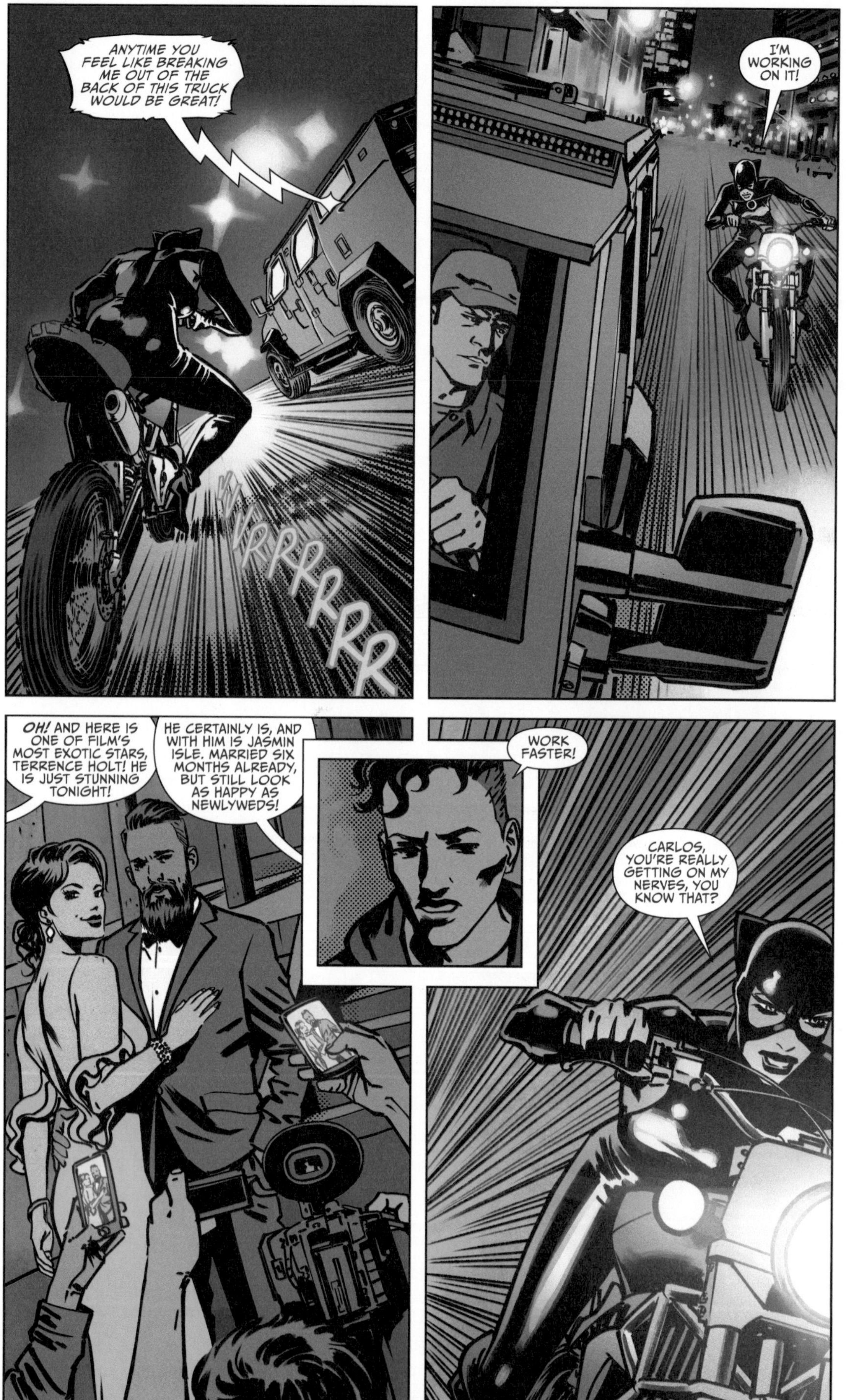
ANYTIME YOU FEEL LIKE BREAKING ME OUT OF THE BACK OF THIS TRUCK WOULD BE GREAT!
VRRRRRRRR
I'M WORKING ON IT!
OH! AND HERE IS ONE OF FILM'S MOST EXOTIC STARS, TERRENCE HOLT! HE IS JUST STUNNING TONIGHT!
HE CERTAINLY IS, AND WITH HIM IS JASMIN ISLE. MARRIED SIX MONTHS ALREADY, BUT STILL LOOK AS HAPPY AS NEWLYWEDS!
WORK FASTER!
CARLOS, YOU'RE REALLY GETTING ON MY NERVES, YOU KNOW THAT?

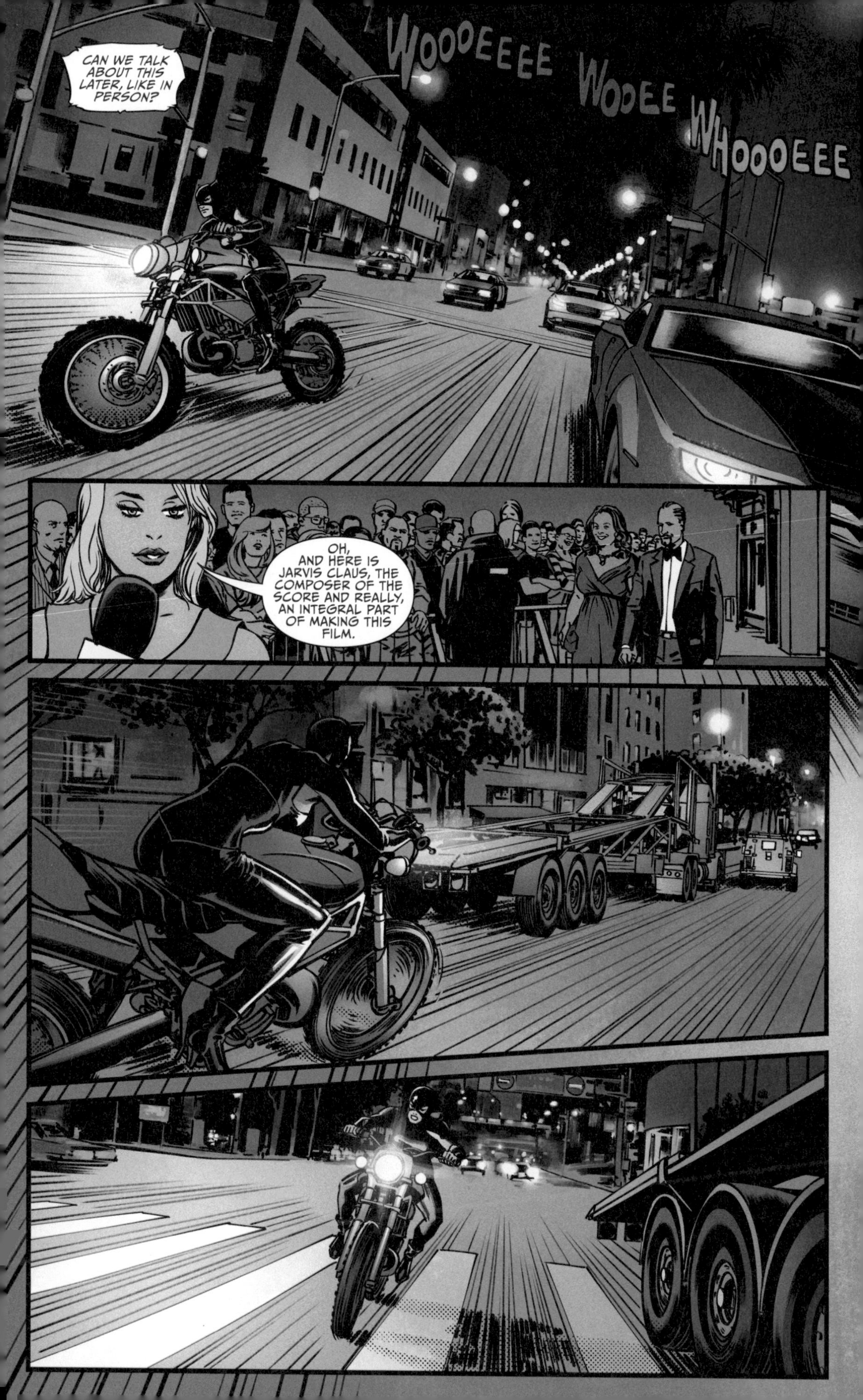
WOOOEEEE WOOEE WHOOOEEE
CAN WE TALK ABOUT THIS LATER, LIKE IN PERSON?
OH, AND HERE IS JARVIS CLAUS, THE COMPOSER OF THE SCORE AND REALLY, AN INTEGRAL PART OF MAKING THIS FILM.

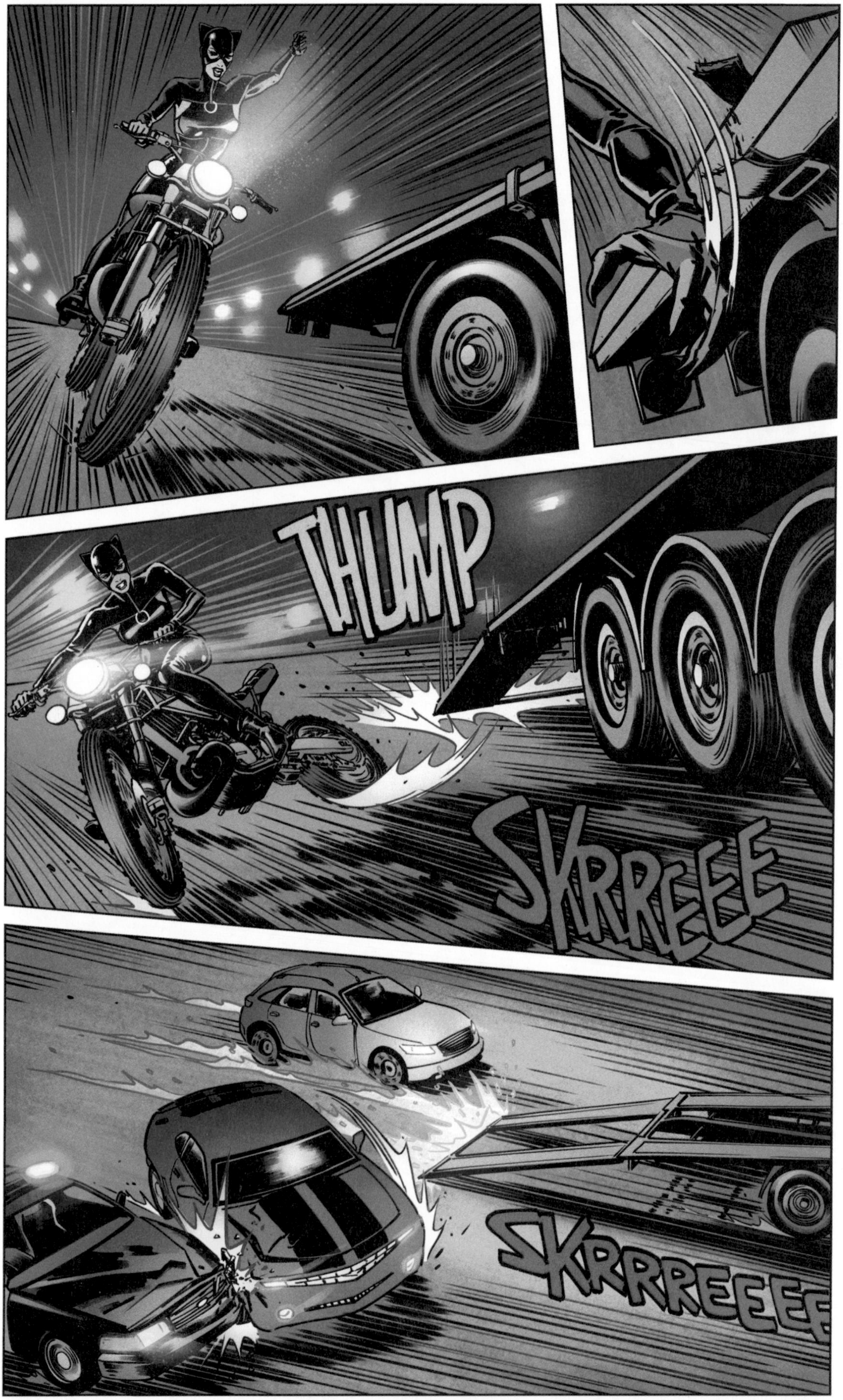
THUMP
SKRREEE
SKRRREEEE

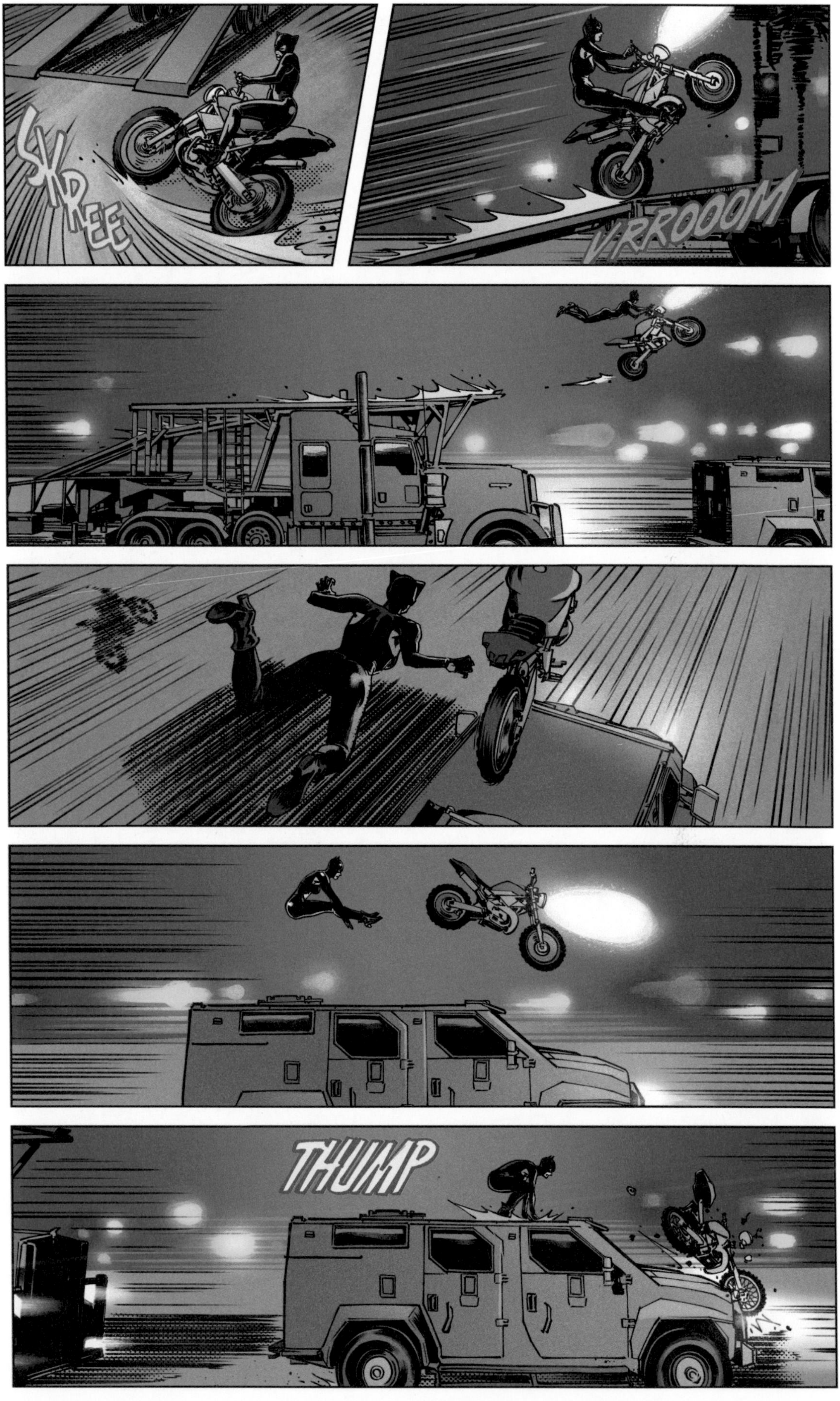
SKREE
VRROOOM
THUMP

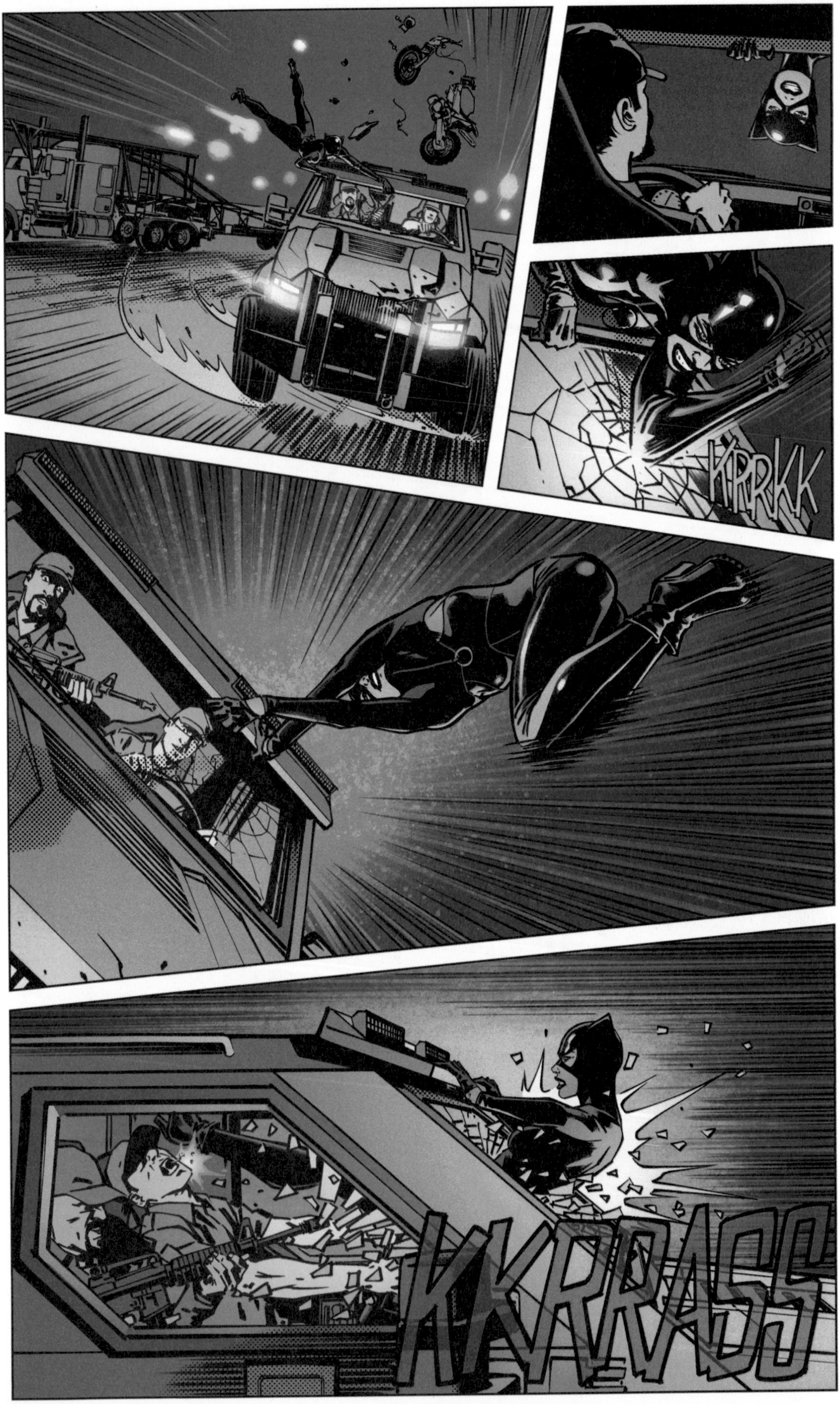
KRRKK
KKRRASS

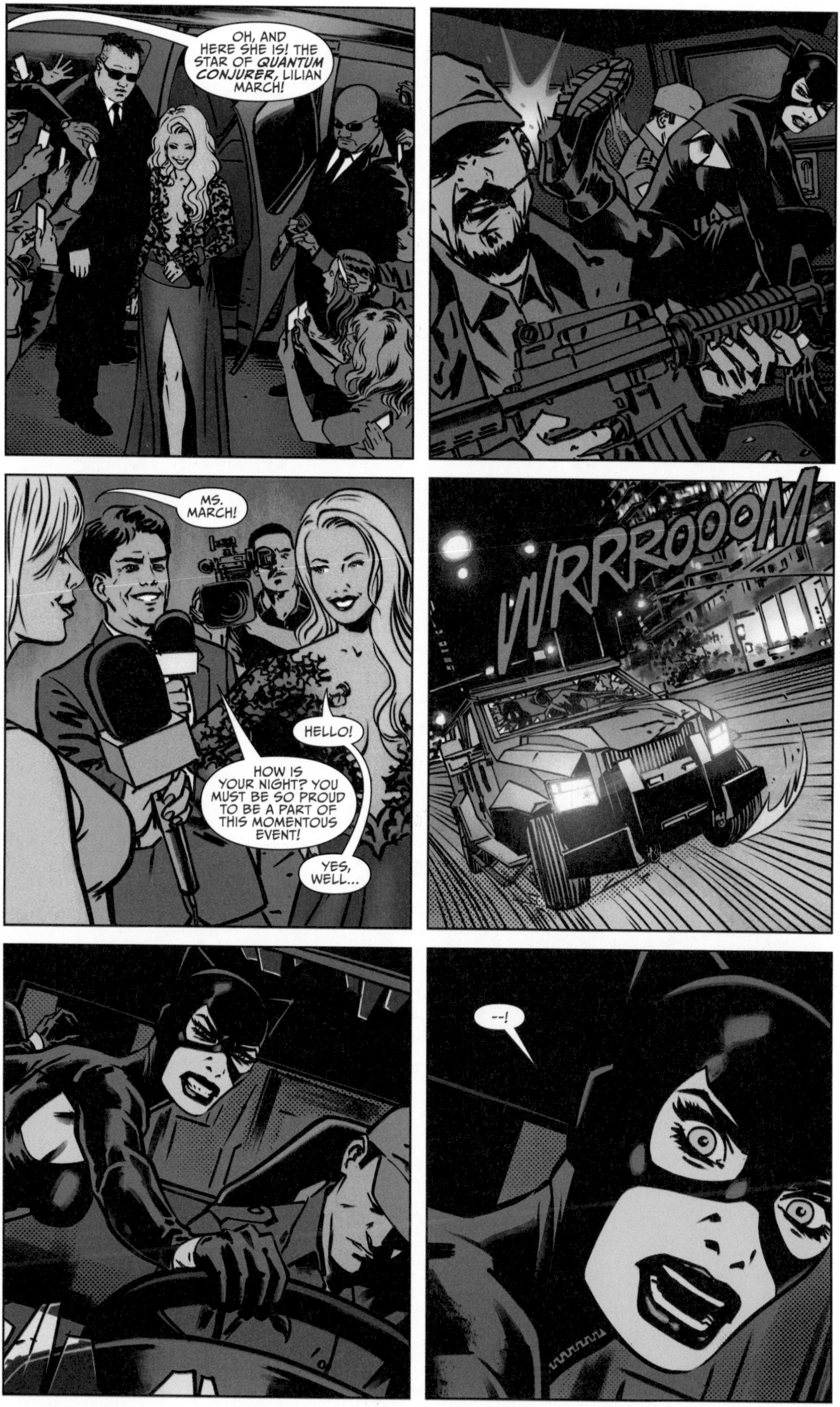
OH, AND HERE SHE IS! THE STAR OF *QUANTUM CONJURER*, LILIAN MARCH!
MS. MARCH!
HELLO!
HOW IS YOUR NIGHT? YOU MUST BE SO PROUD TO BE A PART OF THIS MOMENTOUS EVENT!
YES, WELL...
WRRROOOM
--!

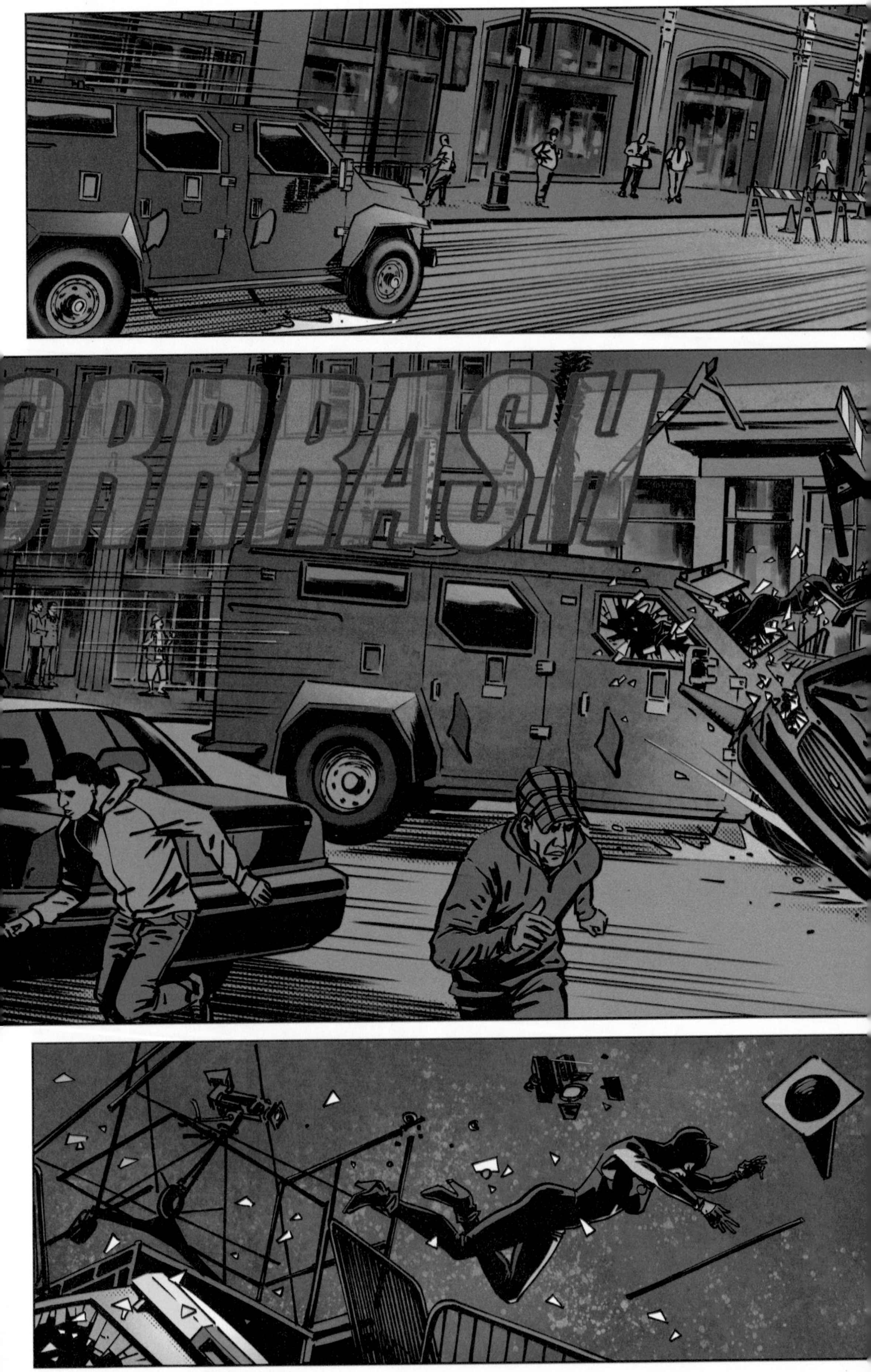
CRRASH

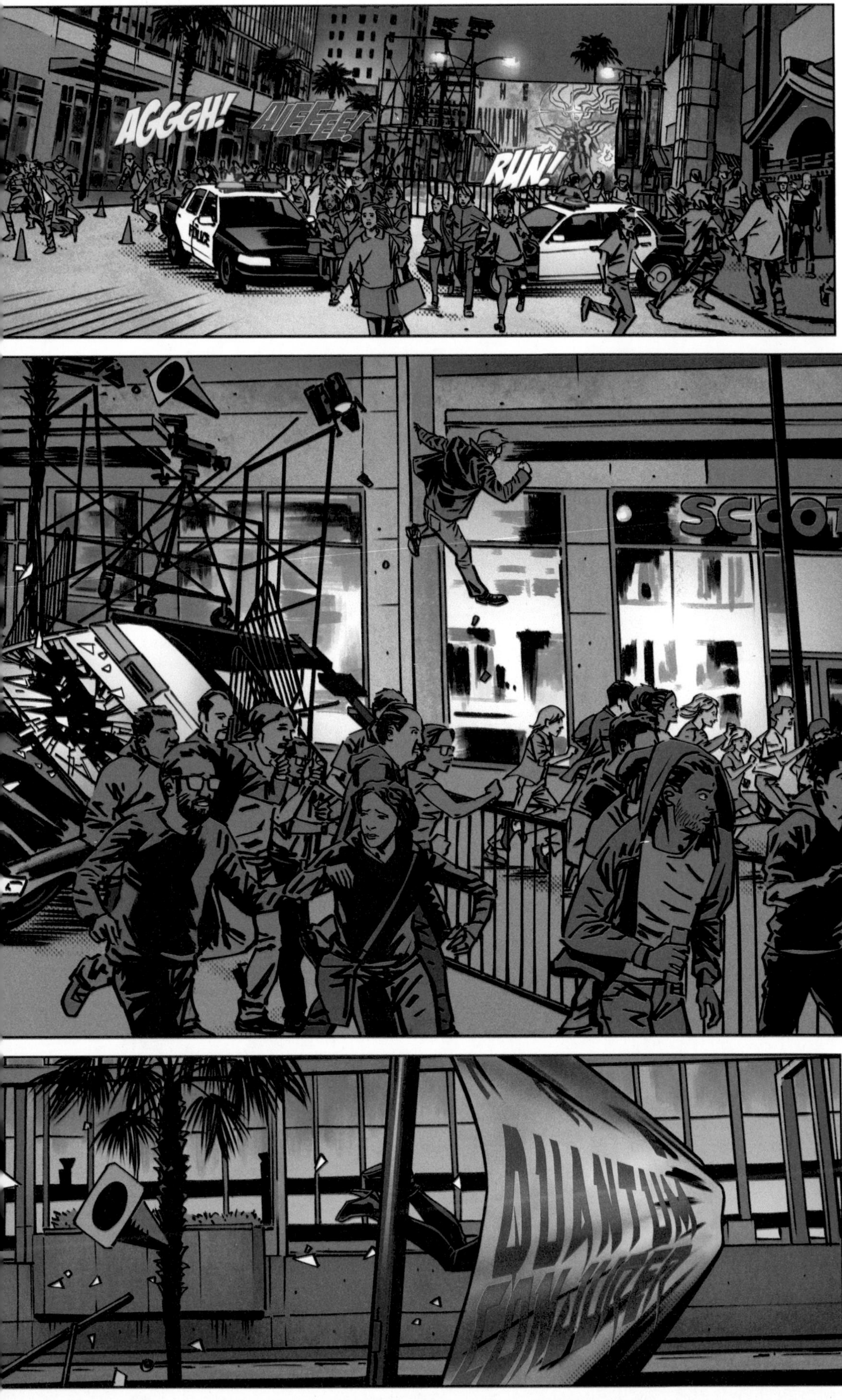

AGGGH!
AIEEEEE!
RUN!
POLICE
QUANTUM

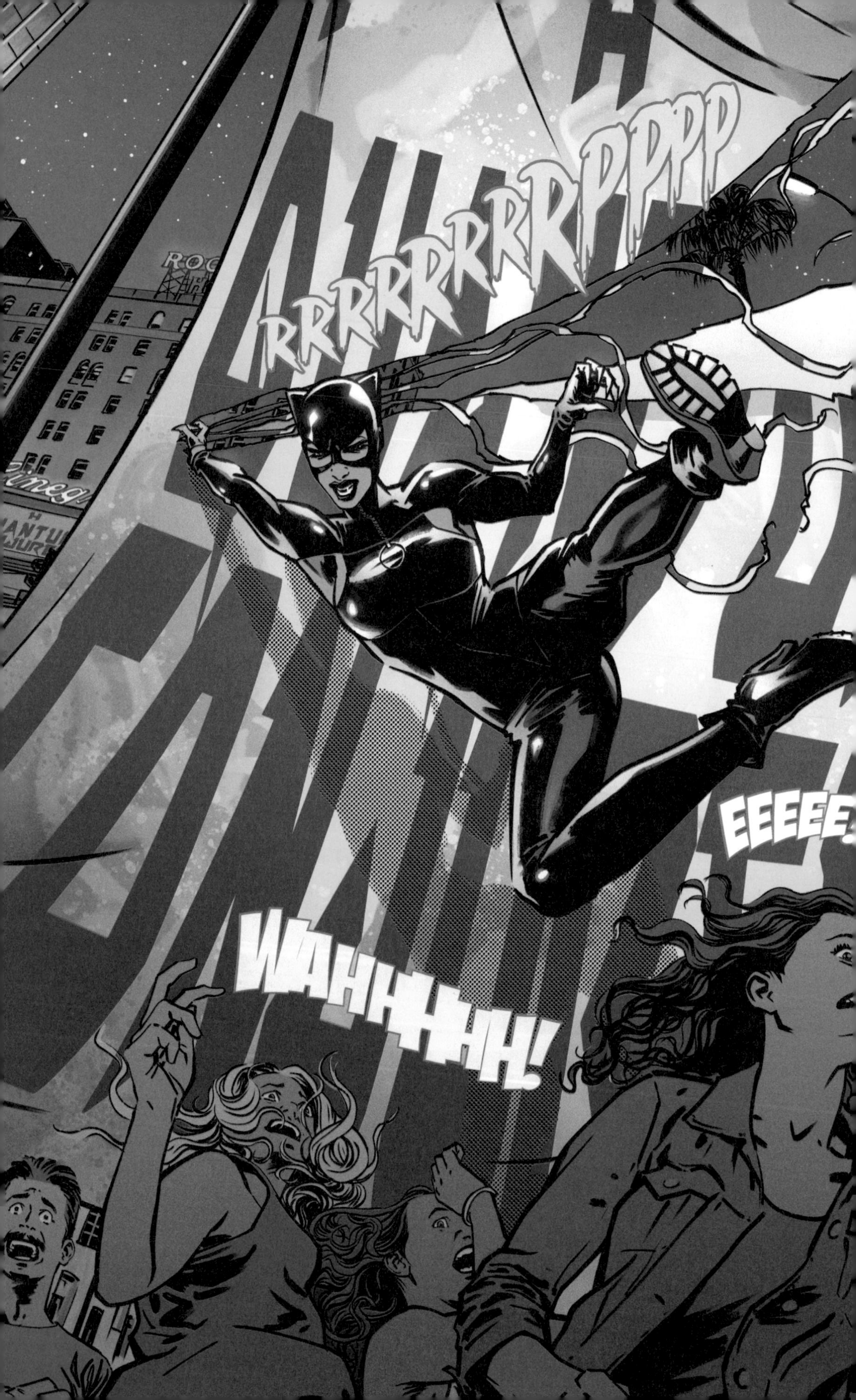
RRRRRRRRPPPP
EEEEE
WAHHHHHH!

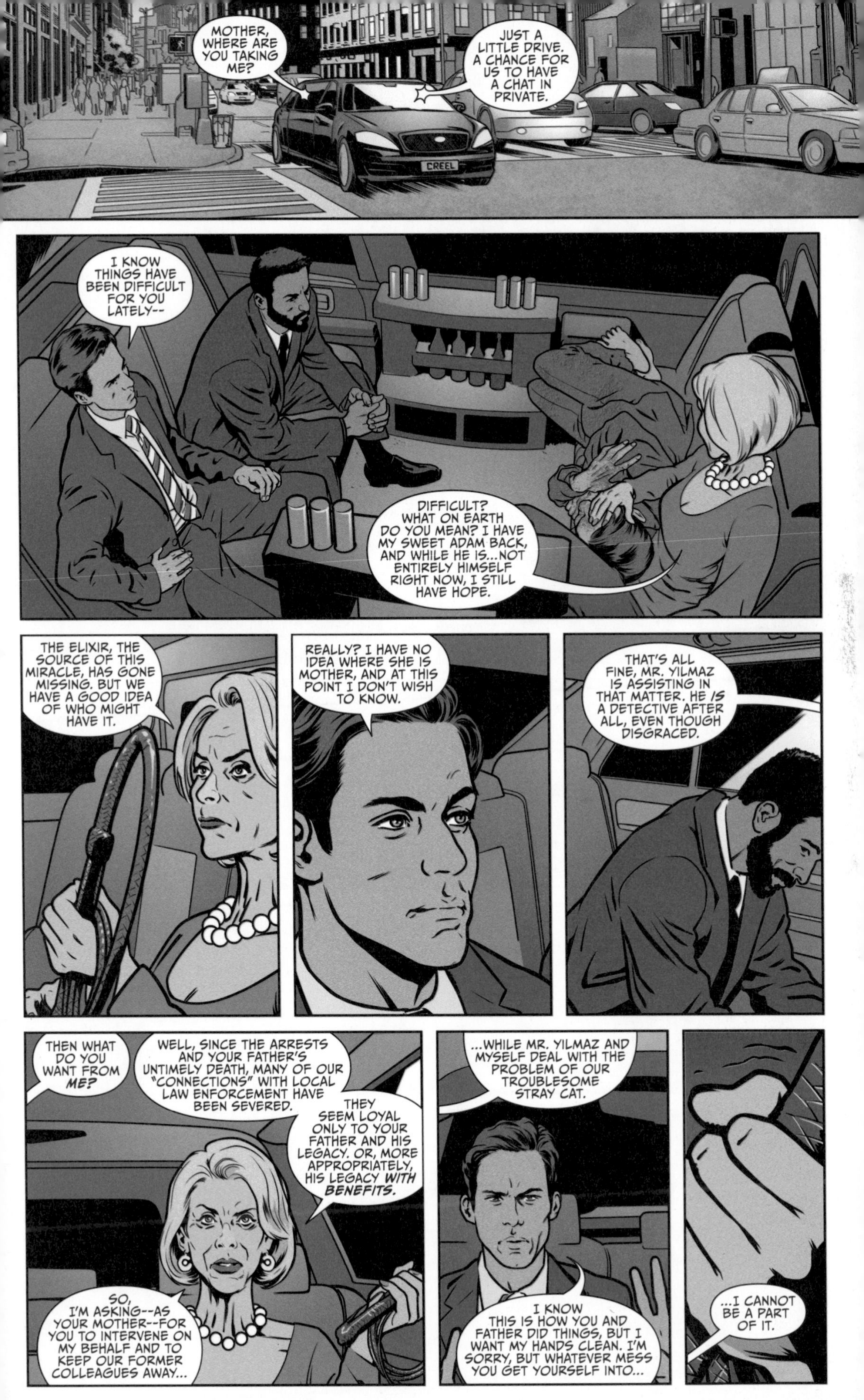
MOTHER, WHERE ARE YOU TAKING ME?
JUST A LITTLE DRIVE. A CHANCE FOR US TO HAVE A CHAT IN PRIVATE.
CREEL
I KNOW THINGS HAVE BEEN DIFFICULT FOR YOU LATELY--
DIFFICULT? WHAT ON EARTH DO YOU MEAN? I HAVE MY SWEET ADAM BACK, AND WHILE HE IS...NOT ENTIRELY HIMSELF RIGHT NOW, I STILL HAVE HOPE.
THE ELIXIR, THE SOURCE OF THIS MIRACLE, HAS GONE MISSING. BUT WE HAVE A GOOD IDEA OF WHO MIGHT HAVE IT.
REALLY? I HAVE NO IDEA WHERE SHE IS MOTHER, AND AT THIS POINT I DON'T WISH TO KNOW.
THAT'S ALL FINE, MR. YILMAZ IS ASSISTING IN THAT MATTER. HE *IS* A DETECTIVE AFTER ALL, EVEN THOUGH DISGRACED.
THEN WHAT DO YOU WANT FROM ***ME?***
WELL, SINCE THE ARRESTS AND YOUR FATHER'S UNTIMELY DEATH, MANY OF OUR "CONNECTIONS" WITH LOCAL LAW ENFORCEMENT HAVE BEEN SEVERED.
THEY SEEM LOYAL ONLY TO YOUR FATHER AND HIS LEGACY. OR, MORE APPROPRIATELY, HIS LEGACY ***WITH BENEFITS.***
SO, I'M ASKING--AS YOUR MOTHER--FOR YOU TO INTERVENE ON MY BEHALF AND TO KEEP OUR FORMER COLLEAGUES AWAY...
...WHILE MR. YILMAZ AND MYSELF DEAL WITH THE PROBLEM OF OUR TROUBLESOME STRAY CAT.
I KNOW THIS IS HOW YOU AND FATHER DID THINGS, BUT I WANT MY HANDS CLEAN. I'M SORRY, BUT WHATEVER MESS YOU GET YOURSELF INTO...
...I CANNOT BE A PART OF IT.

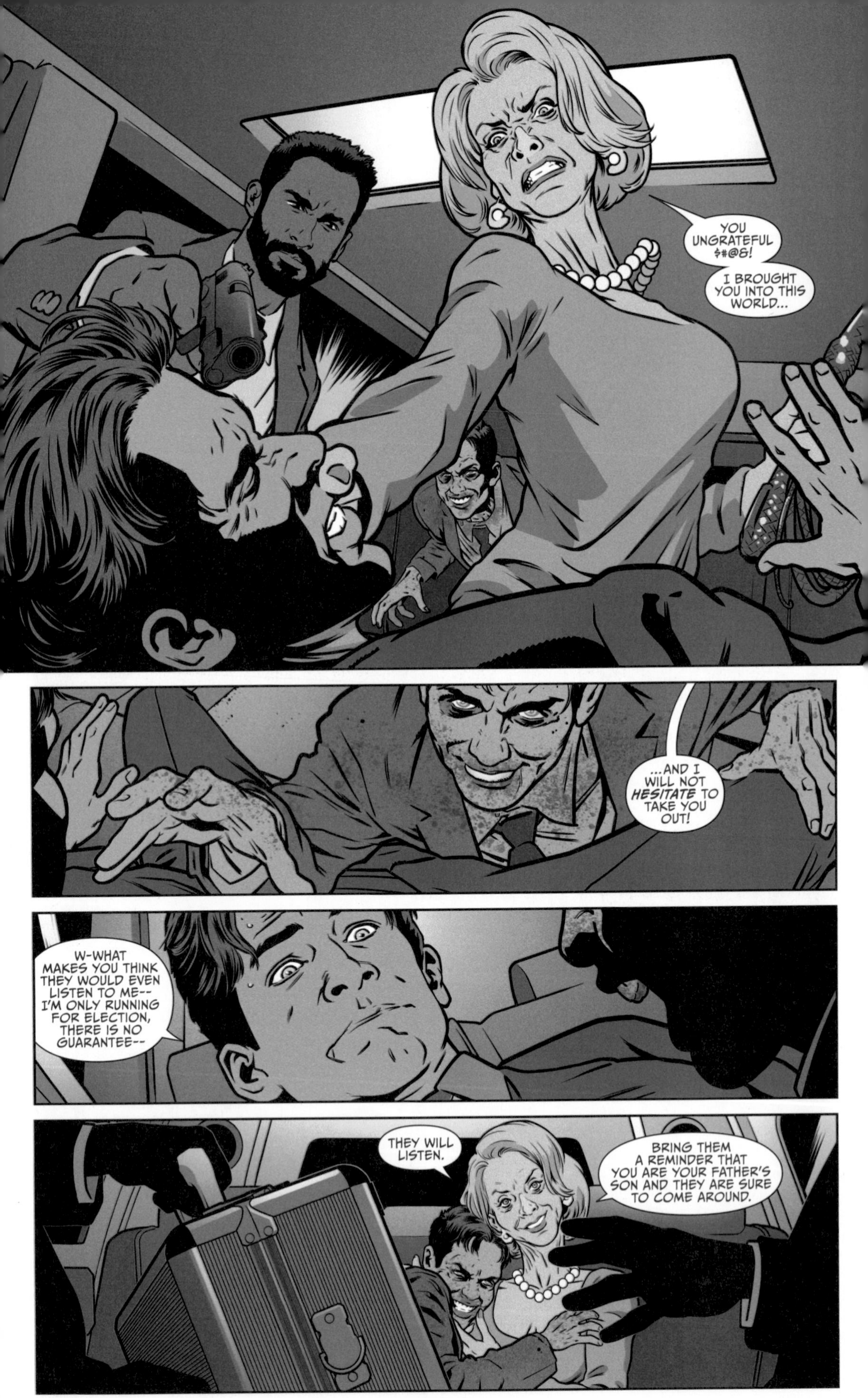
YOU UNGRATEFUL $#@&!
I BROUGHT YOU INTO THIS WORLD...
...AND I WILL NOT HESITATE TO TAKE YOU OUT!
W-WHAT MAKES YOU THINK THEY WOULD EVEN LISTEN TO ME--I'M ONLY RUNNING FOR ELECTION, THERE IS NO GUARANTEE--
THEY WILL LISTEN.
BRING THEM A REMINDER THAT YOU ARE YOUR FATHER'S SON AND THEY ARE SURE TO COME AROUND.

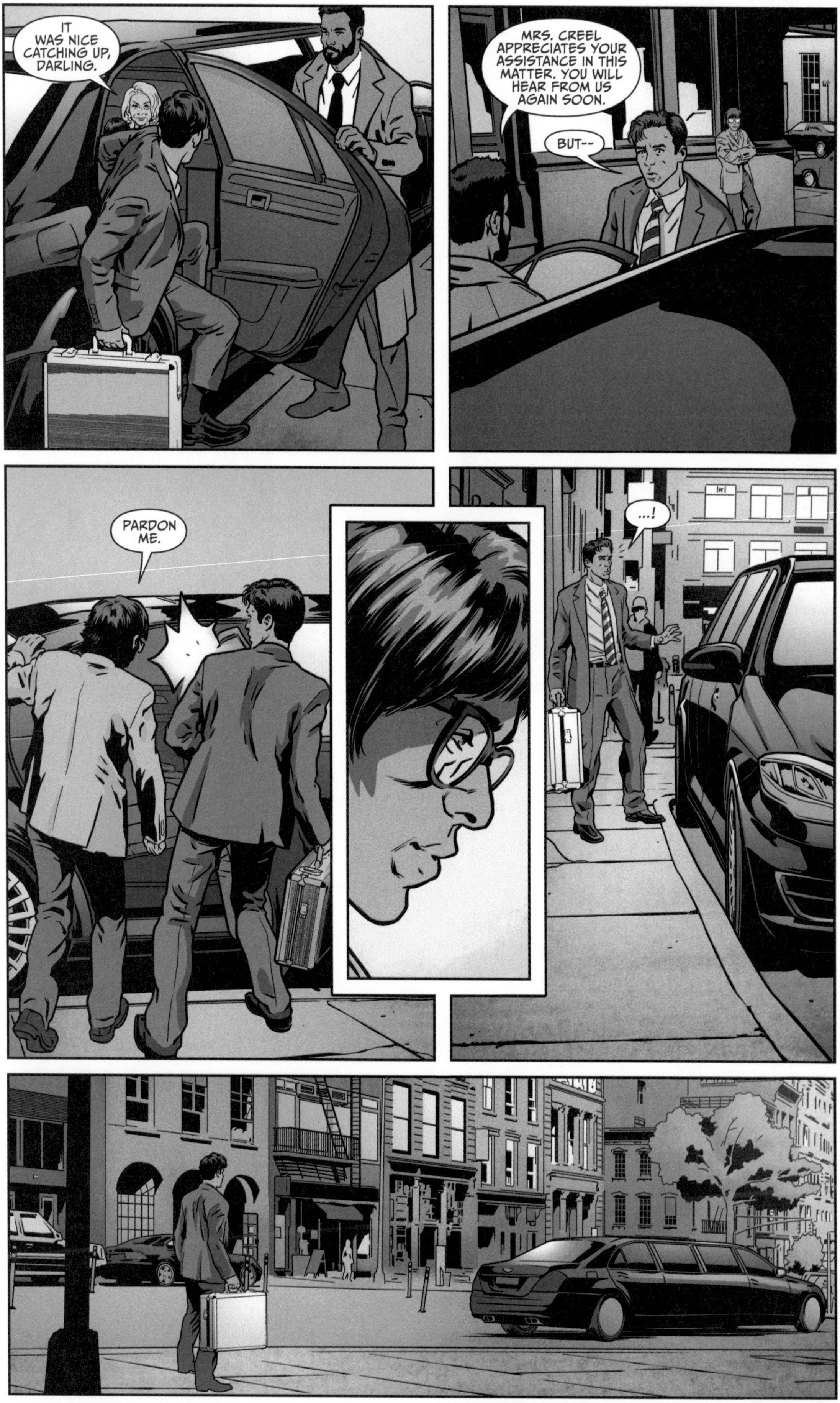
IT WAS NICE CATCHING UP, DARLING.
MRS. CREEL APPRECIATES YOUR ASSISTANCE IN THIS MATTER. YOU WILL HEAR FROM US AGAIN SOON.
BUT--
PARDON ME.
...!

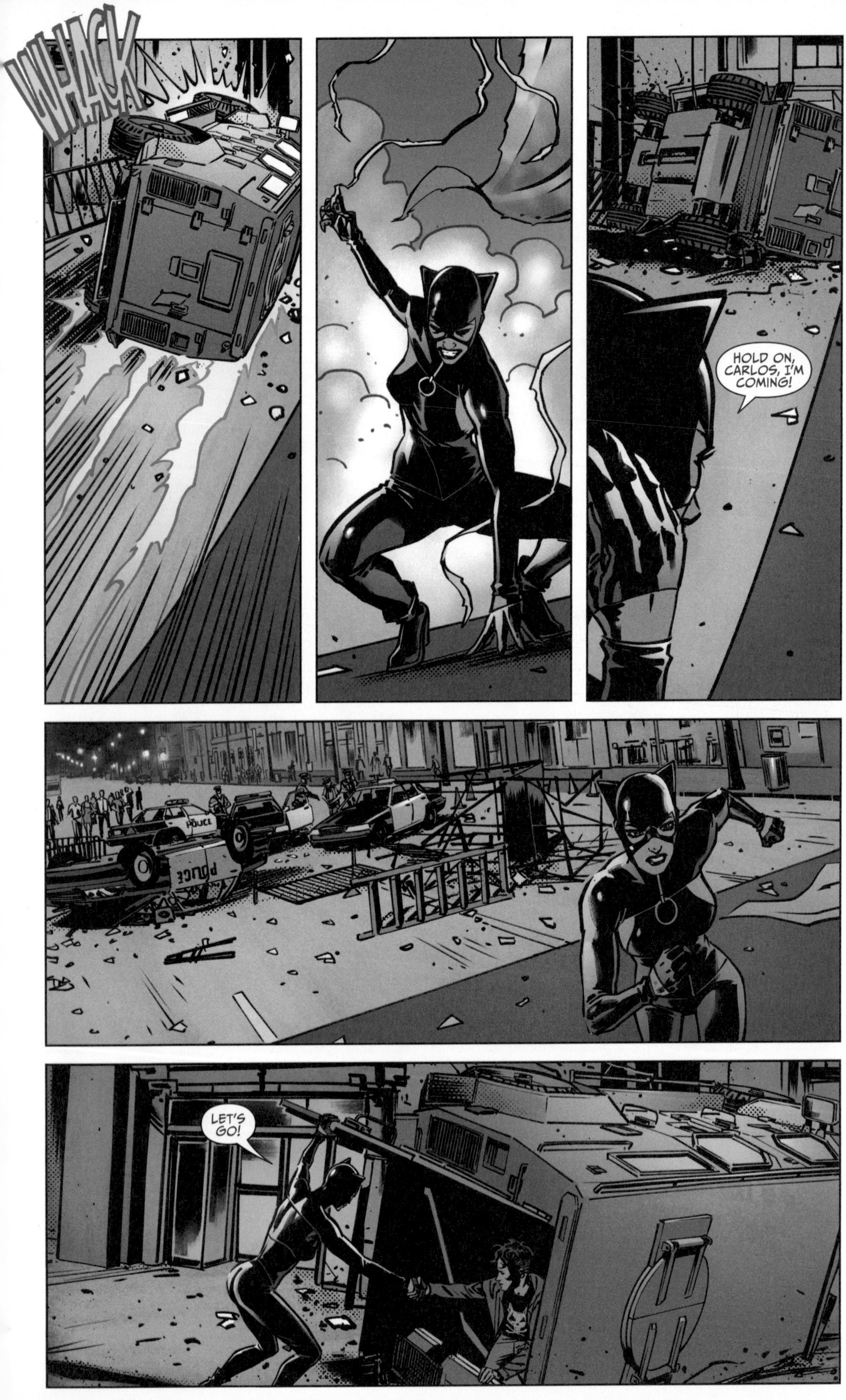

WHACK
HOLD ON, CARLOS, I'M COMING!
POLICE
POLICE
LET'S GO!

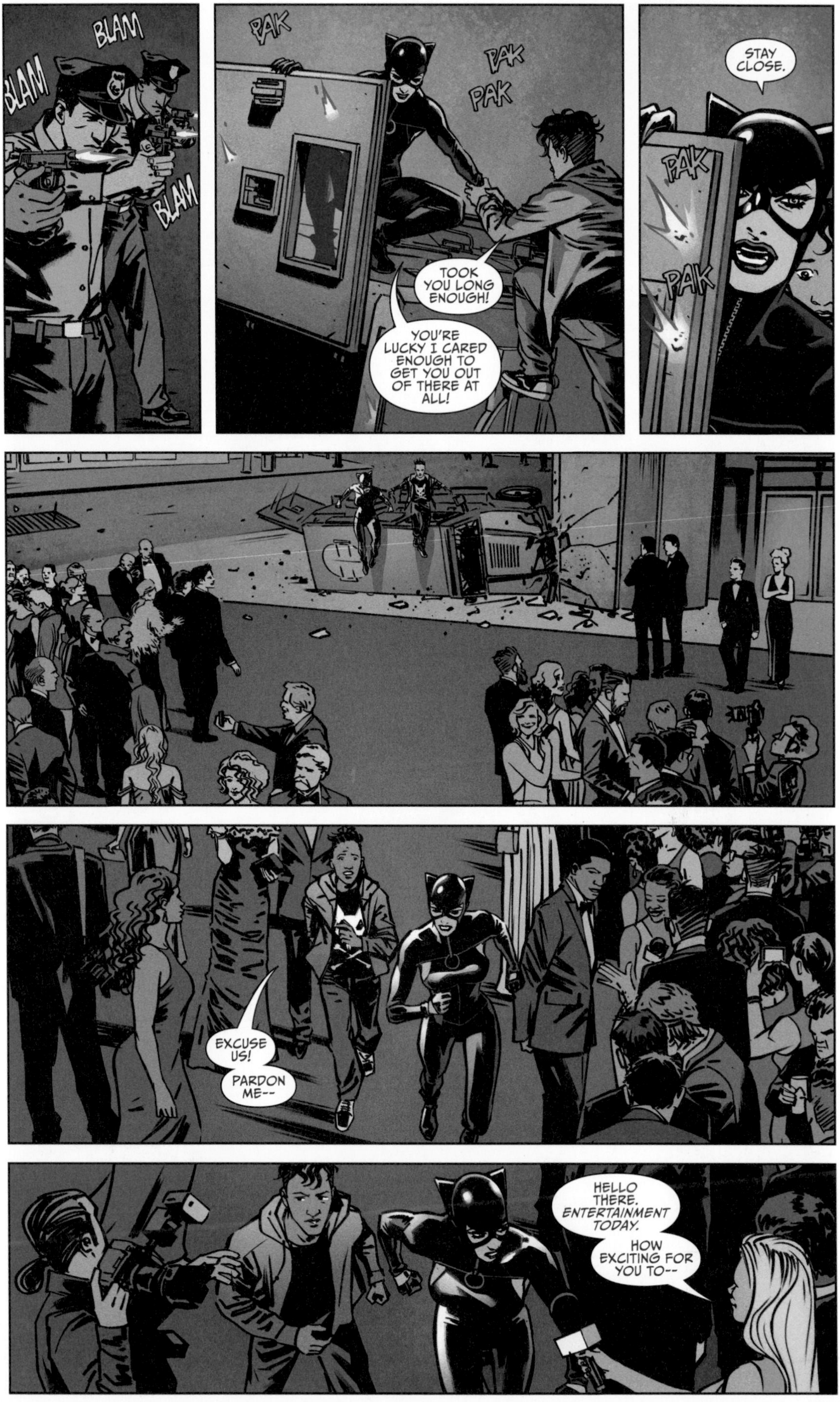
BLAM
BLAM
BLAM
PAK
PAK
PAK
TOOK YOU LONG ENOUGH!
YOU'RE LUCKY I CARED ENOUGH TO GET YOU OUT OF THERE AT ALL!
STAY CLOSE.
PAK
PAK
EXCUSE US!
PARDON ME--
HELLO THERE. ENTERTAINMENT TODAY.
HOW EXCITING FOR YOU TO--

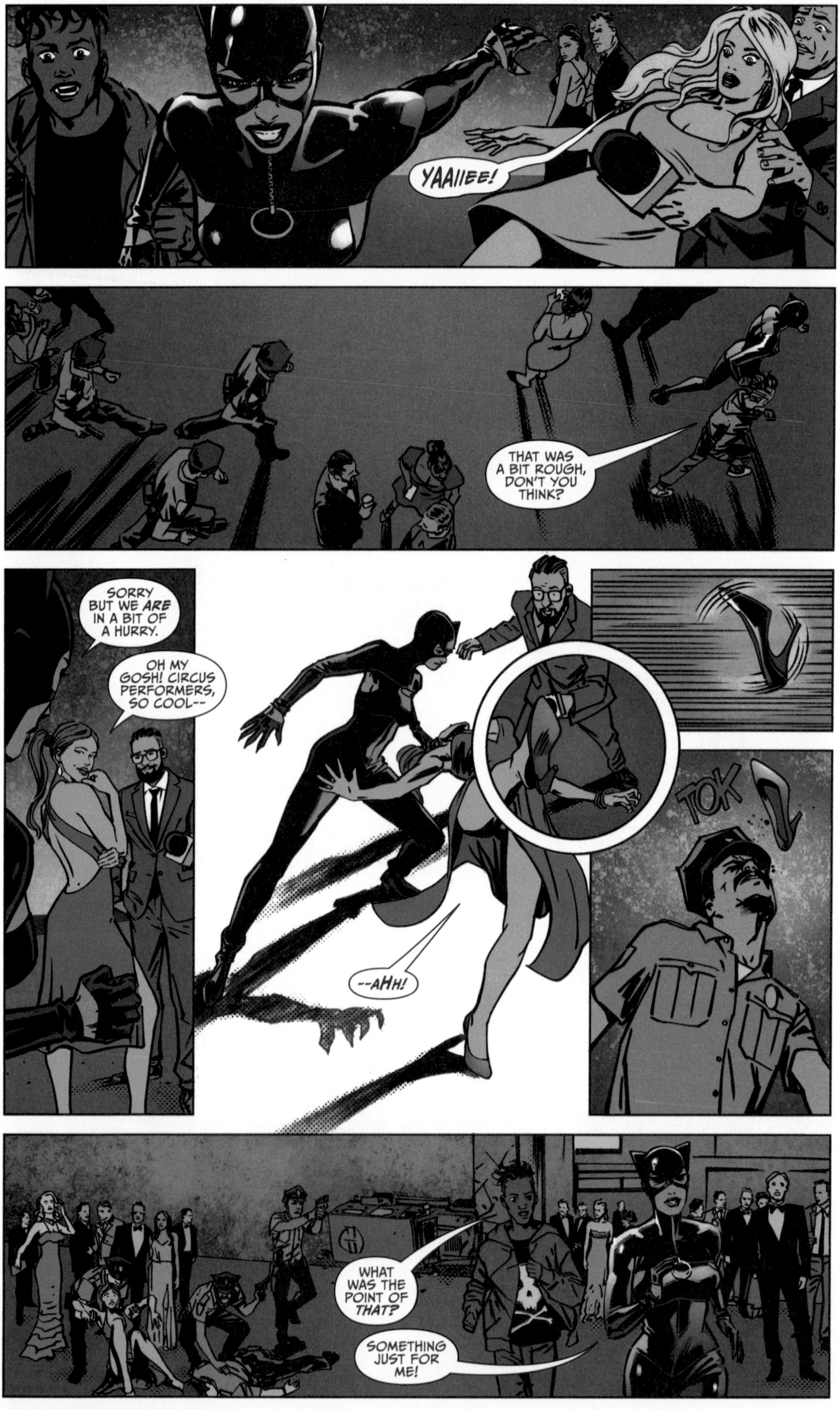
YAAIIEE!
THAT WAS A BIT ROUGH, DON'T YOU THINK?
SORRY BUT WE *ARE* IN A BIT OF A HURRY.
OH MY GOSH! CIRCUS PERFORMERS, SO COOL--
--AHH!
TOK
WHAT WAS THE POINT OF *THAT?*
SOMETHING JUST FOR ME!

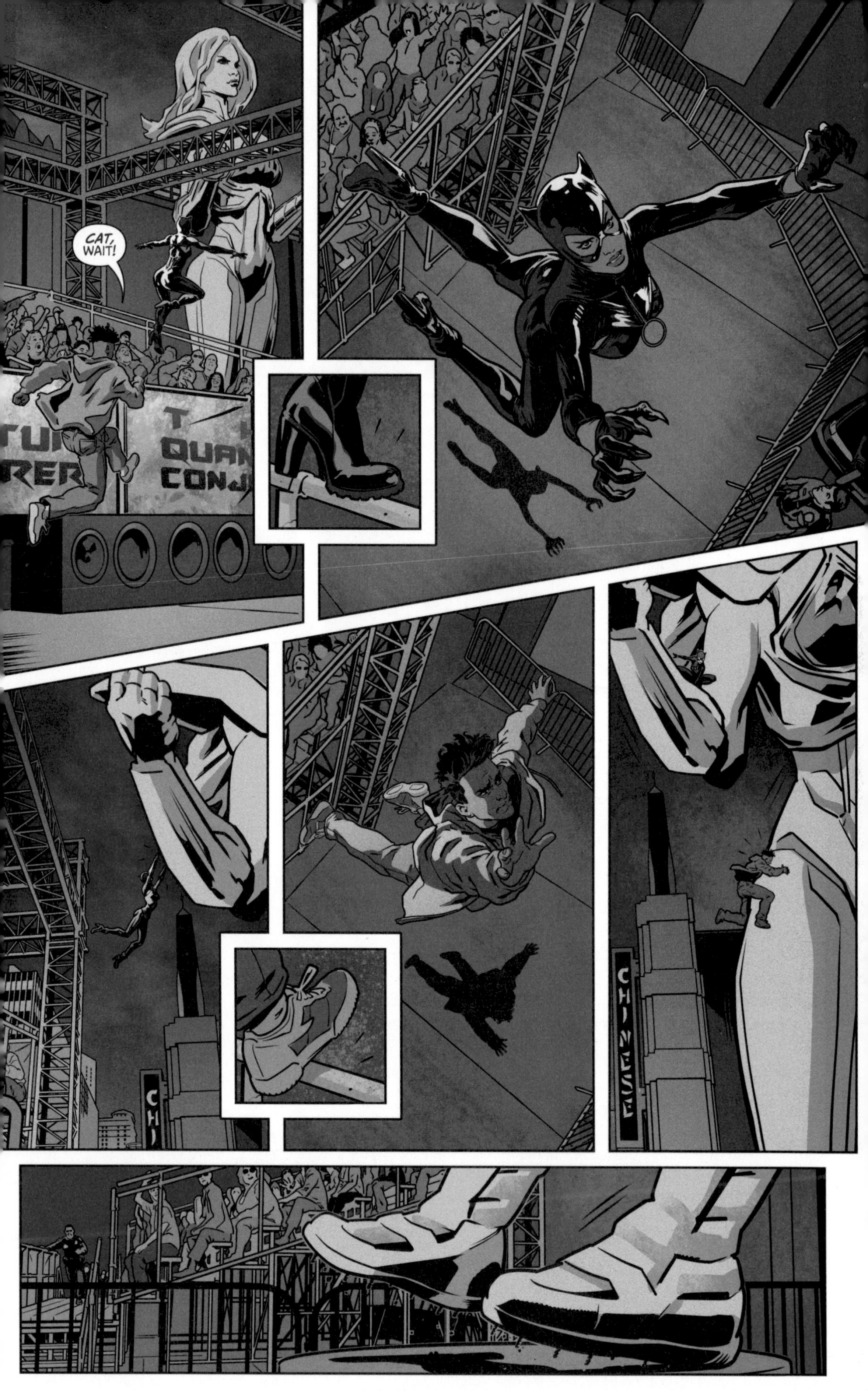
CAT, WAIT!
CHINESE

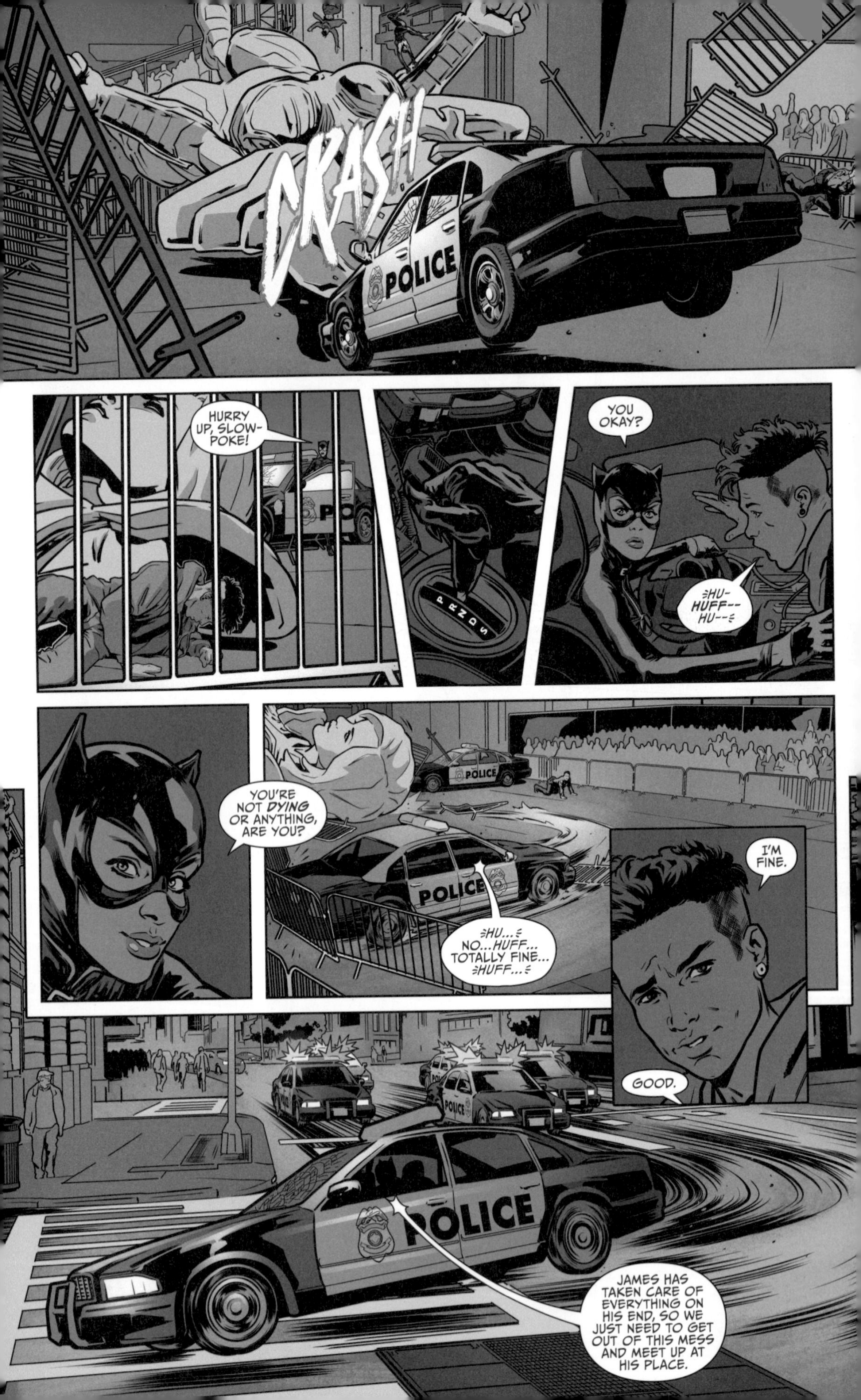
CRASH
POLICE
HURRY UP, SLOW-POKE!
P R N D S
YOU OKAY?
HU-HUFF--HU--
YOU'RE NOT *DYING* OR ANYTHING, ARE YOU?
POLICE
HU... NO...HUFF... TOTALLY FINE... HUFF...
I'M FINE.
GOOD.
POLICE
JAMES HAS TAKEN CARE OF EVERYTHING ON HIS END, SO WE JUST NEED TO GET OUT OF THIS MESS AND MEET UP AT HIS PLACE.

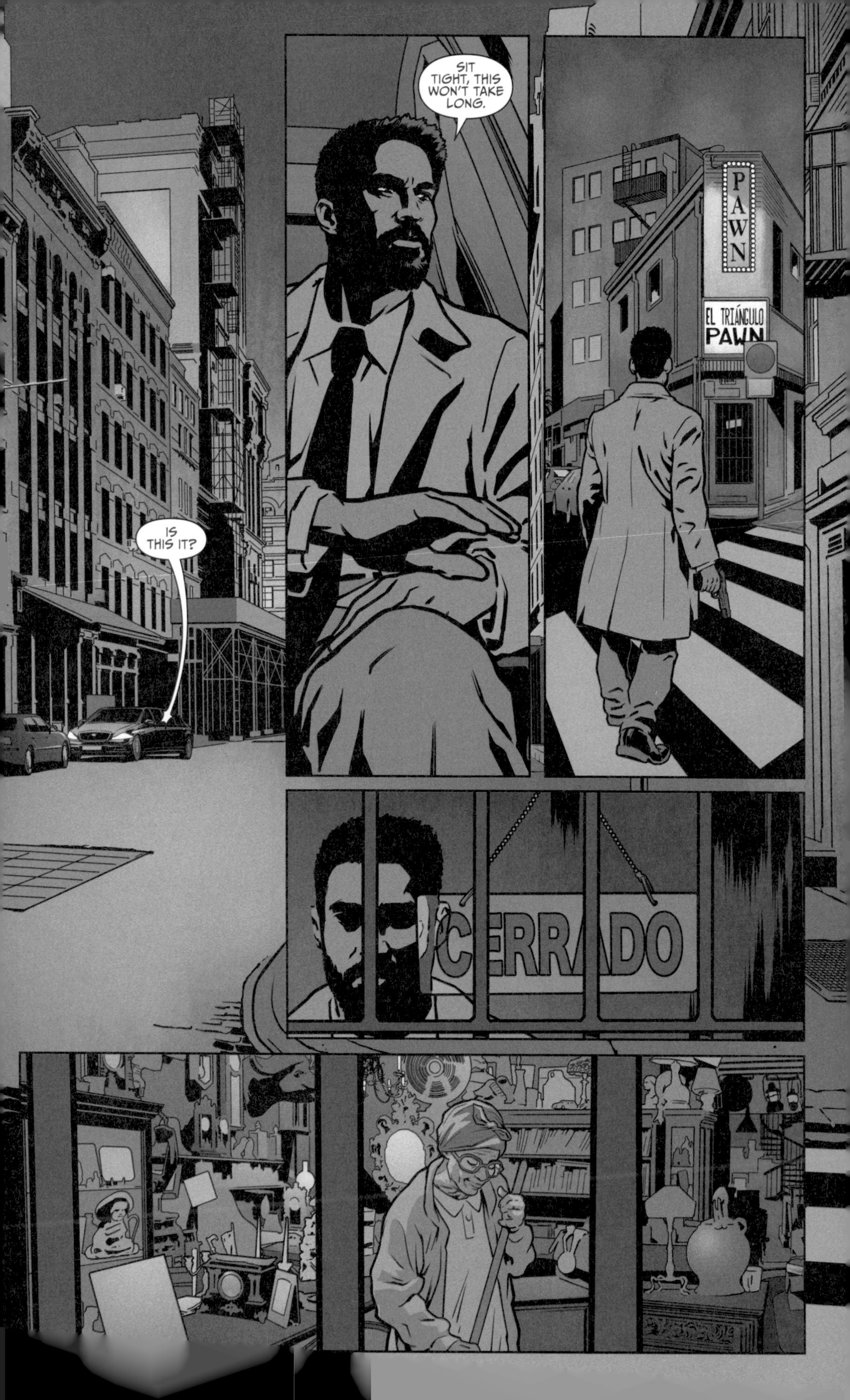

IS THIS IT?
SIT TIGHT, THIS WON'T TAKE LONG.
PAWN
EL TRIÁNGULO PAWN
CERRADO

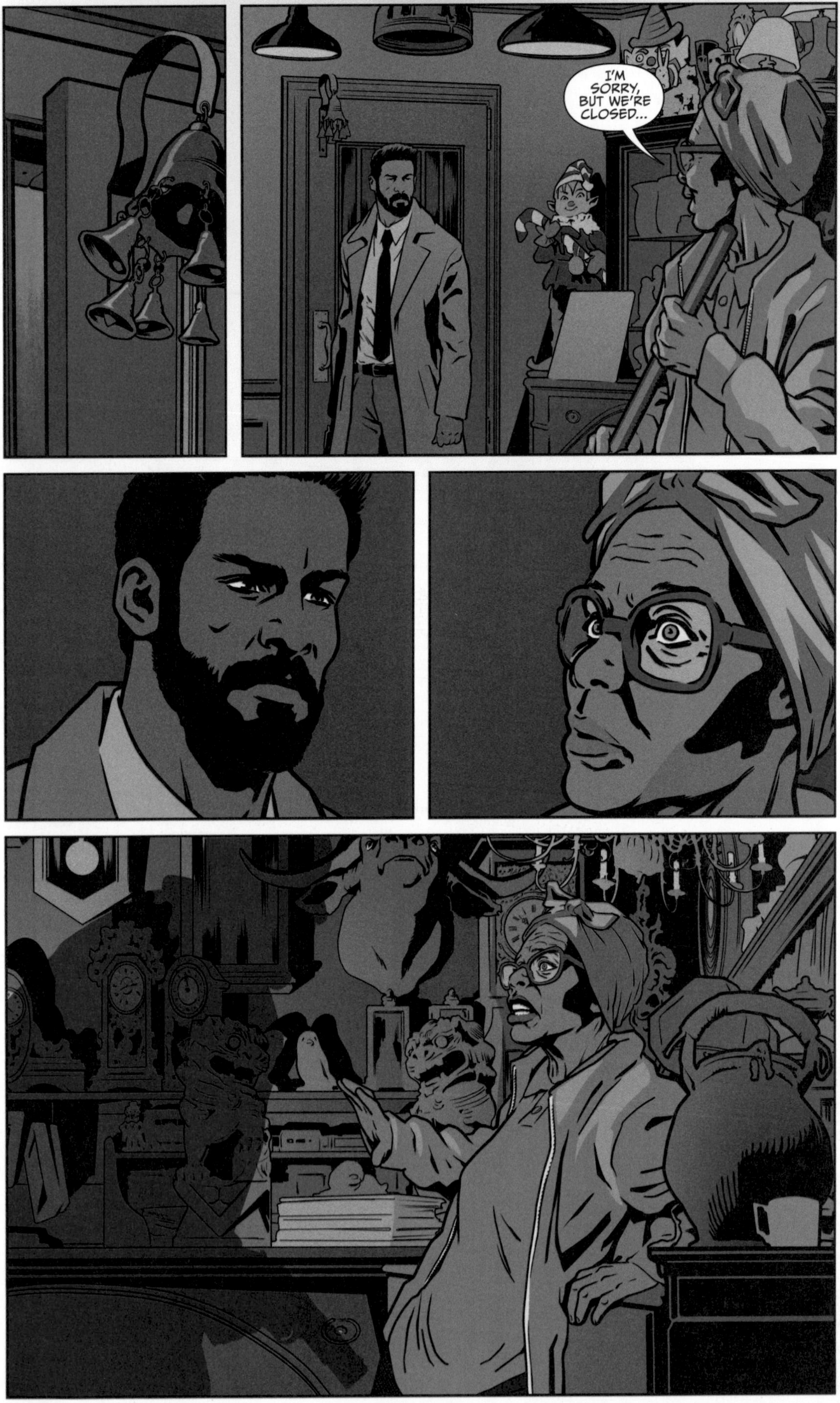
I'M SORRY, BUT WE'RE CLOSED...

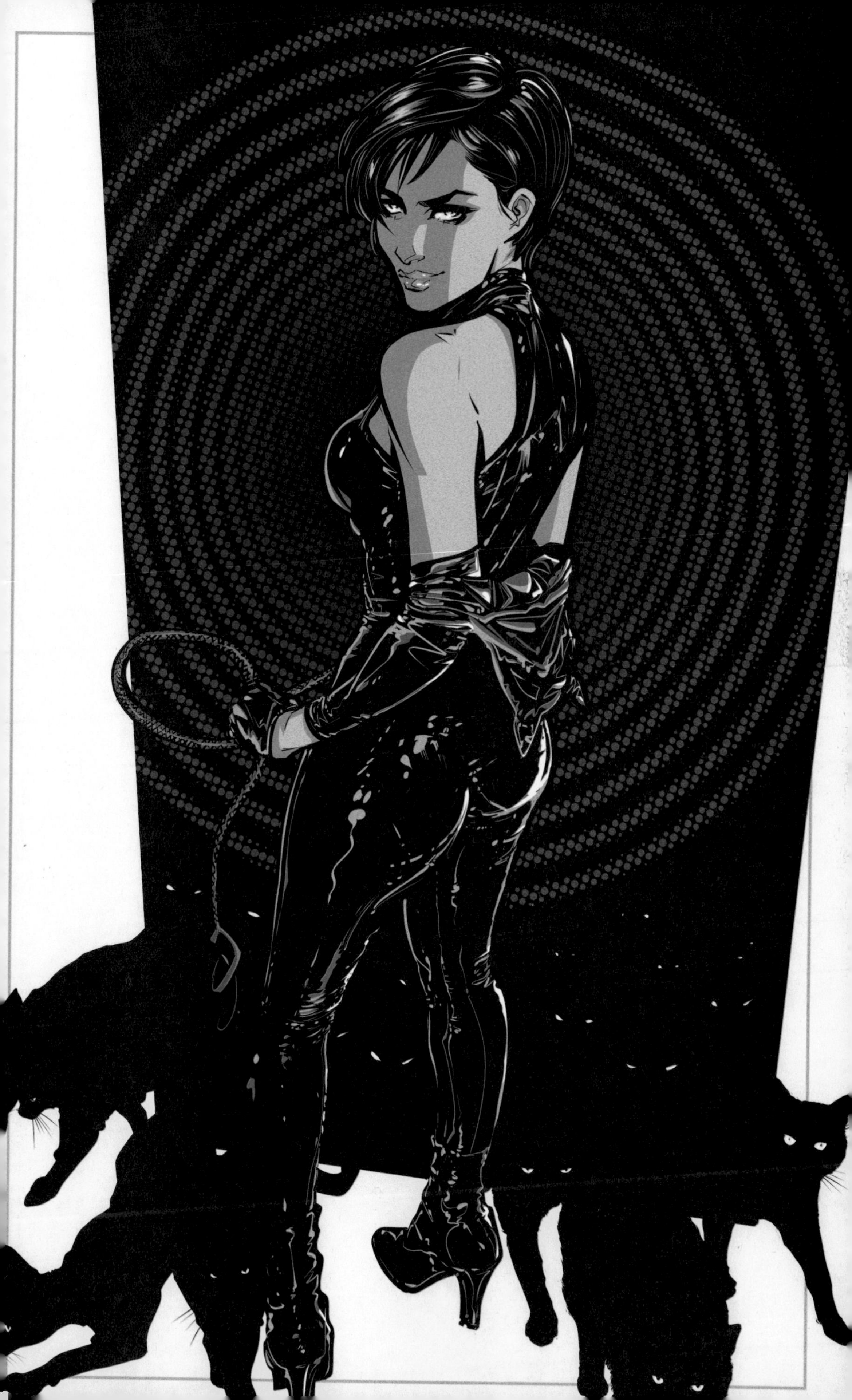

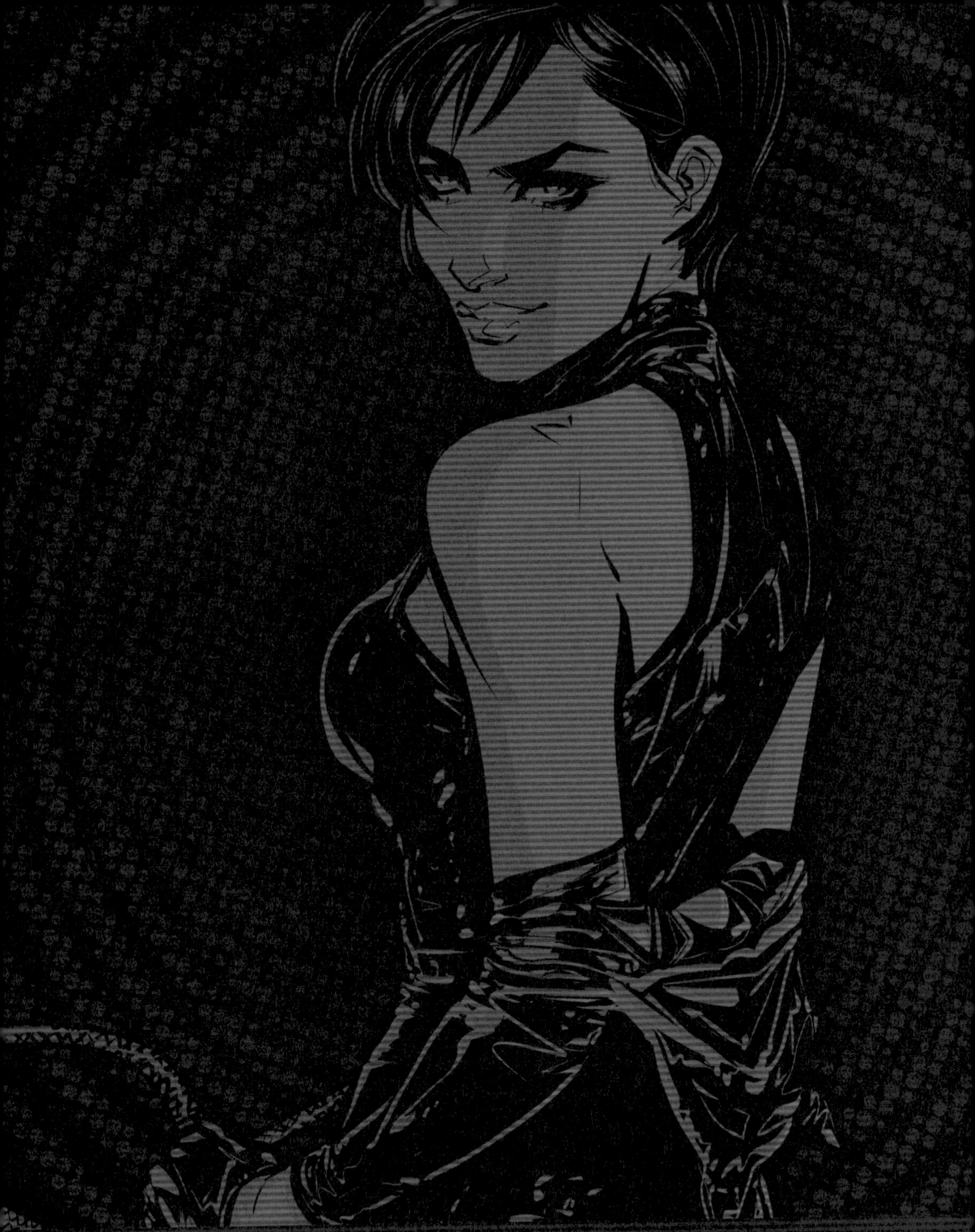

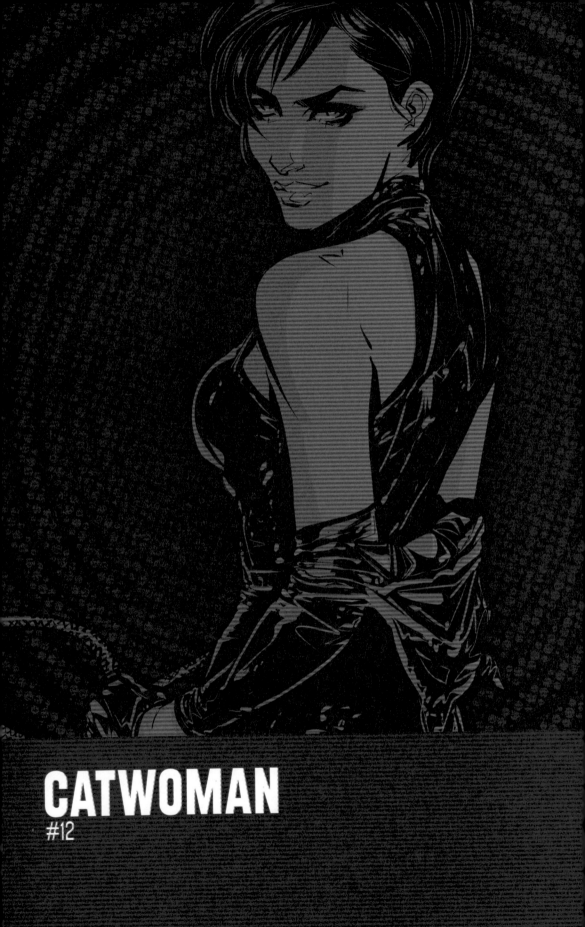

# CATWOMAN
#12

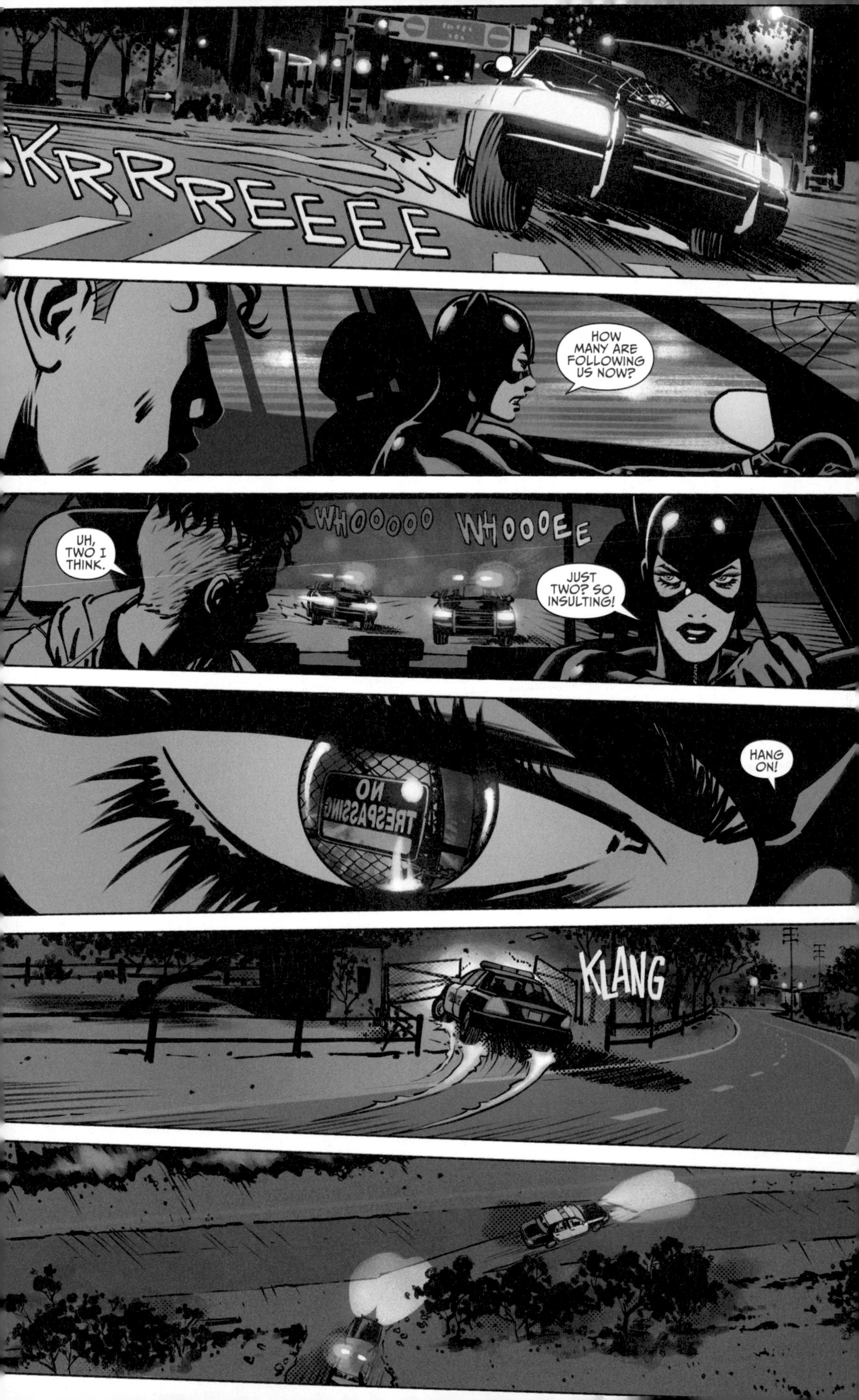
KRRREEEEE
HOW MANY ARE FOLLOWING US NOW?
UH, TWO I THINK.
WHOOOOO WHOOOEE
JUST TWO? SO INSULTING!
NO TRESPASSING
HANG ON!
KLANG

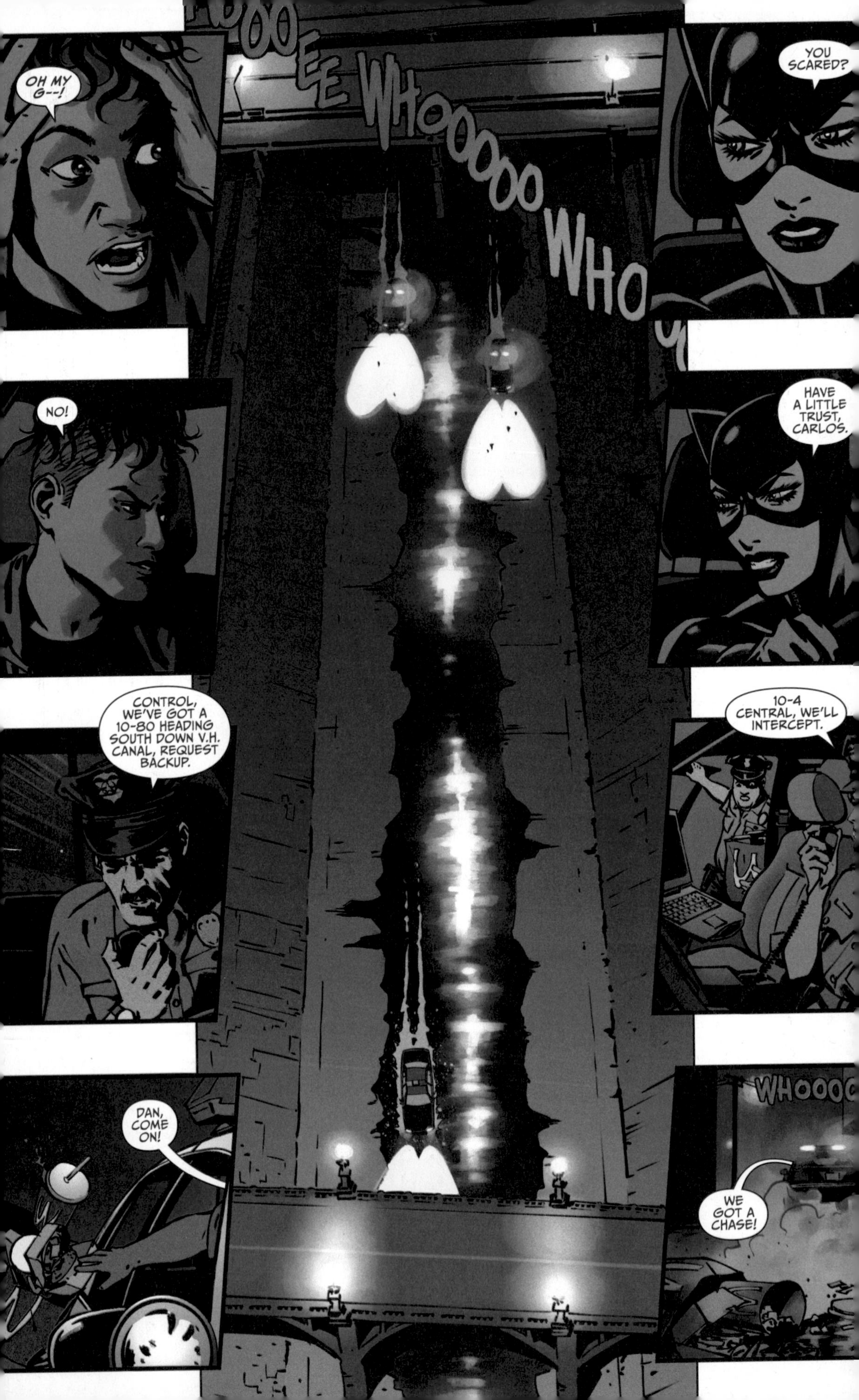
WHOOOEE WHOOOOOO WHOO
OH MY G--!
YOU SCARED?
NO!
HAVE A LITTLE TRUST, CARLOS.
CONTROL, WE'VE GOT A 10-80 HEADING SOUTH DOWN V.H. CANAL, REQUEST BACKUP.
10-4 CENTRAL, WE'LL INTERCEPT.
DAN, COME ON!
WHOOOO
WE GOT A CHASE!

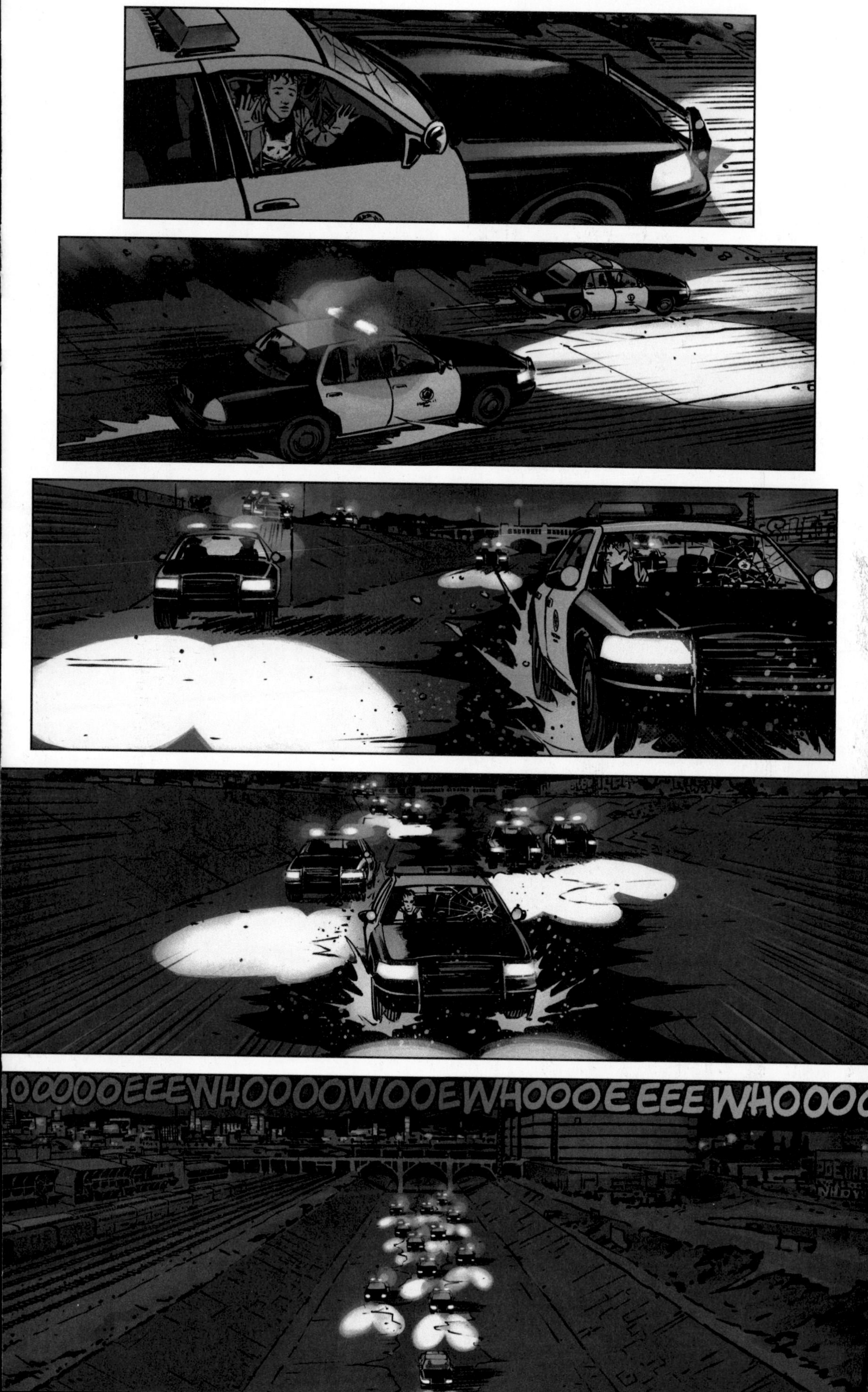
OOOOOEEEWHOOOOOWOOEWHOOOE EEE WHOOO

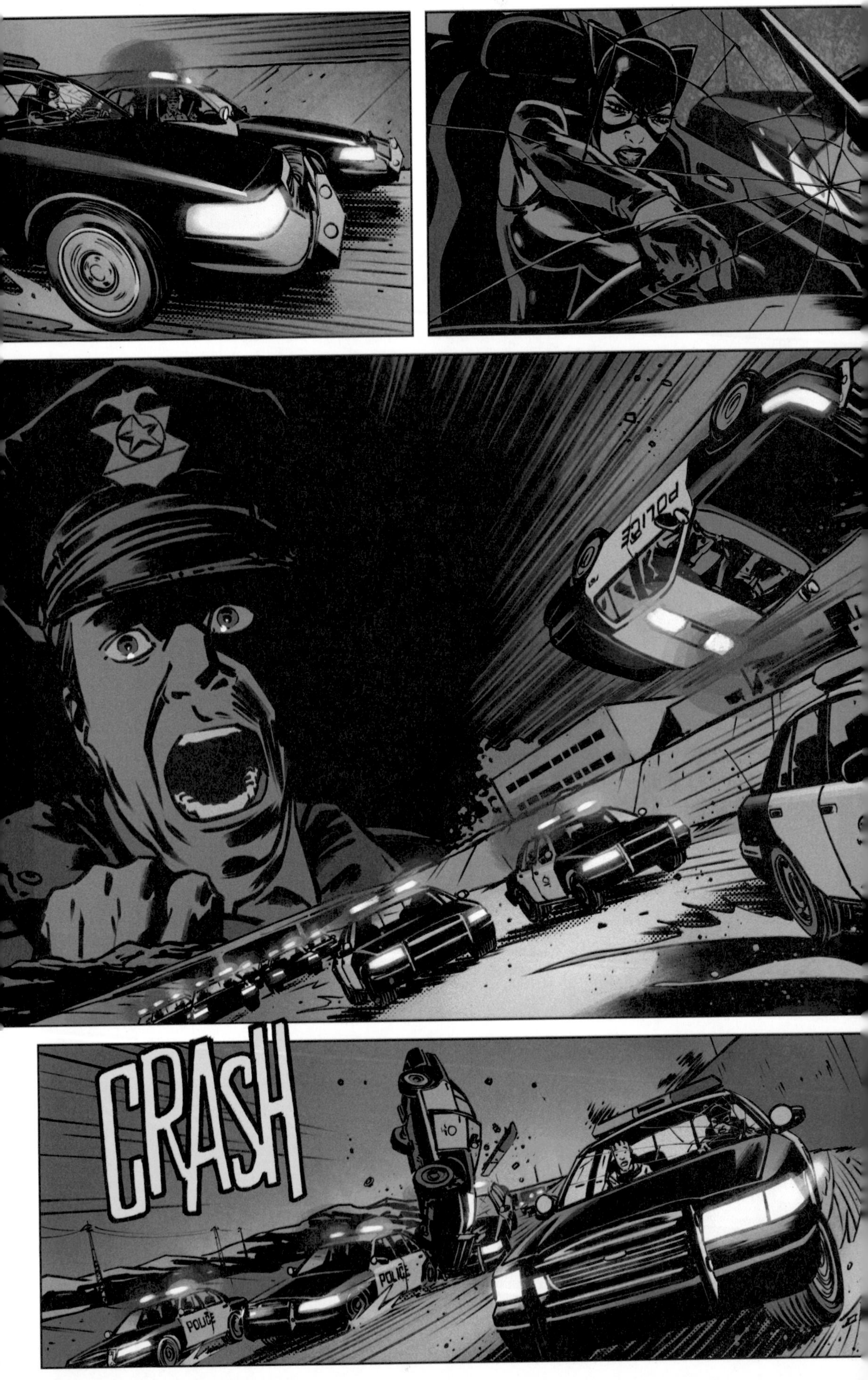
POLICE
CRASH
POLICE
POLICE

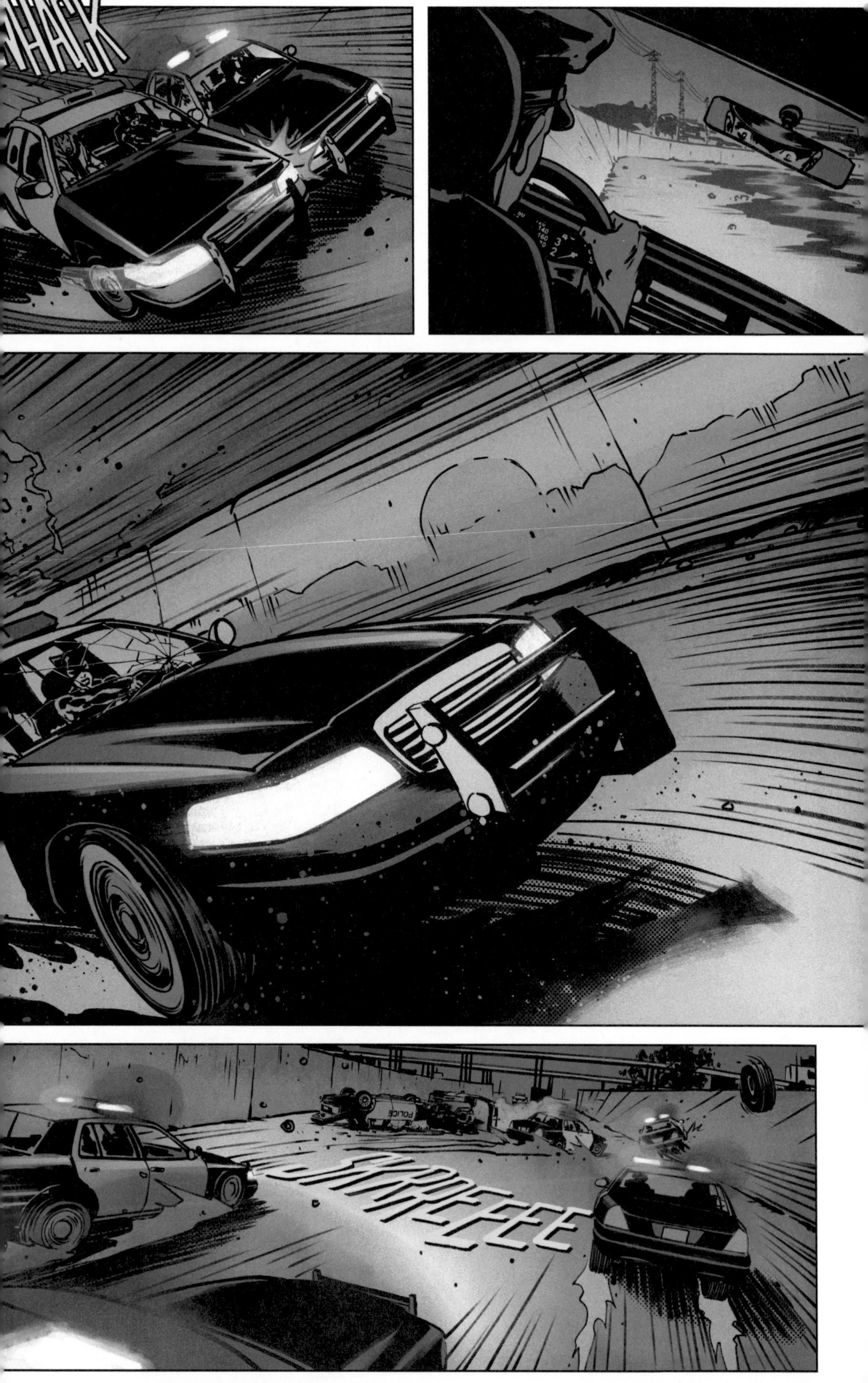
WHACK
POLICE
SKREEEE

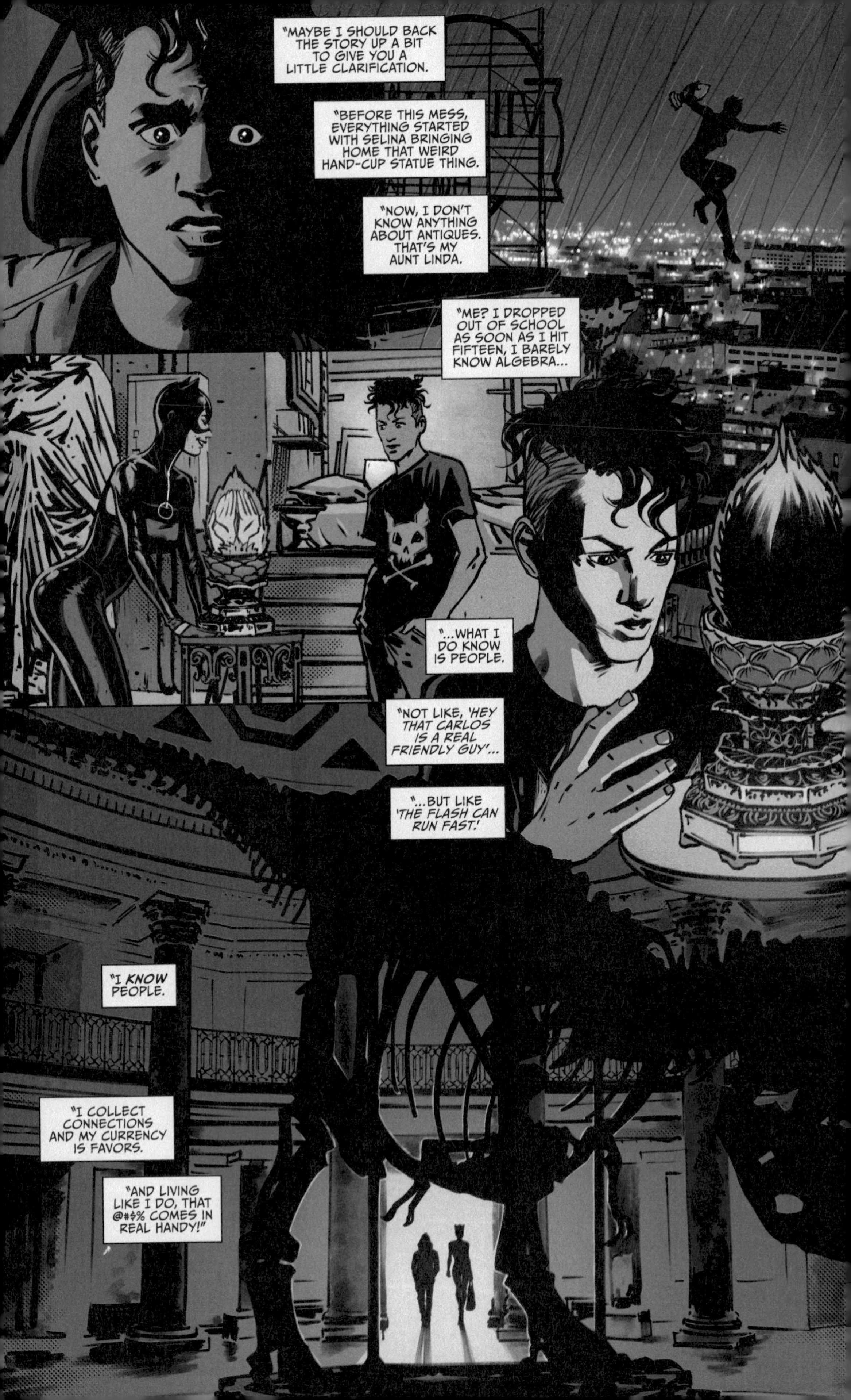
"MAYBE I SHOULD BACK THE STORY UP A BIT TO GIVE YOU A LITTLE CLARIFICATION.
"BEFORE THIS MESS, EVERYTHING STARTED WITH SELINA BRINGING HOME THAT WEIRD HAND-CUP STATUE THING.
"NOW, I DON'T KNOW ANYTHING ABOUT ANTIQUES. THAT'S MY AUNT LINDA.
"ME? I DROPPED OUT OF SCHOOL AS SOON AS I HIT FIFTEEN, I BARELY KNOW ALGEBRA...
"...WHAT I DO KNOW IS PEOPLE.
"NOT LIKE, *'HEY THAT CARLOS IS A REAL FRIENDLY GUY'*...
"...BUT LIKE *'THE FLASH CAN RUN FAST.'*
"I *KNOW* PEOPLE.
"I COLLECT CONNECTIONS AND MY CURRENCY IS FAVORS.
"AND LIVING LIKE I DO, THAT @#$% COMES IN REAL HANDY!"

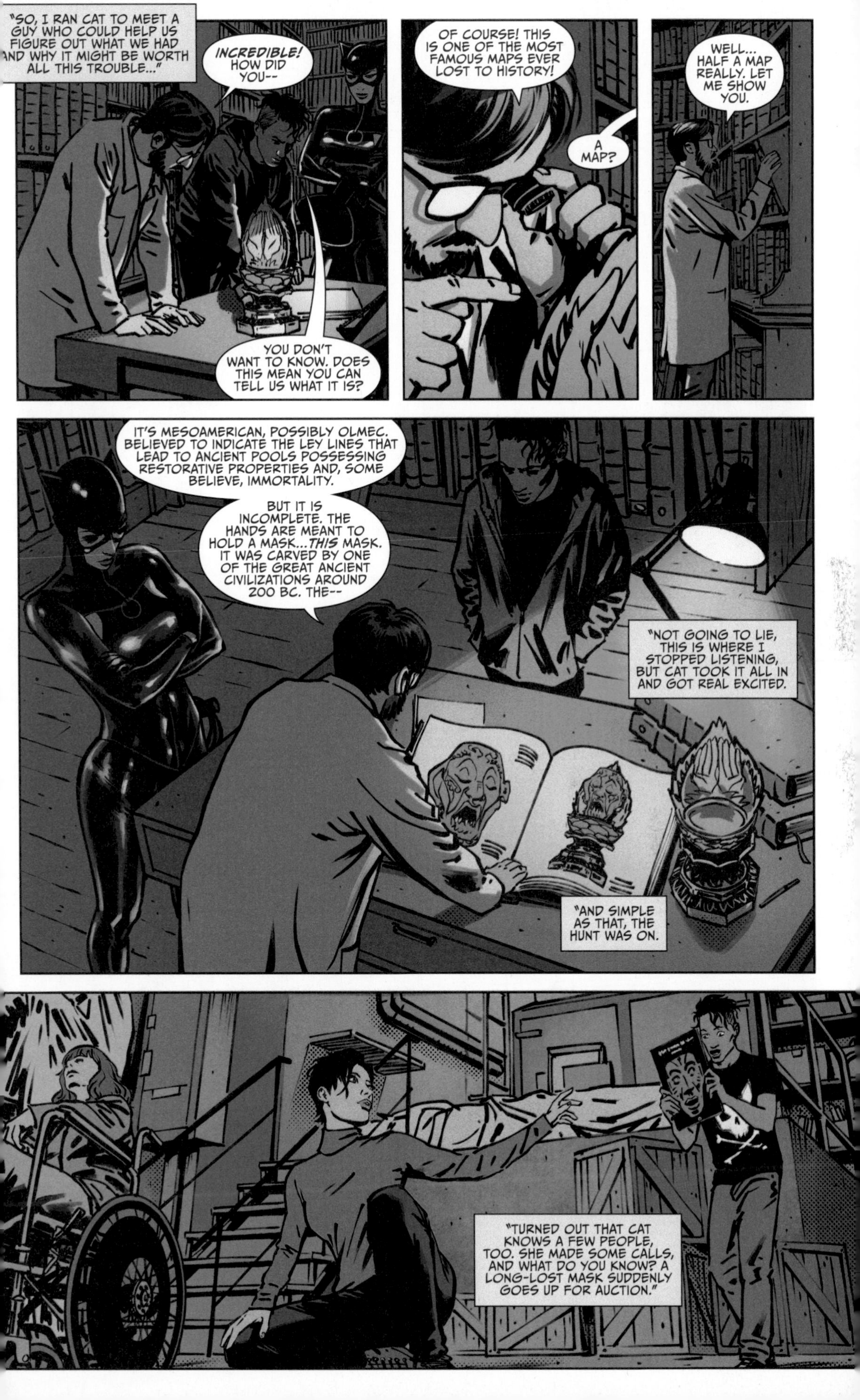
"SO, I RAN CAT TO MEET A GUY WHO COULD HELP US FIGURE OUT WHAT WE HAD AND WHY IT MIGHT BE WORTH ALL THIS TROUBLE..."
INCREDIBLE! HOW DID YOU--
YOU DON'T WANT TO KNOW. DOES THIS MEAN YOU CAN TELL US WHAT IT IS?
OF COURSE! THIS IS ONE OF THE MOST FAMOUS MAPS EVER LOST TO HISTORY!
A MAP?
WELL... HALF A MAP REALLY. LET ME SHOW YOU.
IT'S MESOAMERICAN, POSSIBLY OLMEC. BELIEVED TO INDICATE THE LEY LINES THAT LEAD TO ANCIENT POOLS POSSESSING RESTORATIVE PROPERTIES AND, SOME BELIEVE, IMMORTALITY.
BUT IT IS INCOMPLETE. THE HANDS ARE MEANT TO HOLD A MASK...THIS MASK. IT WAS CARVED BY ONE OF THE GREAT ANCIENT CIVILIZATIONS AROUND 200 BC. THE--
"NOT GOING TO LIE, THIS IS WHERE I STOPPED LISTENING, BUT CAT TOOK IT ALL IN AND GOT REAL EXCITED.
"AND SIMPLE AS THAT, THE HUNT WAS ON.
"TURNED OUT THAT CAT KNOWS A FEW PEOPLE, TOO. SHE MADE SOME CALLS, AND WHAT DO YOU KNOW? A LONG-LOST MASK SUDDENLY GOES UP FOR AUCTION."

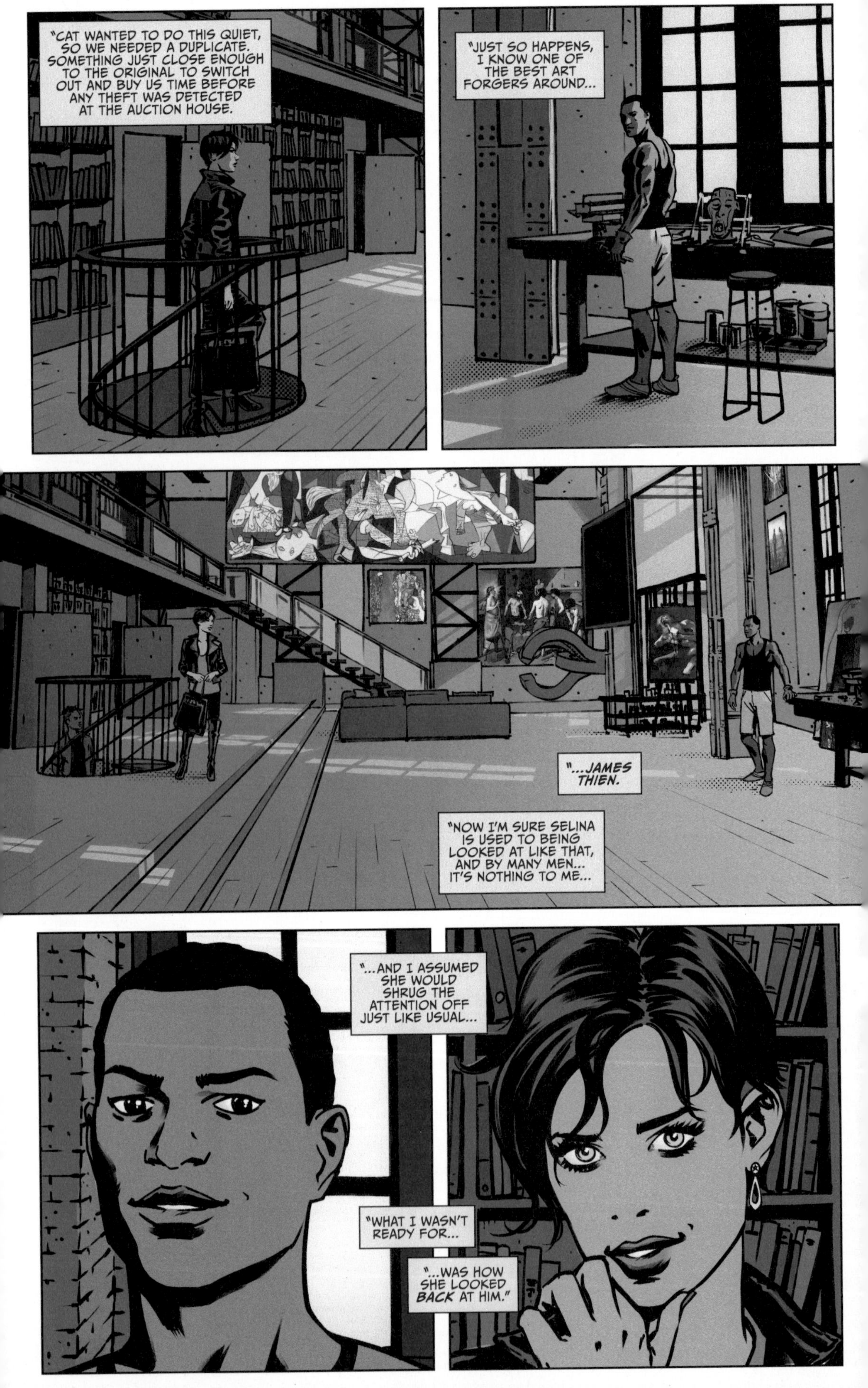
"CAT WANTED TO DO THIS QUIET, SO WE NEEDED A DUPLICATE. SOMETHING JUST CLOSE ENOUGH TO THE ORIGINAL TO SWITCH OUT AND BUY US TIME BEFORE ANY THEFT WAS DETECTED AT THE AUCTION HOUSE.
"JUST SO HAPPENS, I KNOW ONE OF THE BEST ART FORGERS AROUND...
"...JAMES THIEN.
"NOW I'M SURE SELINA IS USED TO BEING LOOKED AT LIKE THAT, AND BY MANY MEN... IT'S NOTHING TO ME...
"...AND I ASSUMED SHE WOULD SHRUG THE ATTENTION OFF JUST LIKE USUAL...
"WHAT I WASN'T READY FOR...
"...WAS HOW SHE LOOKED BACK AT HIM."

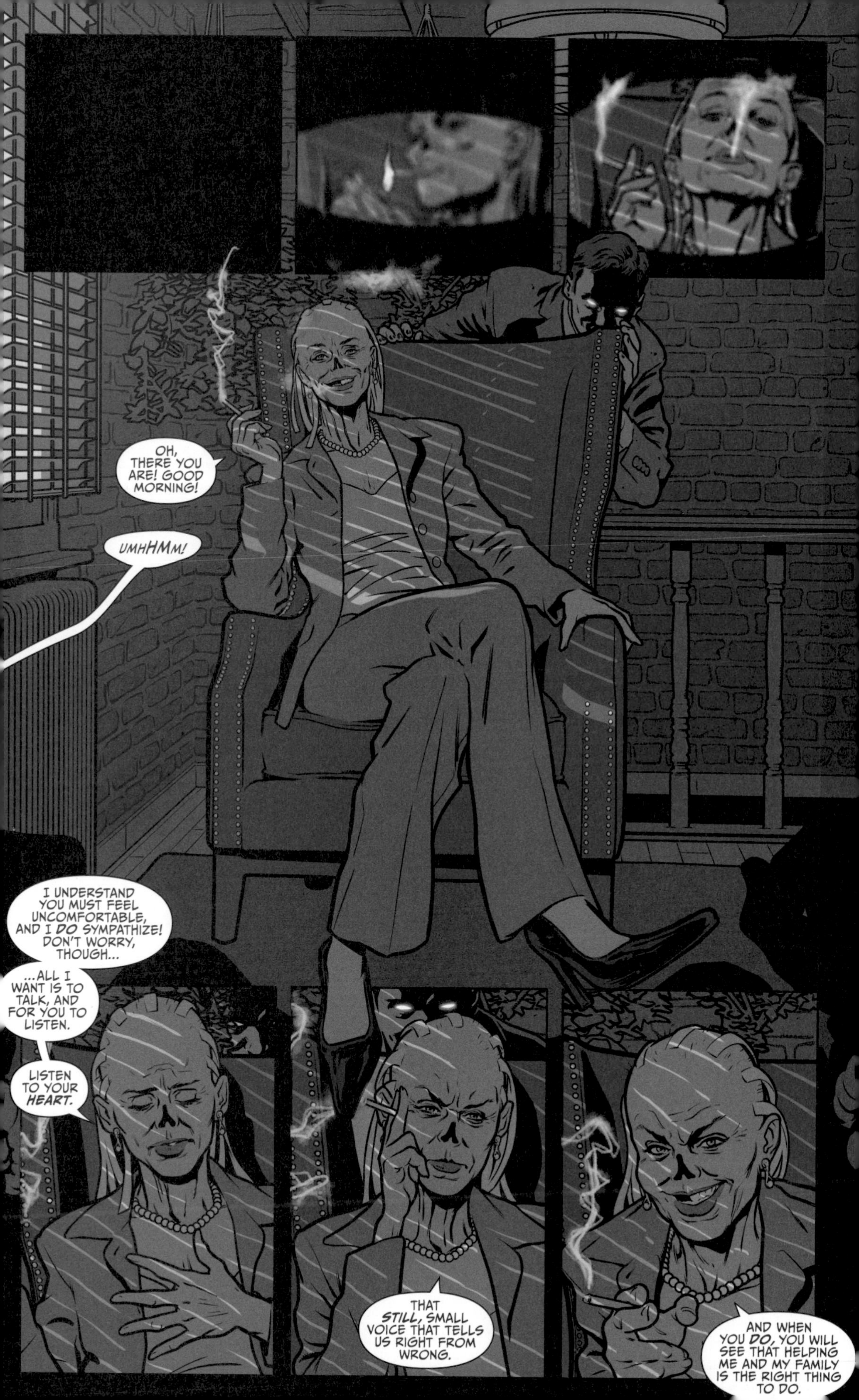
OH, THERE YOU ARE! GOOD MORNING!
UMHHMM!
I UNDERSTAND YOU MUST FEEL UNCOMFORTABLE, AND I *DO* SYMPATHIZE! DON'T WORRY, THOUGH...
...ALL I WANT IS TO TALK, AND FOR YOU TO LISTEN.
LISTEN TO YOUR *HEART.*
THAT *STILL,* SMALL VOICE THAT TELLS US RIGHT FROM WRONG.
AND WHEN YOU *DO,* YOU WILL SEE THAT HELPING ME AND MY FAMILY IS THE RIGHT THING TO DO.

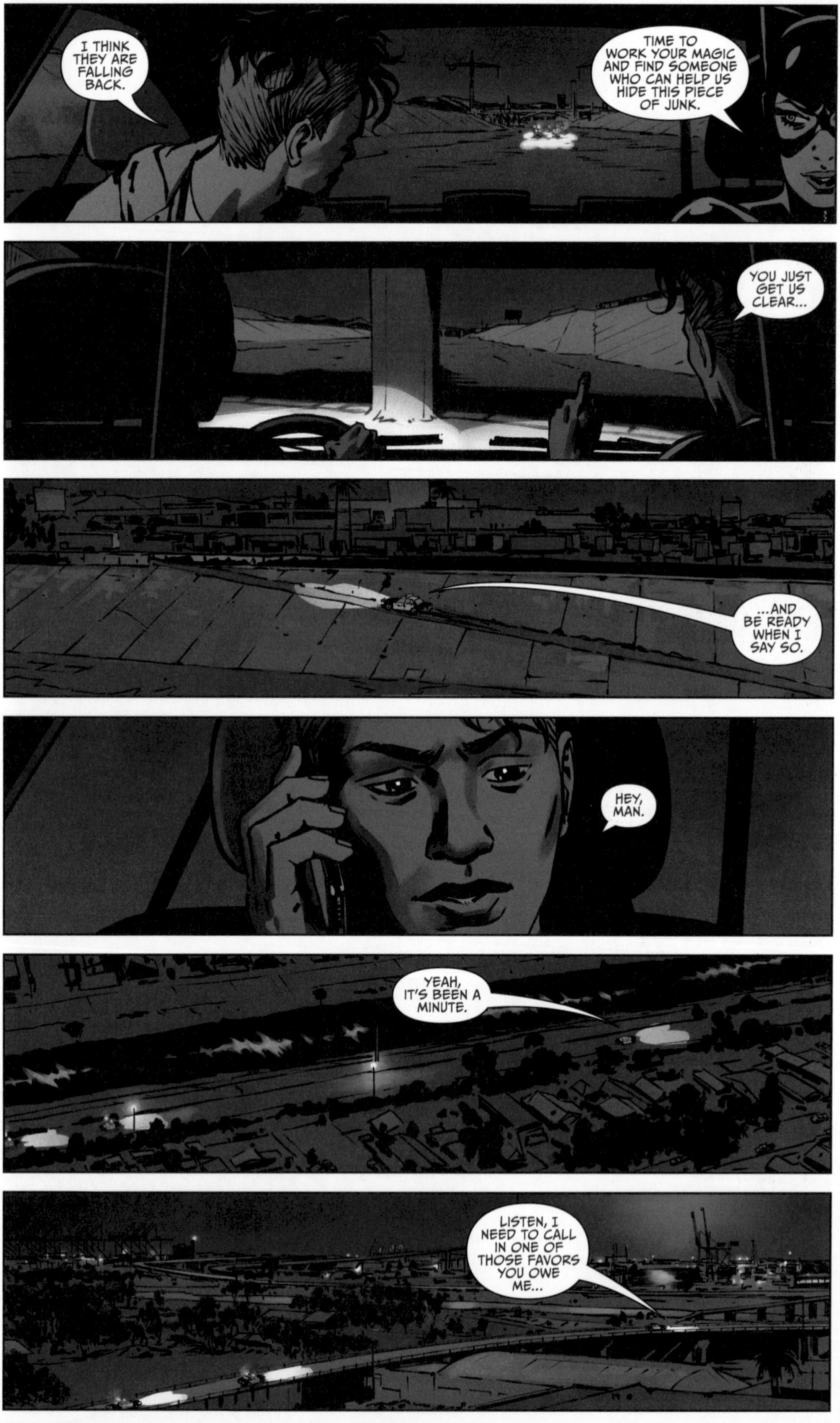
I THINK THEY ARE FALLING BACK.
TIME TO WORK YOUR MAGIC AND FIND SOMEONE WHO CAN HELP US HIDE THIS PIECE OF JUNK.
YOU JUST GET US CLEAR...
...AND BE READY WHEN I SAY SO.
HEY, MAN.
YEAH, IT'S BEEN A MINUTE.
LISTEN, I NEED TO CALL IN ONE OF THOSE FAVORS YOU OWE ME...

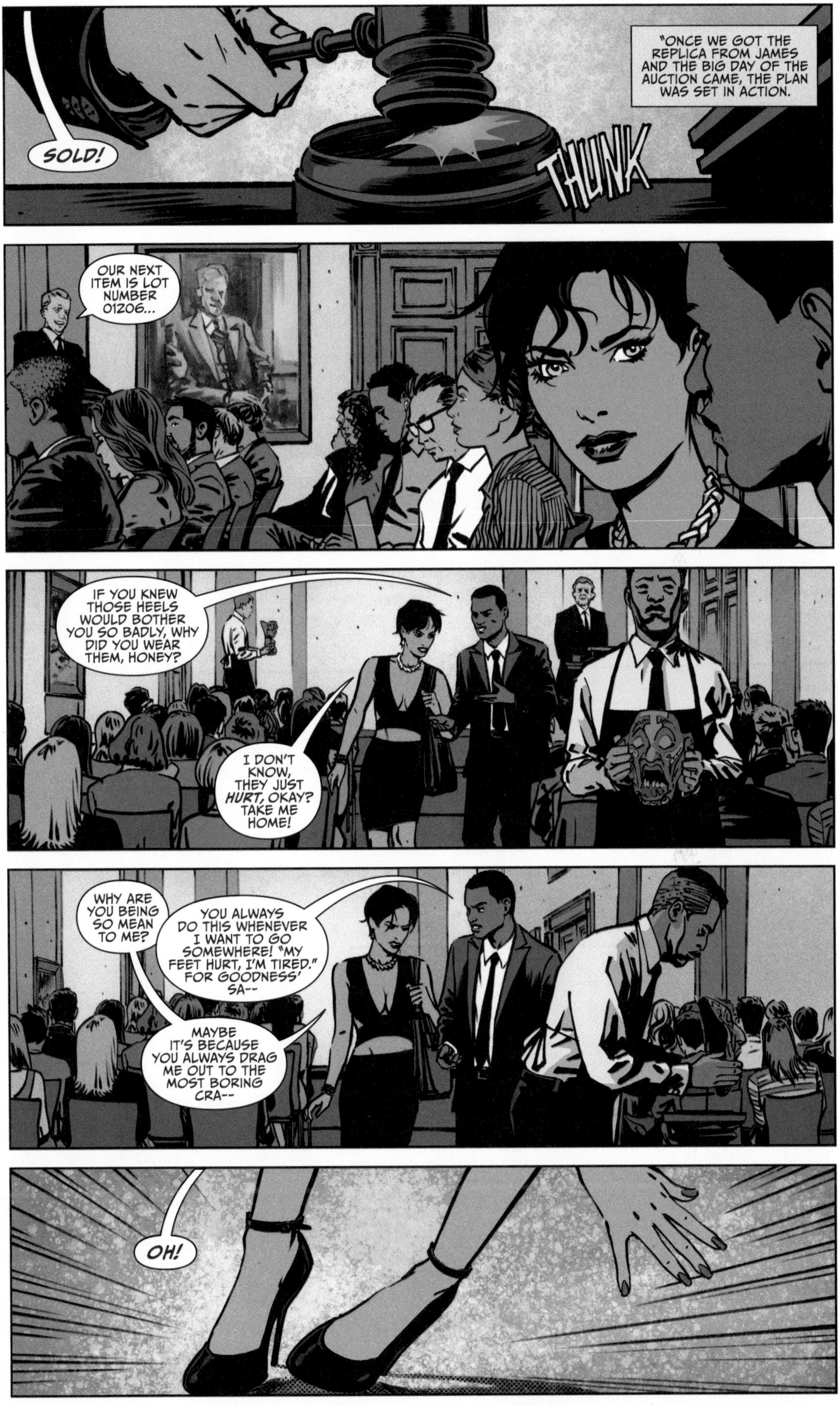
"ONCE WE GOT THE REPLICA FROM JAMES AND THE BIG DAY OF THE AUCTION CAME, THE PLAN WAS SET IN ACTION.
SOLD!
THUNK
OUR NEXT ITEM IS LOT NUMBER 01206...
IF YOU KNEW THOSE HEELS WOULD BOTHER YOU SO BADLY, WHY DID YOU WEAR THEM, HONEY?
I DON'T KNOW, THEY JUST HURT, OKAY? TAKE ME HOME!
WHY ARE YOU BEING SO MEAN TO ME?
YOU ALWAYS DO THIS WHENEVER I WANT TO GO SOMEWHERE! "MY FEET HURT, I'M TIRED." FOR GOODNESS' SA--
MAYBE IT'S BECAUSE YOU ALWAYS DRAG ME OUT TO THE MOST BORING CRA--
OH!

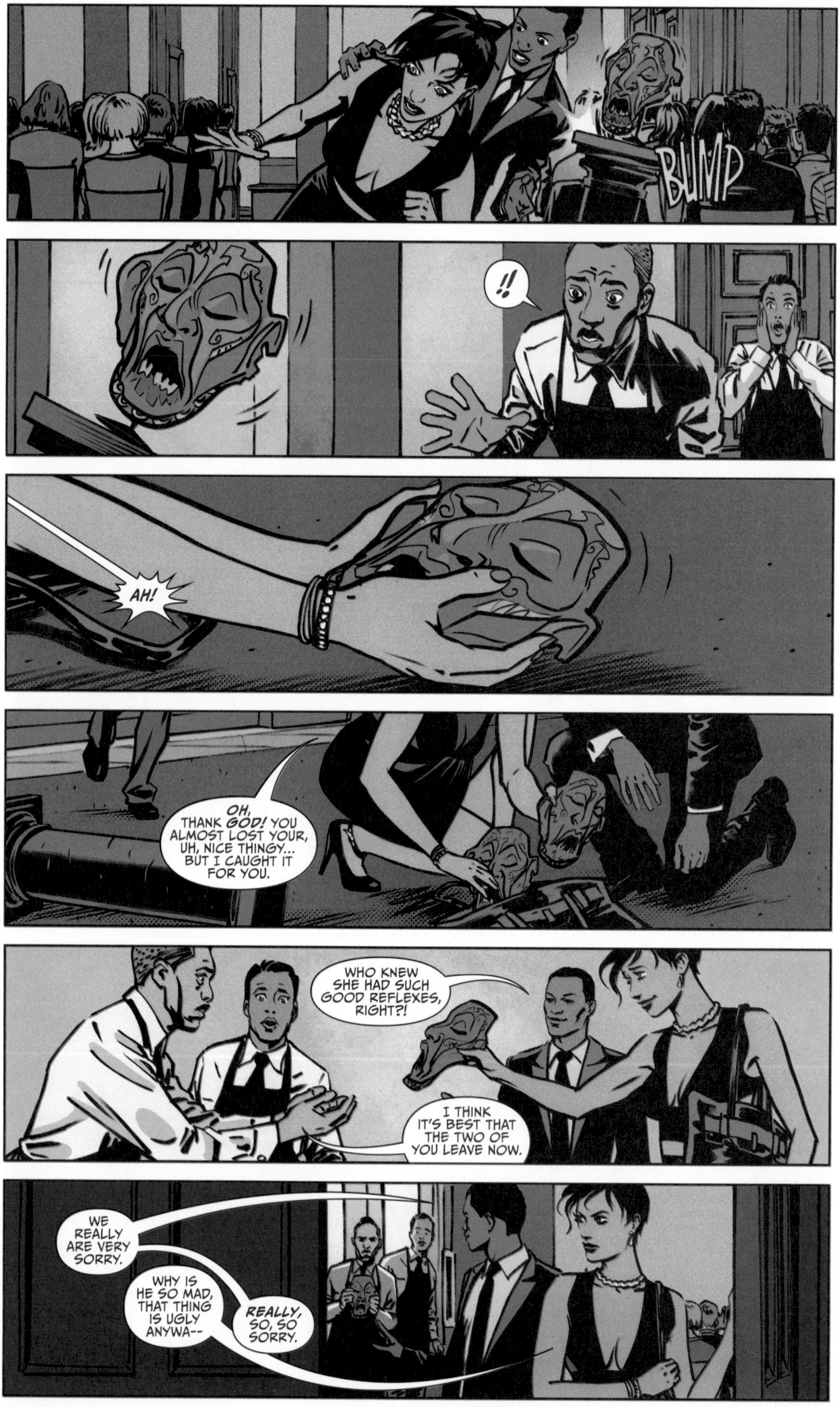
BUMP
!!
AH!
OH, THANK GOD! YOU ALMOST LOST YOUR, UH, NICE THINGY... BUT I CAUGHT IT FOR YOU.
WHO KNEW SHE HAD SUCH GOOD REFLEXES, RIGHT?!
I THINK IT'S BEST THAT THE TWO OF YOU LEAVE NOW.
WE REALLY ARE VERY SORRY.
WHY IS HE SO MAD, THAT THING IS UGLY ANYWA--
REALLY, SO, SO SORRY.

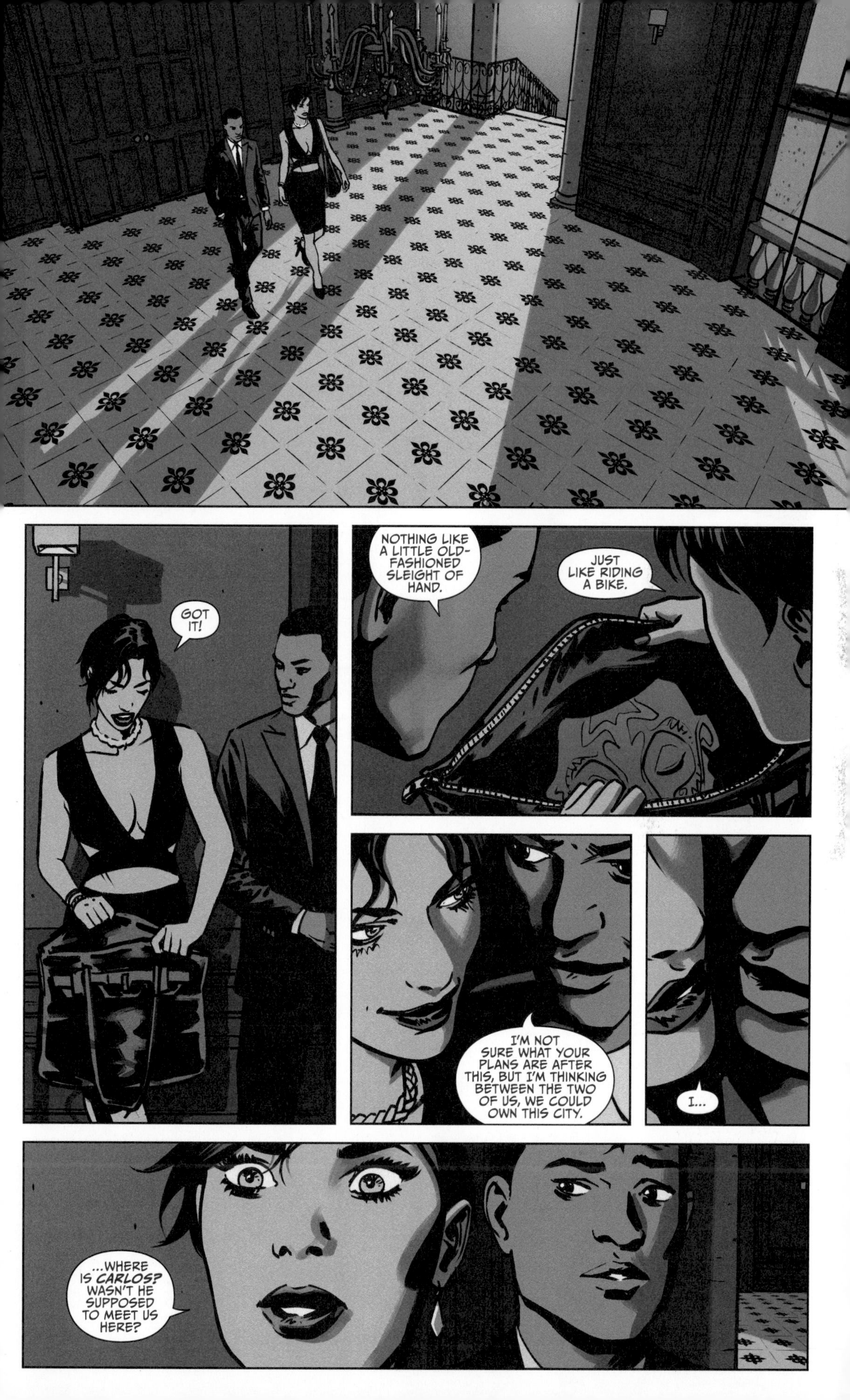
GOT IT!
NOTHING LIKE A LITTLE OLD-FASHIONED SLEIGHT OF HAND.
JUST LIKE RIDING A BIKE.
I'M NOT SURE WHAT YOUR PLANS ARE AFTER THIS, BUT I'M THINKING BETWEEN THE TWO OF US, WE COULD OWN THIS CITY.
I...
...WHERE IS CARLOS? WASN'T HE SUPPOSED TO MEET US HERE?

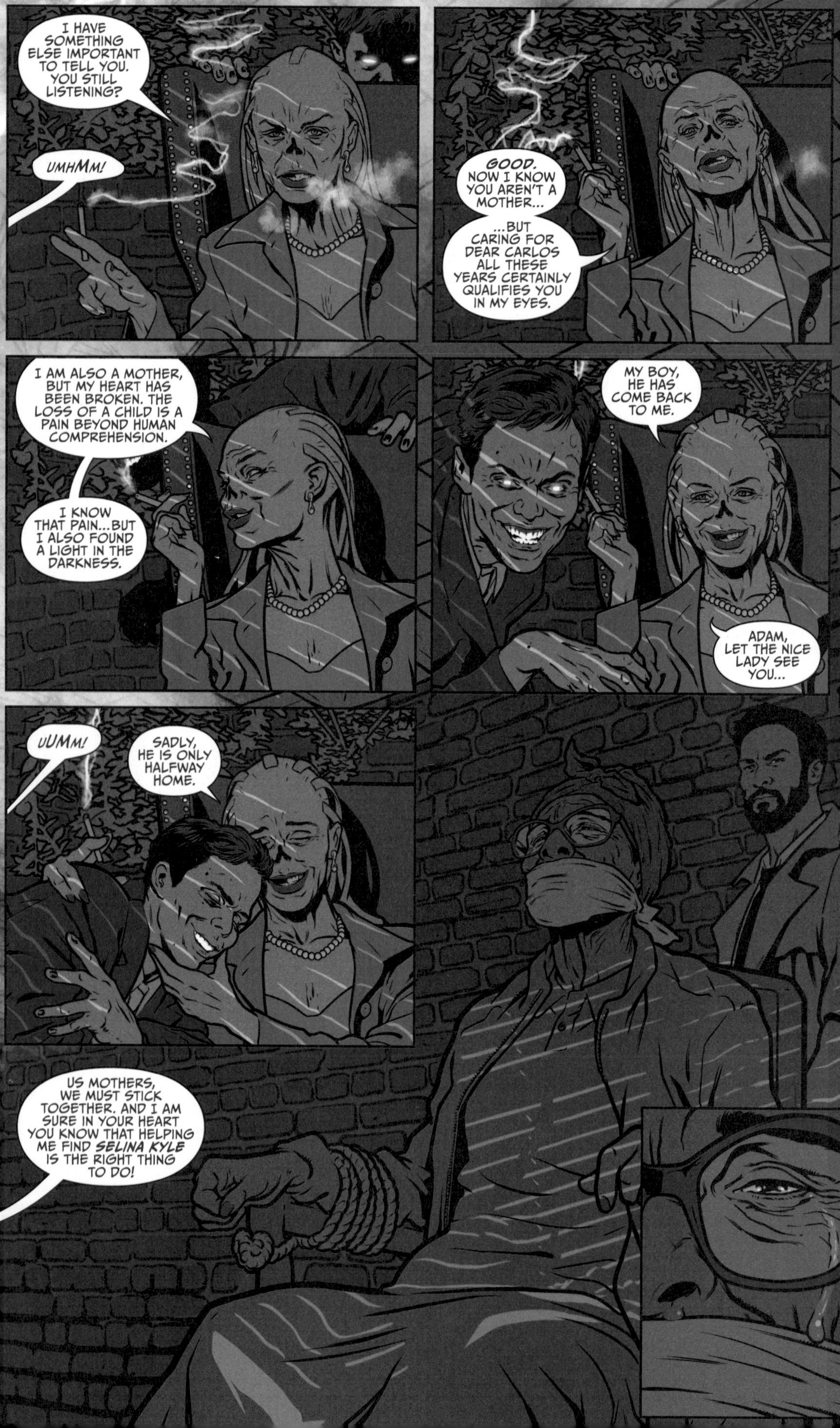
I HAVE SOMETHING ELSE IMPORTANT TO TELL YOU. YOU STILL LISTENING?
UMHMM!
GOOD. NOW I KNOW YOU AREN'T A MOTHER...
...BUT CARING FOR DEAR CARLOS ALL THESE YEARS CERTAINLY QUALIFIES YOU IN MY EYES.
I AM ALSO A MOTHER, BUT MY HEART HAS BEEN BROKEN. THE LOSS OF A CHILD IS A PAIN BEYOND HUMAN COMPREHENSION.
I KNOW THAT PAIN...BUT I ALSO FOUND A LIGHT IN THE DARKNESS.
MY BOY, HE HAS COME BACK TO ME.
ADAM, LET THE NICE LADY SEE YOU...
UUMM!
SADLY, HE IS ONLY HALFWAY HOME.
US MOTHERS, WE MUST STICK TOGETHER. AND I AM SURE IN YOUR HEART YOU KNOW THAT HELPING ME FIND SELINA KYLE IS THE RIGHT THING TO DO!

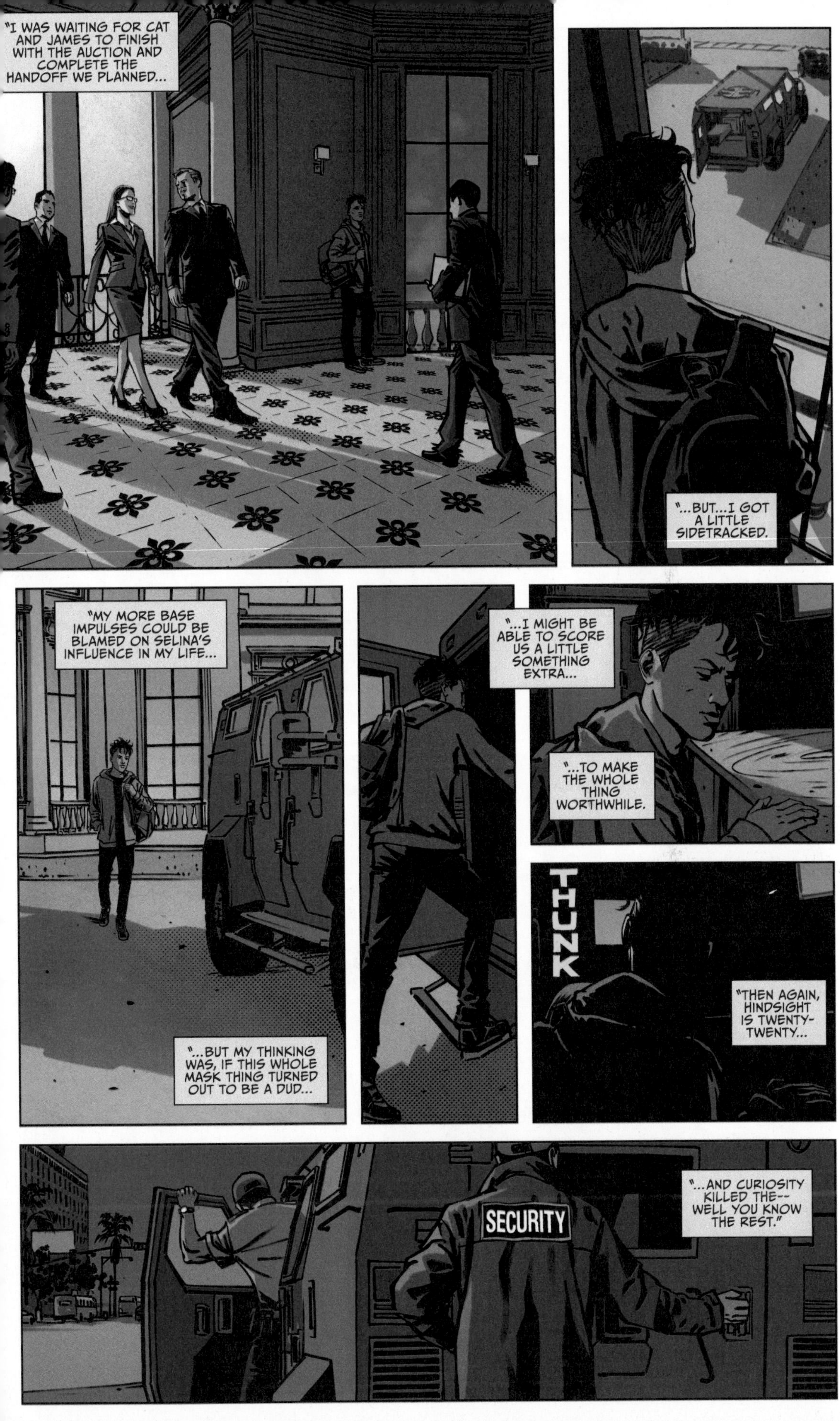
"I WAS WAITING FOR CAT AND JAMES TO FINISH WITH THE AUCTION AND COMPLETE THE HANDOFF WE PLANNED...
"...BUT...I GOT A LITTLE SIDETRACKED.
"MY MORE BASE IMPULSES COULD BE BLAMED ON SELINA'S INFLUENCE IN MY LIFE...
"...BUT MY THINKING WAS, IF THIS WHOLE MASK THING TURNED OUT TO BE A DUD...
"...I MIGHT BE ABLE TO SCORE US A LITTLE SOMETHING EXTRA...
"...TO MAKE THE WHOLE THING WORTHWHILE.
THUNK
"THEN AGAIN, HINDSIGHT IS TWENTY-TWENTY...
SECURITY
"...AND CURIOSITY KILLED THE-- WELL YOU KNOW THE REST."

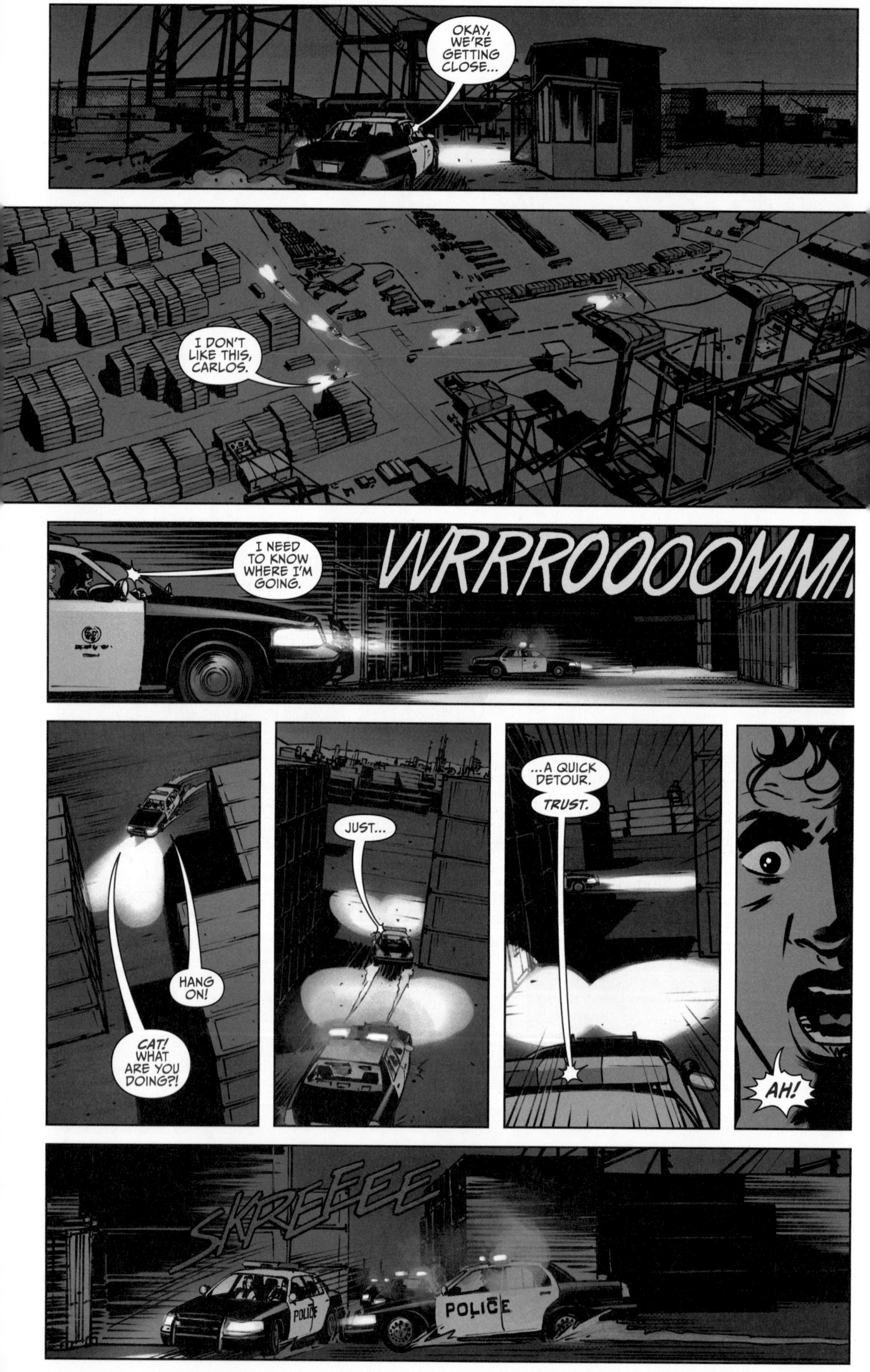
OKAY, WE'RE GETTING CLOSE...
I DON'T LIKE THIS, CARLOS.
I NEED TO KNOW WHERE I'M GOING.
VVRRROOOOMM
HANG ON!
CAT! WHAT ARE YOU DOING?!
JUST...
...A QUICK DETOUR.
TRUST.
AH!
SKREEEEE
POLICE
POLICE

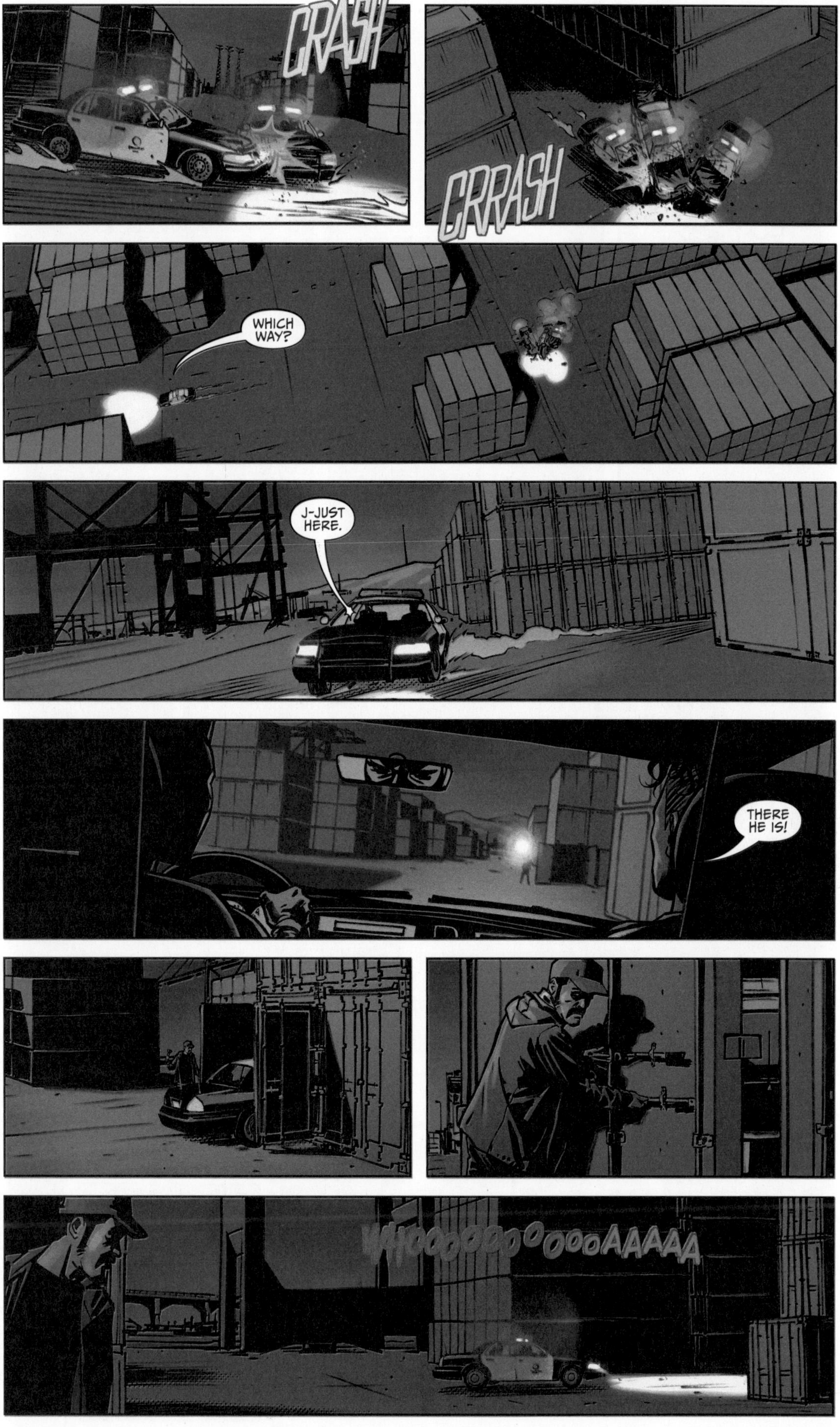
CRASH
CRRASH
WHICH WAY?
J-JUST HERE.
THERE HE IS!
WHOOOOOOOOOOOAAAAA

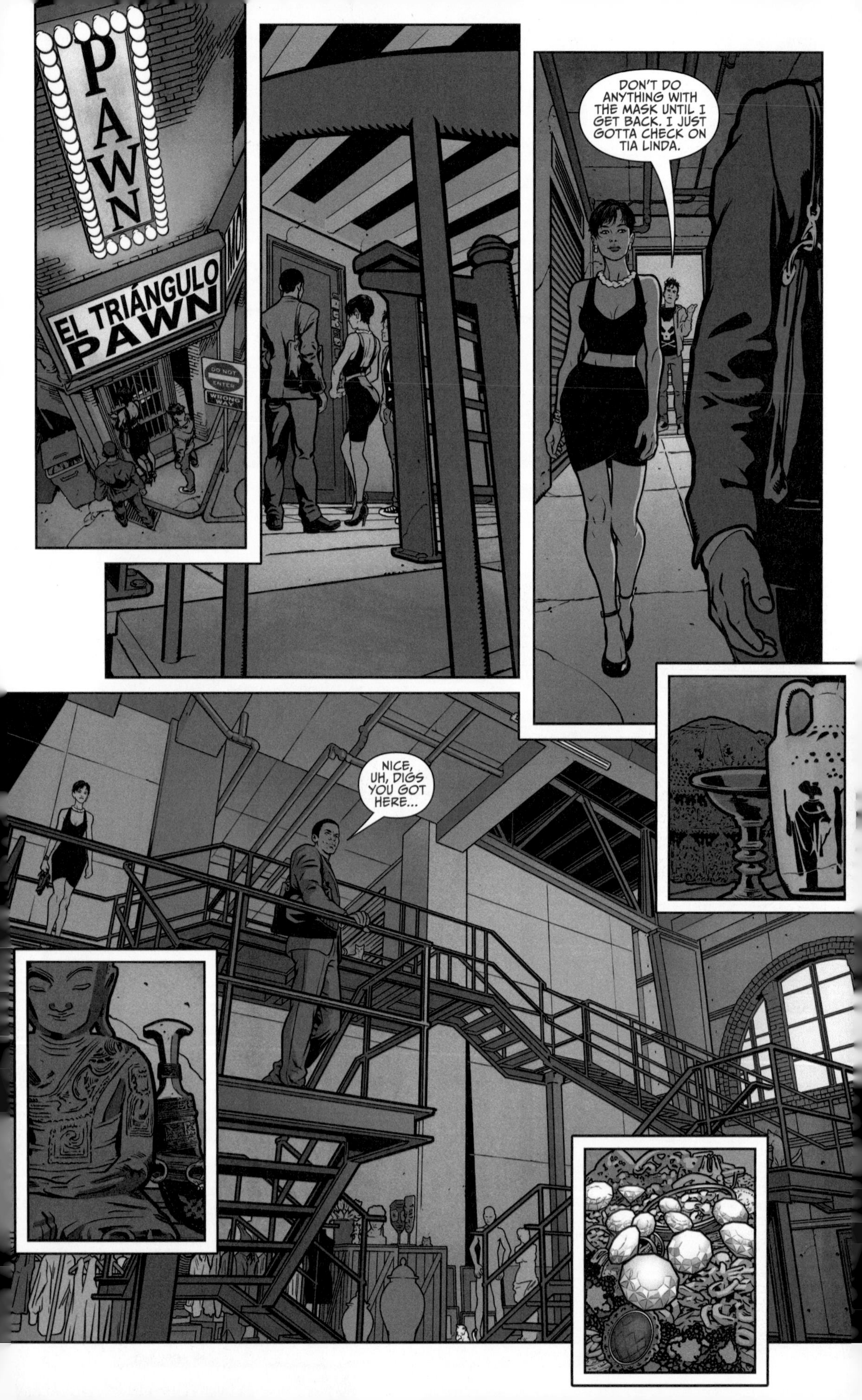
PAWN
EL TRIÁNGULO PAWN
DO NOT ENTER
WRONG WAY
DON'T DO ANYTHING WITH THE MASK UNTIL I GET BACK. I JUST GOTTA CHECK ON TIA LINDA.
NICE, UH, DIGS YOU GOT HERE...

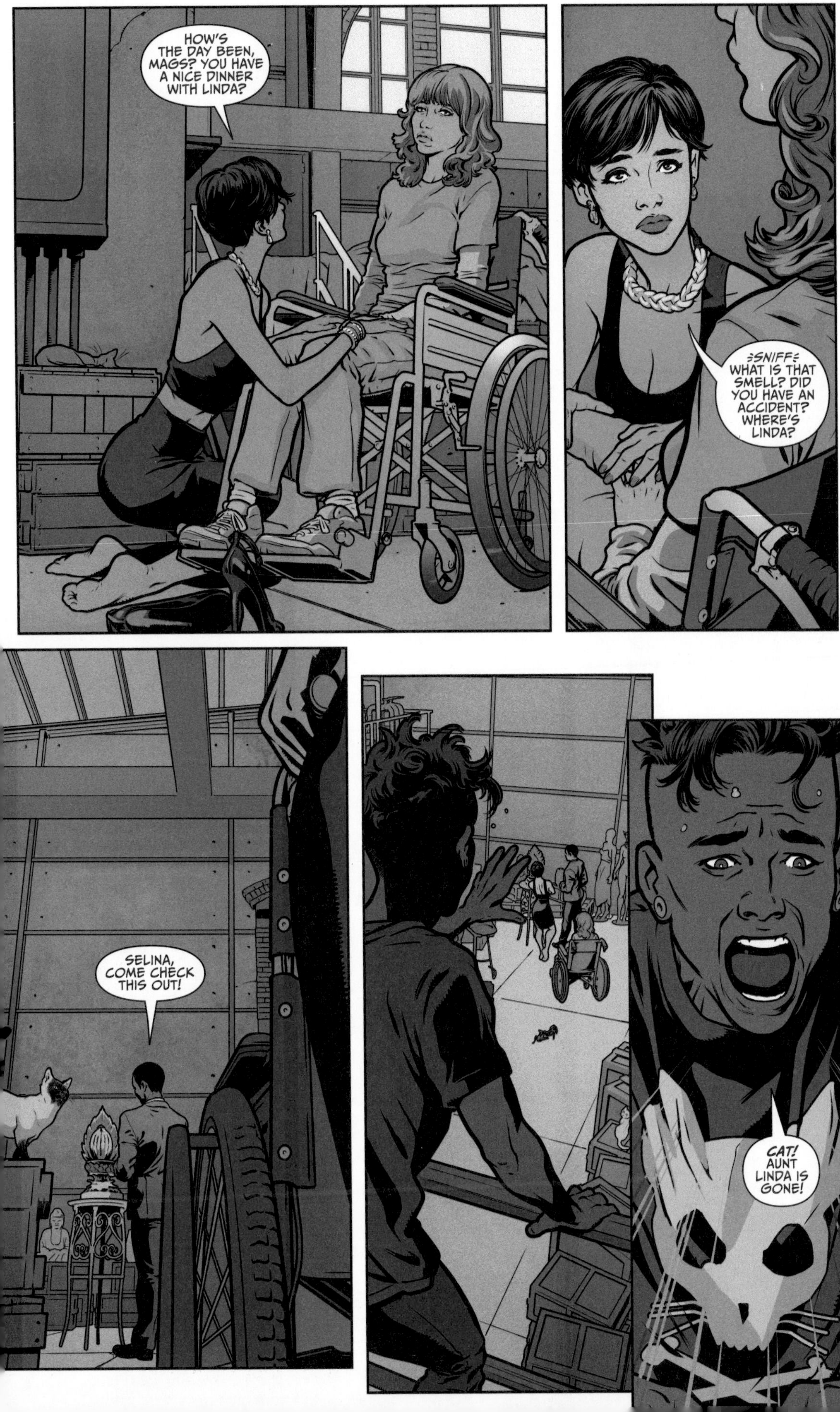
HOW'S THE DAY BEEN, MAGS? YOU HAVE A NICE DINNER WITH LINDA?
=SNIFF= WHAT IS THAT SMELL? DID YOU HAVE AN ACCIDENT? WHERE'S LINDA?
SELINA, COME CHECK THIS OUT!
CAT! AUNT LINDA IS GONE!

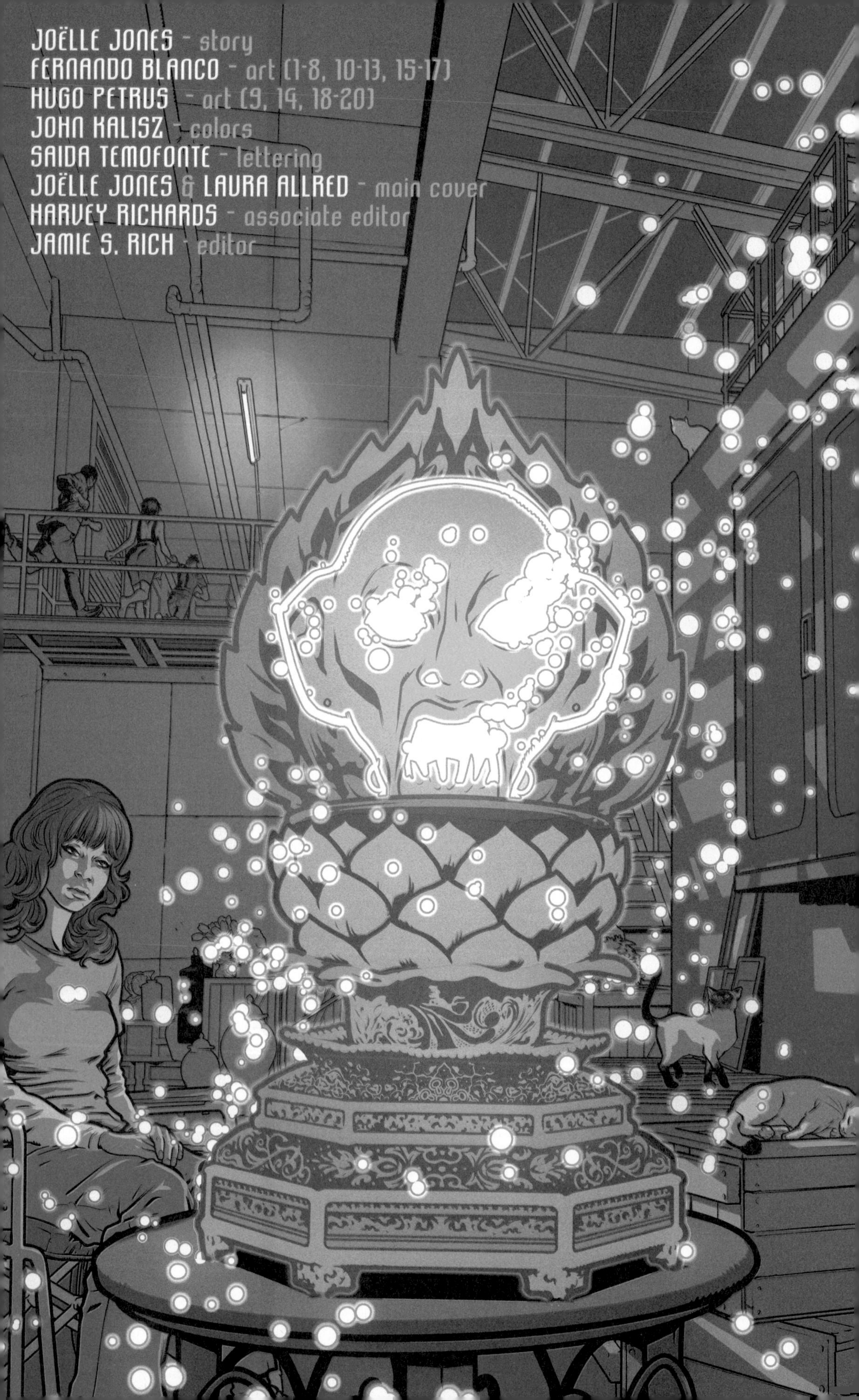
JOËLLE JONES - story
FERNANDO BLANCO - art (1-8, 10-13, 15-17)
HUGO PETRUS - art (9, 14, 18-20)
JOHN KALISZ - colors
SAIDA TEMOFONTE - lettering
JOËLLE JONES & LAURA ALLRED - main cover
HARVEY RICHARDS - associate editor
JAMIE S. RICH - editor

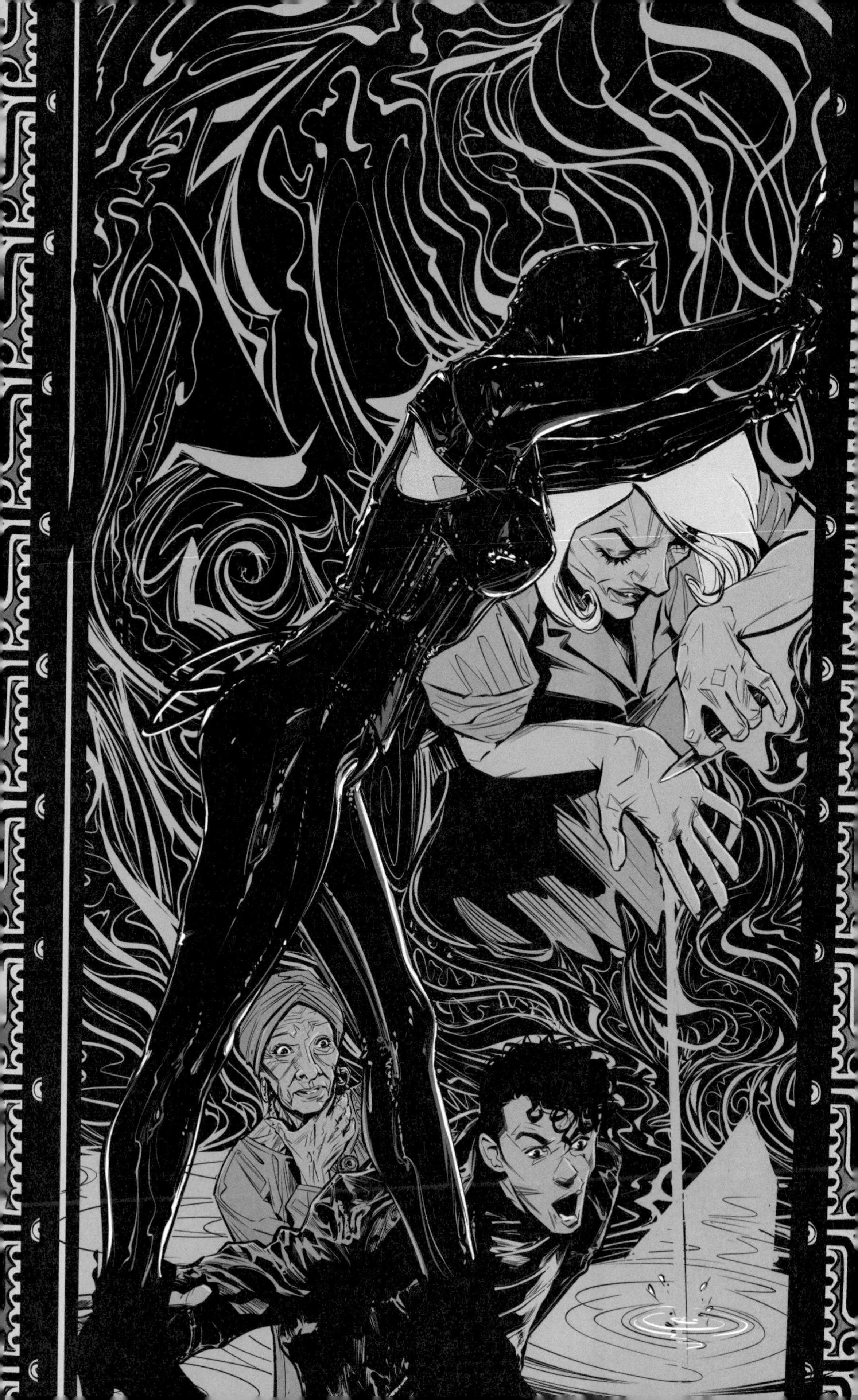

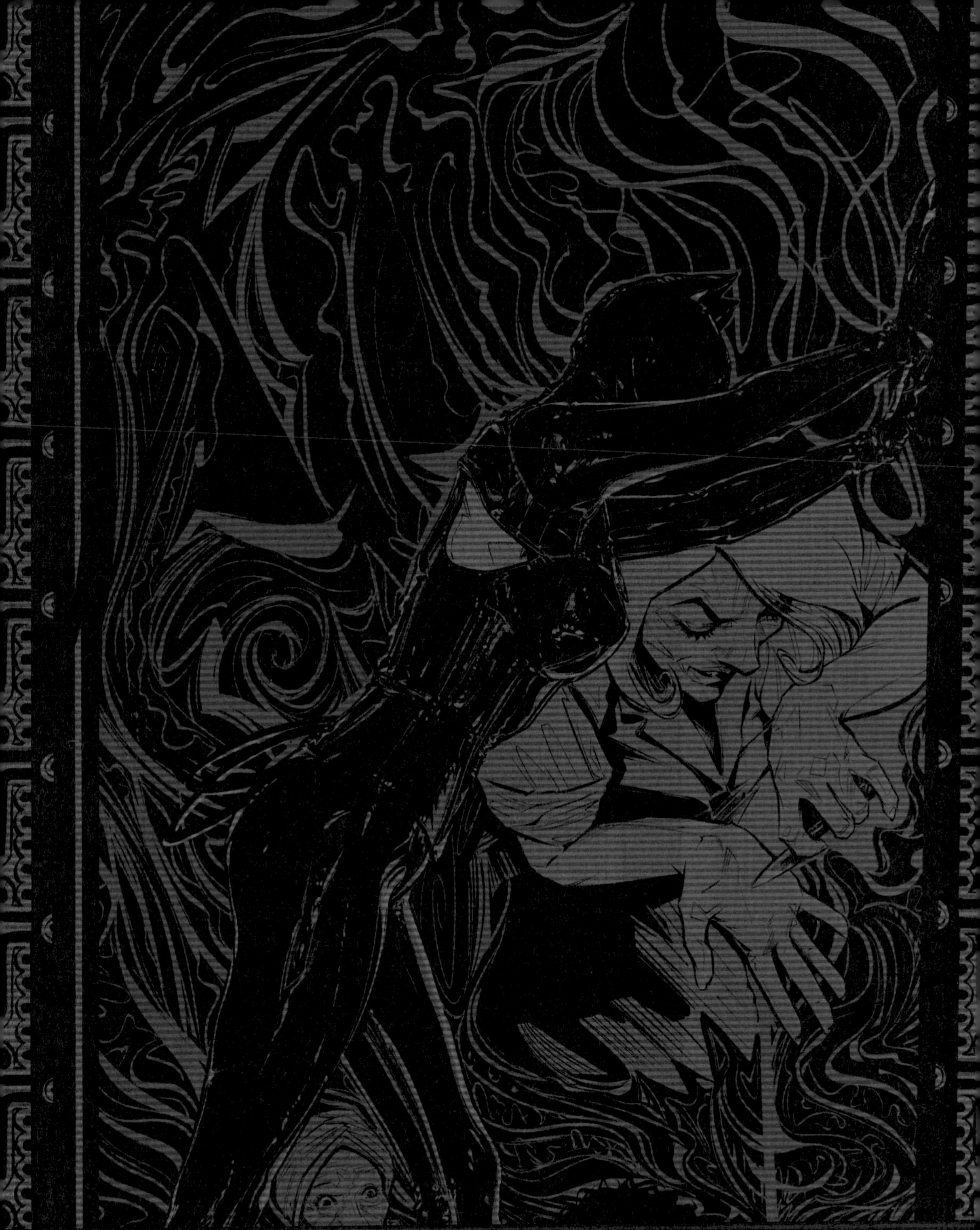

# CATWOMAN
#13

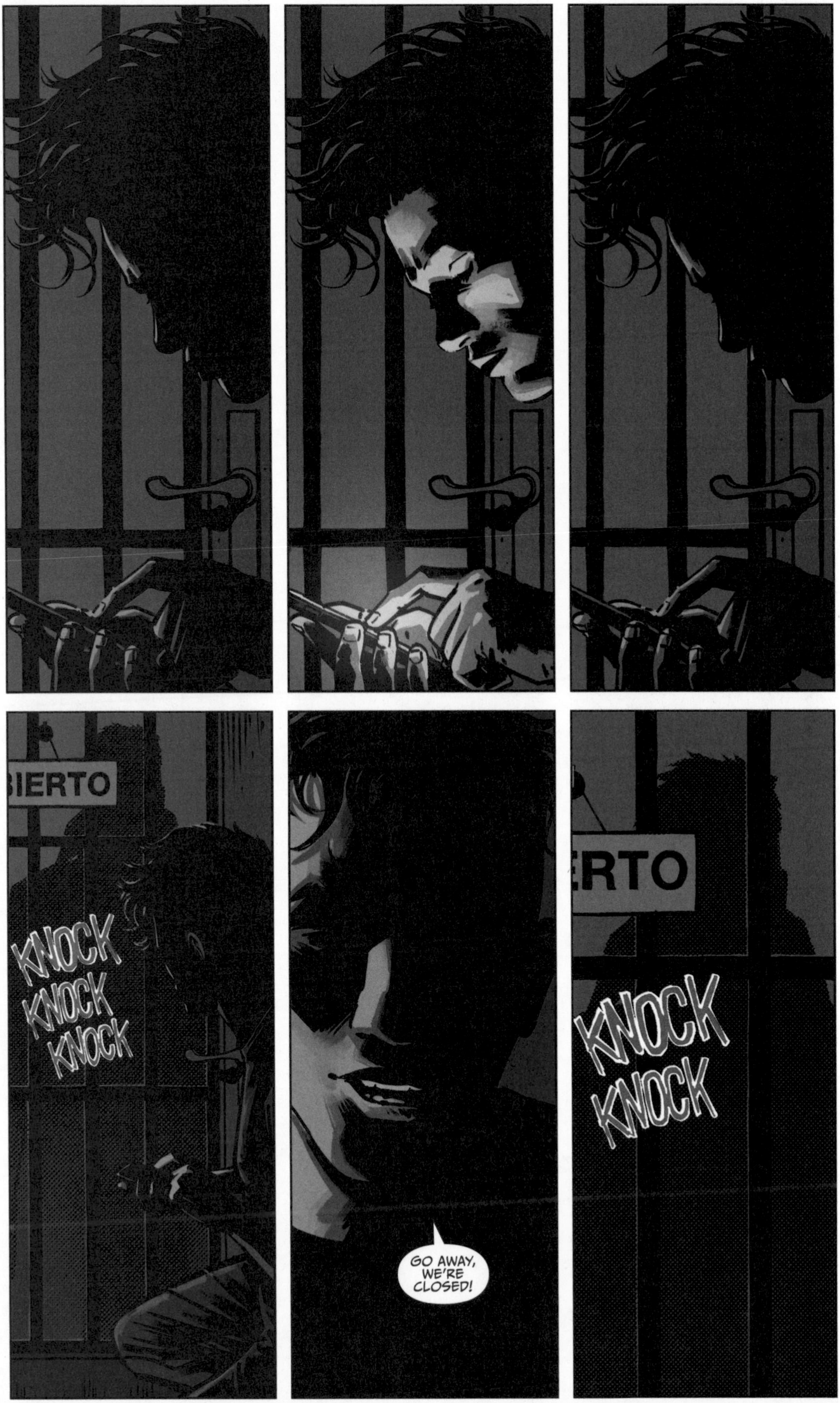
BIERTO
KNOCK KNOCK KNOCK
GO AWAY, WE'RE CLOSED!
ERTO
KNOCK KNOCK

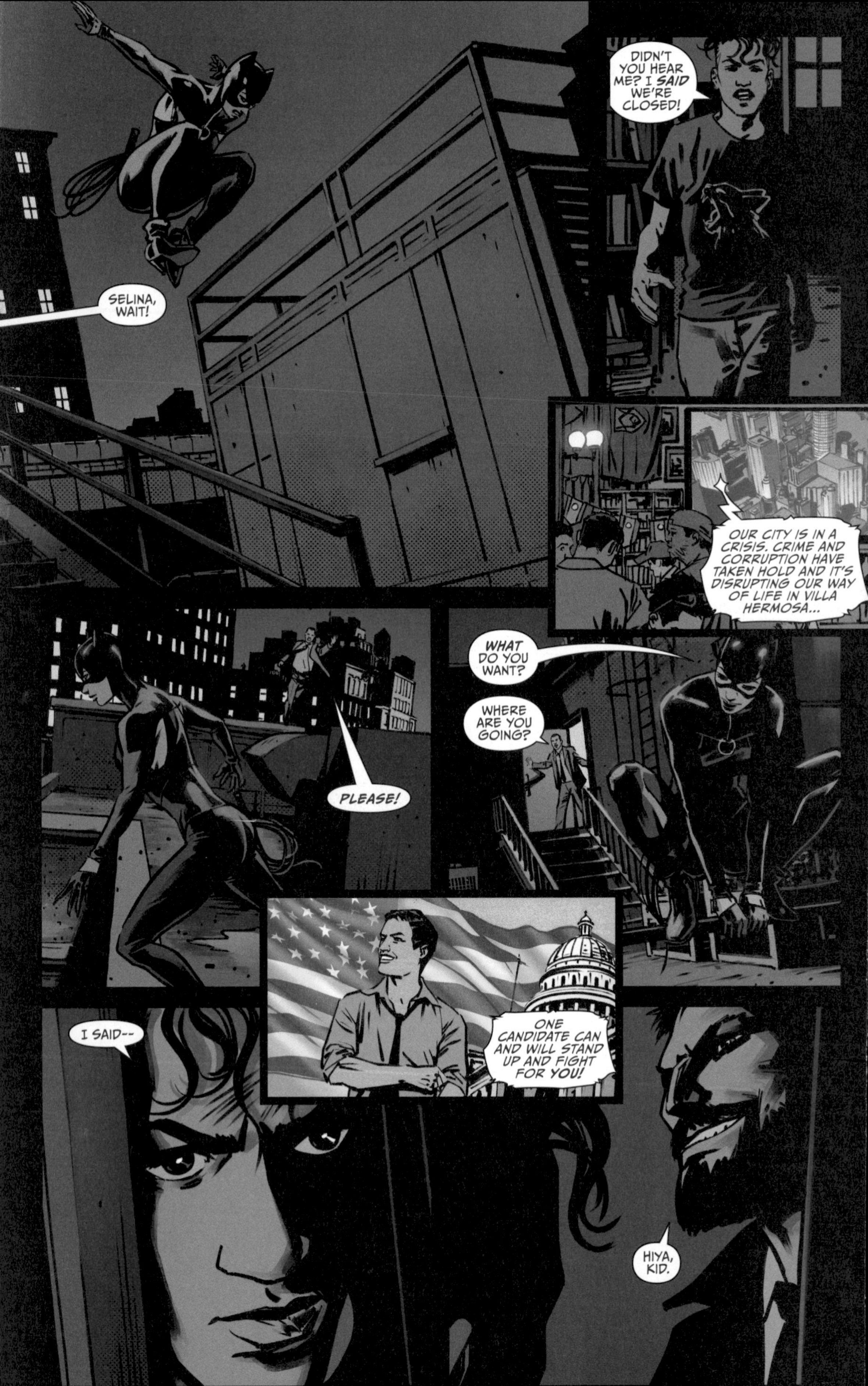

SELINA, WAIT!
DIDN'T YOU HEAR ME? I SAID WE'RE CLOSED!
OUR CITY IS IN A CRISIS. CRIME AND CORRUPTION HAVE TAKEN HOLD AND IT'S DISRUPTING OUR WAY OF LIFE IN VILLA HERMOSA...
PLEASE!
WHAT DO YOU WANT?
WHERE ARE YOU GOING?
ONE CANDIDATE CAN AND WILL STAND UP AND FIGHT FOR YOU!
I SAID--
HIYA, KID.

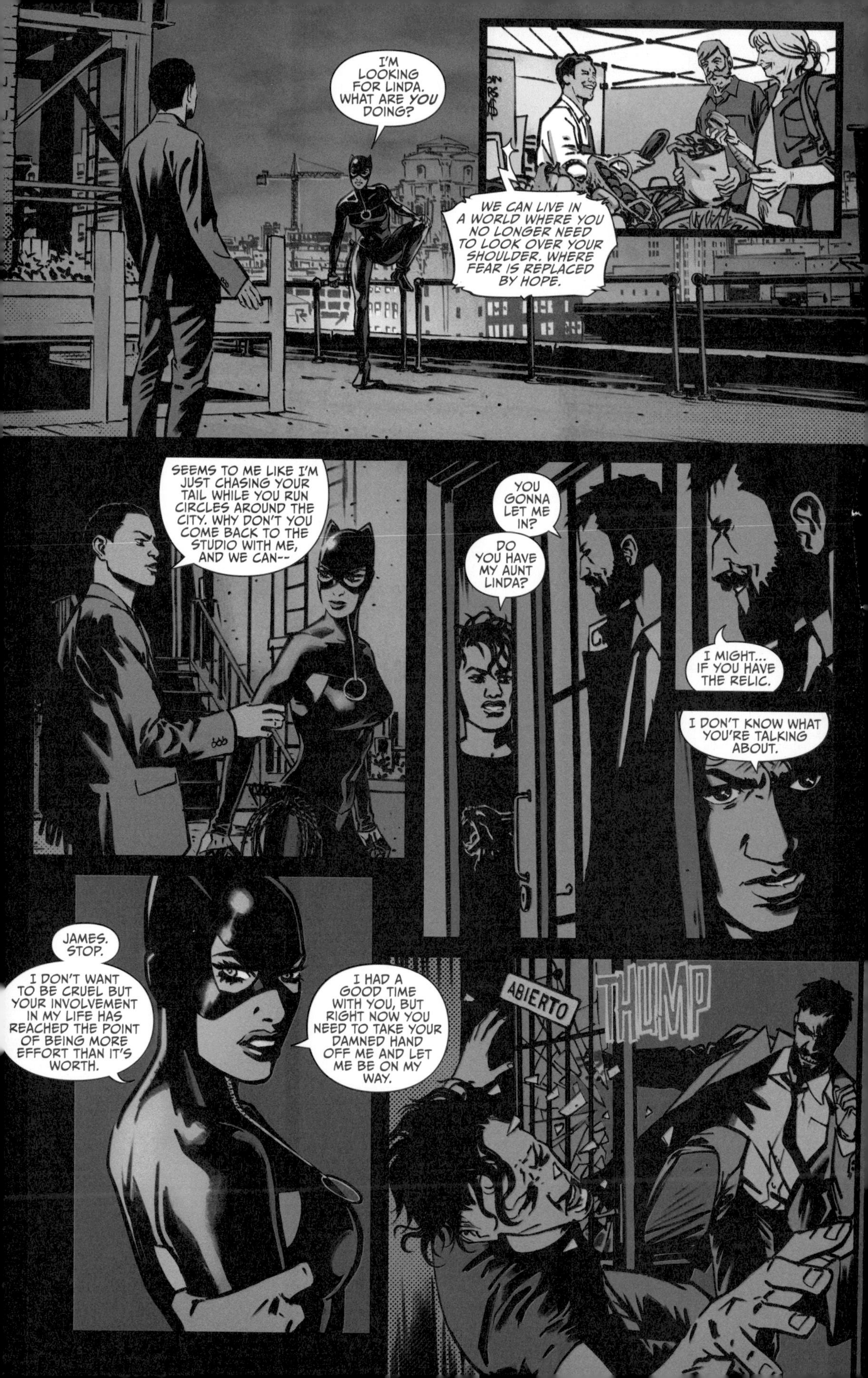
I'M LOOKING FOR LINDA. WHAT ARE YOU DOING?
WE CAN LIVE IN A WORLD WHERE YOU NO LONGER NEED TO LOOK OVER YOUR SHOULDER. WHERE FEAR IS REPLACED BY HOPE.
SEEMS TO ME LIKE I'M JUST CHASING YOUR TAIL WHILE YOU RUN CIRCLES AROUND THE CITY. WHY DON'T YOU COME BACK TO THE STUDIO WITH ME, AND WE CAN--
YOU GONNA LET ME IN?
DO YOU HAVE MY AUNT LINDA?
I MIGHT... IF YOU HAVE THE RELIC.
I DON'T KNOW WHAT YOU'RE TALKING ABOUT.
JAMES. STOP.
I DON'T WANT TO BE CRUEL BUT YOUR INVOLVEMENT IN MY LIFE HAS REACHED THE POINT OF BEING MORE EFFORT THAN IT'S WORTH.
I HAD A GOOD TIME WITH YOU, BUT RIGHT NOW YOU NEED TO TAKE YOUR DAMNED HAND OFF ME AND LET ME BE ON MY WAY.
ABIERTO
THUMP

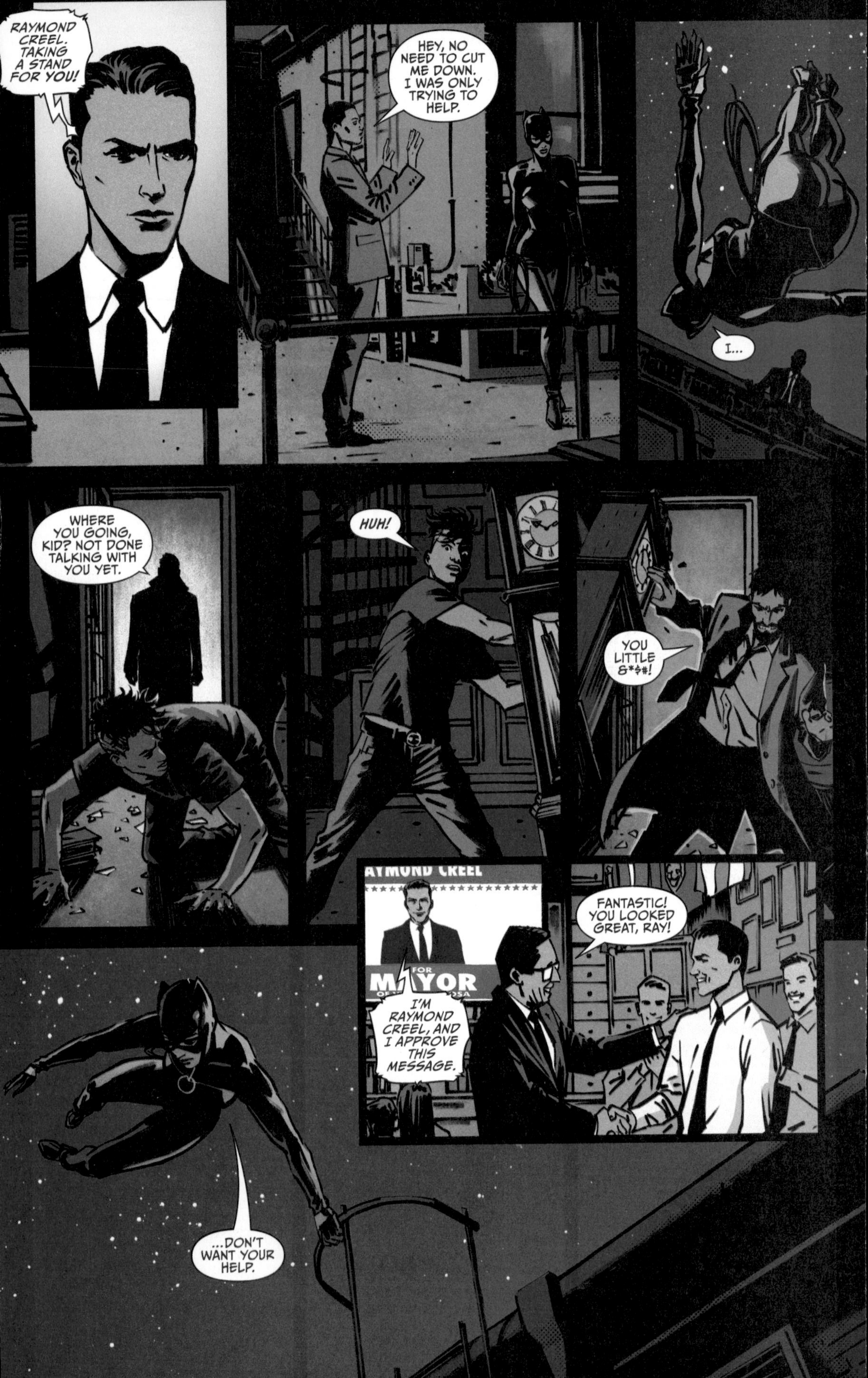
RAYMOND CREEL. TAKING A STAND FOR YOU!
HEY, NO NEED TO CUT ME DOWN. I WAS ONLY TRYING TO HELP.
I...
WHERE YOU GOING, KID? NOT DONE TALKING WITH YOU YET.
HUH!
YOU LITTLE &*$#!
AYMOND CREEL
FOR
M YOR
I'M RAYMOND CREEL, AND I APPROVE THIS MESSAGE.
FANTASTIC! YOU LOOKED GREAT, RAY!
...DON'T WANT YOUR HELP.

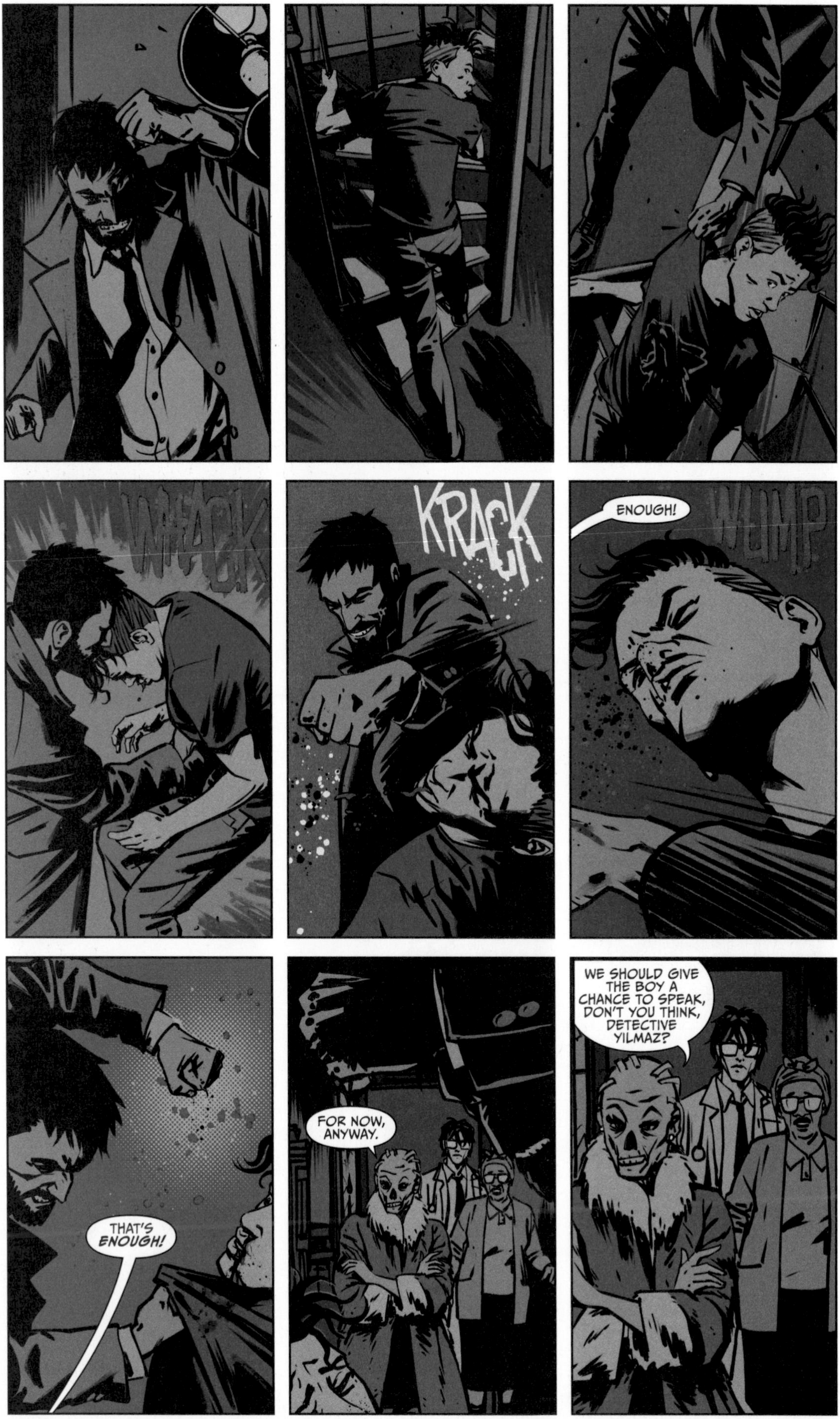
WHACK
KRACK
ENOUGH!
WUMP
THAT'S ENOUGH!
FOR NOW, ANYWAY.
WE SHOULD GIVE THE BOY A CHANCE TO SPEAK, DON'T YOU THINK, DETECTIVE YILMAZ?

*HUFF* *HUFF* READY TO TALK?

SERIOUSLY?! CAN'T YOU TAKE A HINT?

CUT IT OUT, SELINA. I NEVER ASKED YOU FOR ANYTHING. I JUST--

--WE HAD A SPARK, YOU AND ME, AND I KNOW YOU FELT IT--

STOP.

STOP. I DIDN'T COME HERE FOR THIS. FOR *ANY* OF THIS! I...I JUST NEEDED A PLACE TO ESCAPE TO. I NEVER MEANT FOR ANYONE TO GET HURT OR TO GET INVOLVED.

WHAT ARE YOU RUNNING AWAY FROM IN GOTHAM?

SO IS THIS THE PART WHERE WE UNBURDEN OUR SOULS TO EACH OTHER, AND YOU TELL ME EVERYTHING WILL BE ALL RIGHT? AND WHAT? *FIX ME?* FIND A WAY TO CUT OUT THE PART OF ME THAT NEEDS OTHER PEOPLE? THAT NEEDS... WELL...

I'M SORRY, JAMES, I JUST CAN'T PLAY ALONG.

I WISH I COULD...

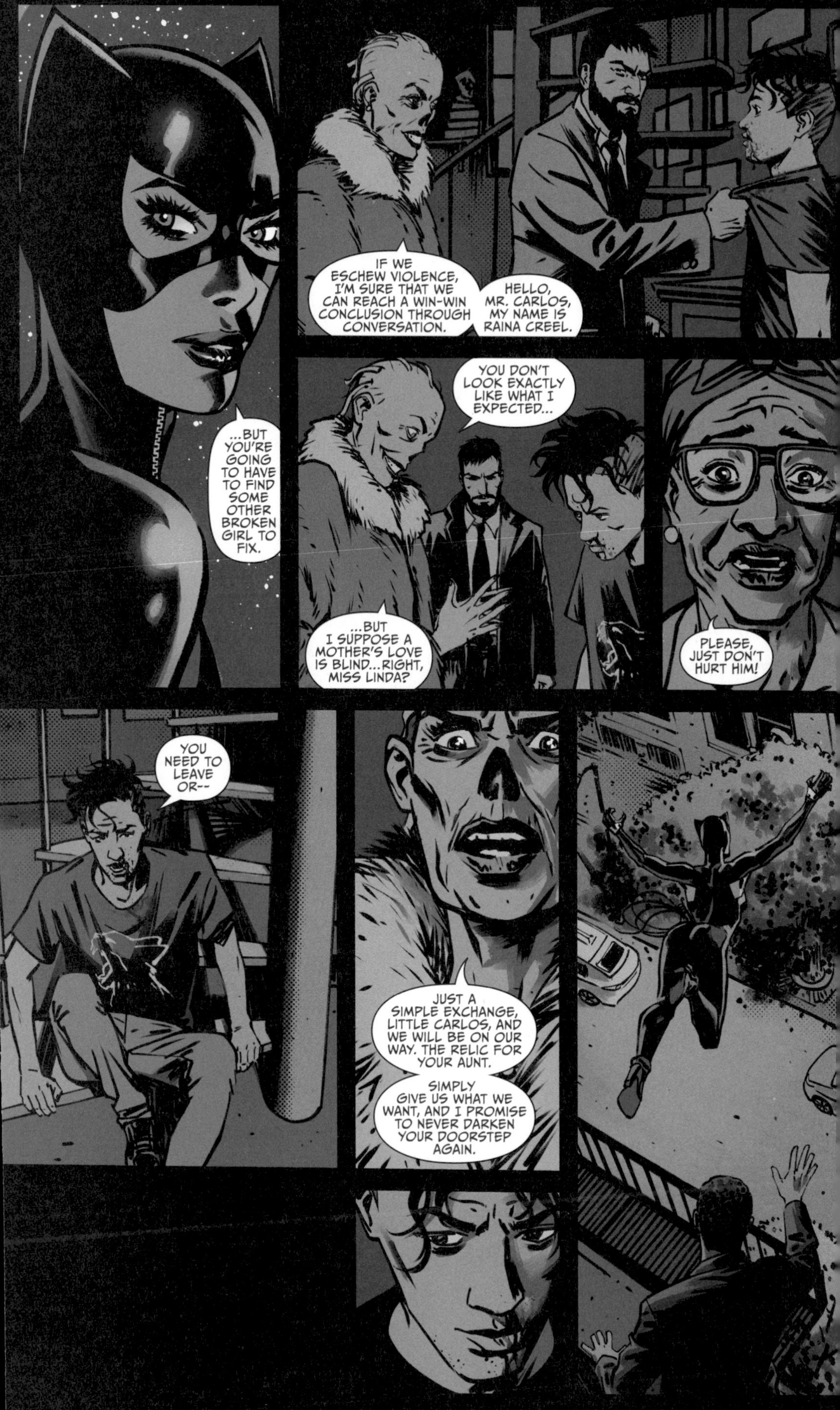
...BUT YOU'RE GOING TO HAVE TO FIND SOME OTHER BROKEN GIRL TO FIX.
HELLO, MR. CARLOS, MY NAME IS RAINA CREEL.
IF WE ESCHEW VIOLENCE, I'M SURE THAT WE CAN REACH A WIN-WIN CONCLUSION THROUGH CONVERSATION.
YOU DON'T LOOK EXACTLY LIKE WHAT I EXPECTED...
...BUT I SUPPOSE A MOTHER'S LOVE IS BLIND...RIGHT, MISS LINDA?
PLEASE, JUST DON'T HURT HIM!
YOU NEED TO LEAVE OR--
JUST A SIMPLE EXCHANGE, LITTLE CARLOS, AND WE WILL BE ON OUR WAY. THE RELIC FOR YOUR AUNT.
SIMPLY GIVE US WHAT WE WANT, AND I PROMISE TO NEVER DARKEN YOUR DOORSTEP AGAIN.

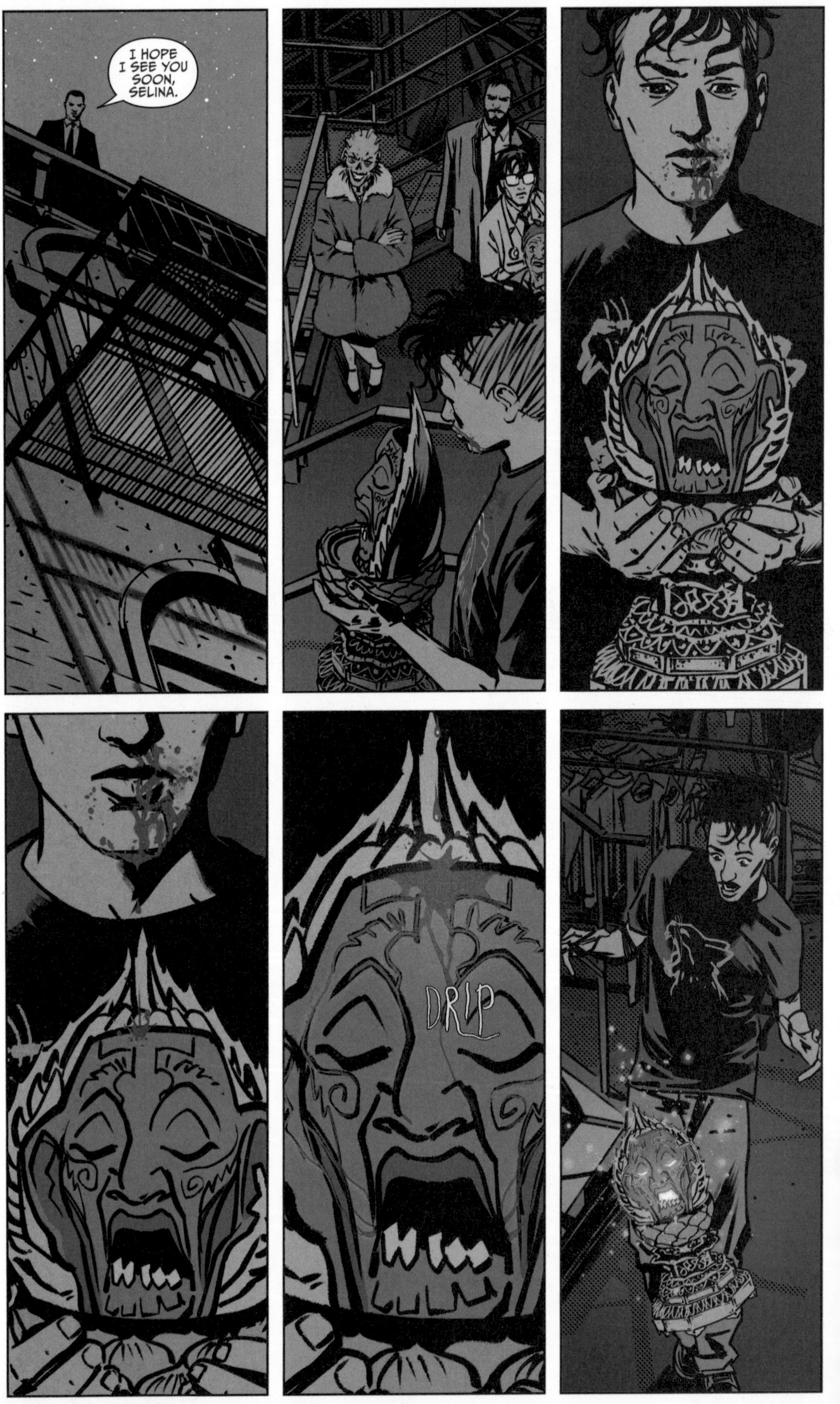
I HOPE I SEE YOU SOON, SELINA.
DRIP

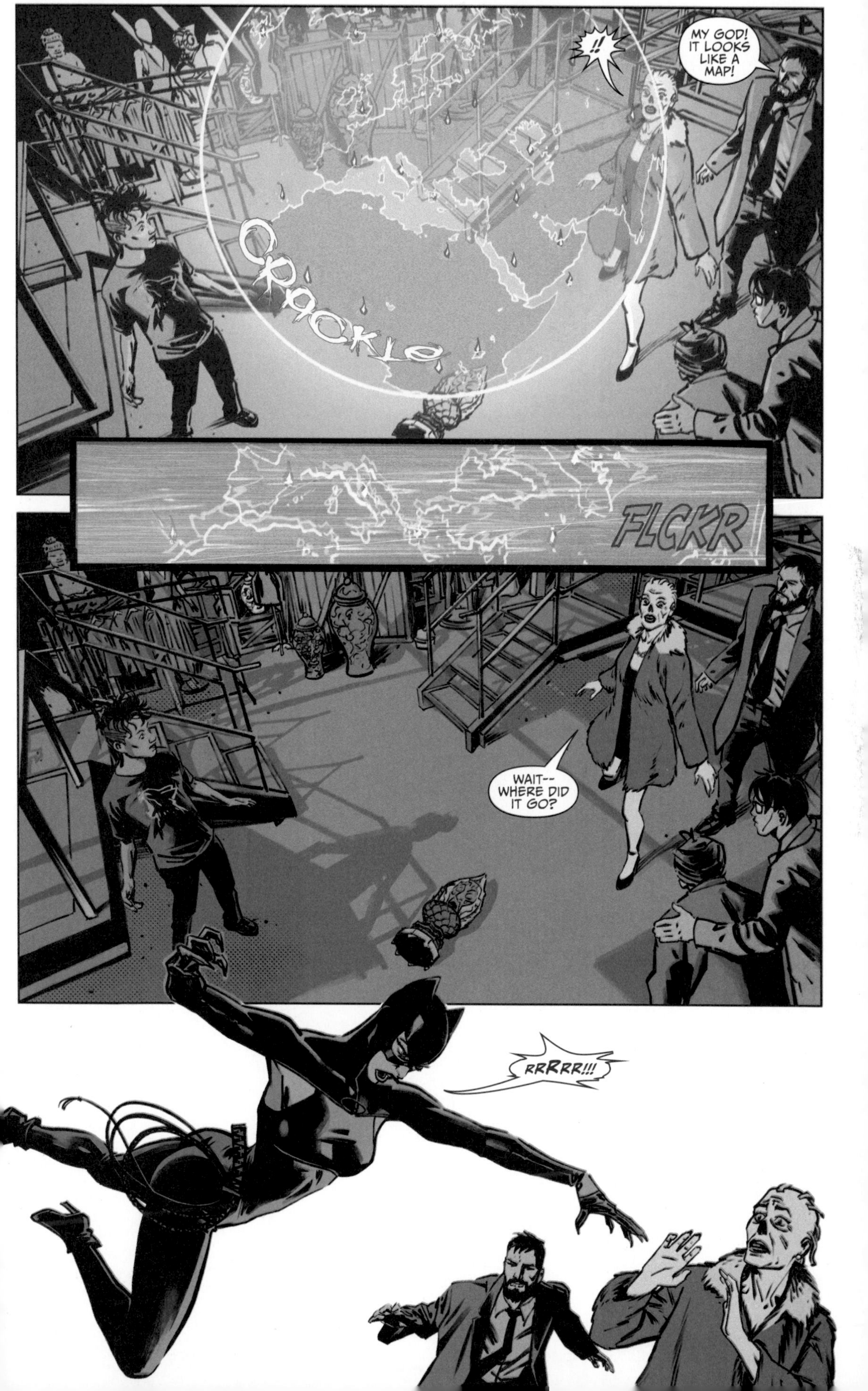
!!
MY GOD! IT LOOKS LIKE A MAP!
CRACKLE
FLCKR
WAIT-- WHERE DID IT GO?
RRRRR!!!

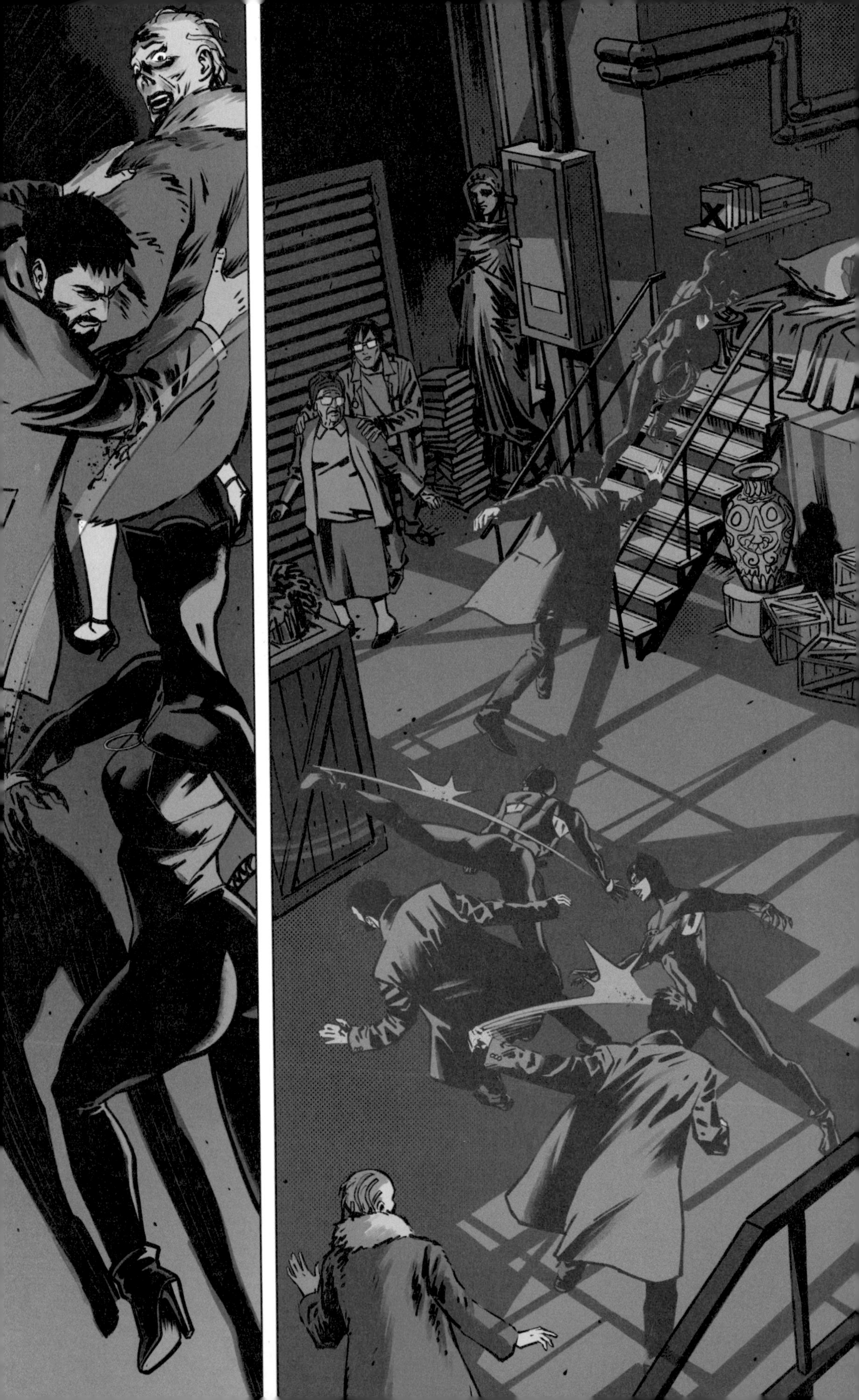

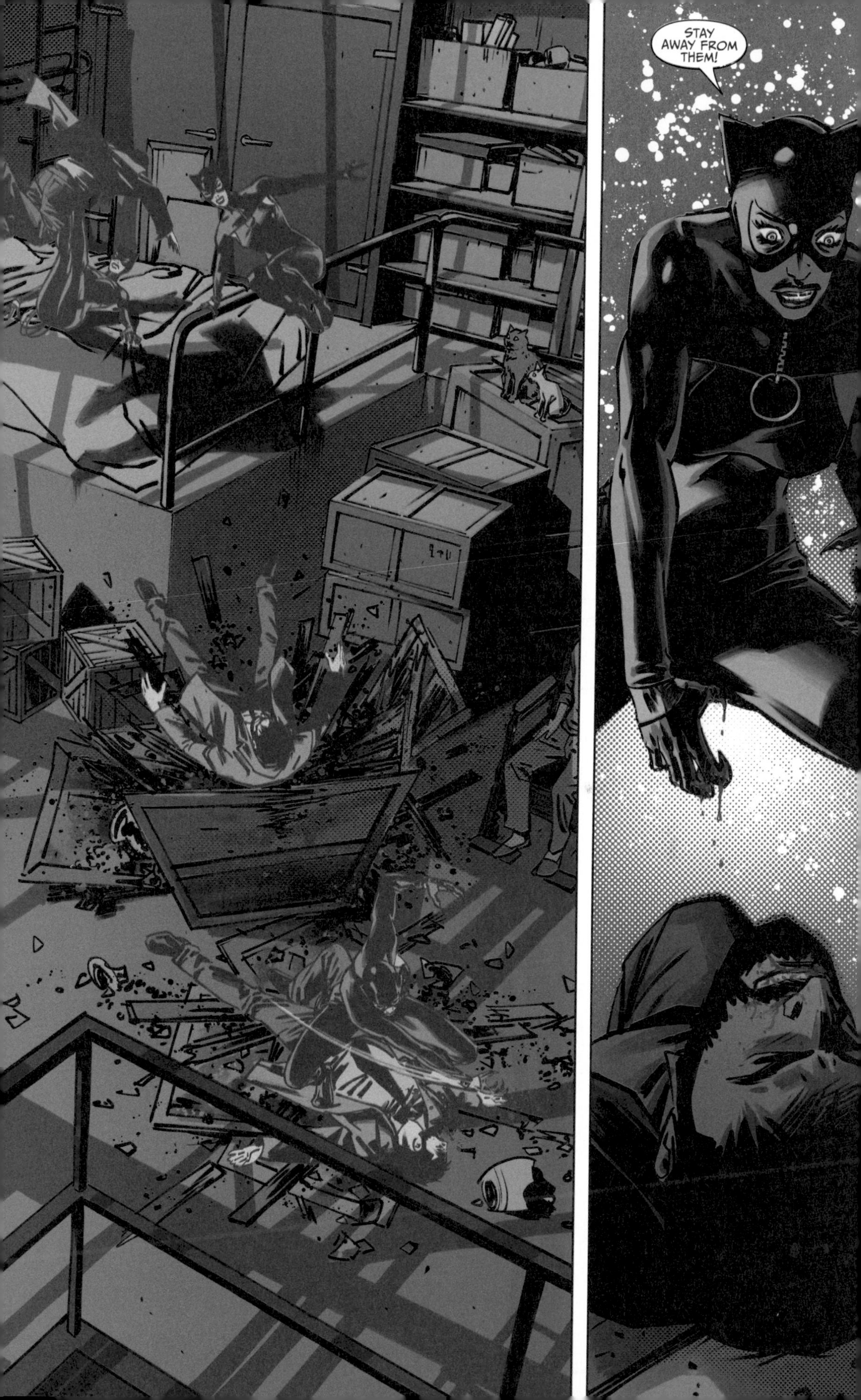
STAY AWAY FROM THEM!

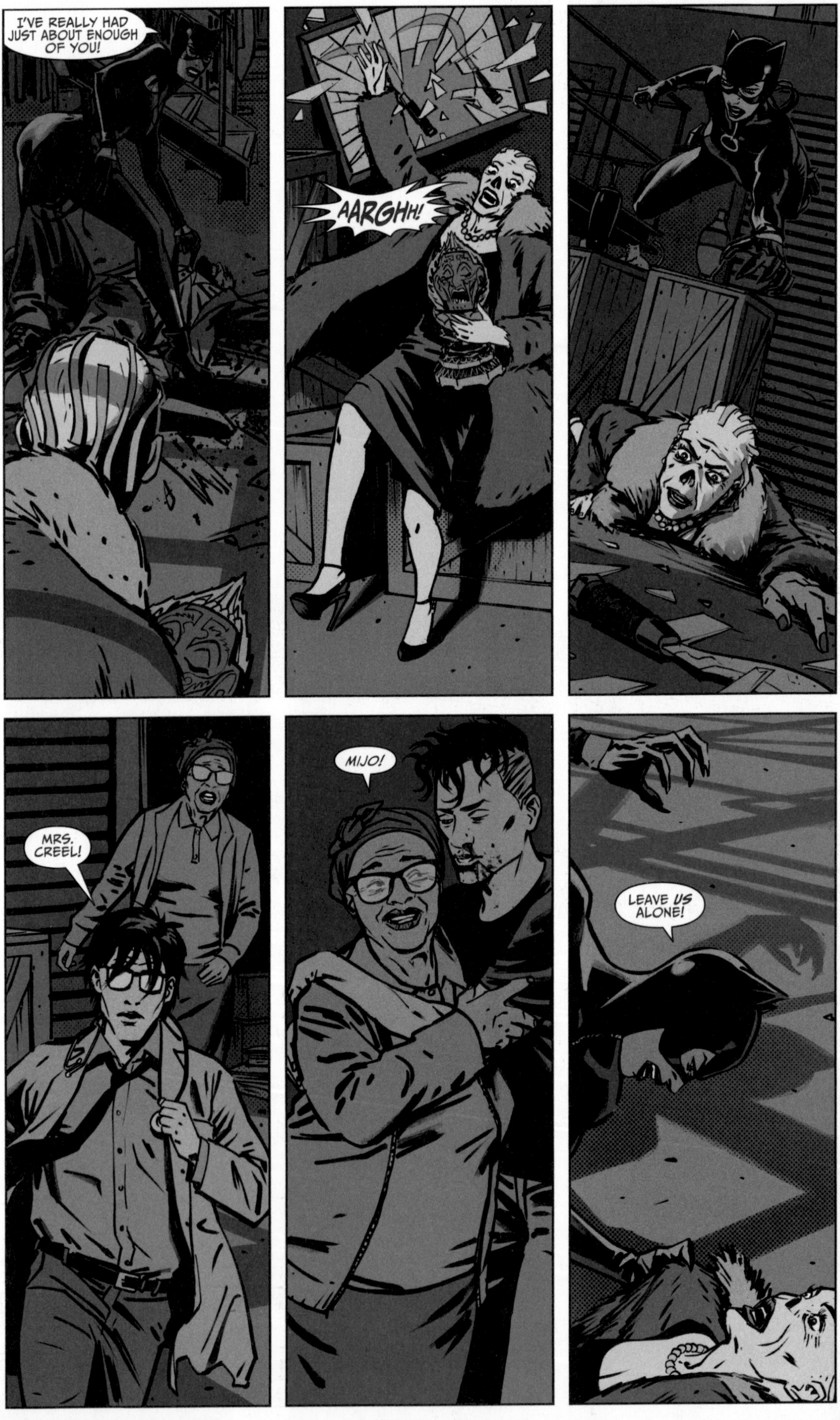
I'VE REALLY HAD JUST ABOUT ENOUGH OF YOU!
AARGHH!
MRS. CREEL!
MIJO!
LEAVE US ALONE!

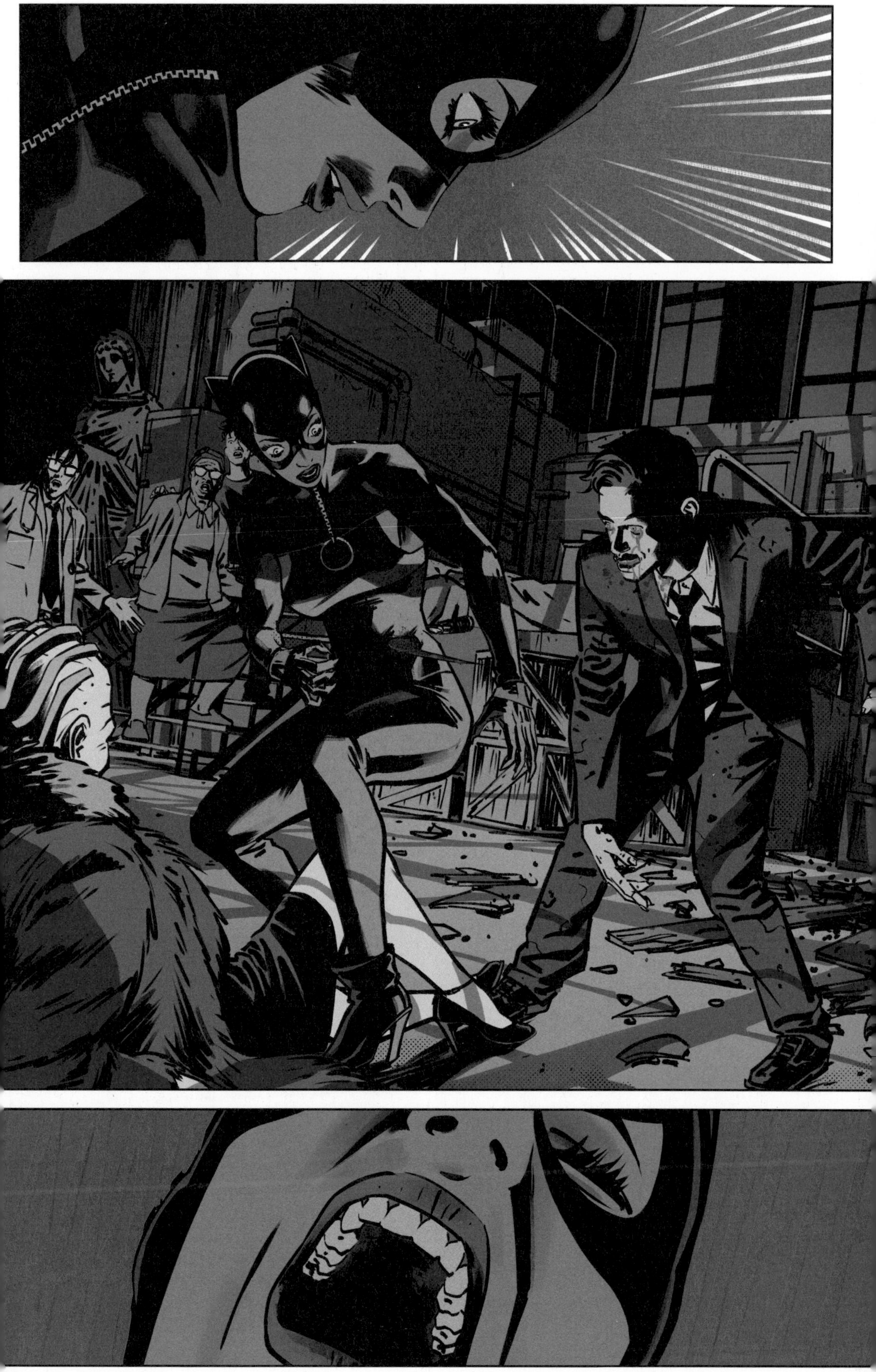

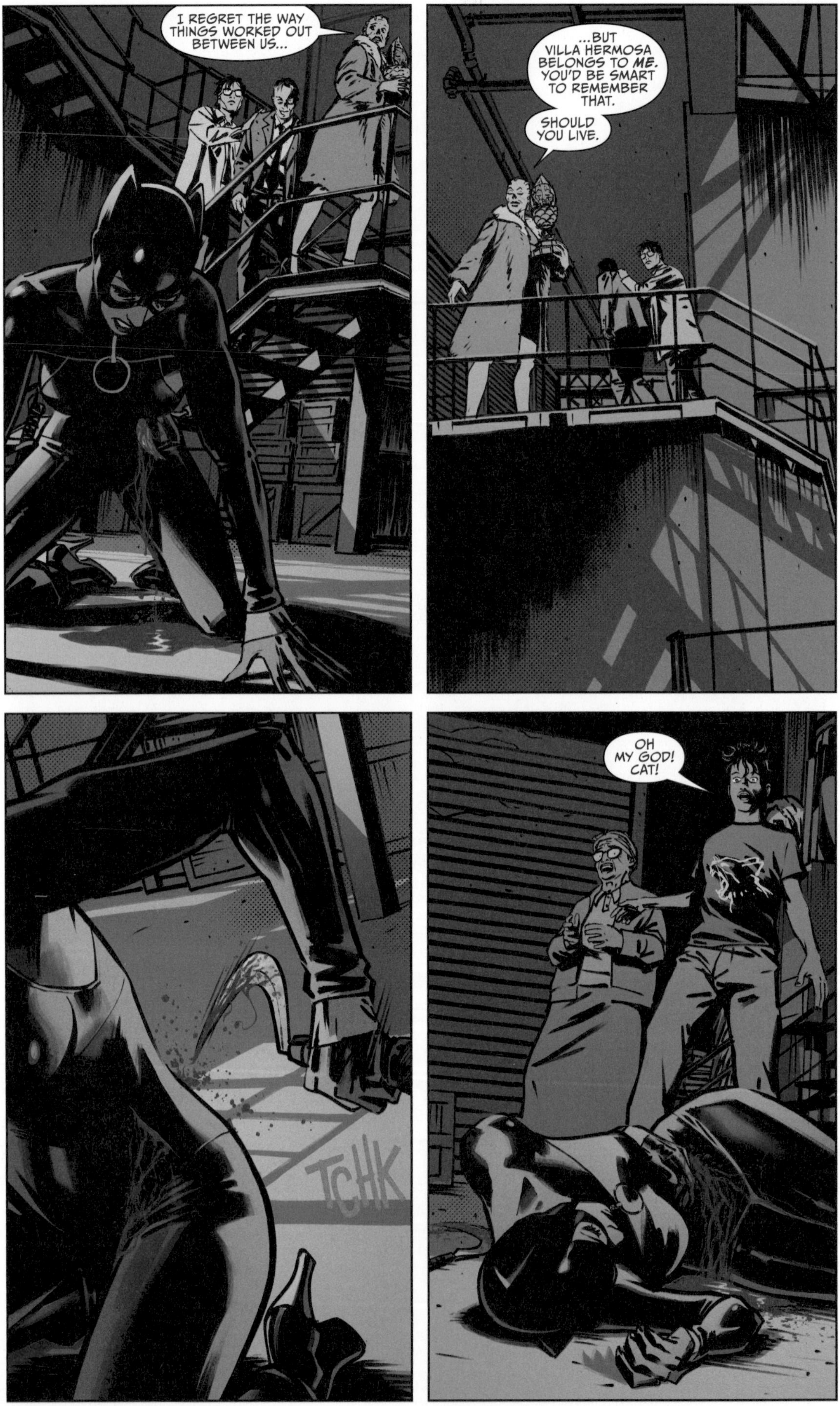
I REGRET THE WAY THINGS WORKED OUT BETWEEN US...
...BUT VILLA HERMOSA BELONGS TO *ME*. YOU'D BE SMART TO REMEMBER THAT.
SHOULD YOU LIVE.
TCHK
OH MY GOD! CAT!

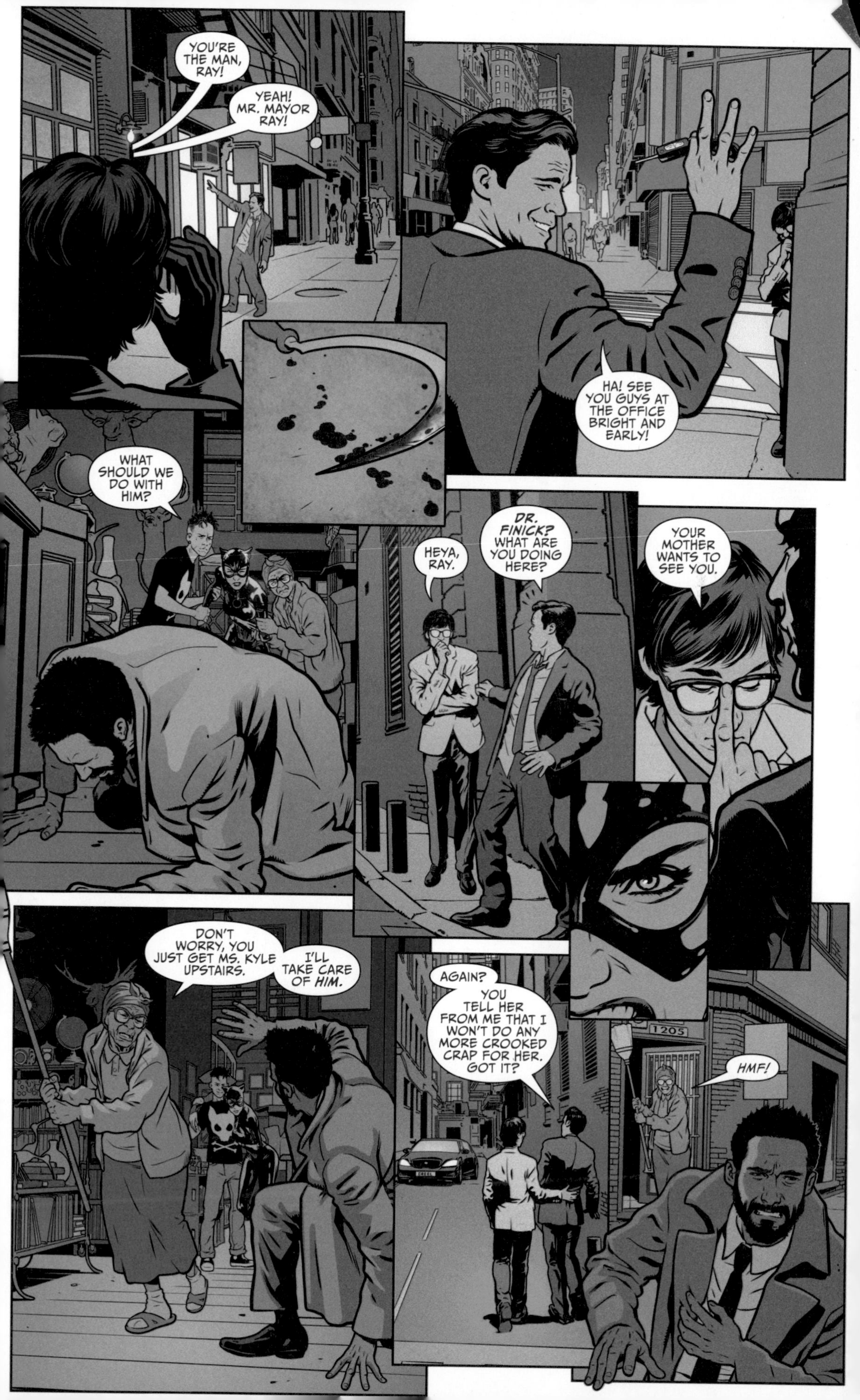
YOU'RE THE MAN, RAY!
YEAH! MR. MAYOR RAY!
HA! SEE YOU GUYS AT THE OFFICE BRIGHT AND EARLY!
WHAT SHOULD WE DO WITH HIM?
HEYA, RAY.
DR. FINICK? WHAT ARE YOU DOING HERE?
YOUR MOTHER WANTS TO SEE YOU.
DON'T WORRY, YOU JUST GET MS. KYLE UPSTAIRS.
I'LL TAKE CARE OF HIM.
AGAIN?
YOU TELL HER FROM ME THAT I WON'T DO ANY MORE CROOKED CRAP FOR HER. GOT IT?
1205
HMF!

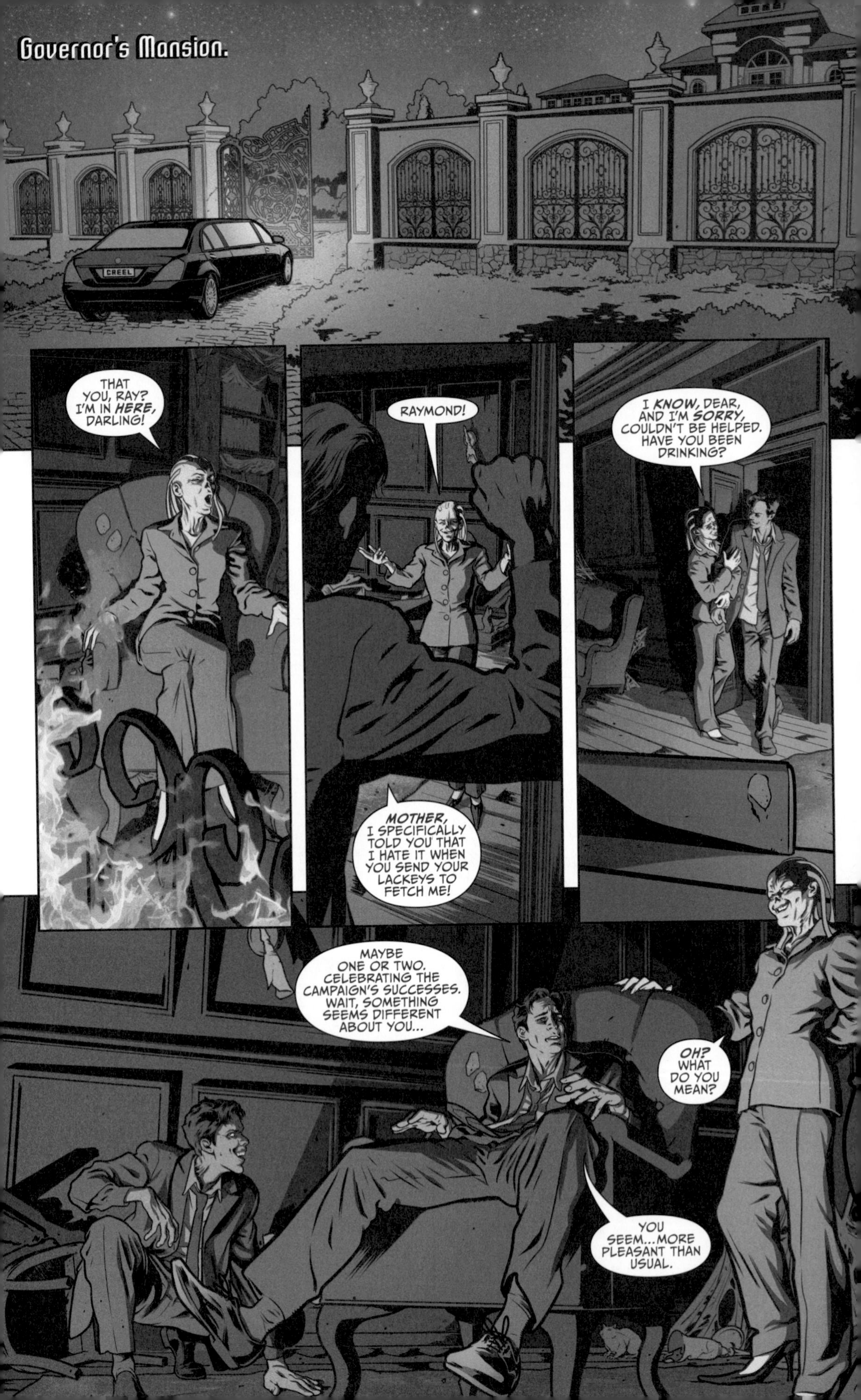
Governor's Mansion.
CREEL
THAT YOU, RAY? I'M IN HERE, DARLING!
RAYMOND!
MOTHER, I SPECIFICALLY TOLD YOU THAT I HATE IT WHEN YOU SEND YOUR LACKEYS TO FETCH ME!
I KNOW, DEAR, AND I'M SORRY, COULDN'T BE HELPED. HAVE YOU BEEN DRINKING?
MAYBE ONE OR TWO. CELEBRATING THE CAMPAIGN'S SUCCESSES. WAIT, SOMETHING SEEMS DIFFERENT ABOUT YOU...
OH? WHAT DO YOU MEAN?
YOU SEEM...MORE PLEASANT THAN USUAL.

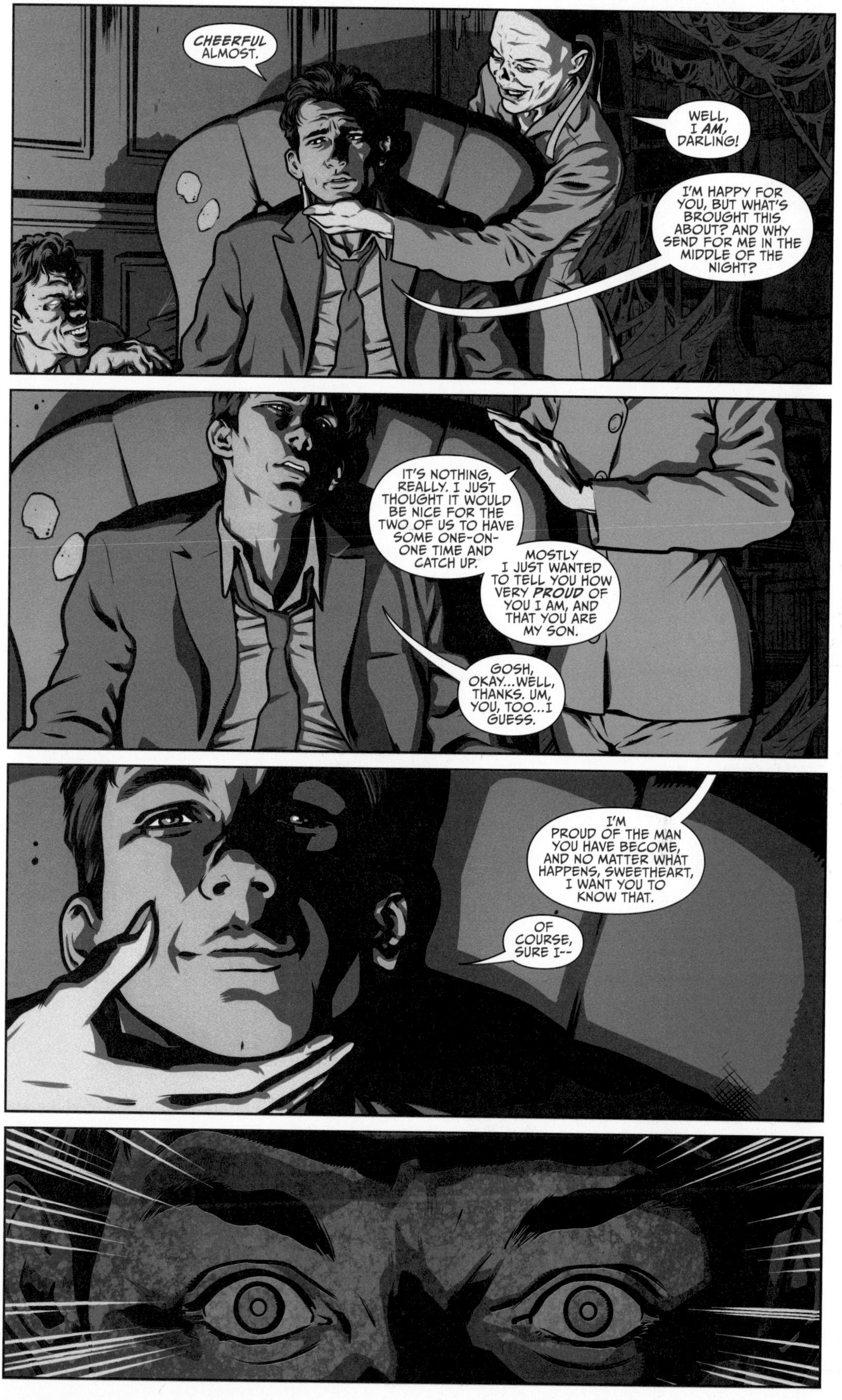

CHEERFUL ALMOST.
WELL, I AM, DARLING!
I'M HAPPY FOR YOU, BUT WHAT'S BROUGHT THIS ABOUT? AND WHY SEND FOR ME IN THE MIDDLE OF THE NIGHT?
IT'S NOTHING, REALLY. I JUST THOUGHT IT WOULD BE NICE FOR THE TWO OF US TO HAVE SOME ONE-ON-ONE TIME AND CATCH UP.
MOSTLY I JUST WANTED TO TELL YOU HOW VERY PROUD OF YOU I AM, AND THAT YOU ARE MY SON.
GOSH, OKAY...WELL, THANKS. UM, YOU, TOO...I GUESS.
I'M PROUD OF THE MAN YOU HAVE BECOME, AND NO MATTER WHAT HAPPENS, SWEETHEART, I WANT YOU TO KNOW THAT.
OF COURSE, SURE I--

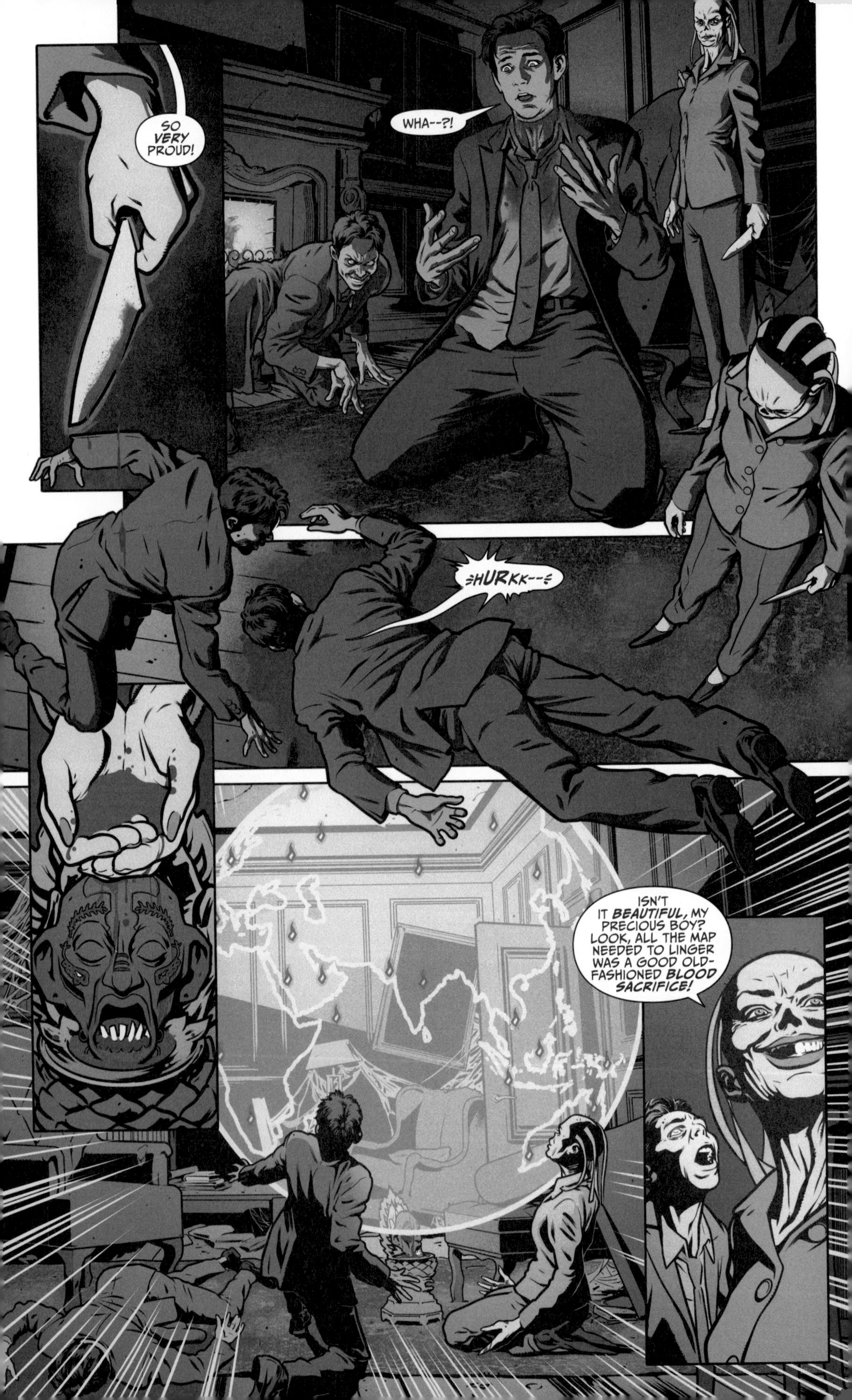
SO VERY PROUD!
WHA--?!
HURKK--
ISN'T IT BEAUTIFUL, MY PRECIOUS BOY? LOOK, ALL THE MAP NEEDED TO LINGER WAS A GOOD OLD-FASHIONED BLOOD SACRIFICE!

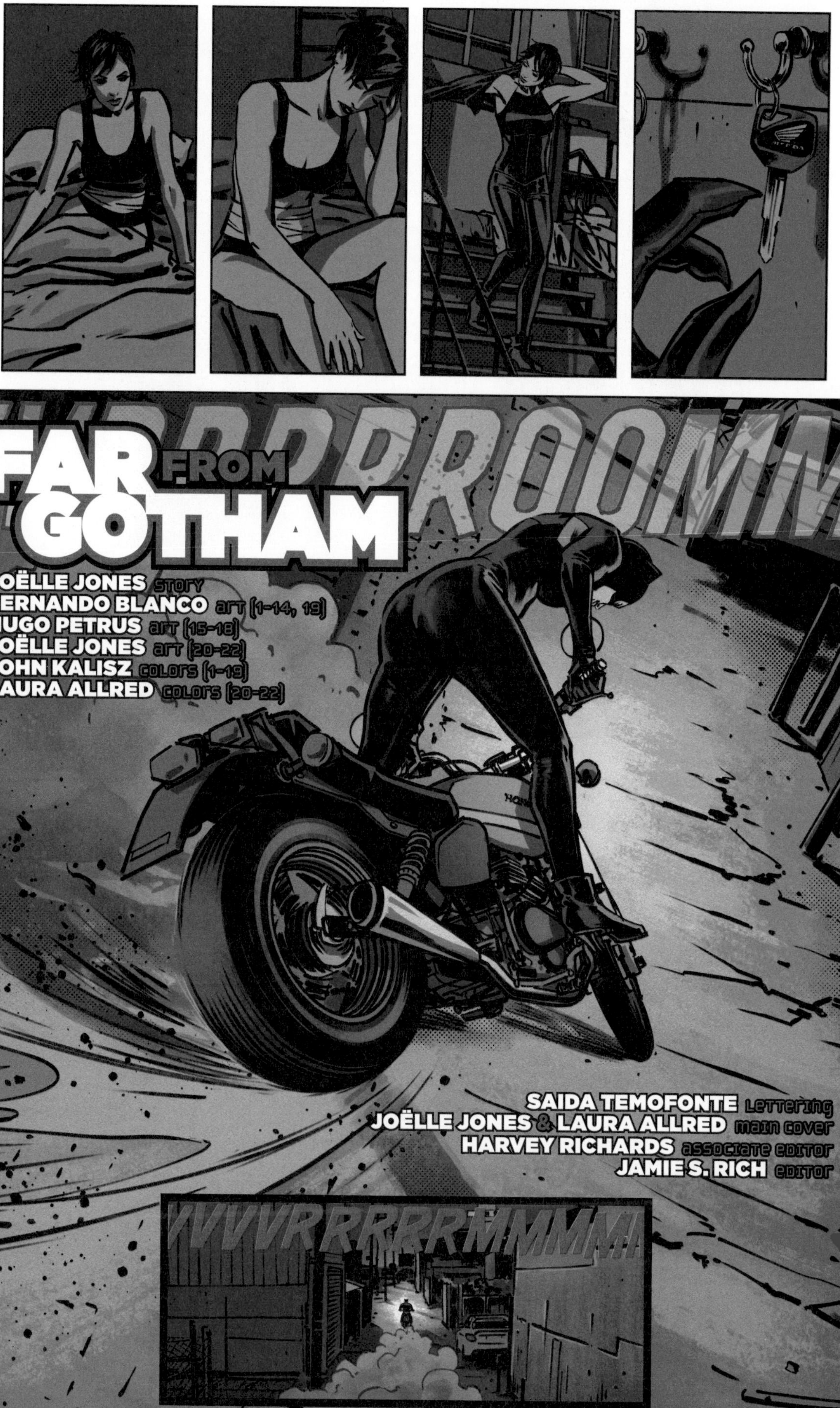

FAR FROM GOTHAM
JOËLLE JONES story
FERNANDO BLANCO art (1-14, 19)
HUGO PETRUS art (15-18)
JOËLLE JONES art (20-22)
JOHN KALISZ colors (1-19)
LAURA ALLRED colors (20-22)
SAIDA TEMOFONTE lettering
JOËLLE JONES & LAURA ALLRED main cover
HARVEY RICHARDS associate editor
JAMIE S. RICH editor
VVVVRRRRRMMMMM

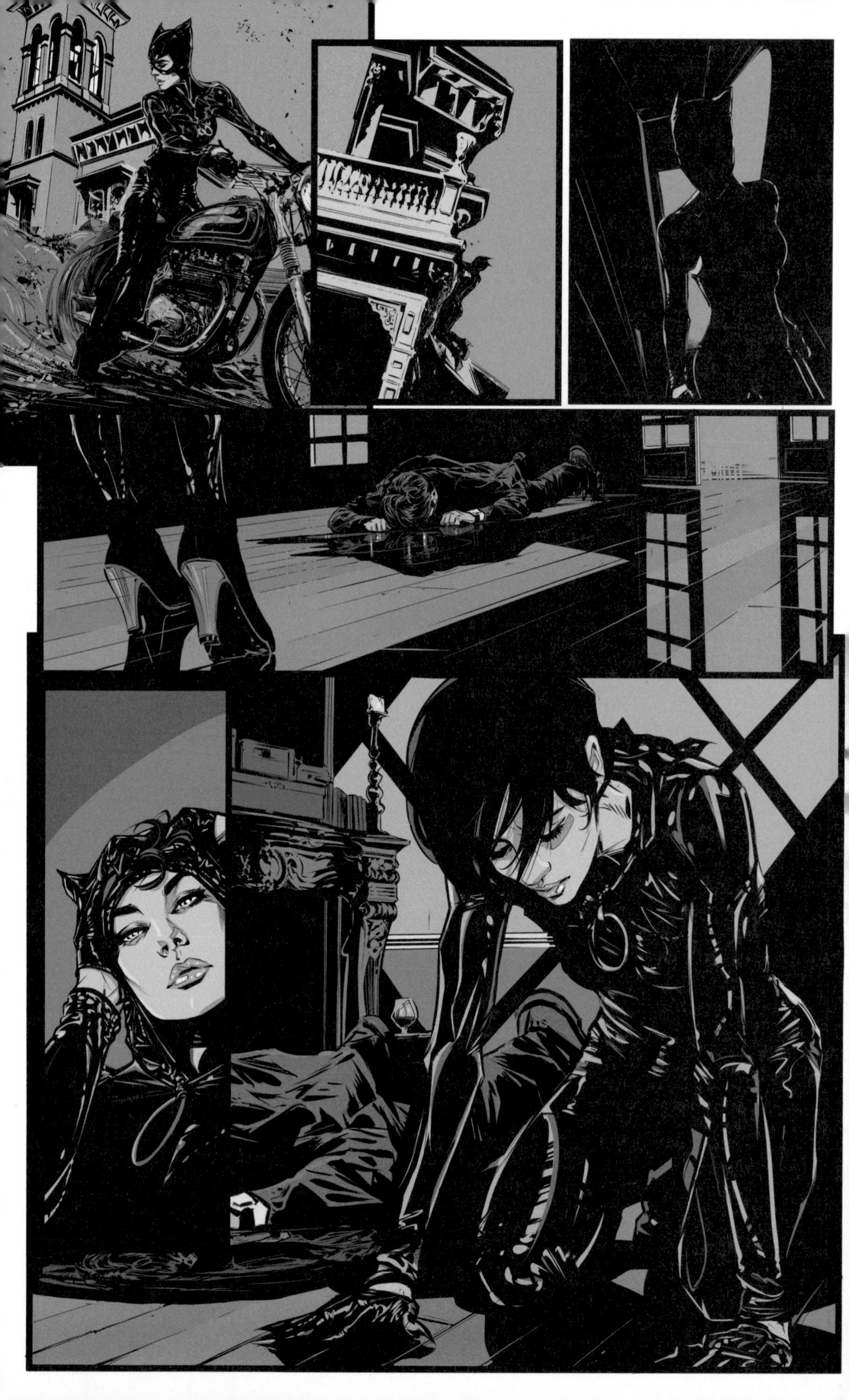

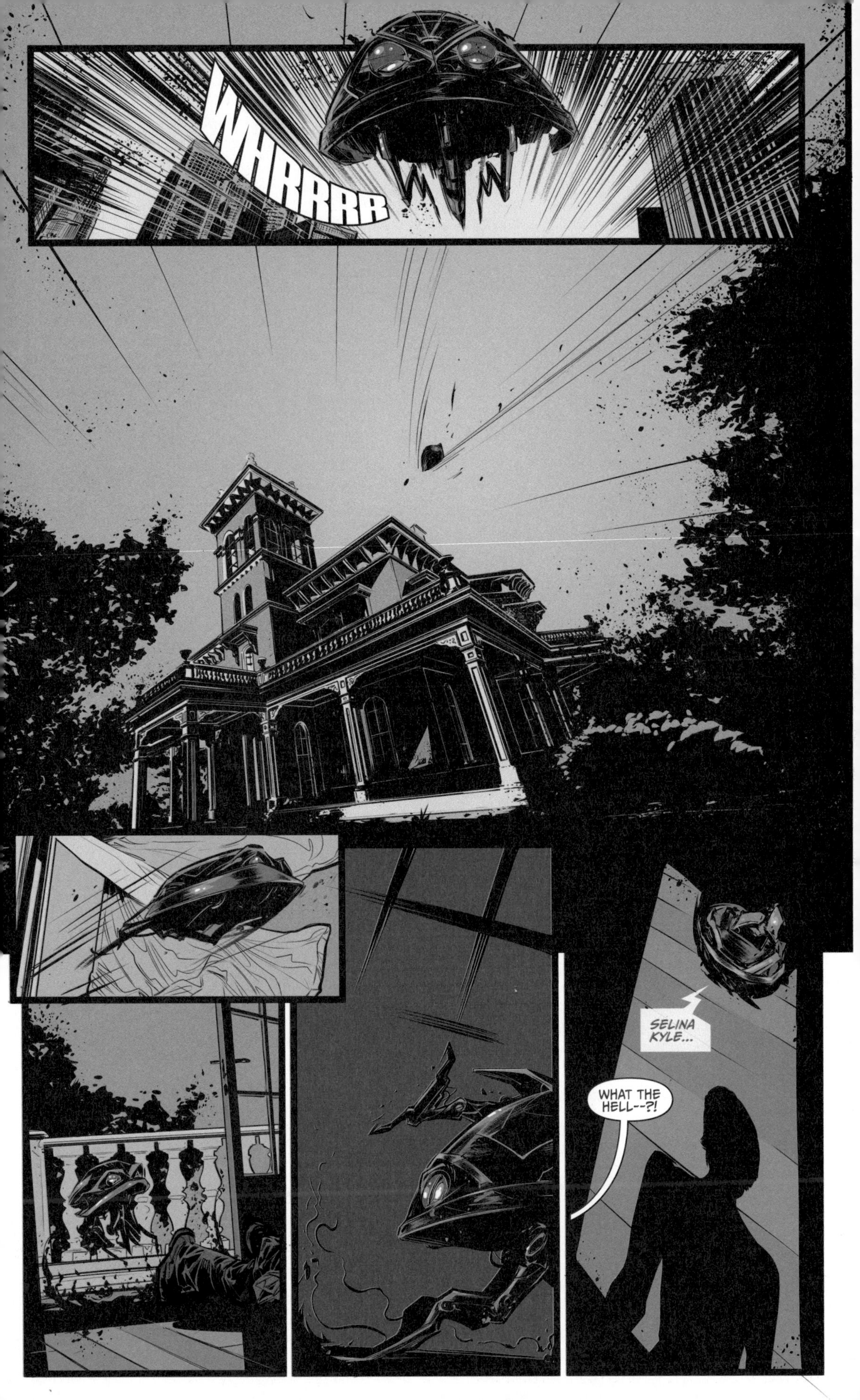
WHRRRRR
SELINA KYLE...
WHAT THE HELL--?!

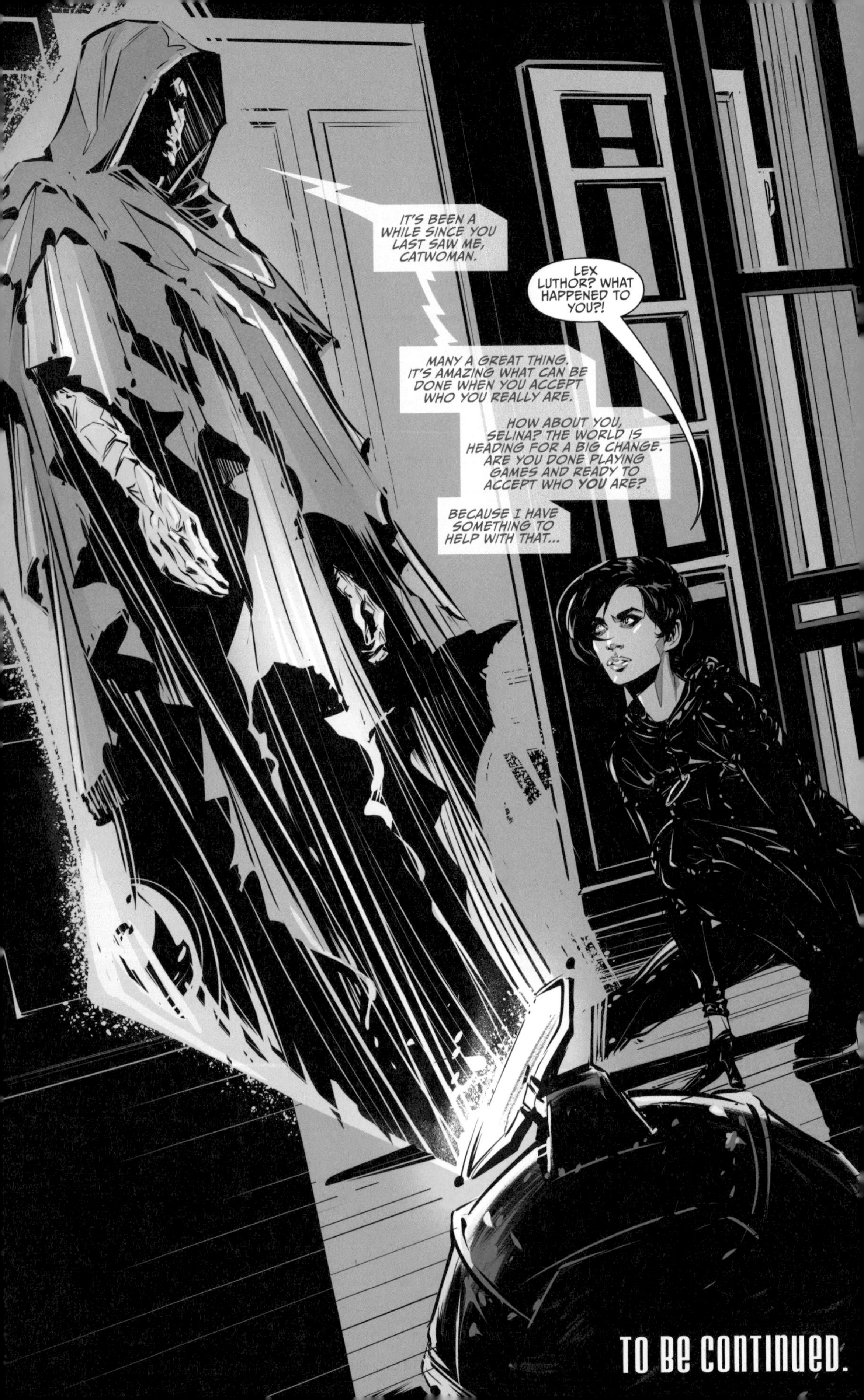
IT'S BEEN A WHILE SINCE YOU LAST SAW ME, CATWOMAN.
LEX LUTHOR? WHAT HAPPENED TO YOU?!
MANY A GREAT THING. IT'S AMAZING WHAT CAN BE DONE WHEN YOU ACCEPT WHO YOU REALLY ARE.
HOW ABOUT YOU, SELINA? THE WORLD IS HEADING FOR A BIG CHANGE. ARE YOU DONE PLAYING GAMES AND READY TO ACCEPT WHO YOU ARE?
BECAUSE I HAVE SOMETHING TO HELP WITH THAT...
TO BE CONTINUED.

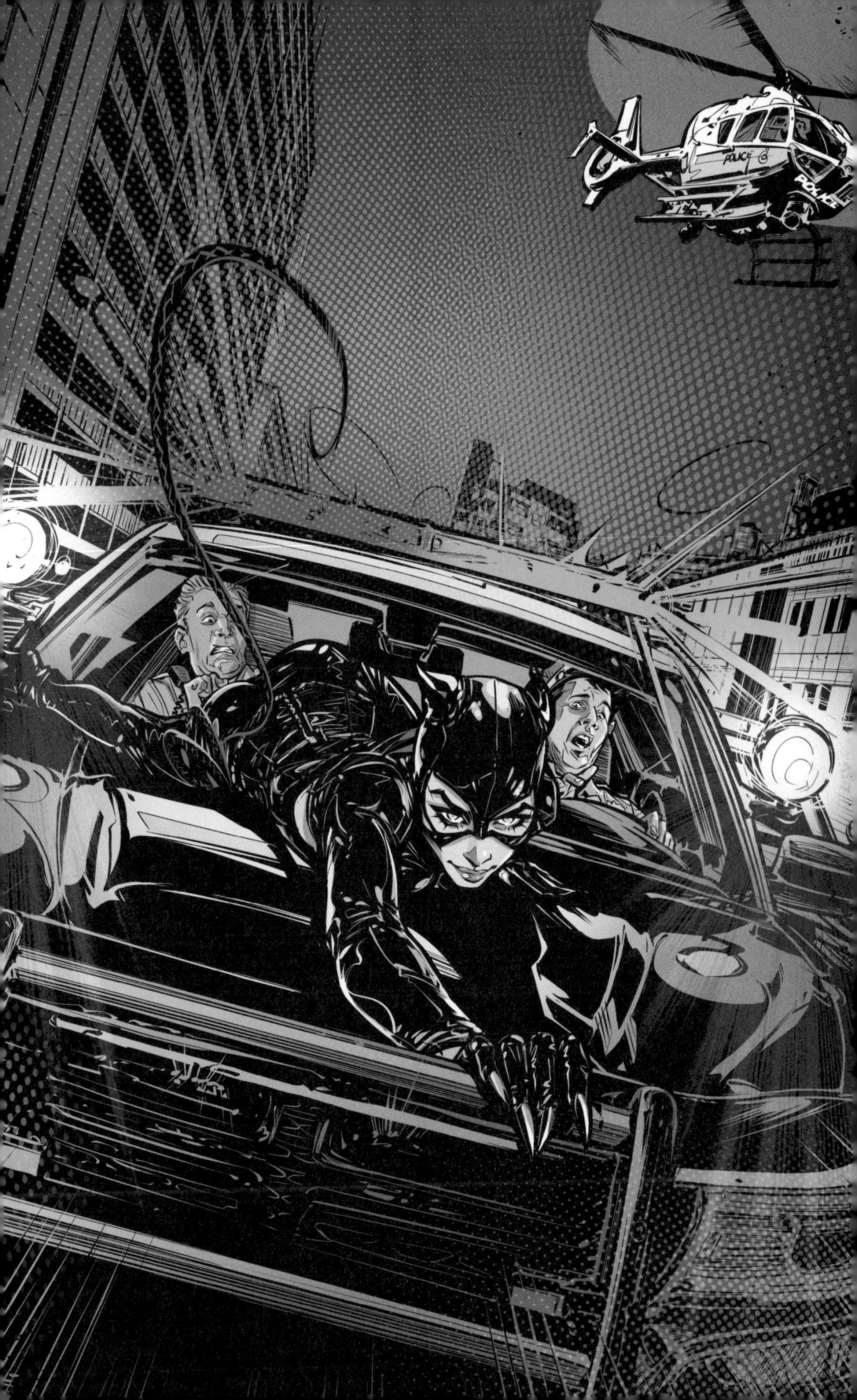
POLICE
POLICE

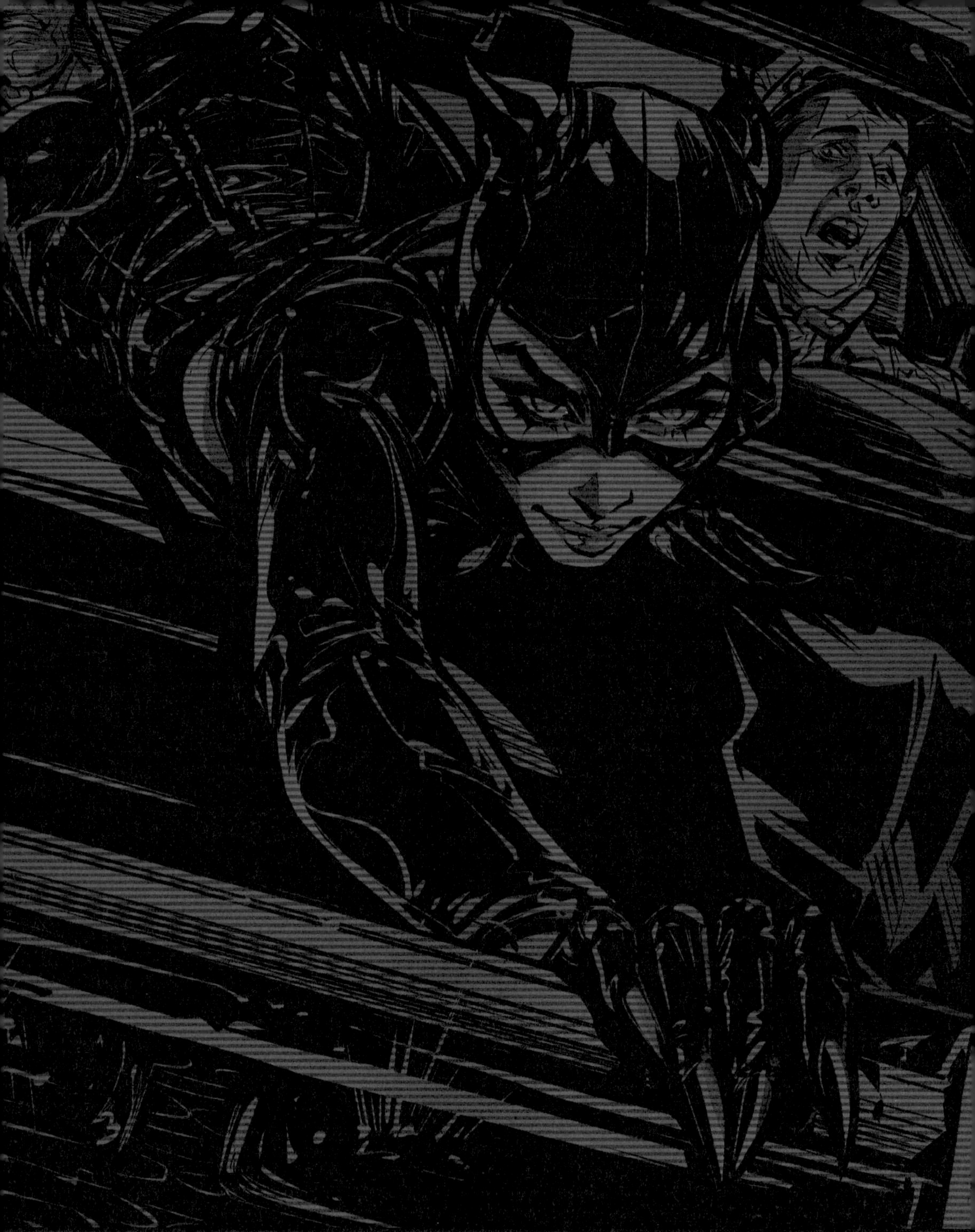

# CATWOMAN
ANNUAL #1

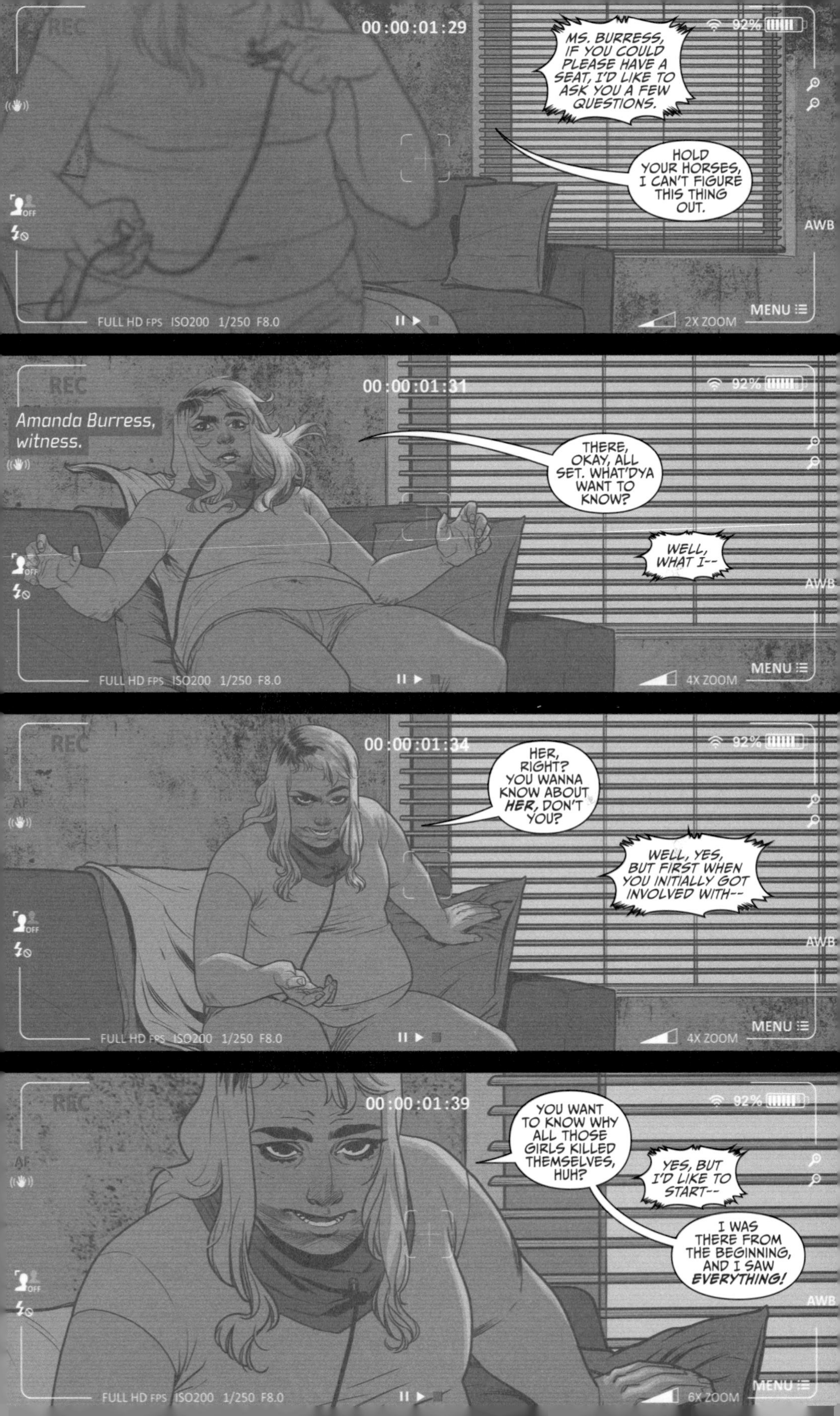
REC
00:00:01:29
92%
MS. BURRESS, IF YOU COULD PLEASE HAVE A SEAT, I'D LIKE TO ASK YOU A FEW QUESTIONS.
HOLD YOUR HORSES, I CAN'T FIGURE THIS THING OUT.
AWB
FULL HD FPS ISO200 1/250 F8.0
2X ZOOM
MENU
REC
00:00:01:31
92%
Amanda Burress, witness.
THERE, OKAY, ALL SET. WHAT'DYA WANT TO KNOW?
WELL, WHAT I--
AWB
FULL HD FPS ISO200 1/250 F8.0
4X ZOOM
MENU
REC
00:00:01:34
92%
HER, RIGHT? YOU WANNA KNOW ABOUT **HER**, DON'T YOU?
WELL, YES, BUT FIRST WHEN YOU INITIALLY GOT INVOLVED WITH--
AWB
FULL HD FPS ISO200 1/250 F8.0
4X ZOOM
MENU
REC
00:00:01:39
92%
YOU WANT TO KNOW WHY ALL THOSE GIRLS KILLED THEMSELVES, HUH?
YES, BUT I'D LIKE TO START--
I WAS THERE FROM THE BEGINNING, AND I SAW **EVERYTHING!**
AWB
FULL HD FPS ISO200 1/250 F8.0
6X ZOOM
MENU

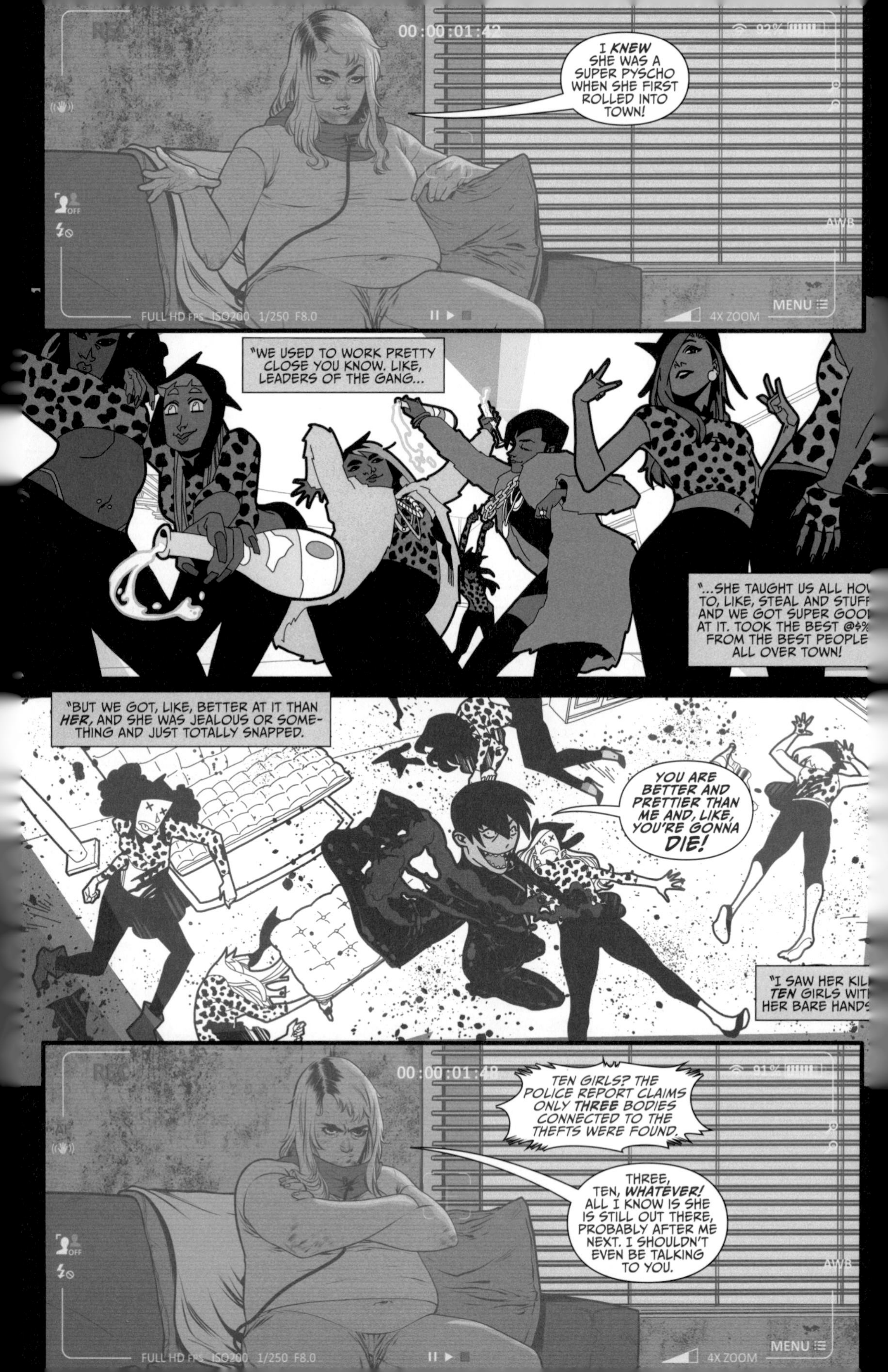
00:00:01:42
92%
I *KNEW* SHE WAS A SUPER PYSCHO WHEN SHE FIRST ROLLED INTO TOWN!
AWB
MENU
FULL HD FPS ISO200 1/250 F8.0
4X ZOOM
"WE USED TO WORK PRETTY CLOSE YOU KNOW. LIKE, LEADERS OF THE GANG...
"...SHE TAUGHT US ALL HOW TO, LIKE, STEAL AND STUFF AND WE GOT SUPER GOOD AT IT. TOOK THE BEST @$% FROM THE BEST PEOPLE ALL OVER TOWN!
"BUT WE GOT, LIKE, BETTER AT IT THAN *HER*, AND SHE WAS JEALOUS OR SOMETHING AND JUST TOTALLY SNAPPED.
YOU ARE BETTER AND PRETTIER THAN ME AND, LIKE, YOU'RE GONNA *DIE!*
"I SAW HER KIL *TEN* GIRLS WIT HER BARE HANDS
00:00:01:48
91%
TEN GIRLS? THE POLICE REPORT CLAIMS ONLY *THREE* BODIES CONNECTED TO THE THEFTS WERE FOUND.
THREE, TEN, *WHATEVER!* ALL I KNOW IS SHE IS STILL OUT THERE, PROBABLY AFTER ME NEXT. I SHOULDN'T EVEN BE TALKING TO YOU.
AWB
MENU
FULL HD FPS ISO200 1/250 F8.0
4X ZOOM

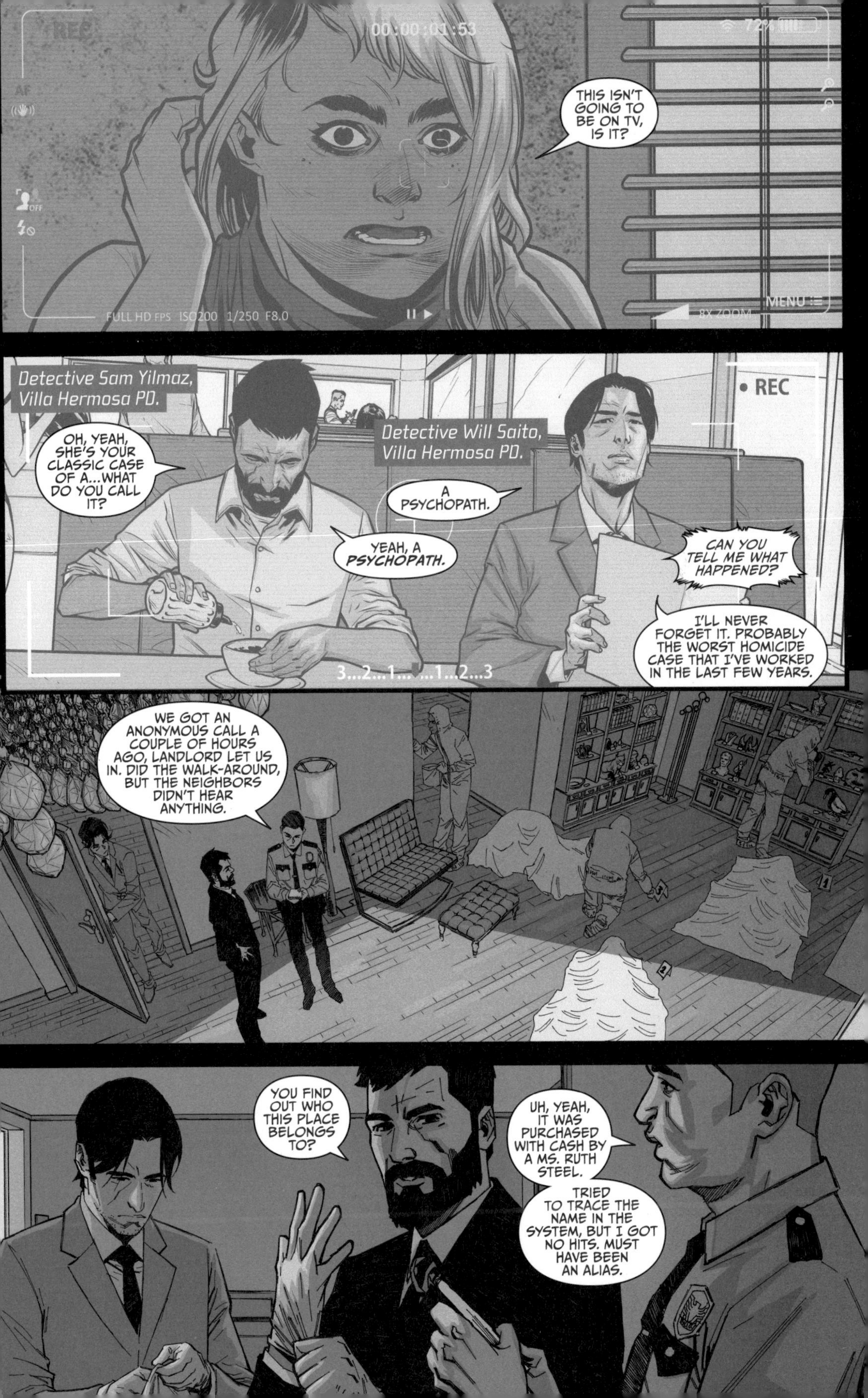
REC
00:00:01:53
72%
THIS ISN'T GOING TO BE ON TV, IS IT?
FULL HD FPS ISO200 1/250 F8.0
8X ZOOM
MENU
Detective Sam Yilmaz, Villa Hermosa PD.
REC
OH, YEAH, SHE'S YOUR CLASSIC CASE OF A...WHAT DO YOU CALL IT?
Detective Will Saito, Villa Hermosa PD.
A PSYCHOPATH.
YEAH, A *PSYCHOPATH.*
CAN YOU TELL ME WHAT HAPPENED?
I'LL NEVER FORGET IT. PROBABLY THE WORST HOMICIDE CASE THAT I'VE WORKED IN THE LAST FEW YEARS.
3...2...1... ...1...2...3
WE GOT AN ANONYMOUS CALL A COUPLE OF HOURS AGO, LANDLORD LET US IN. DID THE WALK-AROUND, BUT THE NEIGHBORS DIDN'T HEAR ANYTHING.
YOU FIND OUT WHO THIS PLACE BELONGS TO?
UH, YEAH, IT WAS PURCHASED WITH CASH BY A MS. RUTH STEEL.
TRIED TO TRACE THE NAME IN THE SYSTEM, BUT I GOT NO HITS. MUST HAVE BEEN AN ALIAS.

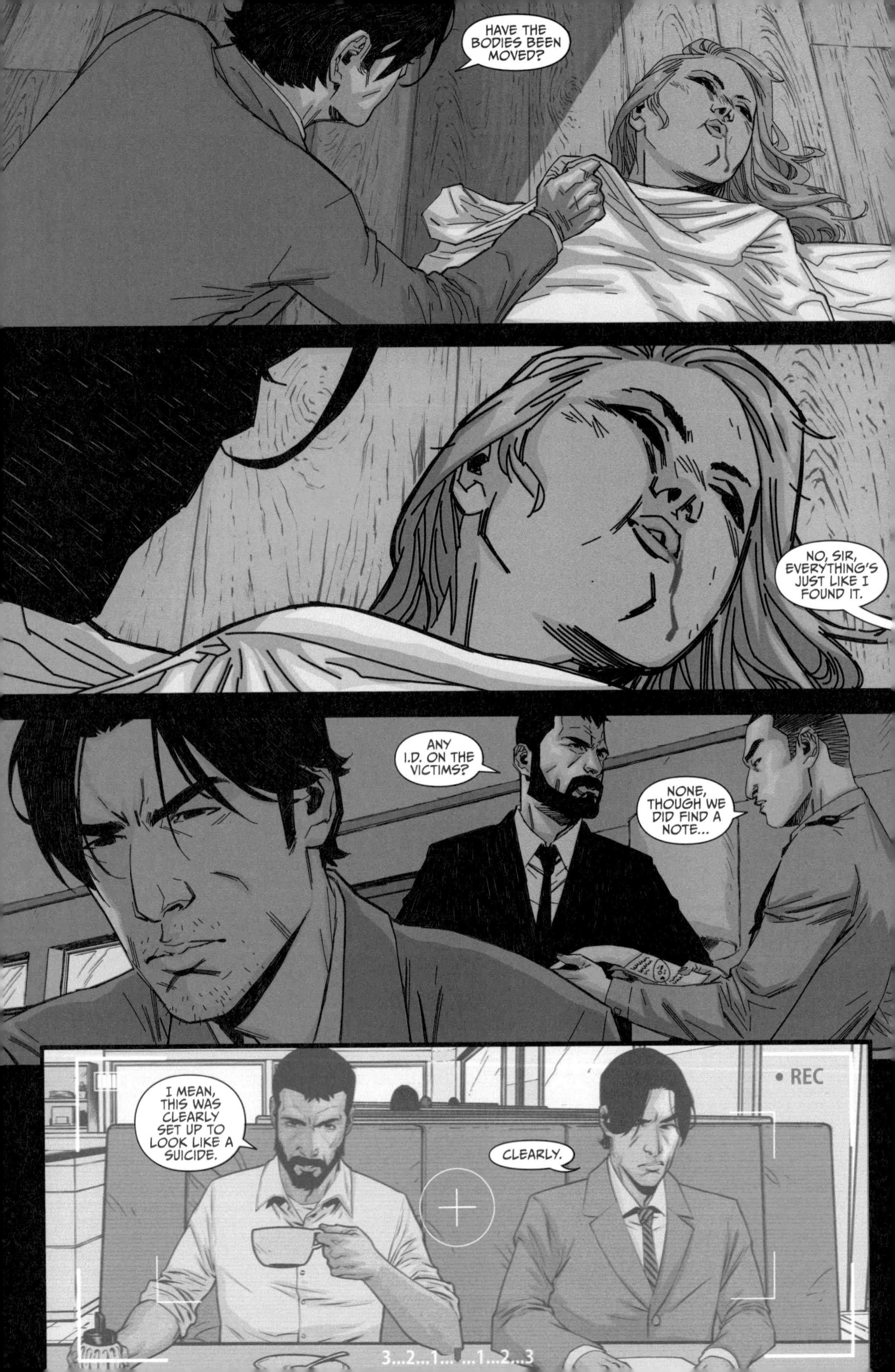
HAVE THE BODIES BEEN MOVED?
NO, SIR, EVERYTHING'S JUST LIKE I FOUND IT.
ANY I.D. ON THE VICTIMS?
NONE, THOUGH WE DID FIND A NOTE...
• REC
I MEAN, THIS WAS CLEARLY SET UP TO LOOK LIKE A SUICIDE.
CLEARLY.
3...2...1......1...2...3

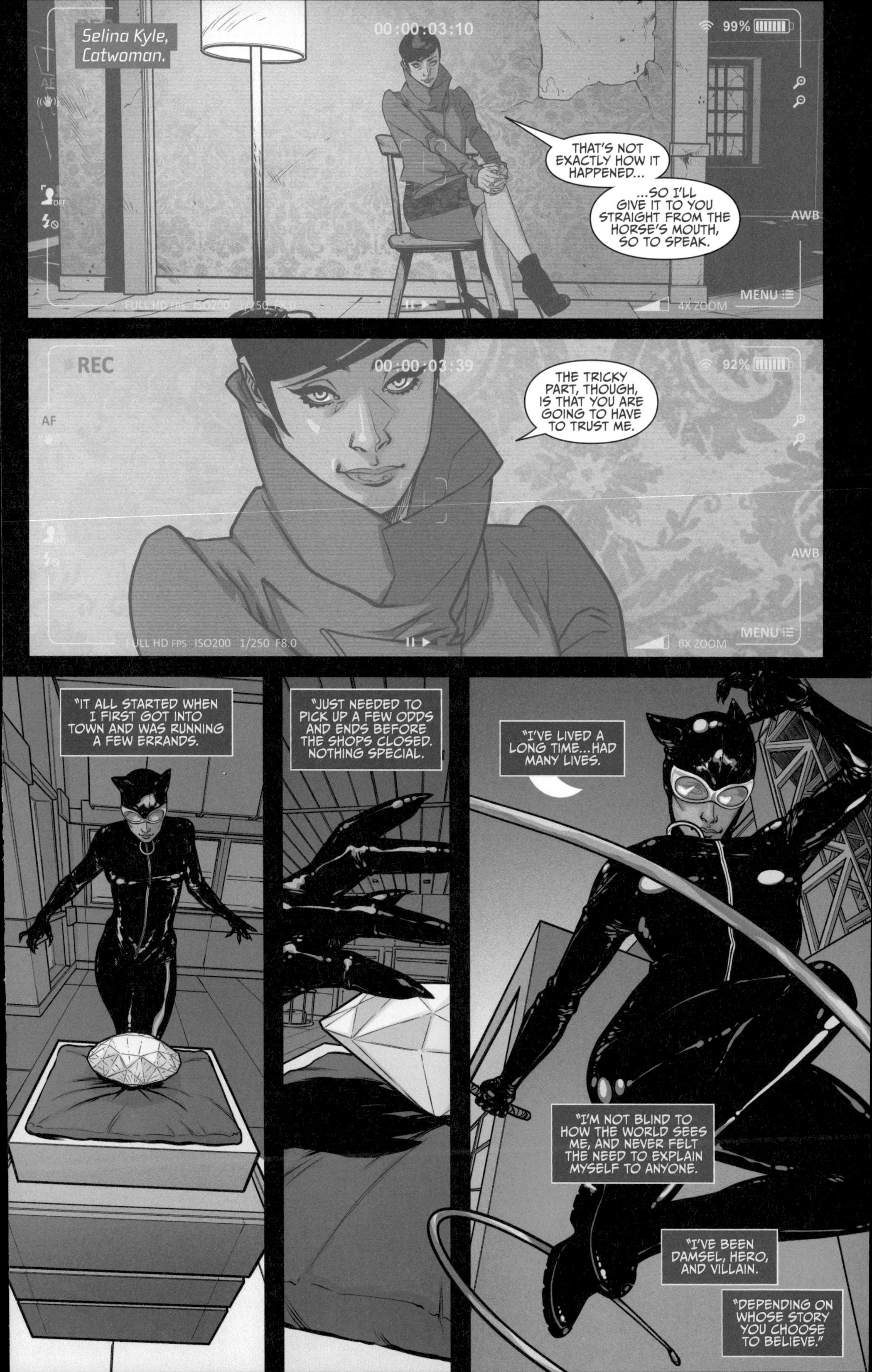
REC
00:00:03:10
99%
Selina Kyle, Catwoman.
THAT'S NOT EXACTLY HOW IT HAPPENED...
...SO I'LL GIVE IT TO YOU STRAIGHT FROM THE HORSE'S MOUTH, SO TO SPEAK.
AWB
MENU
FULL HD FPS ISO200 1/250 F8.0
4X ZOOM
REC
00:00:03:39
92%
AF
THE TRICKY PART, THOUGH, IS THAT YOU ARE GOING TO HAVE TO TRUST ME.
AWB
MENU
FULL HD FPS ISO200 1/250 F8.0
6X ZOOM
"IT ALL STARTED WHEN I FIRST GOT INTO TOWN AND WAS RUNNING A FEW ERRANDS.
"JUST NEEDED TO PICK UP A FEW ODDS AND ENDS BEFORE THE SHOPS CLOSED. NOTHING SPECIAL.
"I'VE LIVED A LONG TIME...HAD MANY LIVES.
"I'M NOT BLIND TO HOW THE WORLD SEES ME, AND NEVER FELT THE NEED TO EXPLAIN MYSELF TO ANYONE.
"I'VE BEEN DAMSEL, HERO, AND VILLAIN.
"DEPENDING ON WHOSE STORY YOU CHOOSE TO BELIEVE."

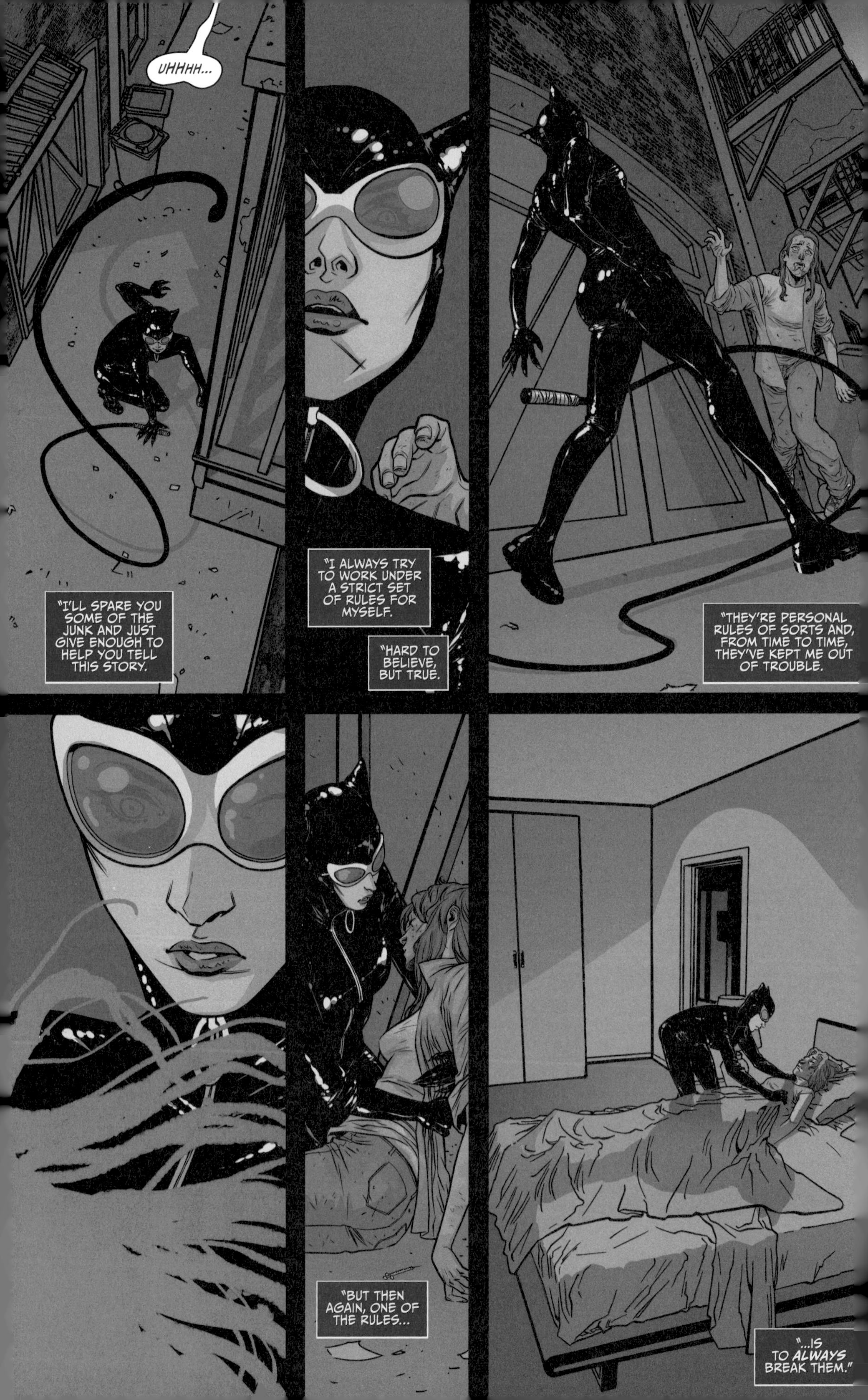
UHHHH...
"I'LL SPARE YOU SOME OF THE JUNK AND JUST GIVE ENOUGH TO HELP YOU TELL THIS STORY.
"I ALWAYS TRY TO WORK UNDER A STRICT SET OF RULES FOR MYSELF.
"HARD TO BELIEVE, BUT TRUE.
"THEY'RE PERSONAL RULES OF SORTS AND, FROM TIME TO TIME, THEY'VE KEPT ME OUT OF TROUBLE.
"BUT THEN AGAIN, ONE OF THE RULES...
"...IS TO *ALWAYS* BREAK THEM."

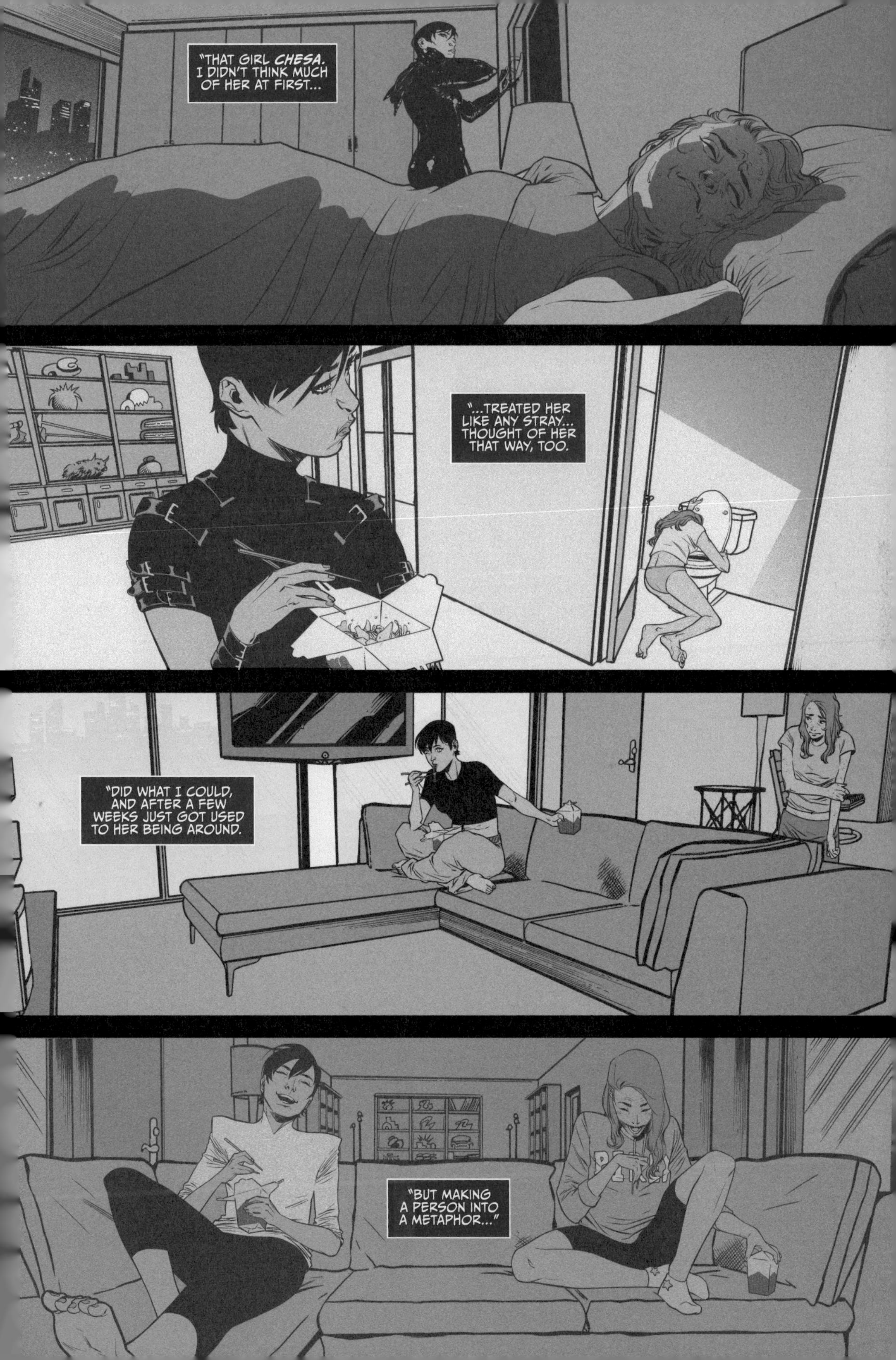
"THAT GIRL CHESA. I DIDN'T THINK MUCH OF HER AT FIRST...
"...TREATED HER LIKE ANY STRAY... THOUGHT OF HER THAT WAY, TOO.
"DID WHAT I COULD, AND AFTER A FEW WEEKS JUST GOT USED TO HER BEING AROUND.
"BUT MAKING A PERSON INTO A METAPHOR..."

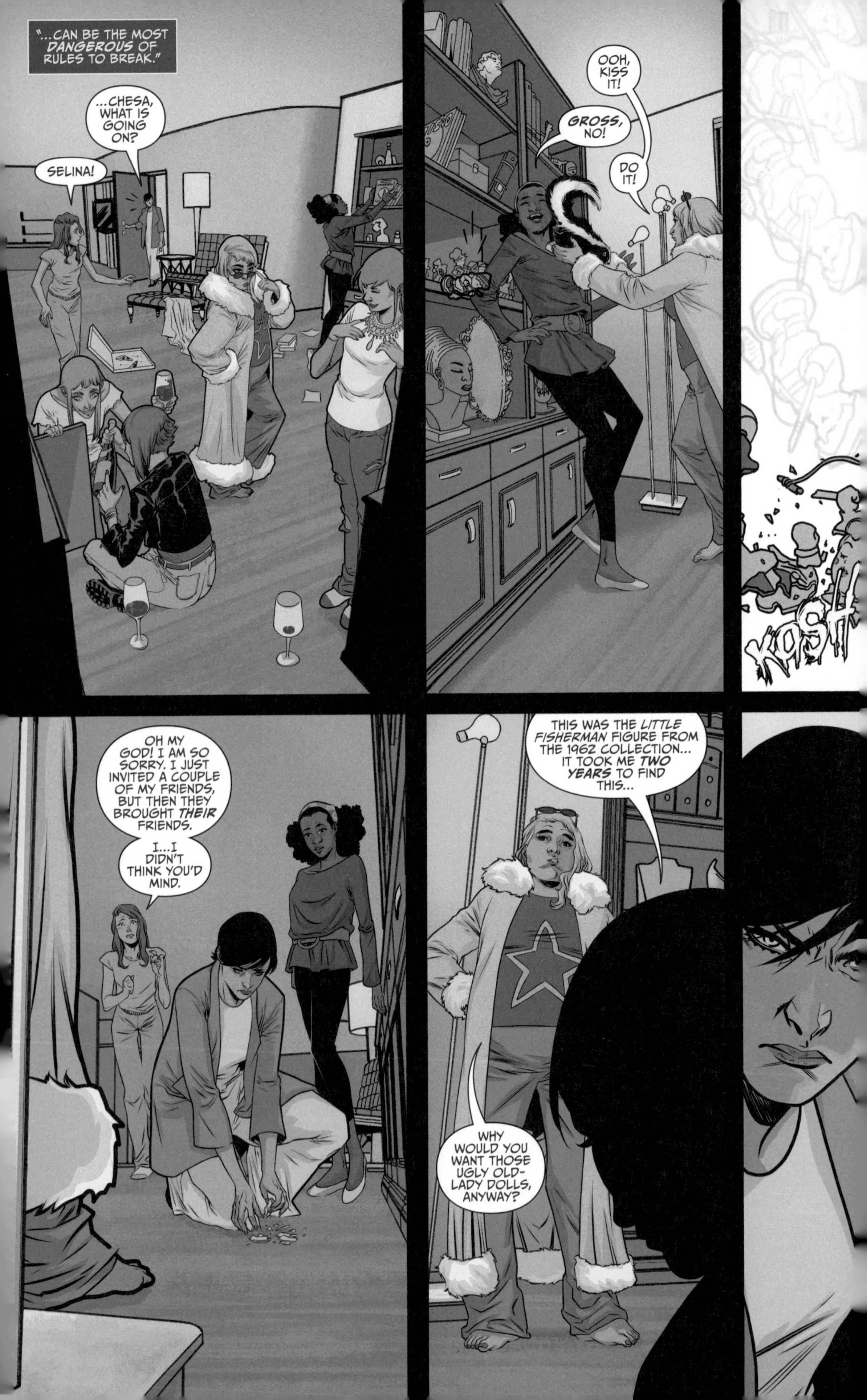
"...CAN BE THE MOST DANGEROUS OF RULES TO BREAK."
...CHESA, WHAT IS GOING ON?
SELINA!
OOH, KISS IT!
GROSS, NO!
DO IT!
KOSH
OH MY GOD! I AM SO SORRY. I JUST INVITED A COUPLE OF MY FRIENDS, BUT THEN THEY BROUGHT THEIR FRIENDS.
I...I DIDN'T THINK YOU'D MIND.
THIS WAS THE LITTLE FISHERMAN FIGURE FROM THE 1962 COLLECTION... IT TOOK ME TWO YEARS TO FIND THIS...
WHY WOULD YOU WANT THOSE UGLY OLD-LADY DOLLS, ANYWAY?

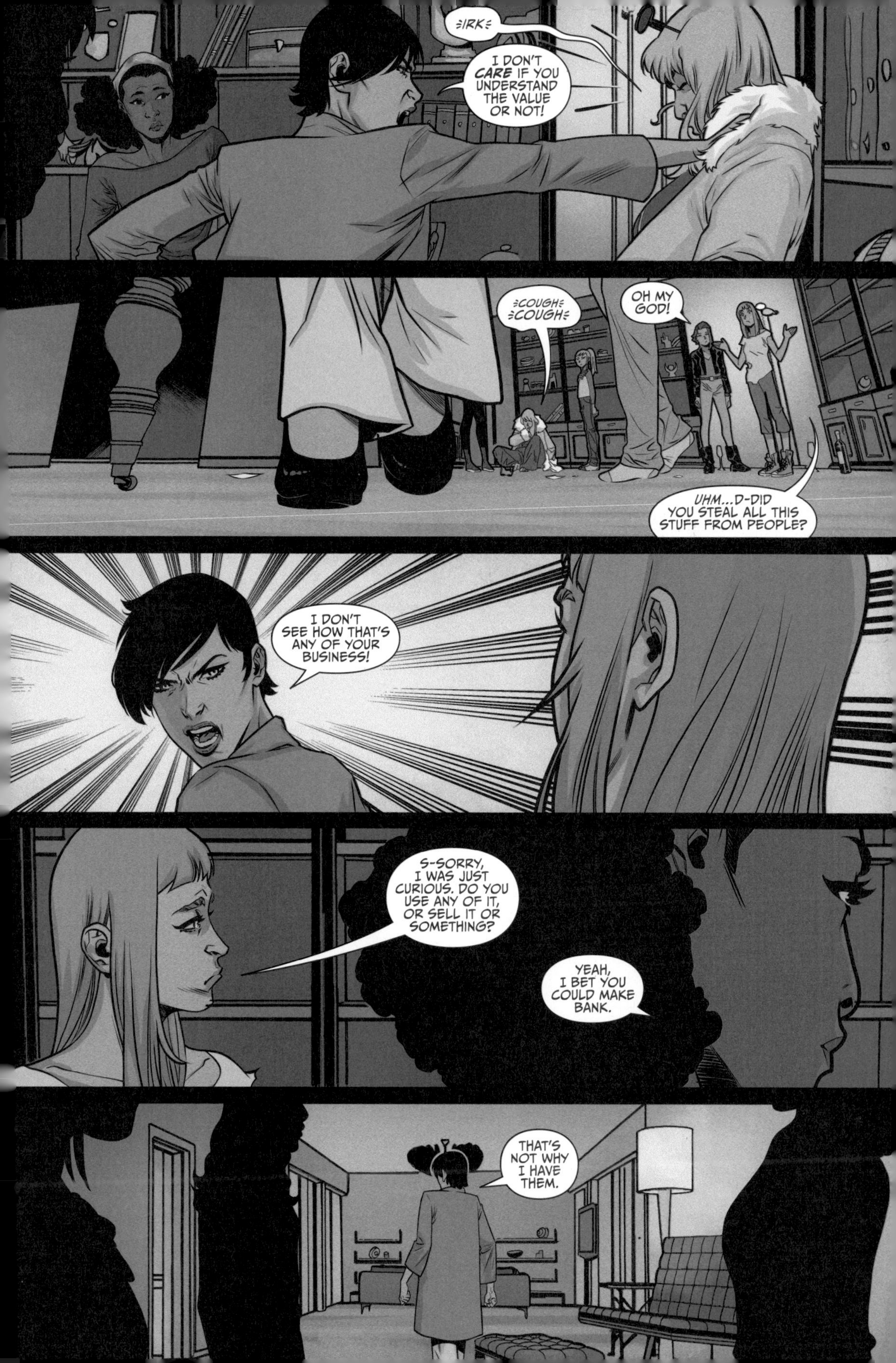
IRK
I DON'T CARE IF YOU UNDERSTAND THE VALUE OR NOT!
COUGH COUGH
OH MY GOD!
UHM...D-DID YOU STEAL ALL THIS STUFF FROM PEOPLE?
I DON'T SEE HOW THAT'S ANY OF YOUR BUSINESS!
S-SORRY, I WAS JUST CURIOUS. DO YOU USE ANY OF IT, OR SELL IT OR SOMETHING?
YEAH, I BET YOU COULD MAKE BANK.
THAT'S NOT WHY I HAVE THEM.

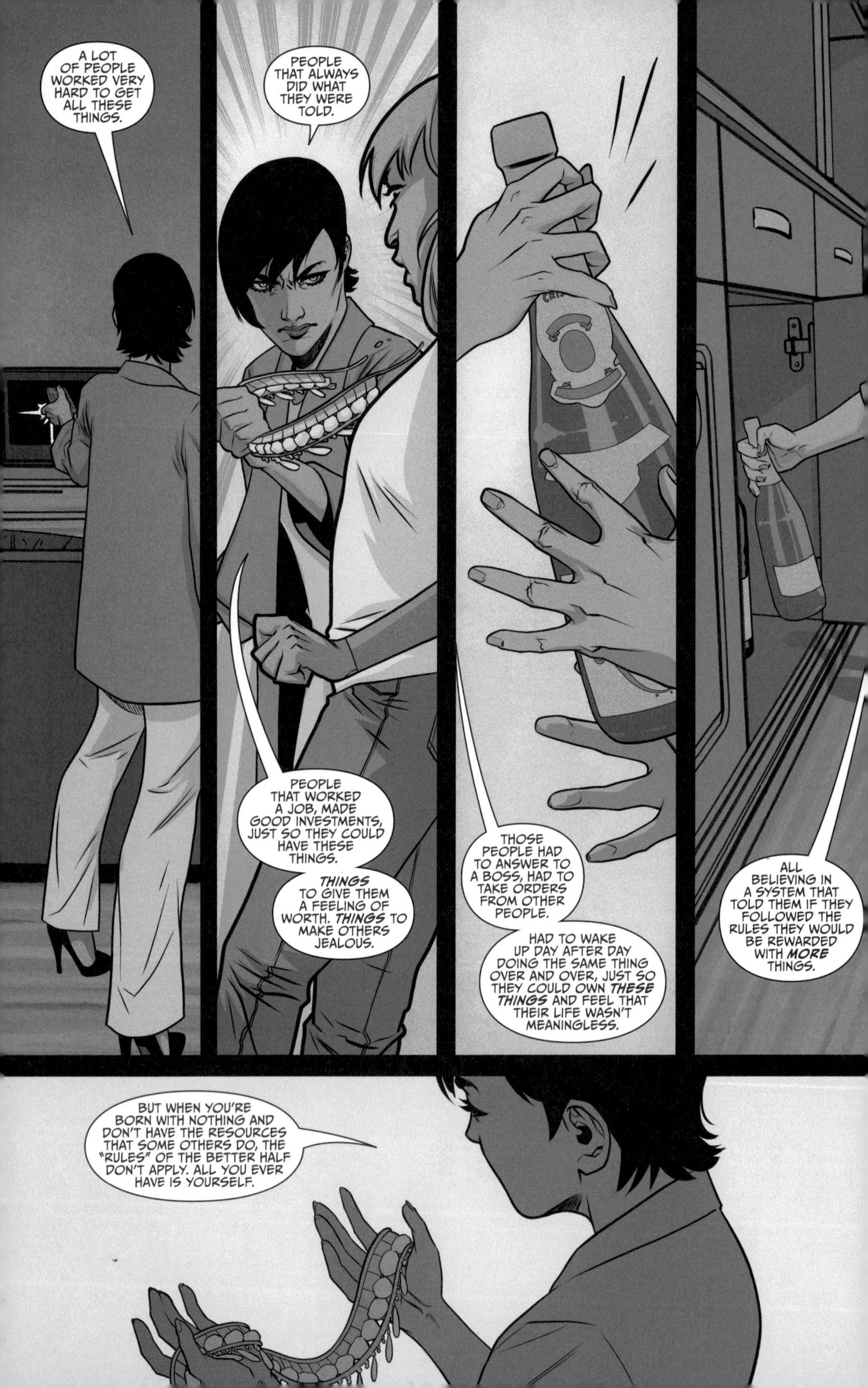
A LOT OF PEOPLE WORKED VERY HARD TO GET ALL THESE THINGS.
PEOPLE THAT ALWAYS DID WHAT THEY WERE TOLD.
PEOPLE THAT WORKED A JOB, MADE GOOD INVESTMENTS, JUST SO THEY COULD HAVE THESE THINGS.
*THINGS* TO GIVE THEM A FEELING OF WORTH. *THINGS* TO MAKE OTHERS JEALOUS.
THOSE PEOPLE HAD TO ANSWER TO A BOSS, HAD TO TAKE ORDERS FROM OTHER PEOPLE.
HAD TO WAKE UP DAY AFTER DAY DOING THE SAME THING OVER AND OVER, JUST SO THEY COULD OWN *THESE THINGS* AND FEEL THAT THEIR LIFE WASN'T MEANINGLESS.
ALL BELIEVING IN A SYSTEM THAT TOLD THEM IF THEY FOLLOWED THE RULES THEY WOULD BE REWARDED WITH *MORE* THINGS.
BUT WHEN YOU'RE BORN WITH NOTHING AND DON'T HAVE THE RESOURCES THAT SOME OTHERS DO, THE "RULES" OF THE BETTER HALF DON'T APPLY. ALL YOU EVER HAVE IS YOURSELF.

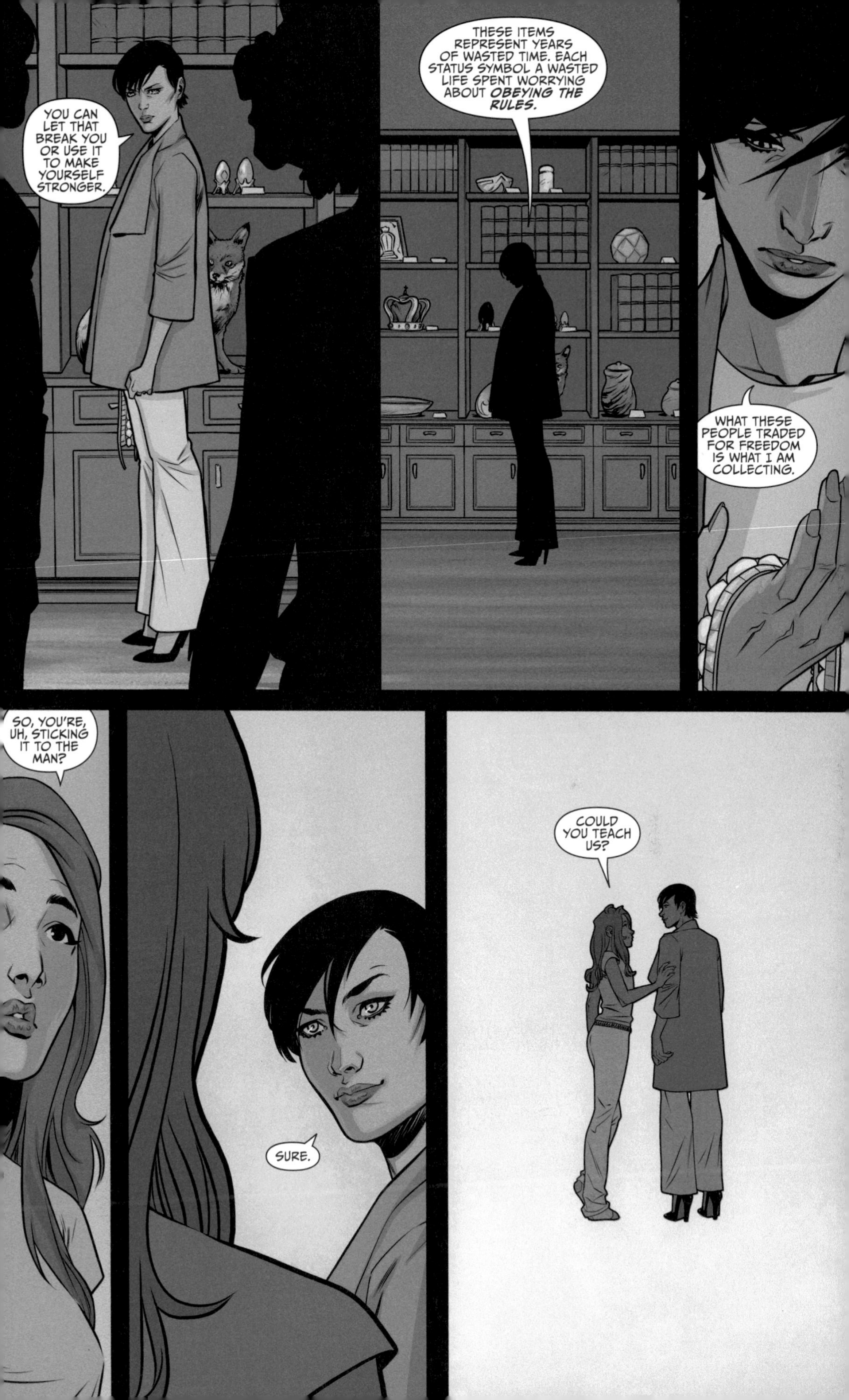
YOU CAN LET THAT BREAK YOU OR USE IT TO MAKE YOURSELF STRONGER.
THESE ITEMS REPRESENT YEARS OF WASTED TIME. EACH STATUS SYMBOL A WASTED LIFE SPENT WORRYING ABOUT OBEYING THE RULES.
WHAT THESE PEOPLE TRADED FOR FREEDOM IS WHAT I AM COLLECTING.
SO, YOU'RE, UH, STICKING IT TO THE MAN?
SURE.
COULD YOU TEACH US?

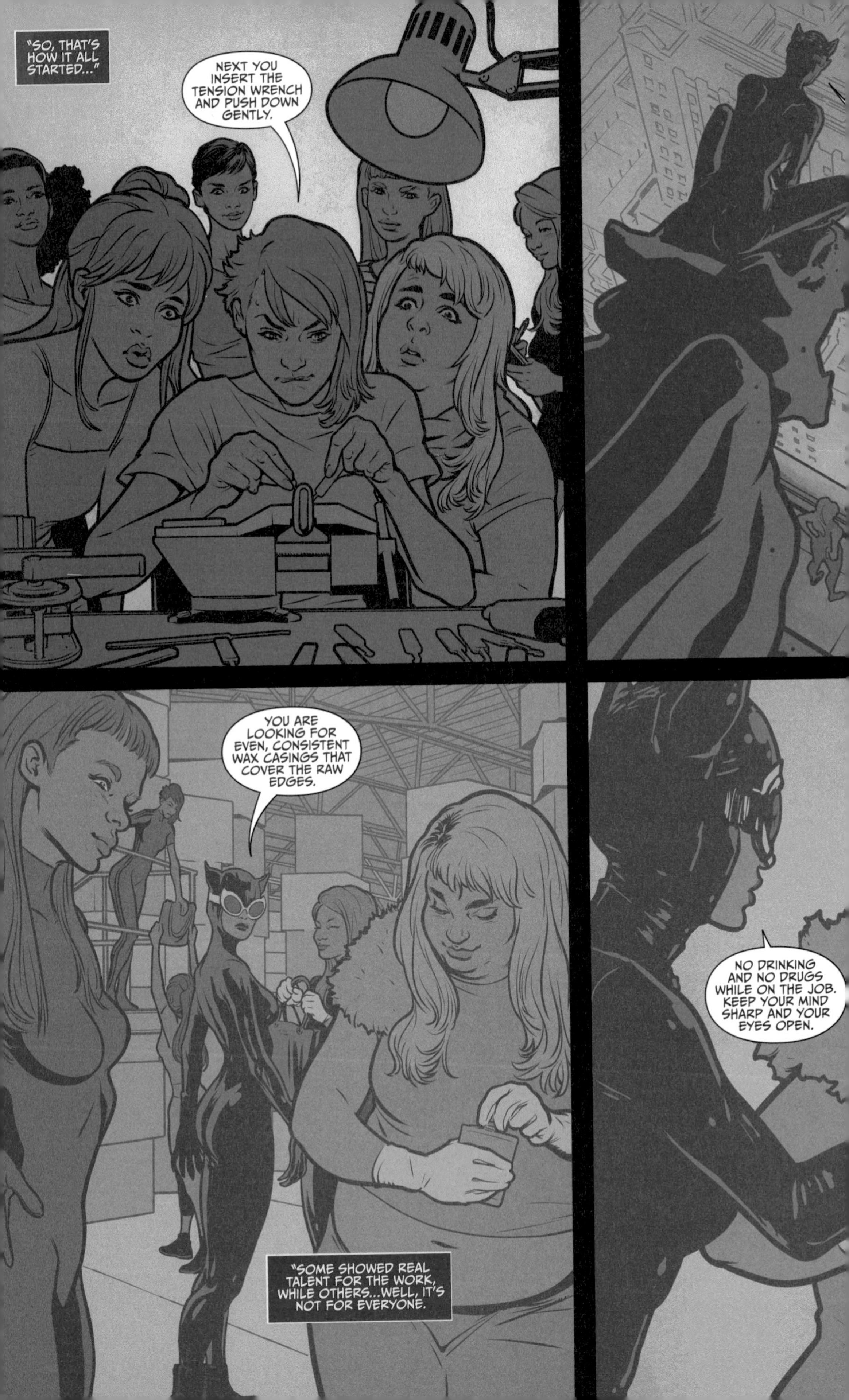
"SO, THAT'S HOW IT ALL STARTED..."
NEXT YOU INSERT THE TENSION WRENCH AND PUSH DOWN GENTLY.
YOU ARE LOOKING FOR EVEN, CONSISTENT WAX CASINGS THAT COVER THE RAW EDGES.
"SOME SHOWED REAL TALENT FOR THE WORK, WHILE OTHERS...WELL, IT'S NOT FOR EVERYONE.
NO DRINKING AND NO DRUGS WHILE ON THE JOB. KEEP YOUR MIND SHARP AND YOUR EYES OPEN.

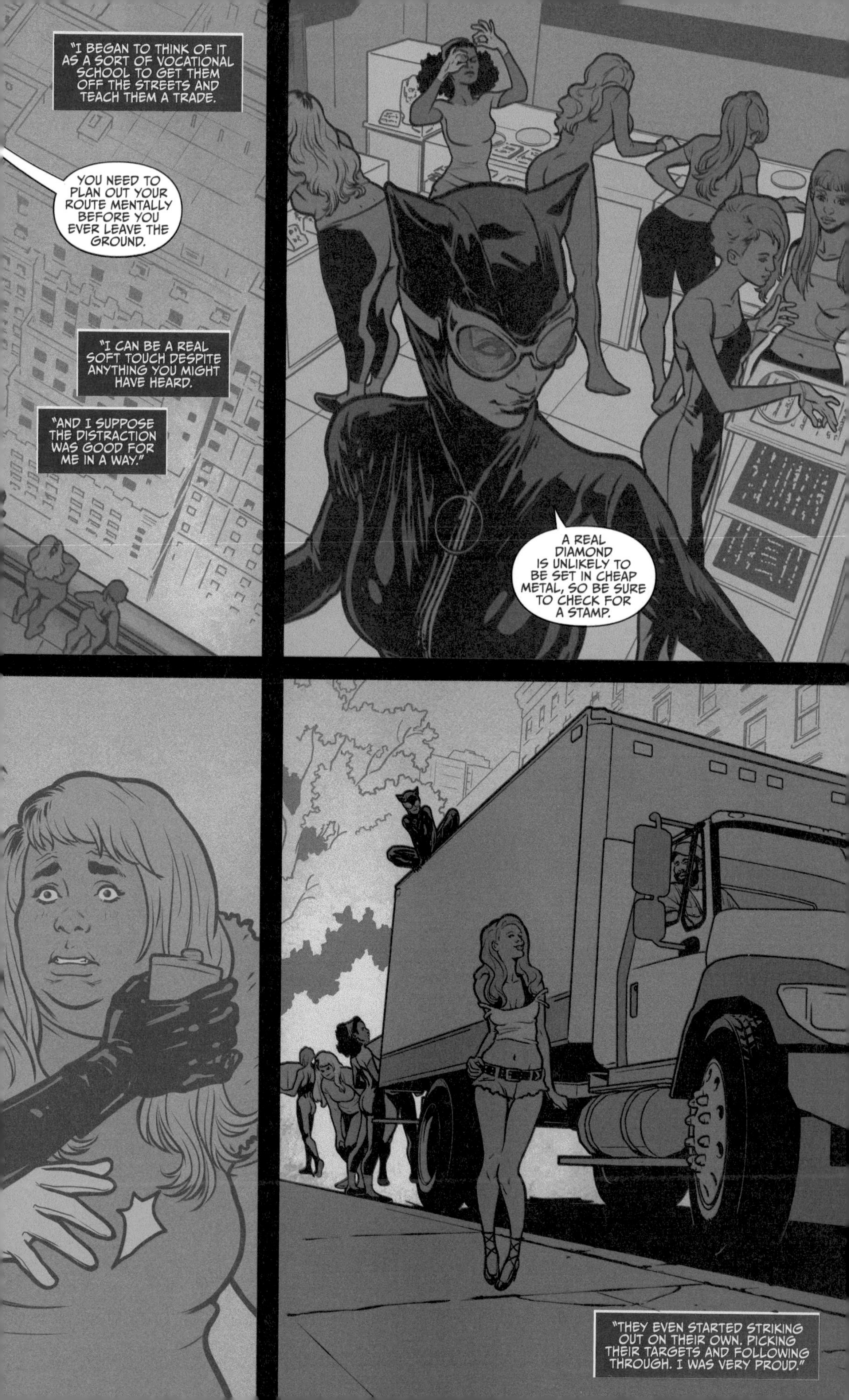
"I BEGAN TO THINK OF IT AS A SORT OF VOCATIONAL SCHOOL TO GET THEM OFF THE STREETS AND TEACH THEM A TRADE.
YOU NEED TO PLAN OUT YOUR ROUTE MENTALLY BEFORE YOU EVER LEAVE THE GROUND.
"I CAN BE A REAL SOFT TOUCH DESPITE ANYTHING YOU MIGHT HAVE HEARD.
"AND I SUPPOSE THE DISTRACTION WAS GOOD FOR ME IN A WAY."
A REAL DIAMOND IS UNLIKELY TO BE SET IN CHEAP METAL, SO BE SURE TO CHECK FOR A STAMP.
"THEY EVEN STARTED STRIKING OUT ON THEIR OWN. PICKING THEIR TARGETS AND FOLLOWING THROUGH. I WAS VERY PROUD."

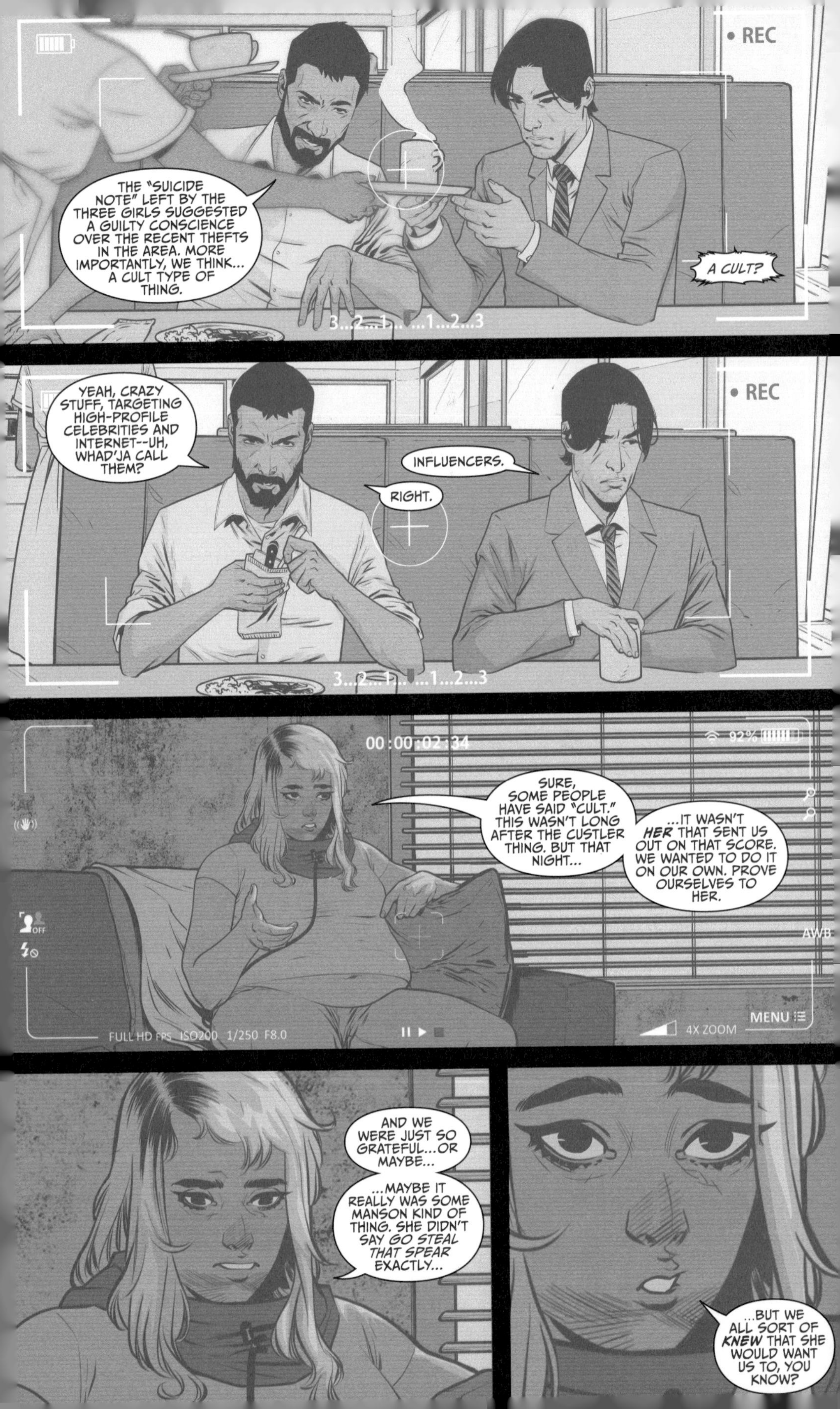
REC
THE "SUICIDE NOTE" LEFT BY THE THREE GIRLS SUGGESTED A GUILTY CONSCIENCE OVER THE RECENT THEFTS IN THE AREA. MORE IMPORTANTLY, WE THINK... A CULT TYPE OF THING.
A CULT?
3...2...1... ...1...2...3
REC
YEAH, CRAZY STUFF, TARGETING HIGH-PROFILE CELEBRITIES AND INTERNET--UH, WHAD'JA CALL THEM?
INFLUENCERS.
RIGHT.
3...2...1... ...1...2...3
00:00:02:34
92%
SURE, SOME PEOPLE HAVE SAID "CULT." THIS WASN'T LONG AFTER THE CUSTLER THING. BUT THAT NIGHT...
...IT WASN'T HER THAT SENT US OUT ON THAT SCORE. WE WANTED TO DO IT ON OUR OWN. PROVE OURSELVES TO HER.
OFF
AWB
MENU
FULL HD FPS ISO200 1/250 F8.0
4X ZOOM
AND WE WERE JUST SO GRATEFUL...OR MAYBE...
...MAYBE IT REALLY WAS SOME MANSON KIND OF THING. SHE DIDN'T SAY GO STEAL THAT SPEAR EXACTLY...
...BUT WE ALL SORT OF KNEW THAT SHE WOULD WANT US TO, YOU KNOW?

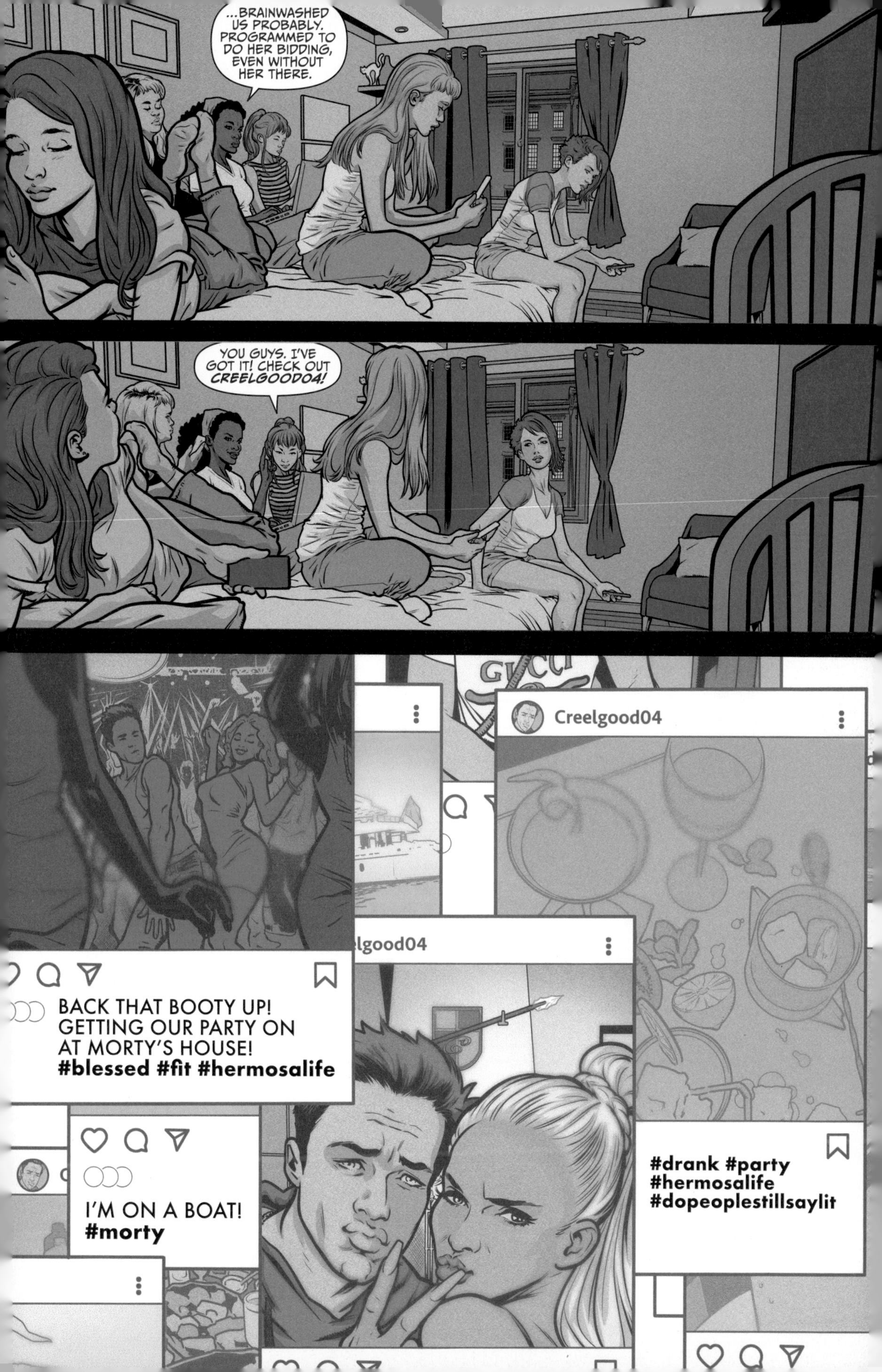
...BRAINWASHED US PROBABLY. PROGRAMMED TO DO HER BIDDING, EVEN WITHOUT HER THERE.
YOU GUYS. I'VE GOT IT! CHECK OUT CREELGOOD04!
BACK THAT BOOTY UP! GETTING OUR PARTY ON AT MORTY'S HOUSE! #blessed #fit #hermosalife
Creelgood04
#drank #party #hermosalife #dopeoplestillsaylit
lgood04
I'M ON A BOAT! #morty

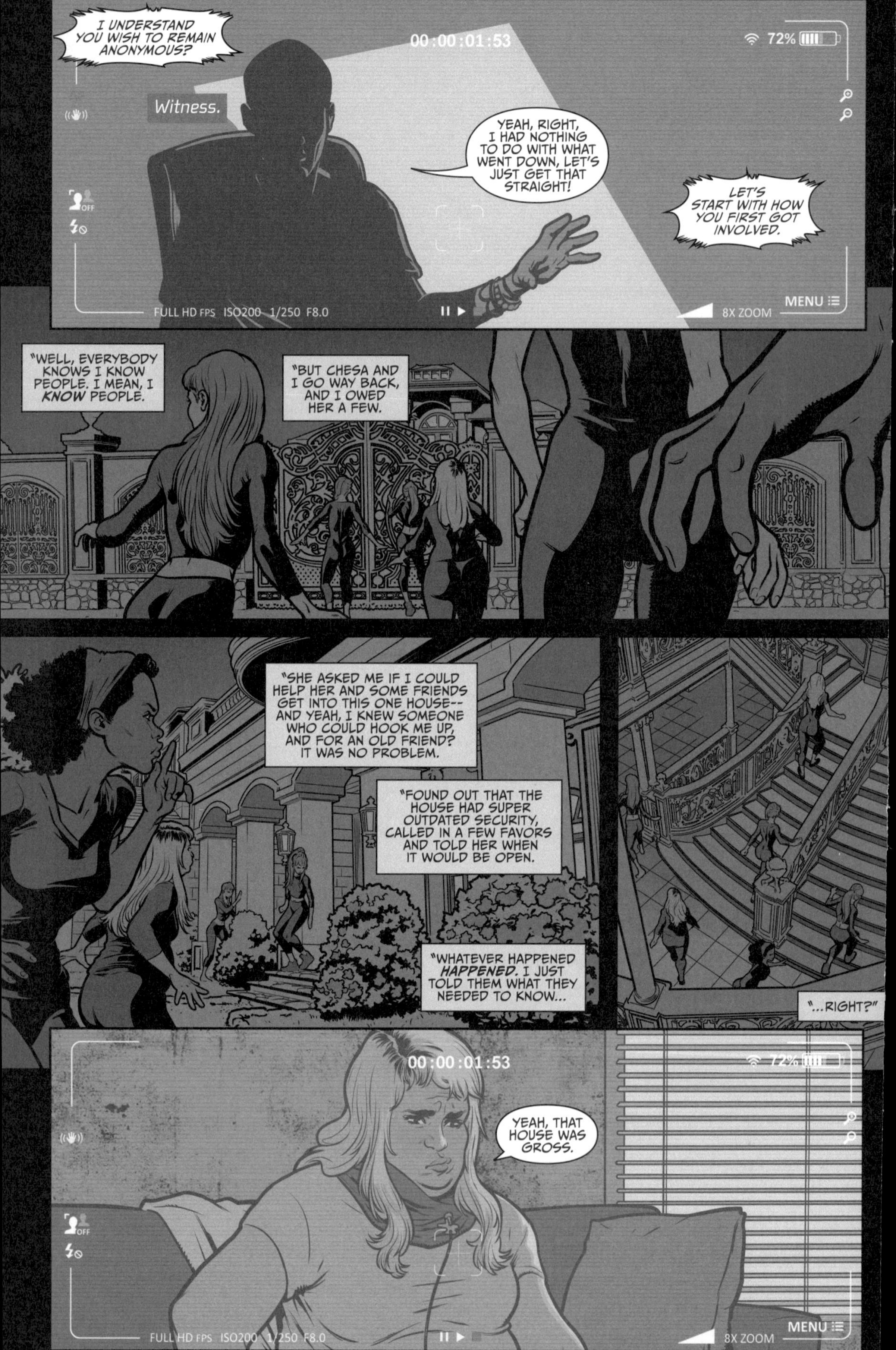

I UNDERSTAND YOU WISH TO REMAIN ANONYMOUS?
00:00:01:53
72%
Witness.
YEAH, RIGHT, I HAD NOTHING TO DO WITH WHAT WENT DOWN, LET'S JUST GET THAT STRAIGHT!
LET'S START WITH HOW YOU FIRST GOT INVOLVED.
FULL HD FPS ISO200 1/250 F8.0
8X ZOOM
MENU
"WELL, EVERYBODY KNOWS I KNOW PEOPLE. I MEAN, I *KNOW* PEOPLE.
"BUT CHESA AND I GO WAY BACK, AND I OWED HER A FEW.
"SHE ASKED ME IF I COULD HELP HER AND SOME FRIENDS GET INTO THIS ONE HOUSE-- AND YEAH, I KNEW SOMEONE WHO COULD HOOK ME UP, AND FOR AN OLD FRIEND? IT WAS NO PROBLEM.
"FOUND OUT THAT THE HOUSE HAD SUPER OUTDATED SECURITY, CALLED IN A FEW FAVORS AND TOLD HER WHEN IT WOULD BE OPEN.
"WHATEVER HAPPENED *HAPPENED.* I JUST TOLD THEM WHAT THEY NEEDED TO KNOW...
"...RIGHT?"
00:00:01:53
72%
YEAH, THAT HOUSE WAS GROSS.
FULL HD FPS ISO200 1/250 F8.0
8X ZOOM
MENU

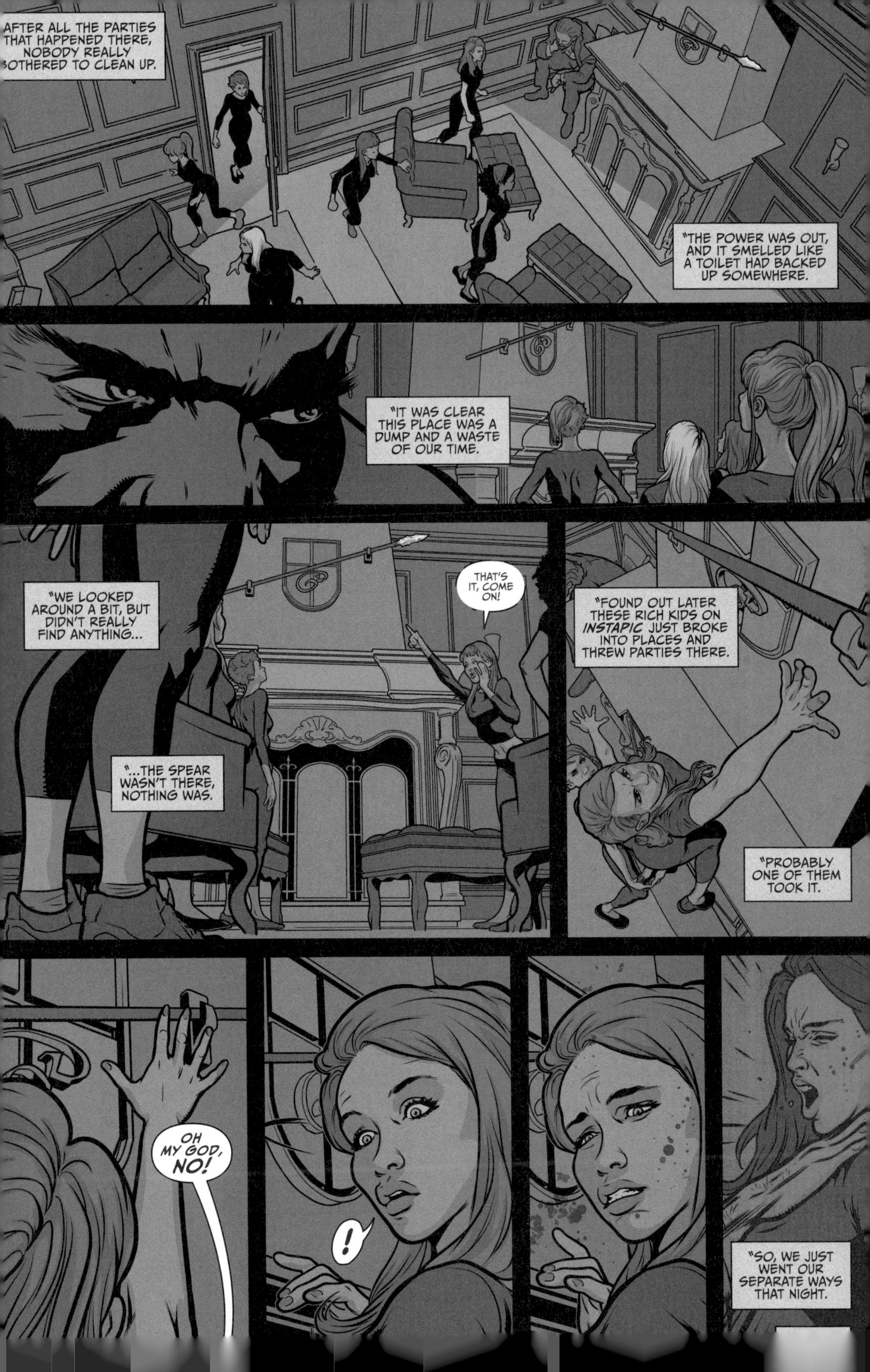
AFTER ALL THE PARTIES THAT HAPPENED THERE, NOBODY REALLY BOTHERED TO CLEAN UP.
"THE POWER WAS OUT, AND IT SMELLED LIKE A TOILET HAD BACKED UP SOMEWHERE.
"IT WAS CLEAR THIS PLACE WAS A DUMP AND A WASTE OF OUR TIME.
"WE LOOKED AROUND A BIT, BUT DIDN'T REALLY FIND ANYTHING...
THAT'S IT, COME ON!
"...THE SPEAR WASN'T THERE, NOTHING WAS.
"FOUND OUT LATER THESE RICH KIDS ON *INSTAPIC* JUST BROKE INTO PLACES AND THREW PARTIES THERE.
"PROBABLY ONE OF THEM TOOK IT.
OH MY GOD, NO!
!
"SO, WE JUST WENT OUR SEPARATE WAYS THAT NIGHT.

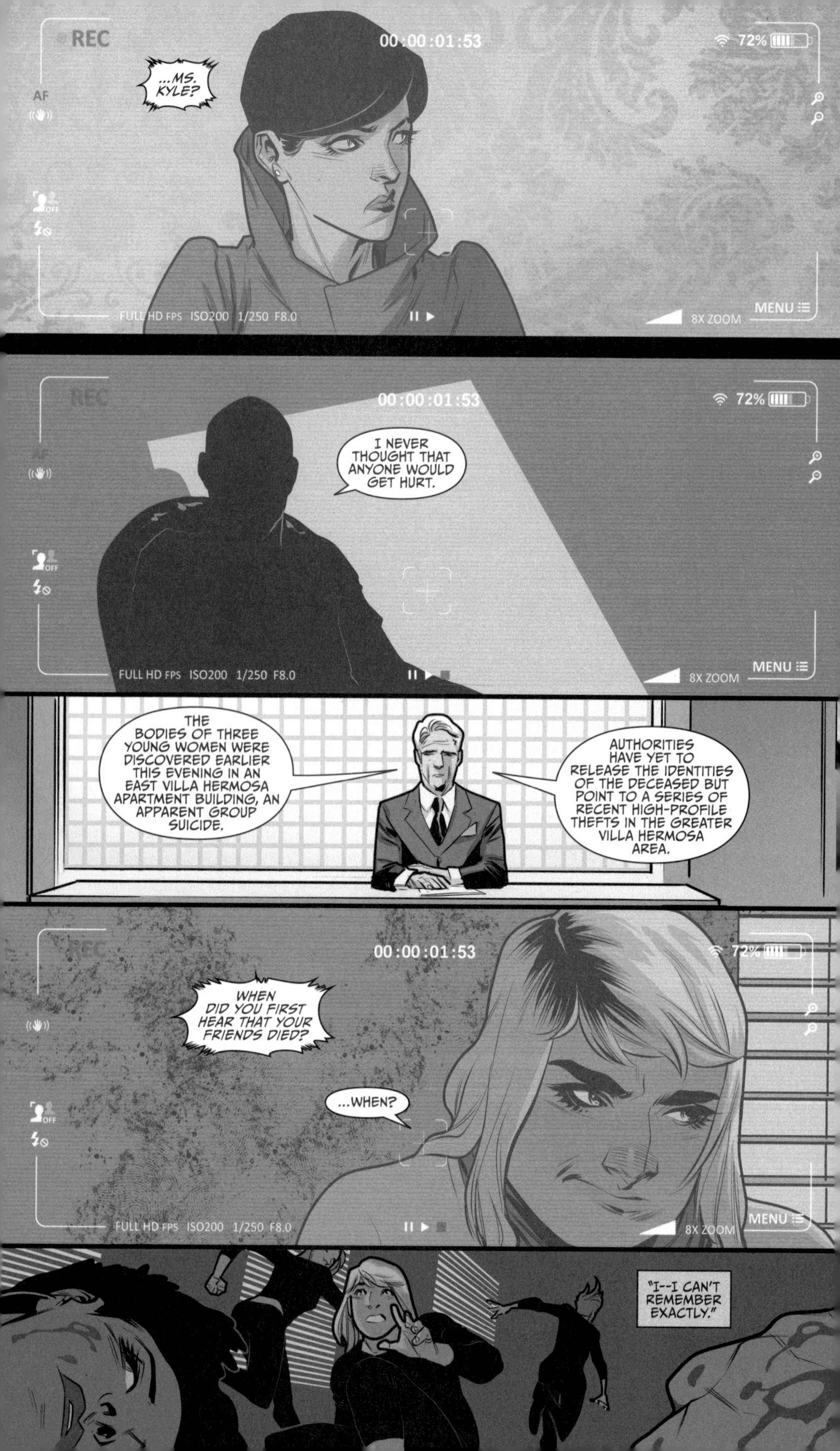
REC
00:00:01:53
72%
...MS. KYLE?
FULL HD FPS ISO200 1/250 F8.0
8X ZOOM
MENU
I NEVER THOUGHT THAT ANYONE WOULD GET HURT.
THE BODIES OF THREE YOUNG WOMEN WERE DISCOVERED EARLIER THIS EVENING IN AN EAST VILLA HERMOSA APARTMENT BUILDING, AN APPARENT GROUP SUICIDE.
AUTHORITIES HAVE YET TO RELEASE THE IDENTITIES OF THE DECEASED BUT POINT TO A SERIES OF RECENT HIGH-PROFILE THEFTS IN THE GREATER VILLA HERMOSA AREA.
WHEN DID YOU FIRST HEAR THAT YOUR FRIENDS DIED?
...WHEN?
"I--I CAN'T REMEMBER EXACTLY."

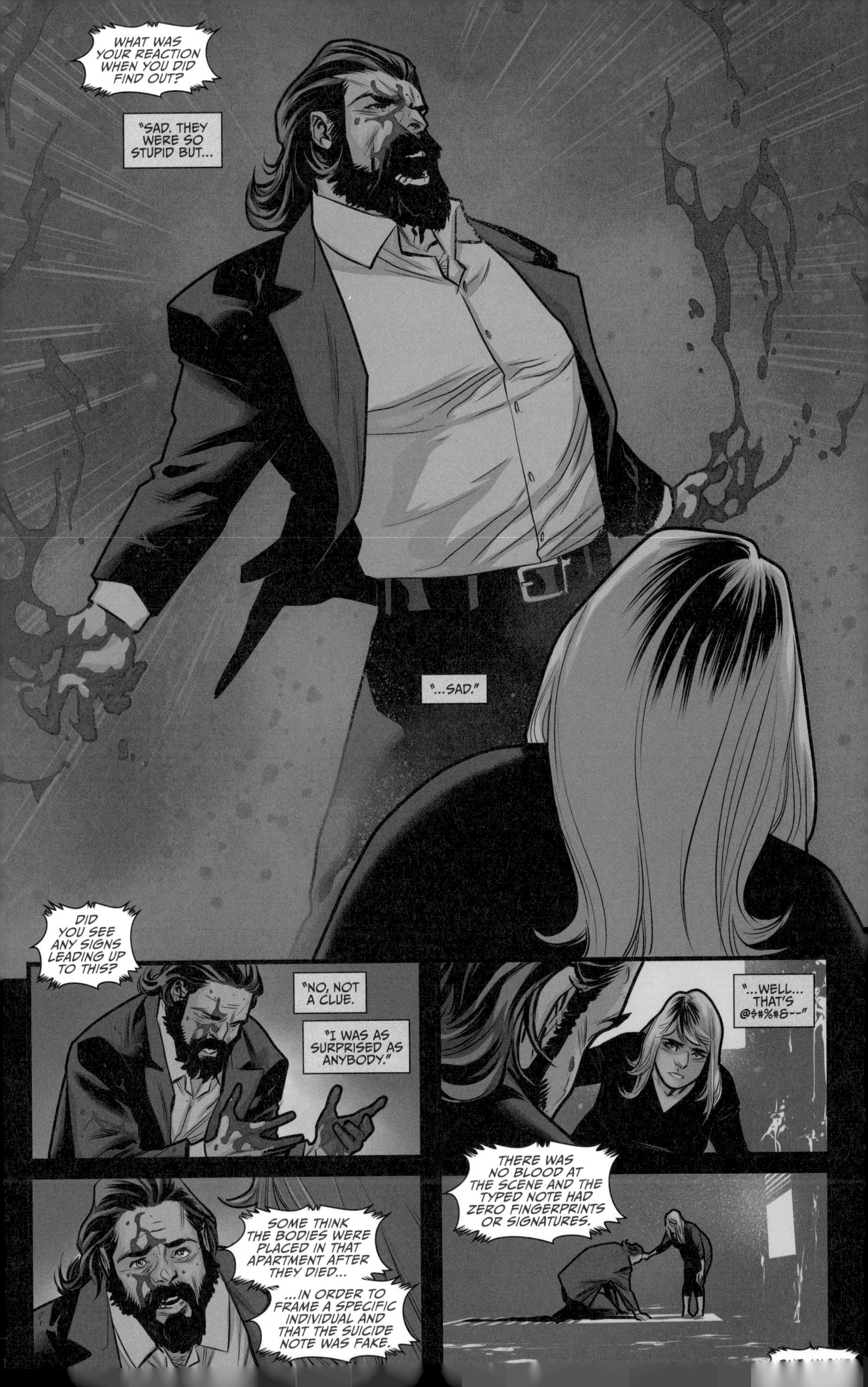
WHAT WAS YOUR REACTION WHEN YOU DID FIND OUT?
"SAD. THEY WERE SO STUPID BUT...
"...SAD."
DID YOU SEE ANY SIGNS LEADING UP TO THIS?
"NO, NOT A CLUE.
"I WAS AS SURPRISED AS ANYBODY."
"...WELL... THAT'S @$#%#&--"
SOME THINK THE BODIES WERE PLACED IN THAT APARTMENT AFTER THEY DIED...
...IN ORDER TO FRAME A SPECIFIC INDIVIDUAL AND THAT THE SUICIDE NOTE WAS FAKE.
THERE WAS NO BLOOD AT THE SCENE AND THE TYPED NOTE HAD ZERO FINGERPRINTS OR SIGNATURES.

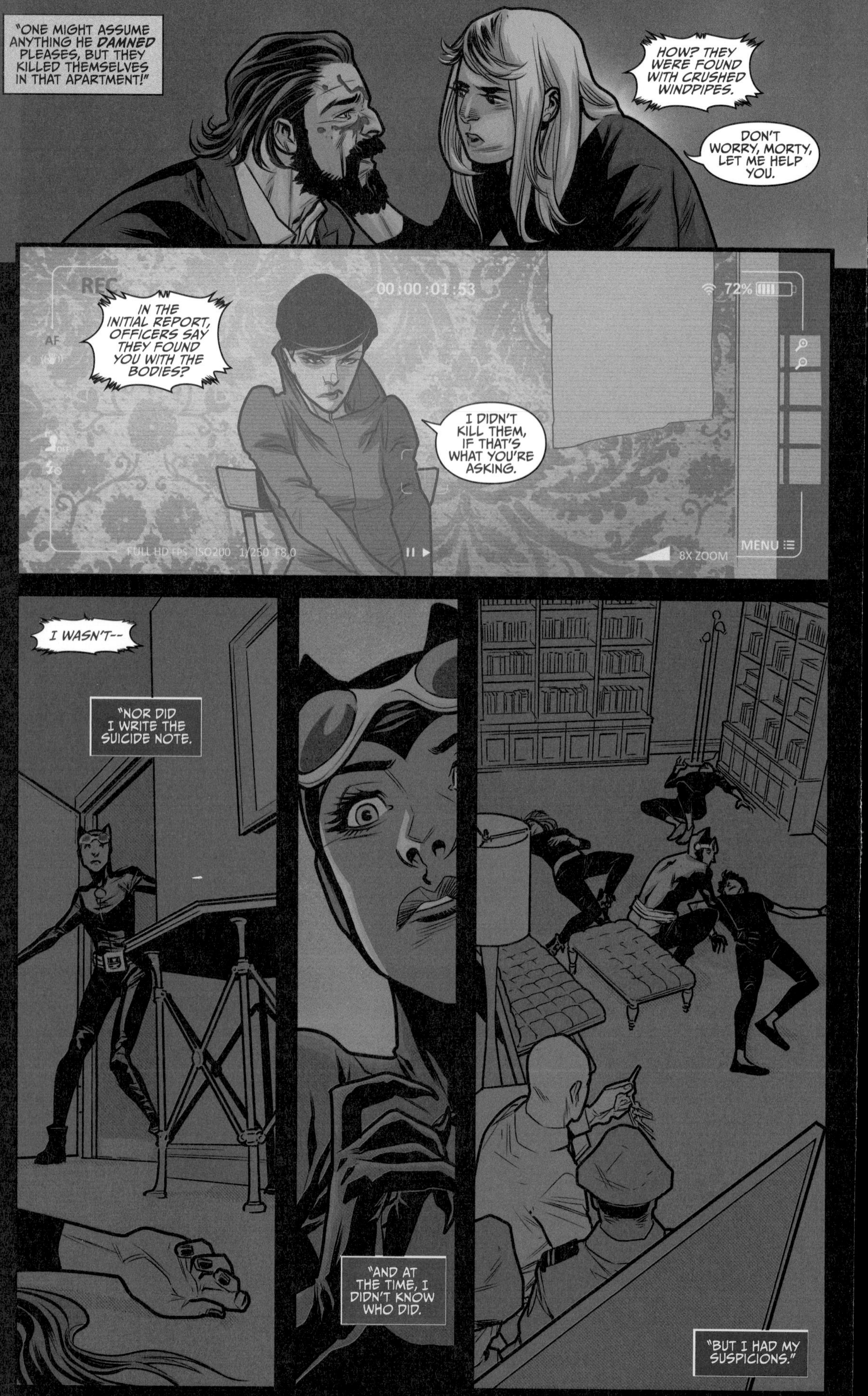
"ONE MIGHT ASSUME ANYTHING HE DAMNED PLEASES, BUT THEY KILLED THEMSELVES IN THAT APARTMENT!"
HOW? THEY WERE FOUND WITH CRUSHED WINDPIPES.
DON'T WORRY, MORTY, LET ME HELP YOU.
REC
00:00:01:53
72%
AF
IN THE INITIAL REPORT, OFFICERS SAY THEY FOUND YOU WITH THE BODIES?
I DIDN'T KILL THEM, IF THAT'S WHAT YOU'RE ASKING.
FULL HD FPS ISO200 1/250 F8.0
8X ZOOM
MENU
I WASN'T--
"NOR DID I WRITE THE SUICIDE NOTE.
"AND AT THE TIME, I DIDN'T KNOW WHO DID.
"BUT I HAD MY SUSPICIONS."

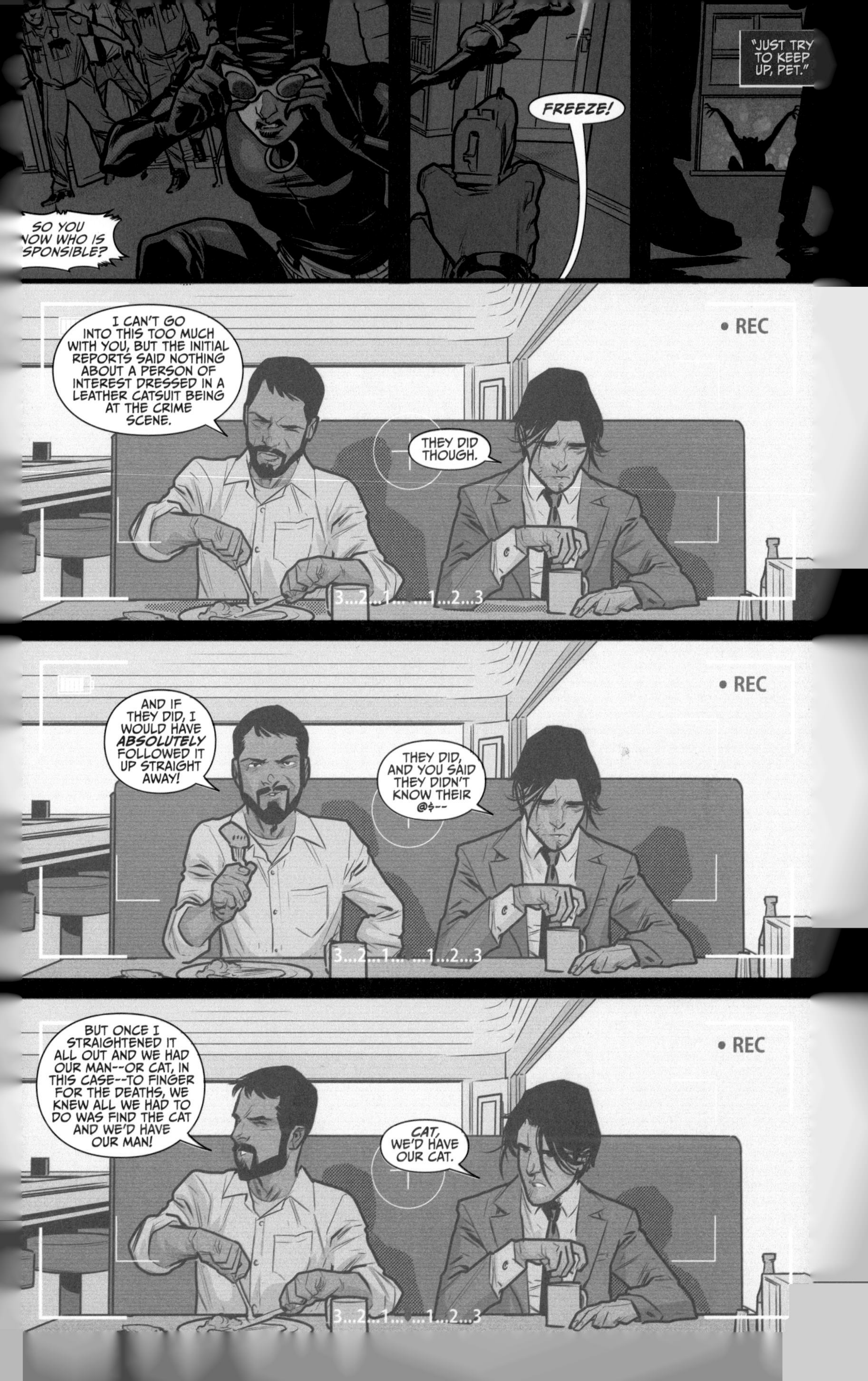
"JUST TRY TO KEEP UP, PET."
FREEZE!
SO YOU NOW WHO IS SPONSIBLE?
• REC
I CAN'T GO INTO THIS TOO MUCH WITH YOU, BUT THE INITIAL REPORTS SAID NOTHING ABOUT A PERSON OF INTEREST DRESSED IN A LEATHER CATSUIT BEING AT THE CRIME SCENE.
THEY DID THOUGH.
3...2...1... ...1...2...3
• REC
AND IF THEY DID, I WOULD HAVE ABSOLUTELY FOLLOWED IT UP STRAIGHT AWAY!
THEY DID, AND YOU SAID THEY DIDN'T KNOW THEIR @$--
3...2...1... ...1...2...3
• REC
BUT ONCE I STRAIGHTENED IT ALL OUT AND WE HAD OUR MAN--OR CAT, IN THIS CASE--TO FINGER FOR THE DEATHS, WE KNEW ALL WE HAD TO DO WAS FIND THE CAT AND WE'D HAVE OUR MAN!
CAT, WE'D HAVE OUR CAT.
3...2...1... ...1...2...3

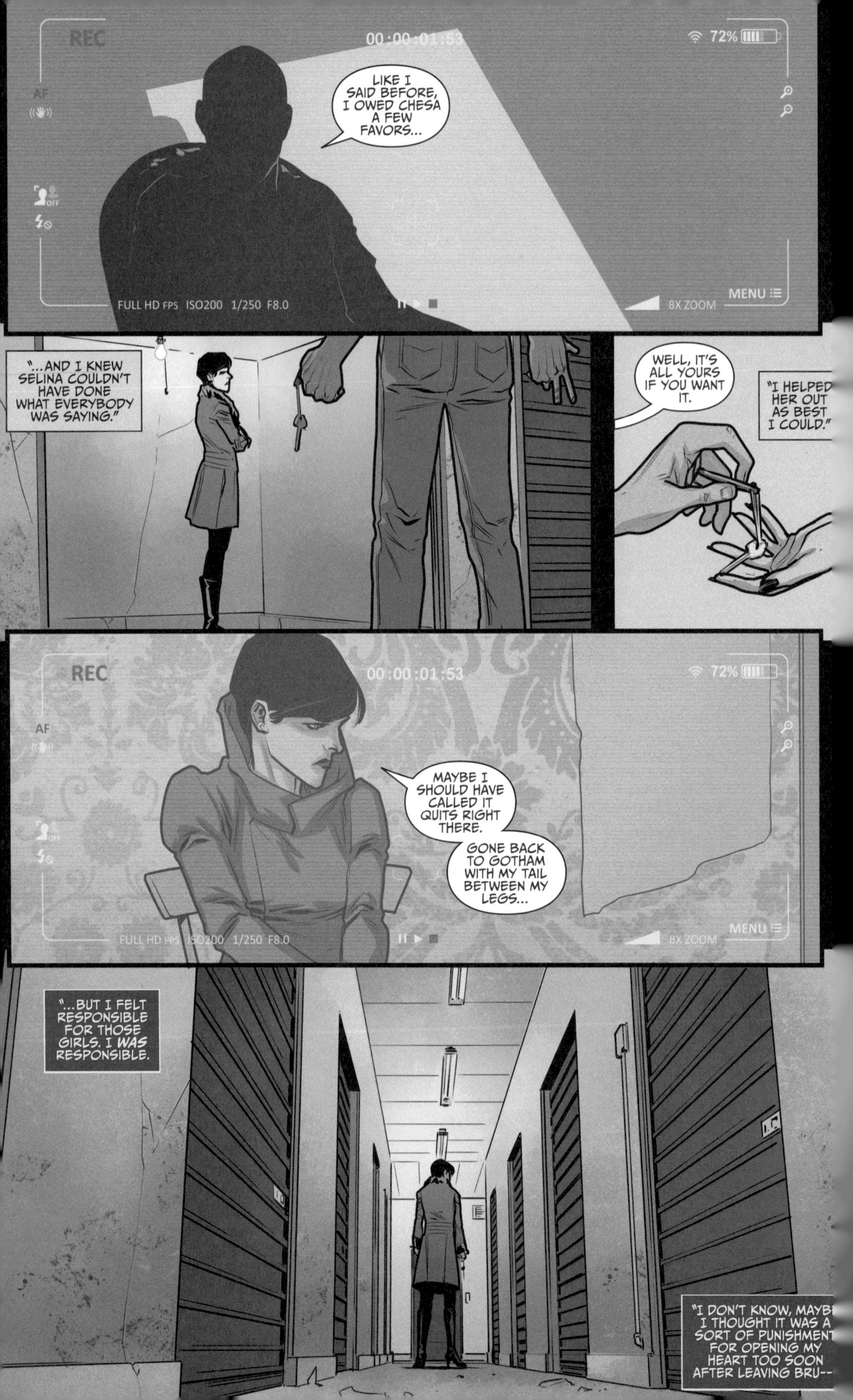
REC
00:00:01:53
72%
AF
LIKE I SAID BEFORE, I OWED CHESA A FEW FAVORS...
FULL HD FPS ISO200 1/250 F8.0
MENU
8X ZOOM
"...AND I KNEW SELINA COULDN'T HAVE DONE WHAT EVERYBODY WAS SAYING."
WELL, IT'S ALL YOURS IF YOU WANT IT.
"I HELPED HER OUT AS BEST I COULD."
REC
00:00:01:53
72%
AF
MAYBE I SHOULD HAVE CALLED IT QUITS RIGHT THERE.
GONE BACK TO GOTHAM WITH MY TAIL BETWEEN MY LEGS...
FULL HD FPS ISO200 1/250 F8.0
MENU
8X ZOOM
"...BUT I FELT RESPONSIBLE FOR THOSE GIRLS. I WAS RESPONSIBLE.
"I DON'T KNOW, MAYB I THOUGHT IT WAS A SORT OF PUNISHMENT FOR OPENING MY HEART TOO SOON AFTER LEAVING BRU--

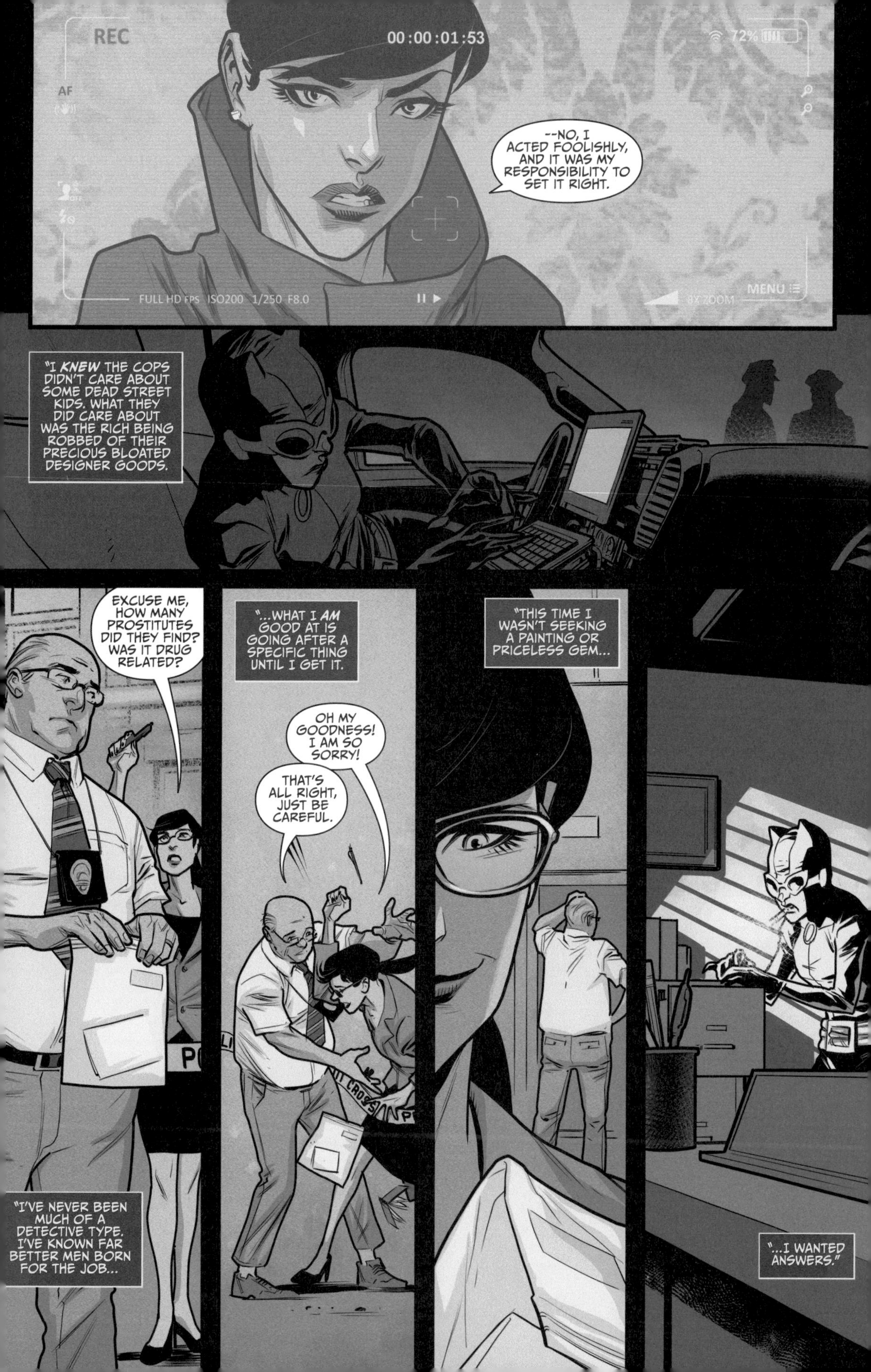
REC
00:00:01:53
72%
AF
--NO, I ACTED FOOLISHLY, AND IT WAS MY RESPONSIBILITY TO SET IT RIGHT.
FULL HD FPS ISO200 1/250 F8.0
MENU
8X ZOOM
"I *KNEW* THE COPS DIDN'T CARE ABOUT SOME DEAD STREET KIDS. WHAT THEY DID CARE ABOUT WAS THE RICH BEING ROBBED OF THEIR PRECIOUS BLOATED DESIGNER GOODS.
EXCUSE ME, HOW MANY PROSTITUTES DID THEY FIND? WAS IT DRUG RELATED?
"I'VE NEVER BEEN MUCH OF A DETECTIVE TYPE. I'VE KNOWN FAR BETTER MEN BORN FOR THE JOB...
"...WHAT I *AM* GOOD AT IS GOING AFTER A SPECIFIC THING UNTIL I GET IT.
OH MY GOODNESS! I AM SO SORRY!
THAT'S ALL RIGHT, JUST BE CAREFUL.
"THIS TIME I WASN'T SEEKING A PAINTING OR PRICELESS GEM...
"...I WANTED ANSWERS."

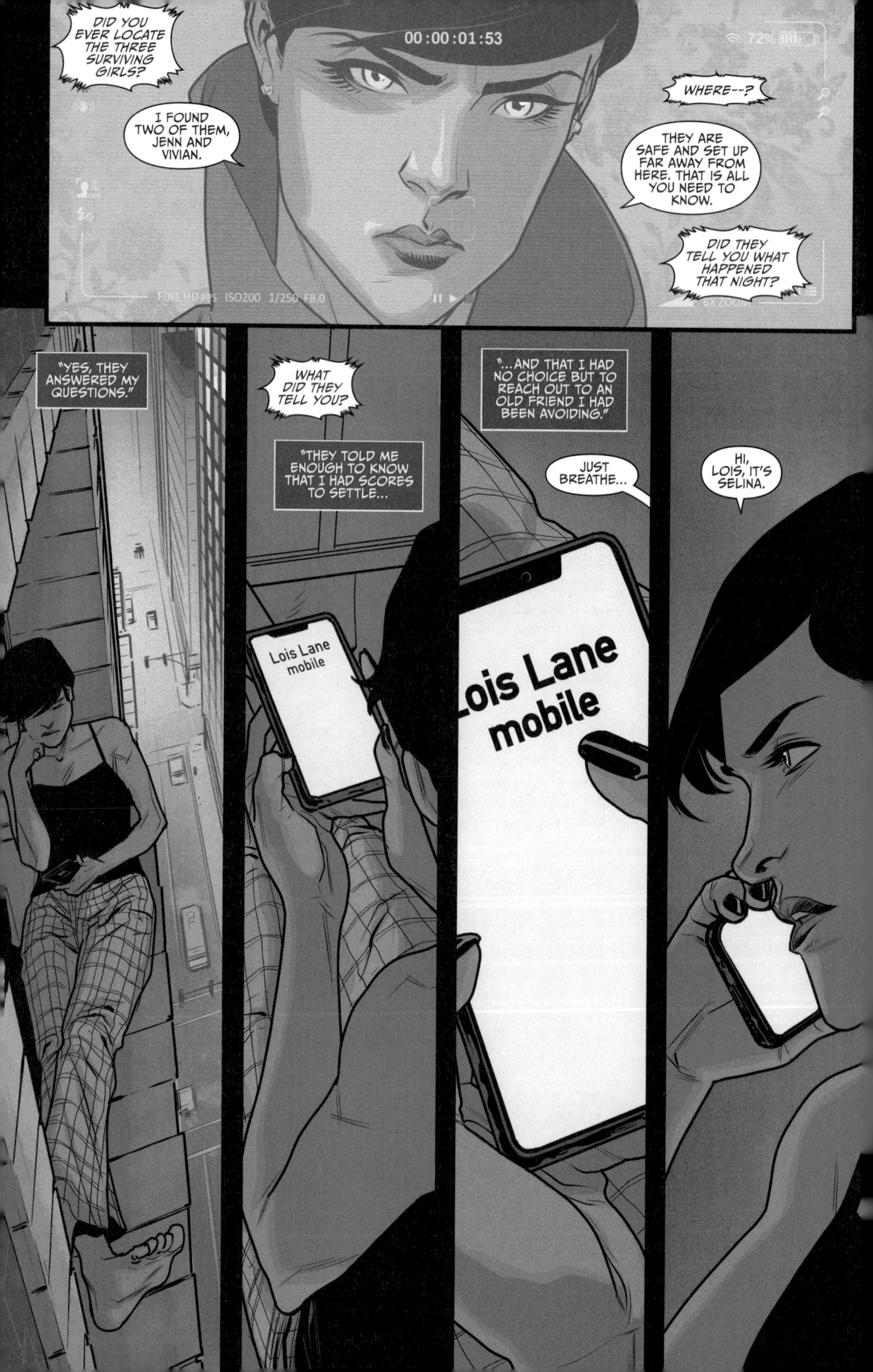
00:00:01:53
72%
DID YOU EVER LOCATE THE THREE SURVIVING GIRLS?
I FOUND TWO OF THEM, JENN AND VIVIAN.
WHERE--?
THEY ARE SAFE AND SET UP FAR AWAY FROM HERE. THAT IS ALL YOU NEED TO KNOW.
DID THEY TELL YOU WHAT HAPPENED THAT NIGHT?
FULL HD FPS ISO200 1/250 F8.0
8X ZOOM
"YES, THEY ANSWERED MY QUESTIONS."
WHAT DID THEY TELL YOU?
"THEY TOLD ME ENOUGH TO KNOW THAT I HAD SCORES TO SETTLE...
Lois Lane
mobile
"...AND THAT I HAD NO CHOICE BUT TO REACH OUT TO AN OLD FRIEND I HAD BEEN AVOIDING."
JUST BREATHE...
Lois Lane
mobile
HI, LOIS, IT'S SELINA.

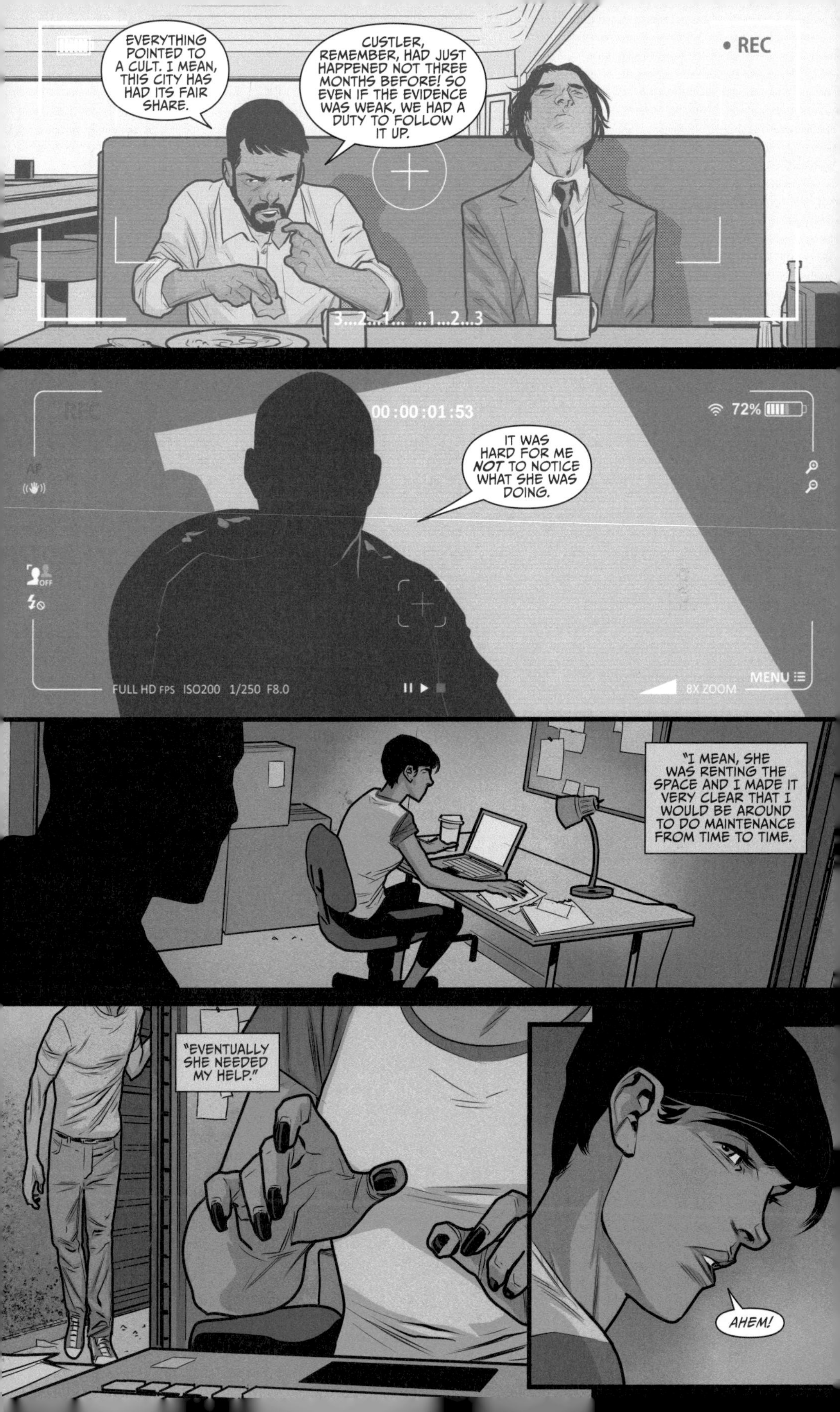

• REC
EVERYTHING POINTED TO A CULT. I MEAN, THIS CITY HAS HAD ITS FAIR SHARE.
CUSTLER, REMEMBER, HAD JUST HAPPENED NOT THREE MONTHS BEFORE! SO EVEN IF THE EVIDENCE WAS WEAK, WE HAD A DUTY TO FOLLOW IT UP.
3...2...1... ...1...2...3
00:00:01:53
72%
IT WAS HARD FOR ME *NOT* TO NOTICE WHAT SHE WAS DOING.
OFF
FULL HD FPS ISO200 1/250 F8.0
MENU
8X ZOOM
"I MEAN, SHE WAS RENTING THE SPACE AND I MADE IT VERY CLEAR THAT I WOULD BE AROUND TO DO MAINTENANCE FROM TIME TO TIME.
"EVENTUALLY SHE NEEDED MY HELP."
AHEM!

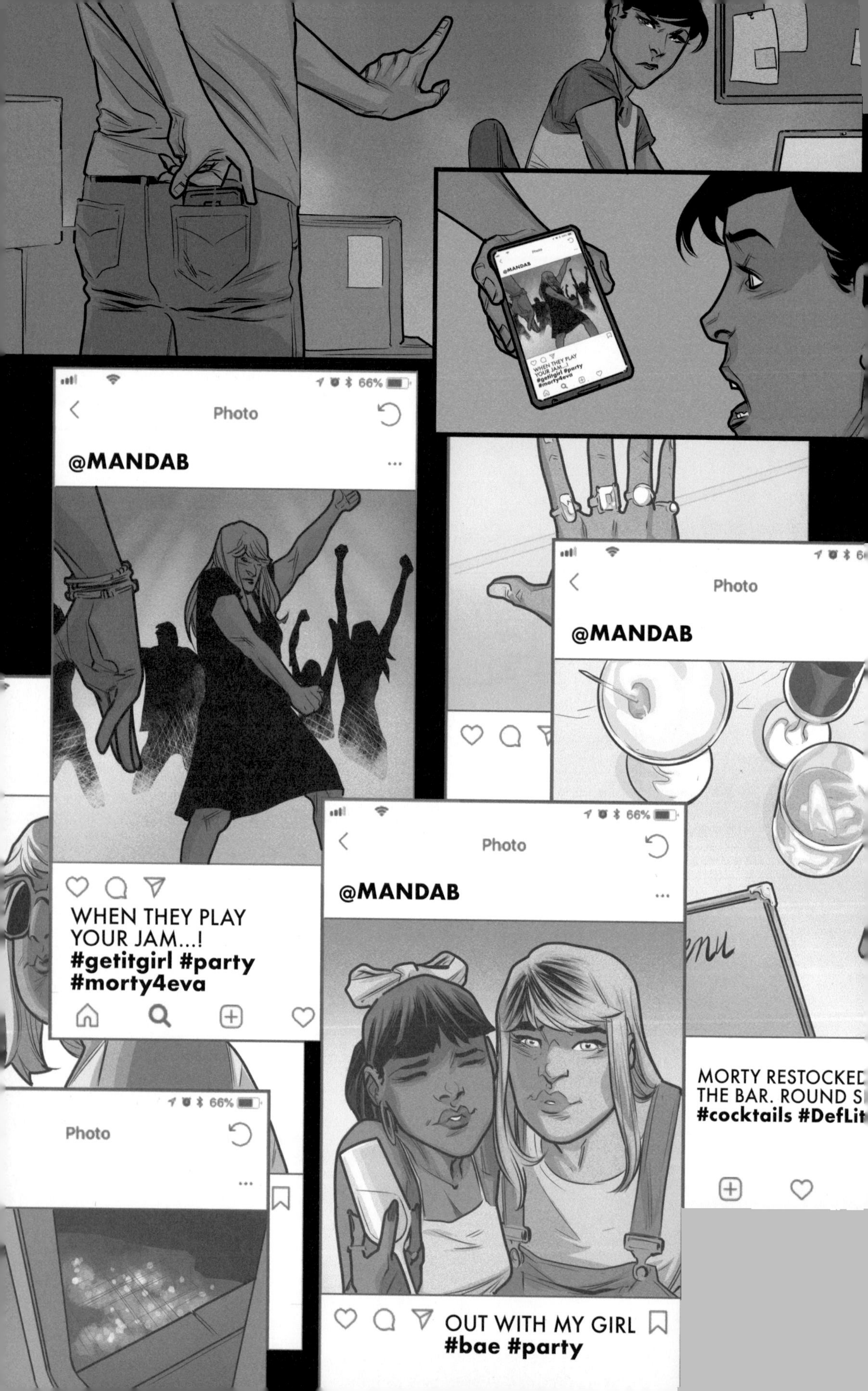
66%
Photo
@MANDAB
WHEN THEY PLAY
YOUR JAM...!
#getitgirl #party
#morty4eva
Photo
@MANDAB
66%
Photo
@MANDAB
OUT WITH MY GIRL
#bae #party
MORTY RESTOCKED
THE BAR. ROUND S
#cocktails #DefLit
66%
Photo

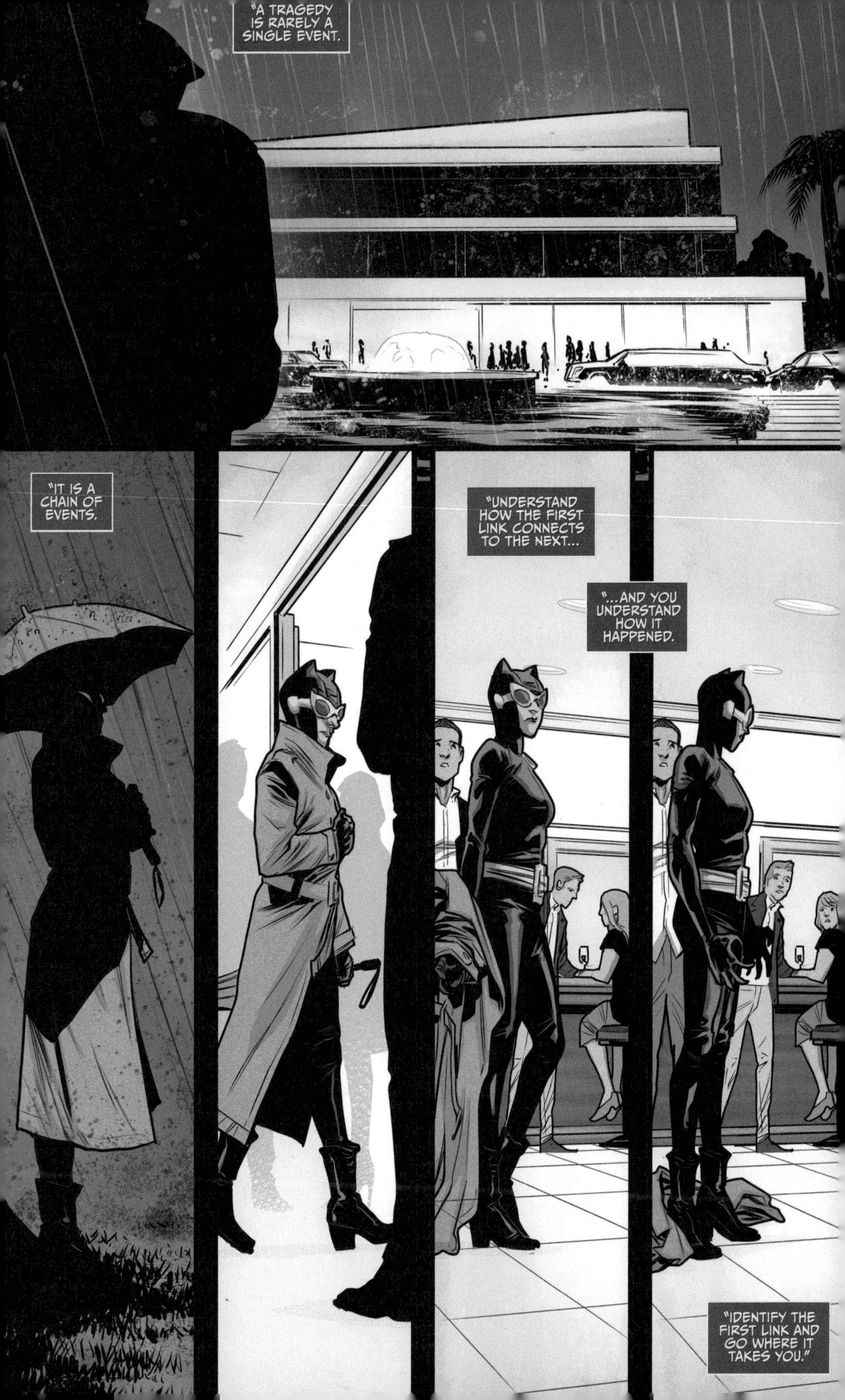
"A TRAGEDY IS RARELY A SINGLE EVENT.
"IT IS A CHAIN OF EVENTS.
"UNDERSTAND HOW THE FIRST LINK CONNECTS TO THE NEXT...
"...AND YOU UNDERSTAND HOW IT HAPPENED.
"IDENTIFY THE FIRST LINK AND GO WHERE IT TAKES YOU."

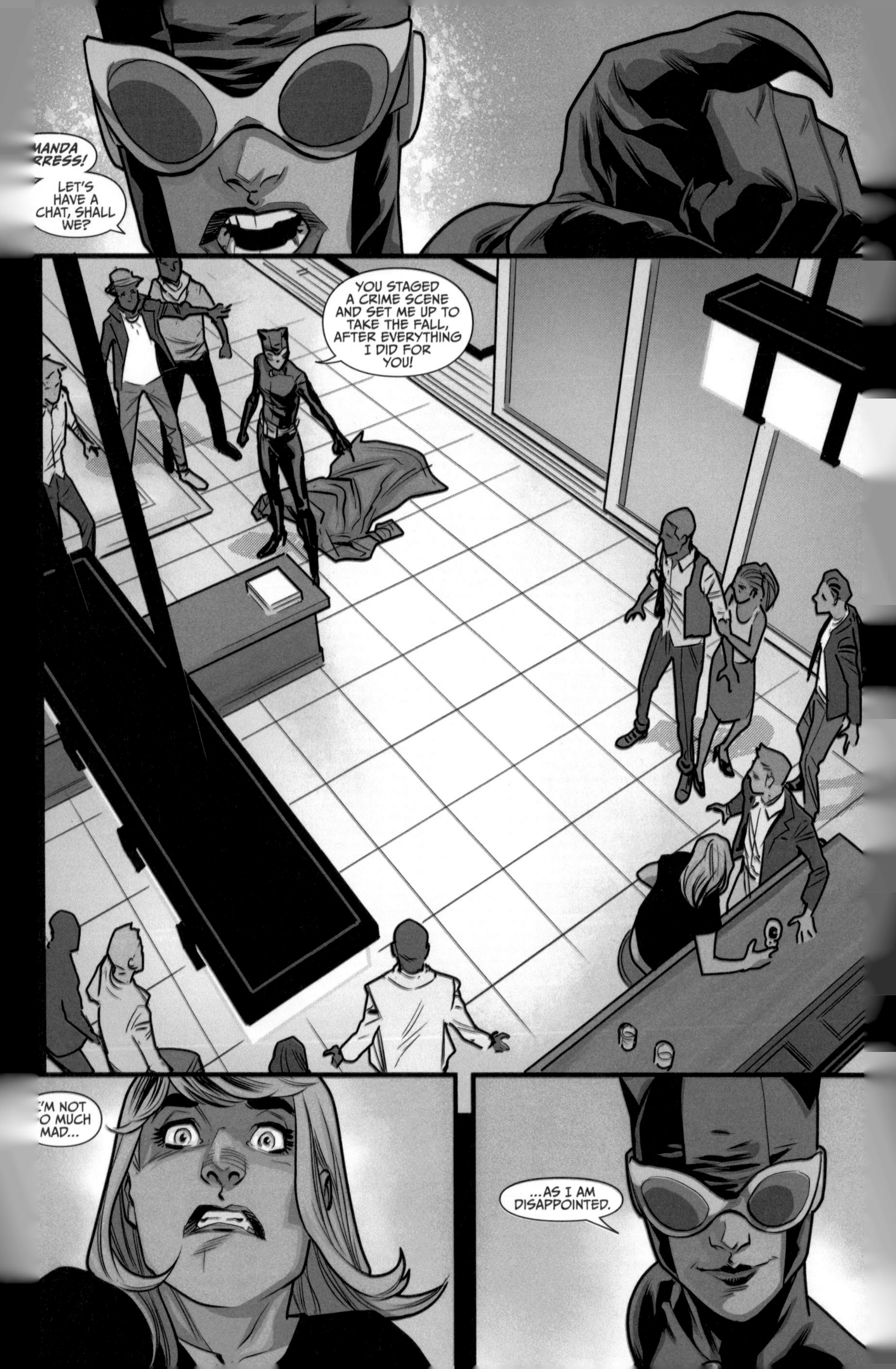
MANDA
RRESS!
LET'S HAVE A CHAT, SHALL WE?
YOU STAGED A CRIME SCENE AND SET ME UP TO TAKE THE FALL, AFTER EVERYTHING I DID FOR YOU!
'M NOT
O MUCH
MAD...
...AS I AM DISAPPOINTED.

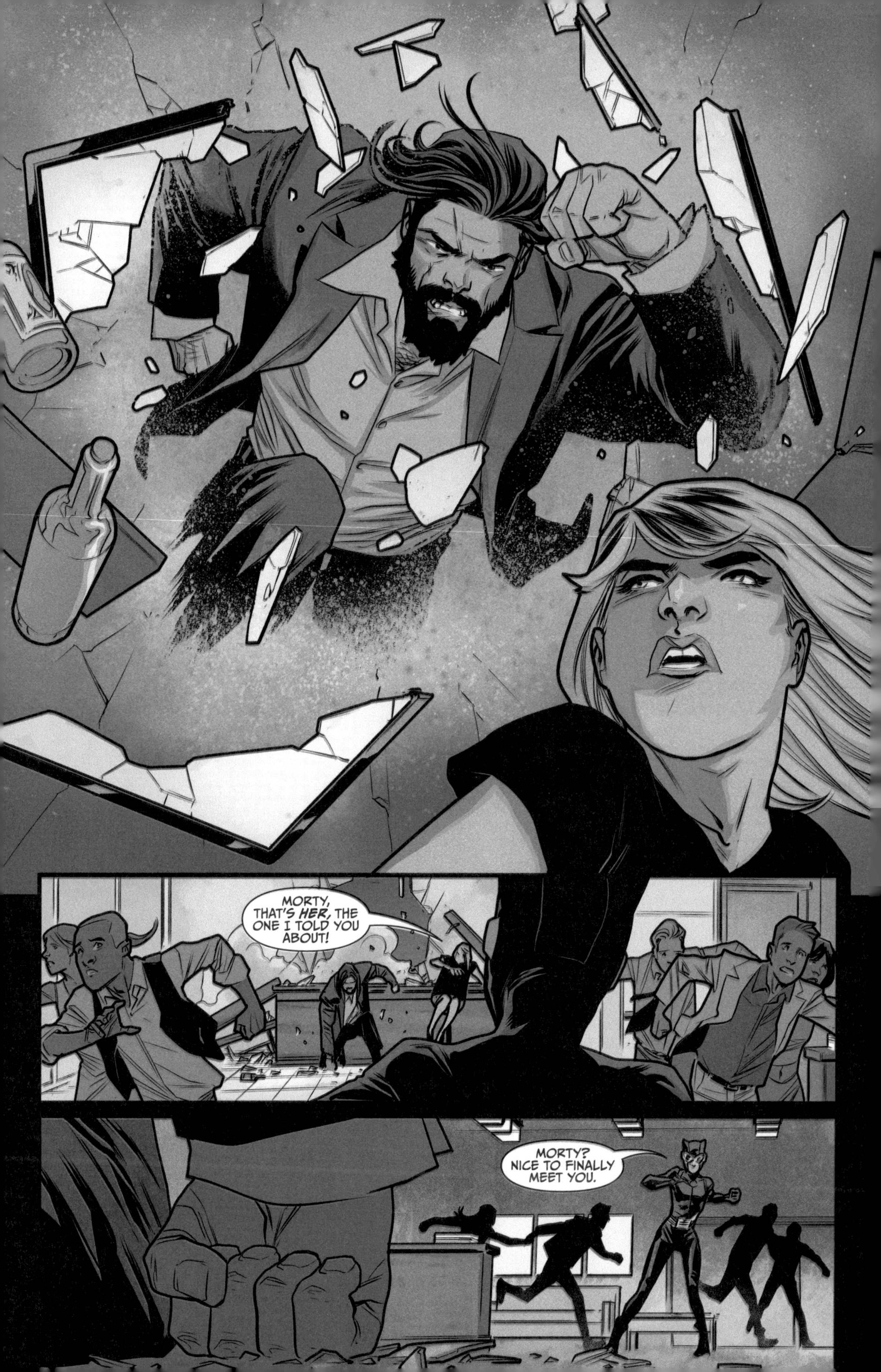
MORTY, THAT'S HER, THE ONE I TOLD YOU ABOUT!
MORTY? NICE TO FINALLY MEET YOU.

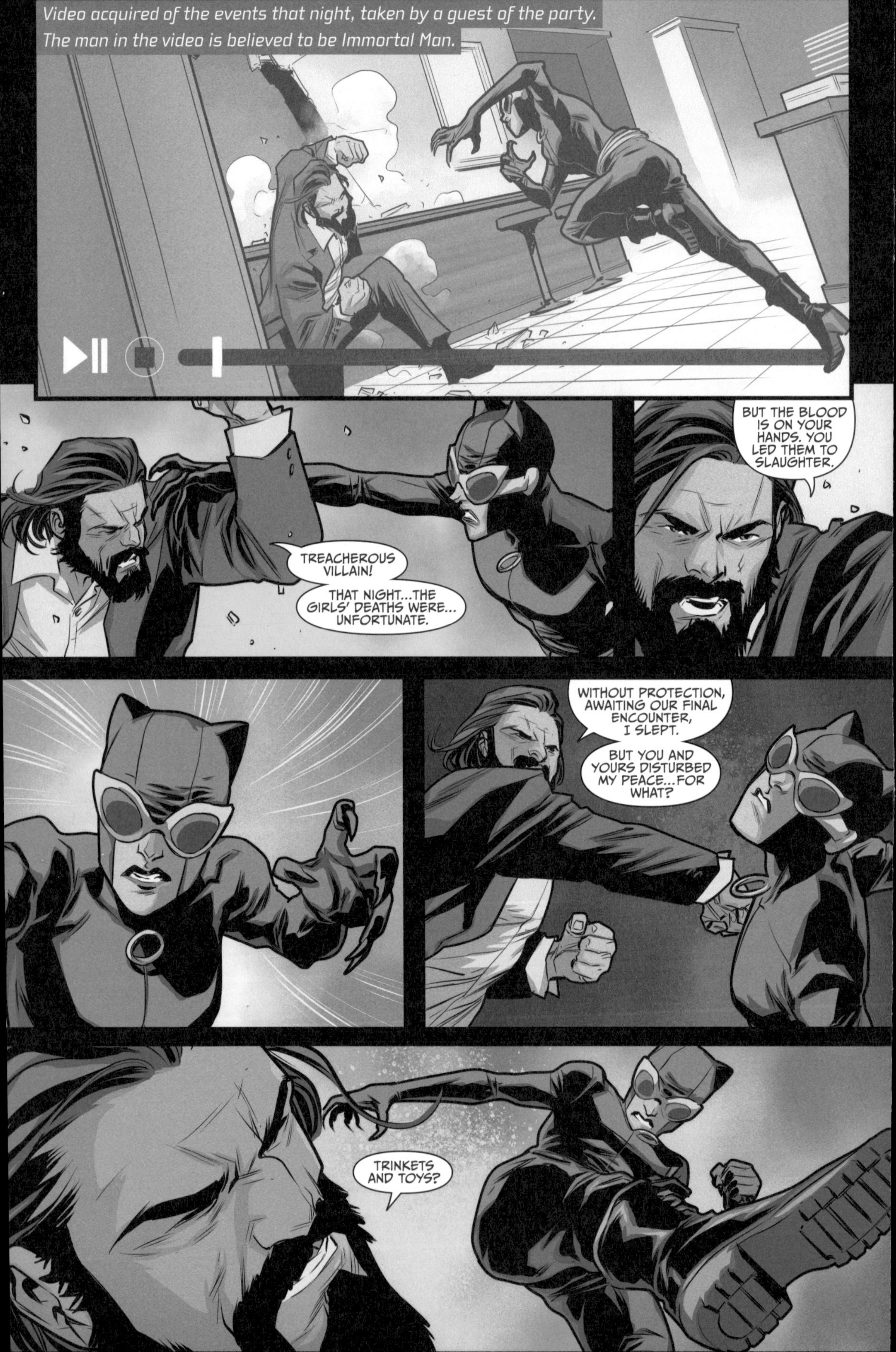
Video acquired of the events that night, taken by a guest of the party.
The man in the video is believed to be Immortal Man.
TREACHEROUS VILLAIN!
THAT NIGHT...THE GIRLS' DEATHS WERE... UNFORTUNATE.
BUT THE BLOOD IS ON YOUR HANDS. YOU LED THEM TO SLAUGHTER.
WITHOUT PROTECTION, AWAITING OUR FINAL ENCOUNTER, I SLEPT.
BUT YOU AND YOURS DISTURBED MY PEACE...FOR WHAT?
TRINKETS AND TOYS?

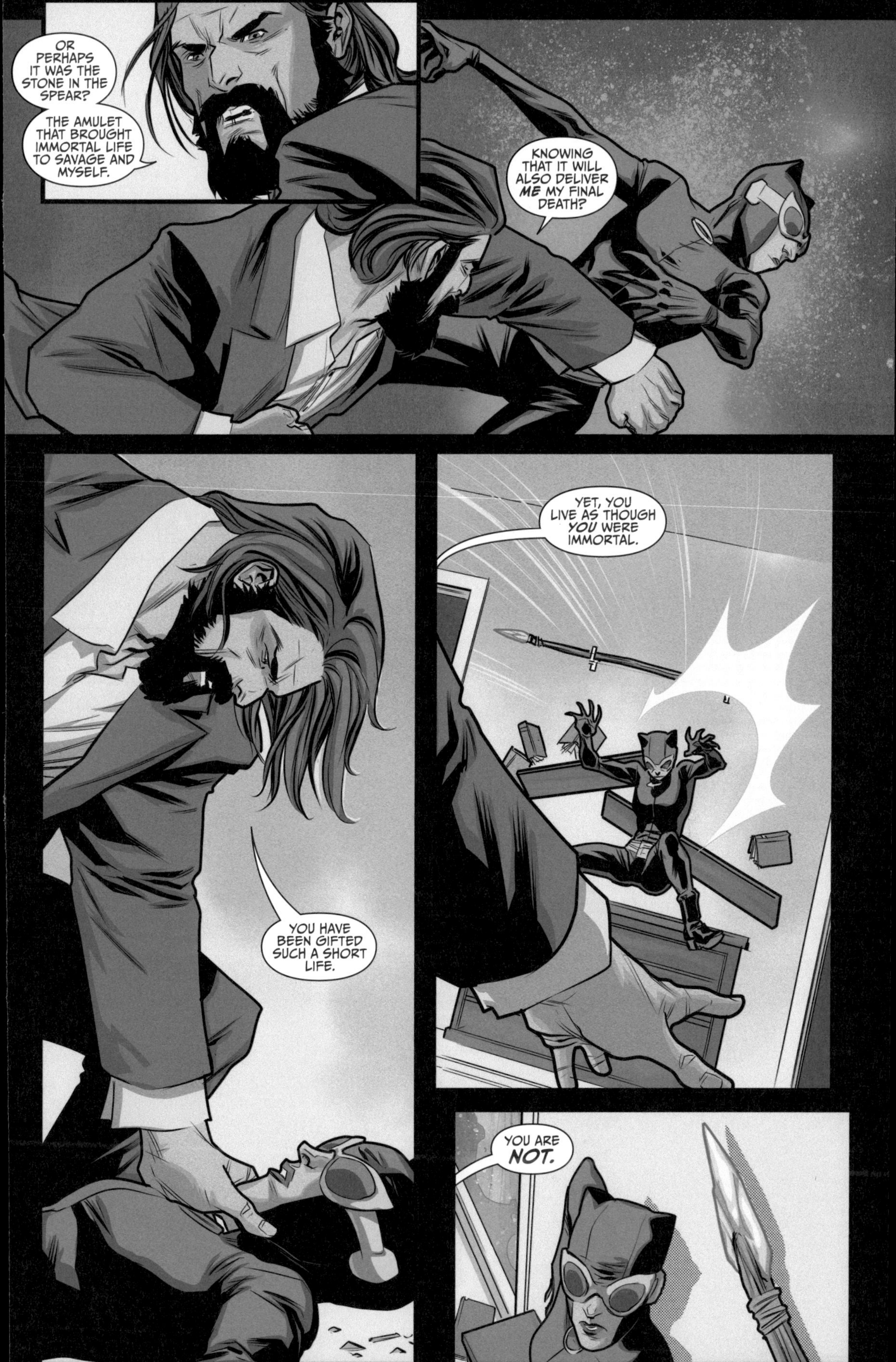
OR PERHAPS IT WAS THE STONE IN THE SPEAR?
THE AMULET THAT BROUGHT IMMORTAL LIFE TO SAVAGE AND MYSELF.
KNOWING THAT IT WILL ALSO DELIVER *ME* MY FINAL DEATH?
YOU HAVE BEEN GIFTED SUCH A SHORT LIFE.
YET, YOU LIVE AS THOUGH *YOU* WERE IMMORTAL.
YOU ARE ***NOT.***

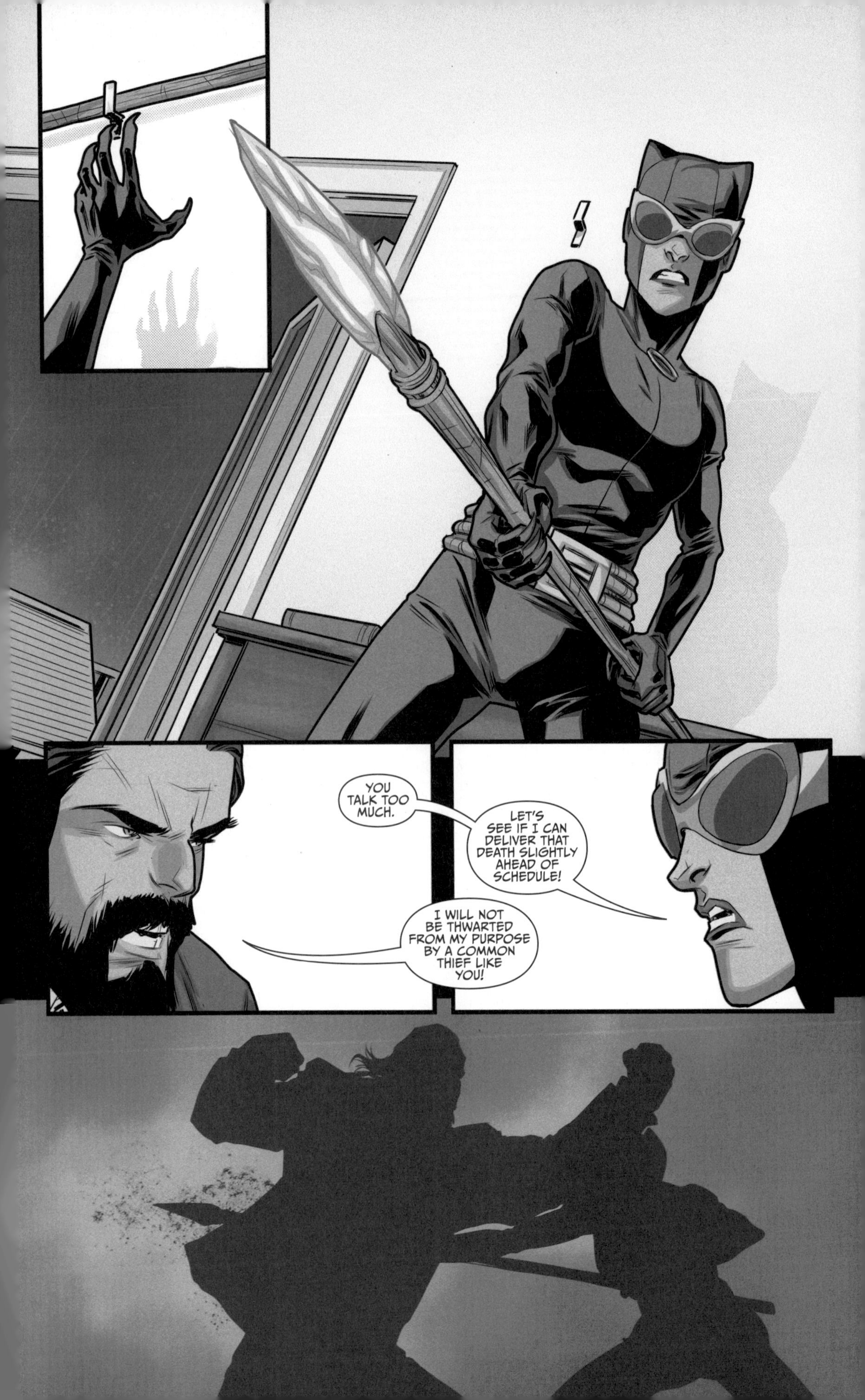
YOU TALK TOO MUCH.
LET'S SEE IF I CAN DELIVER THAT DEATH SLIGHTLY AHEAD OF SCHEDULE!
I WILL NOT BE THWARTED FROM MY PURPOSE BY A COMMON THIEF LIKE YOU!

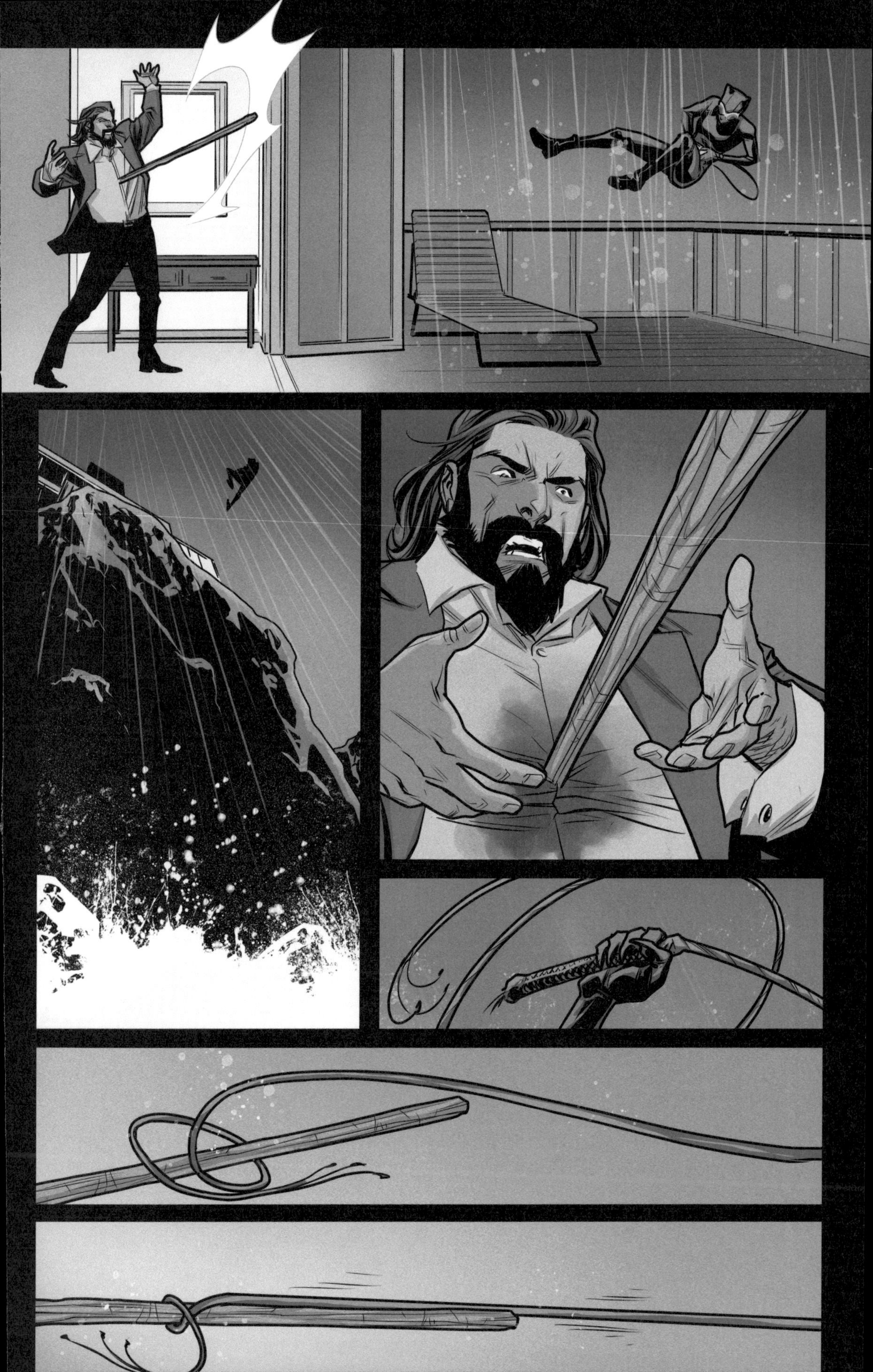

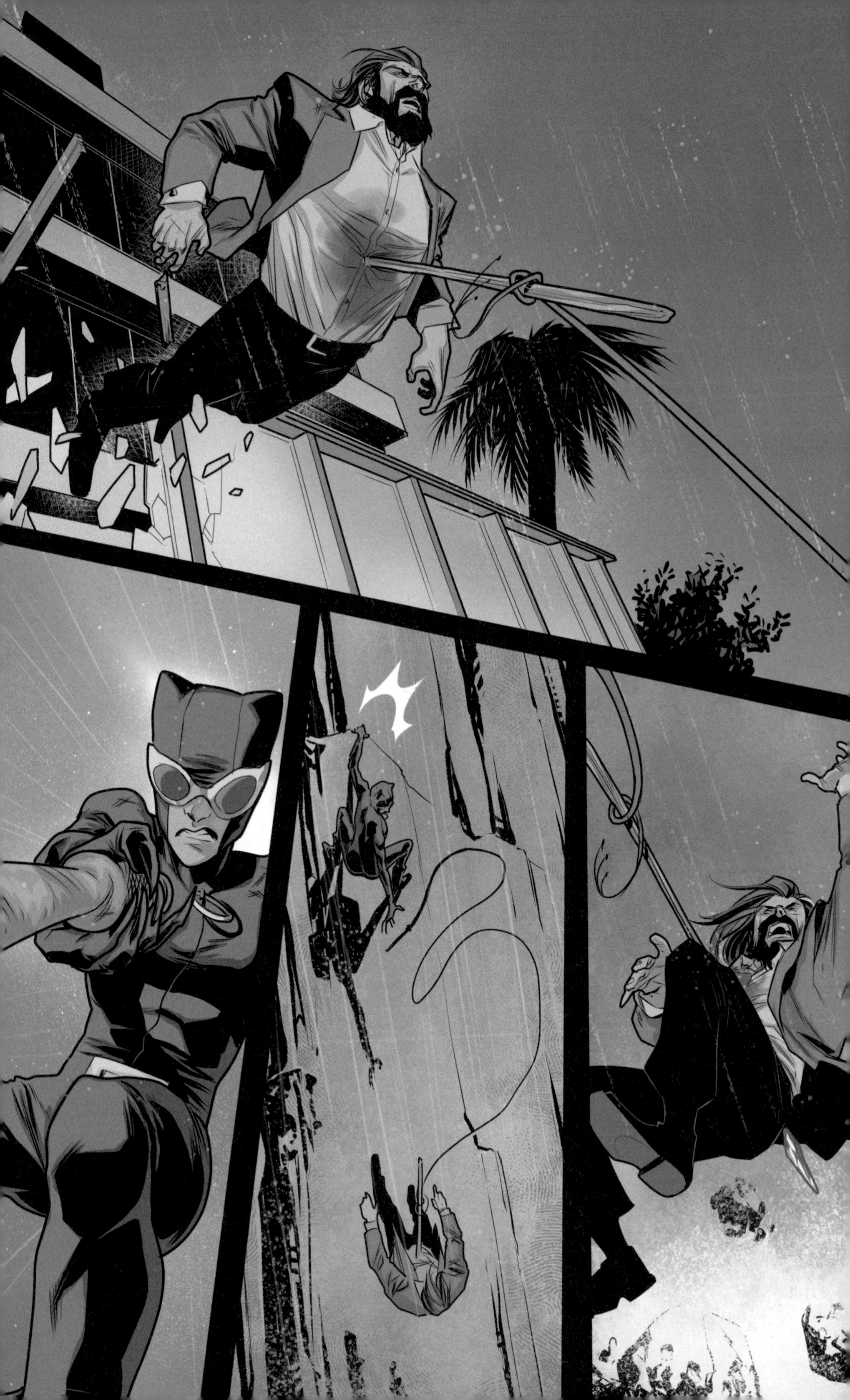

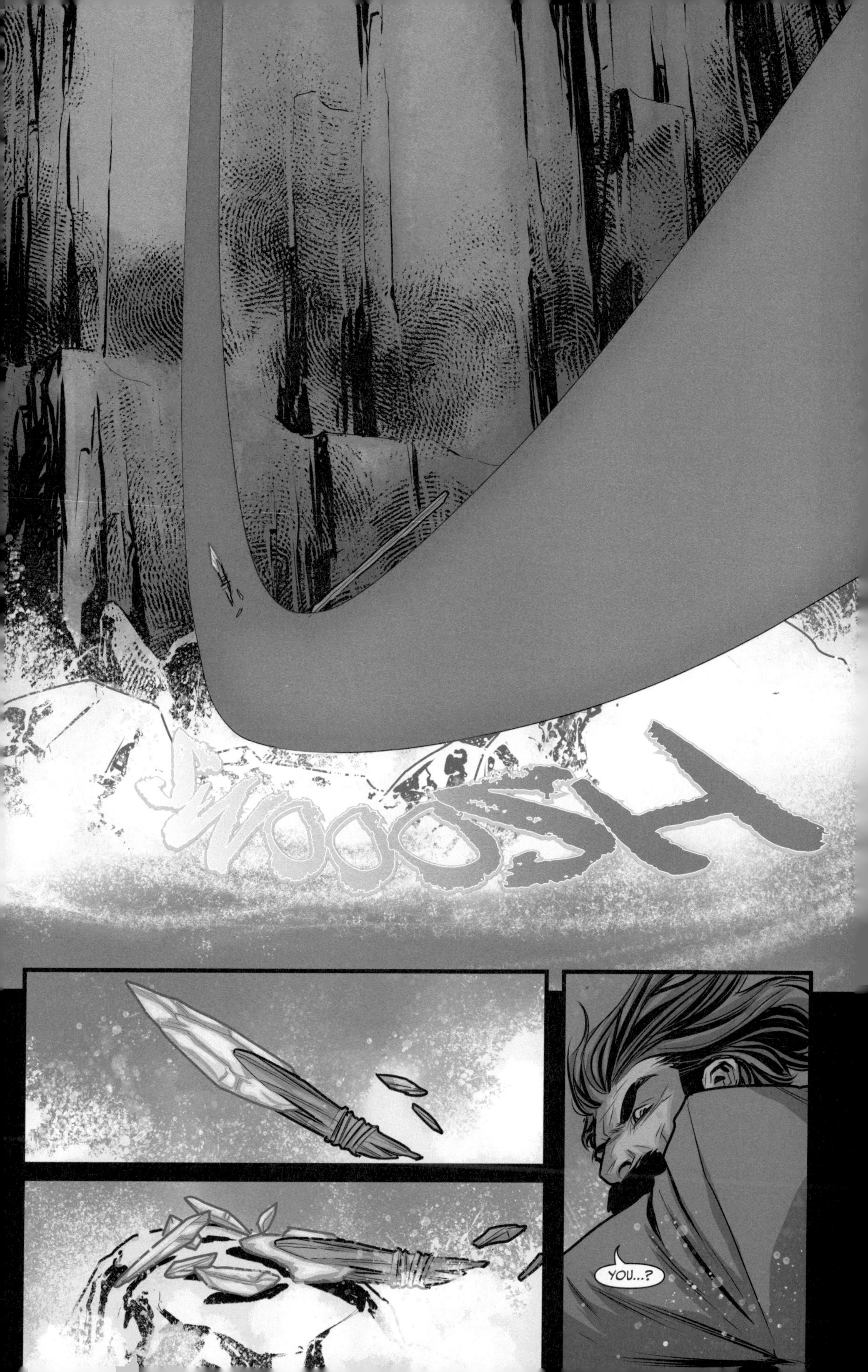
WOOOSH
YOU...?

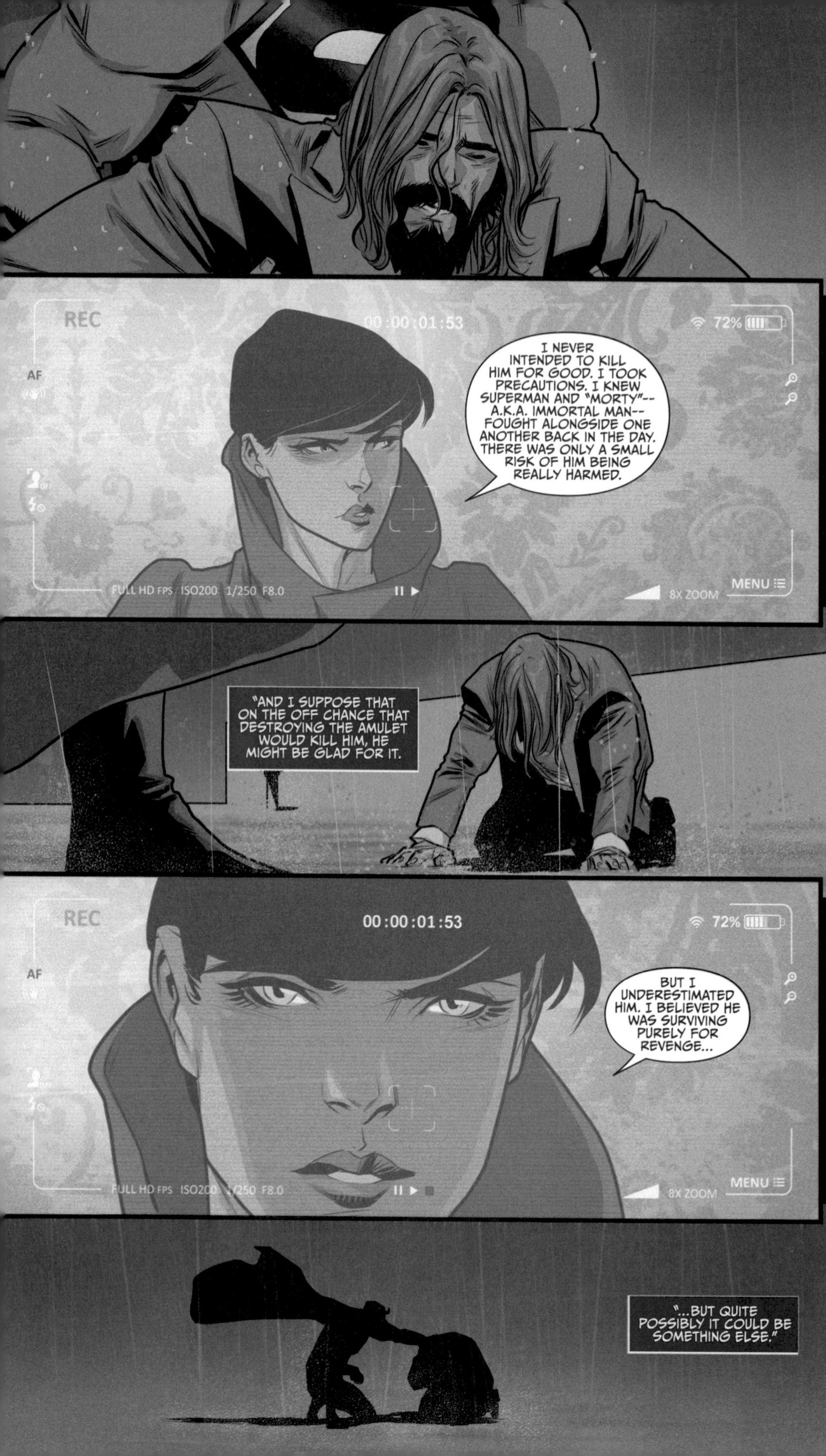
REC
00:00:01:53
72%
AF
I NEVER INTENDED TO KILL HIM FOR GOOD. I TOOK PRECAUTIONS. I KNEW SUPERMAN AND "MORTY"-- A.K.A. IMMORTAL MAN-- FOUGHT ALONGSIDE ONE ANOTHER BACK IN THE DAY. THERE WAS ONLY A SMALL RISK OF HIM BEING REALLY HARMED.
FULL HD FPS ISO200 1/250 F8.0
8X ZOOM
MENU
"AND I SUPPOSE THAT ON THE OFF CHANCE THAT DESTROYING THE AMULET WOULD KILL HIM, HE MIGHT BE GLAD FOR IT.
REC
00:00:01:53
72%
AF
BUT I UNDERESTIMATED HIM. I BELIEVED HE WAS SURVIVING PURELY FOR REVENGE...
FULL HD FPS ISO200 1/250 F8.0
8X ZOOM
MENU
"...BUT QUITE POSSIBLY IT COULD BE SOMETHING ELSE."

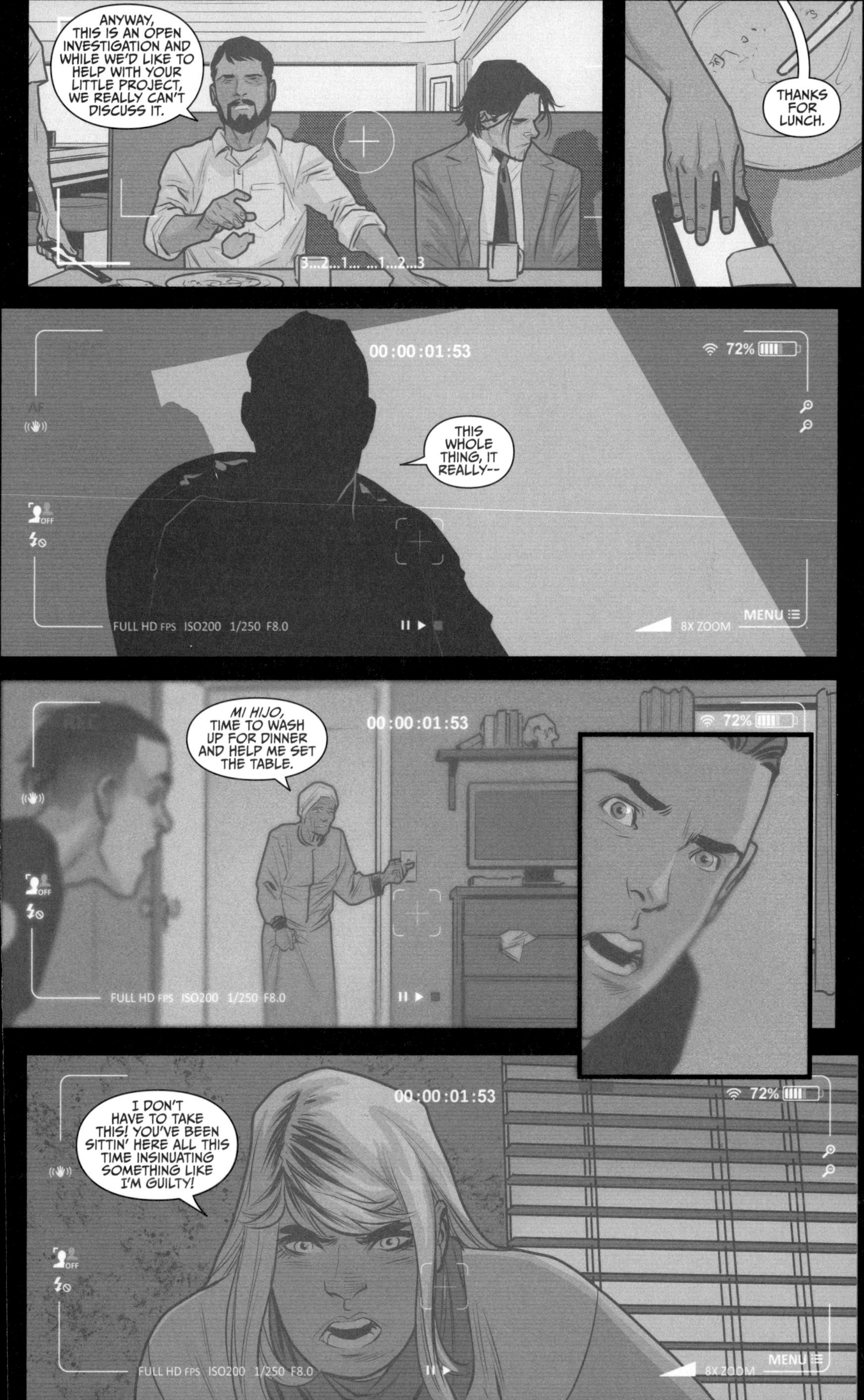
ANYWAY, THIS IS AN OPEN INVESTIGATION AND WHILE WE'D LIKE TO HELP WITH YOUR LITTLE PROJECT, WE REALLY CAN'T DISCUSS IT.
3...2...1... ...1...2...3
THANKS FOR LUNCH.
00:00:01:53
72%
THIS WHOLE THING, IT REALLY--
FULL HD FPS ISO200 1/250 F8.0
8X ZOOM
MENU
MI HIJO, TIME TO WASH UP FOR DINNER AND HELP ME SET THE TABLE.
00:00:01:53
72%
FULL HD FPS ISO200 1/250 F8.0
00:00:01:53
72%
I DON'T HAVE TO TAKE THIS! YOU'VE BEEN SITTIN' HERE ALL THIS TIME INSINUATING SOMETHING LIKE I'M GUILTY!
FULL HD FPS ISO200 1/250 F8.0
8X ZOOM
MENU

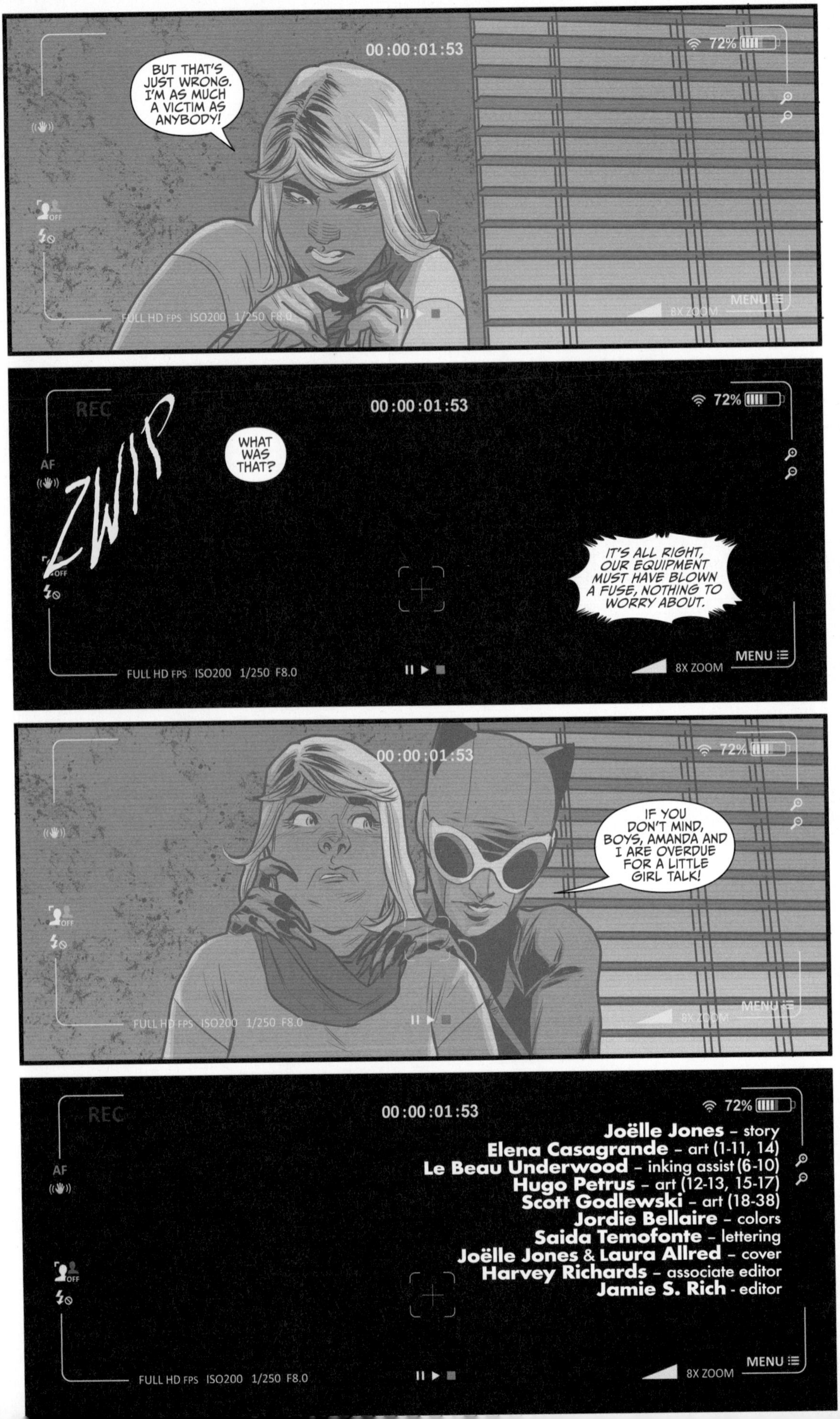
BUT THAT'S JUST WRONG. I'M AS MUCH A VICTIM AS ANYBODY!
ZWIP
WHAT WAS THAT?
IT'S ALL RIGHT, OUR EQUIPMENT MUST HAVE BLOWN A FUSE, NOTHING TO WORRY ABOUT.
IF YOU DON'T MIND, BOYS, AMANDA AND I ARE OVERDUE FOR A LITTLE GIRL TALK!
Joëlle Jones – story
Elena Casagrande – art (1-11, 14)
Le Beau Underwood – inking assist (6-10)
Hugo Petrus – art (12-13, 15-17)
Scott Godlewski – art (18-38)
Jordie Bellaire – colors
Saida Temofonte – lettering
Joëlle Jones & Laura Allred – cover
Harvey Richards – associate editor
Jamie S. Rich - editor

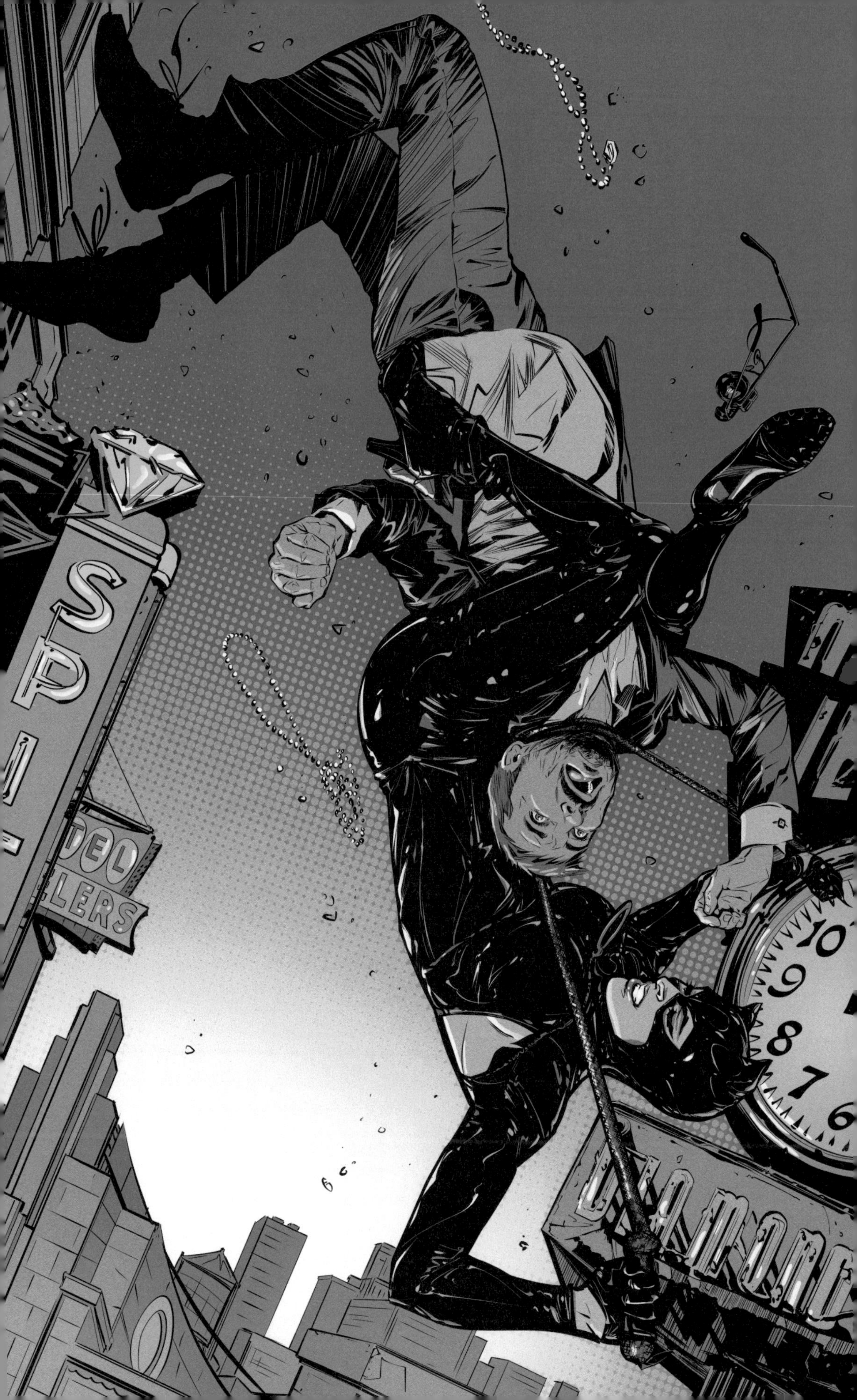

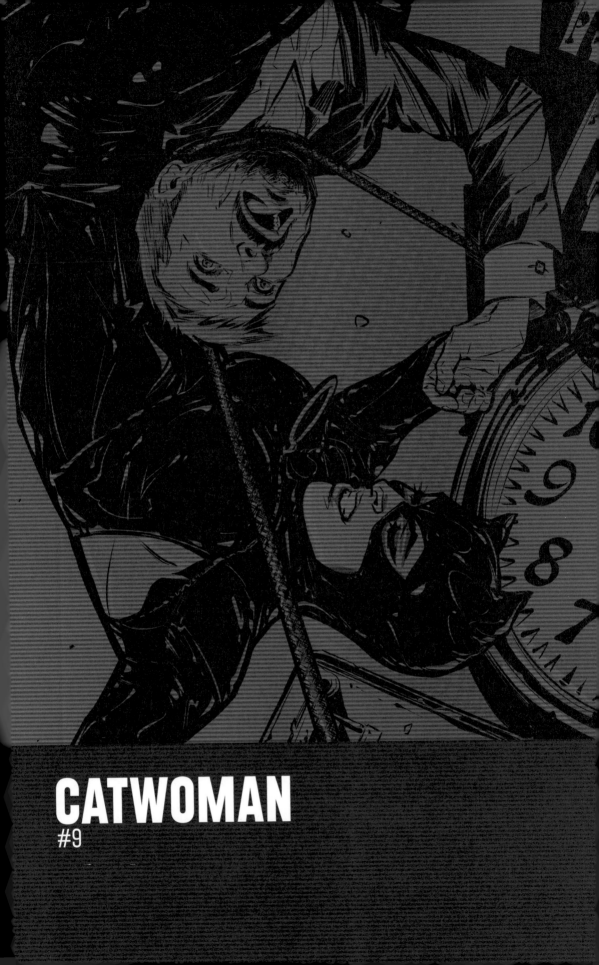

# CATWOMAN
#9

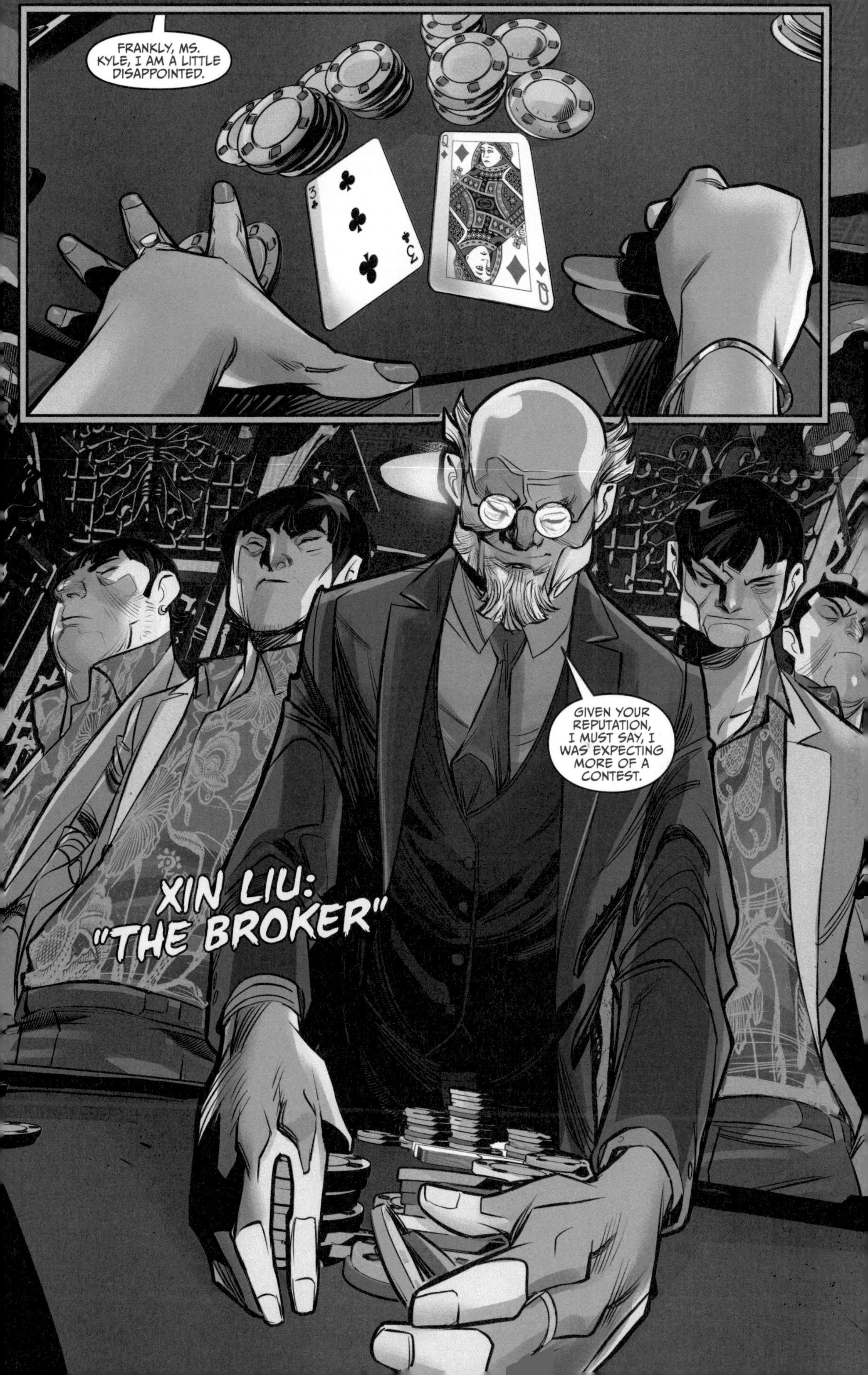
FRANKLY, MS. KYLE, I AM A LITTLE DISAPPOINTED.
GIVEN YOUR REPUTATION, I MUST SAY, I WAS EXPECTING MORE OF A CONTEST.
XIN LIU: "THE BROKER"

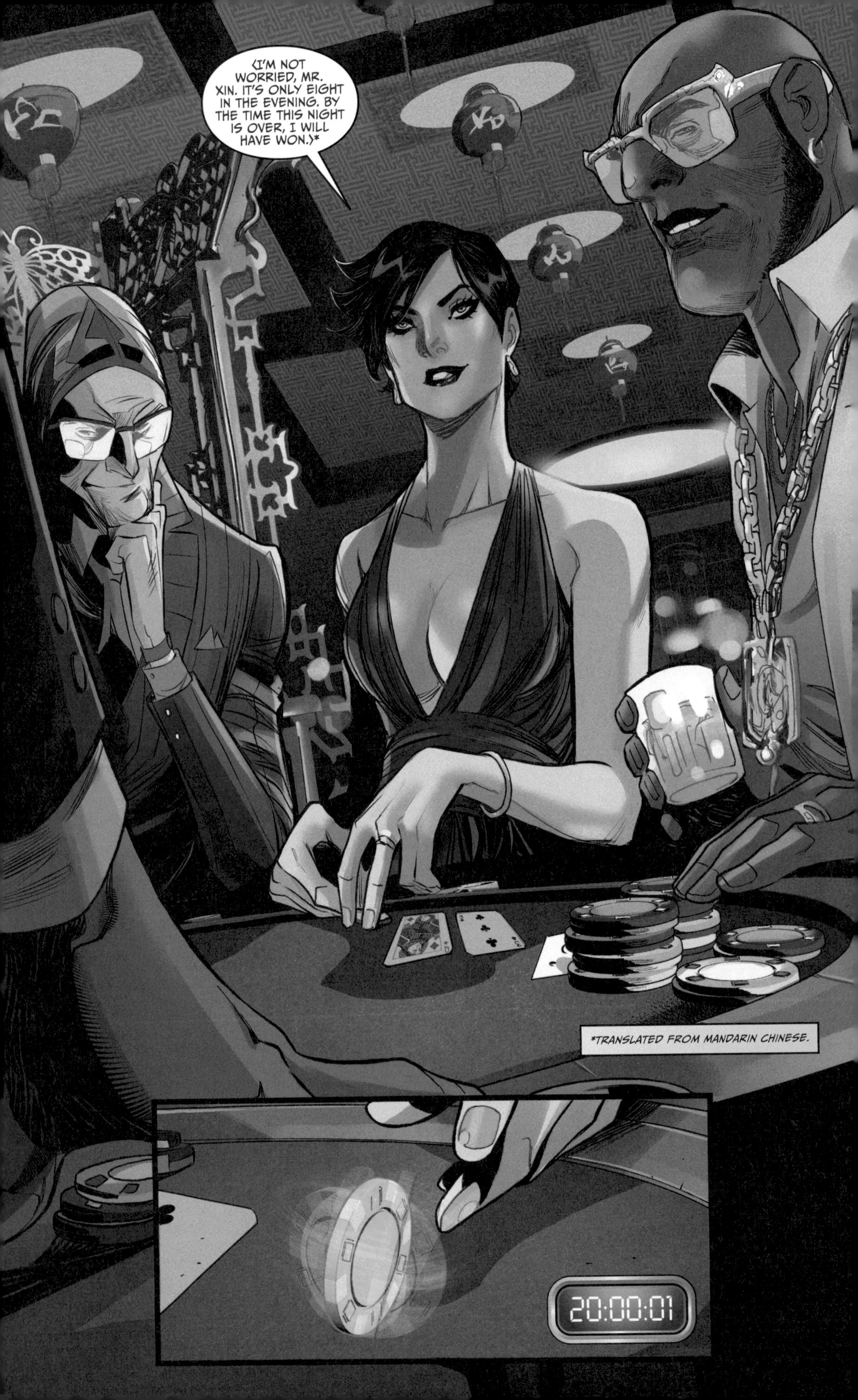
‹I'M NOT WORRIED, MR. XIN. IT'S ONLY EIGHT IN THE EVENING. BY THE TIME THIS NIGHT IS OVER, I WILL HAVE WON.›*
*TRANSLATED FROM MANDARIN CHINESE.
20:00:01

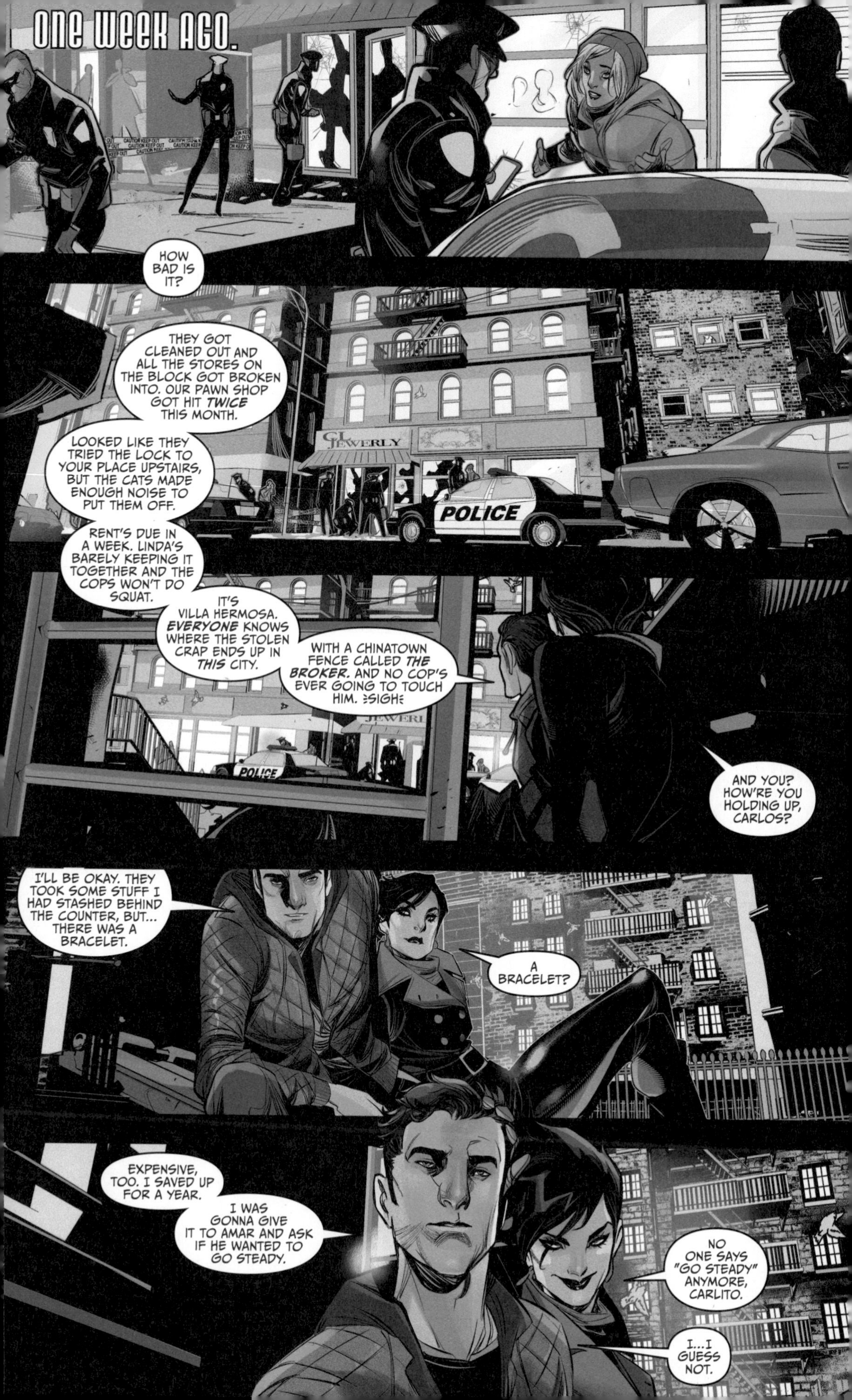
ONE WEEK AGO.
CAUTION KEEP OUT
HOW BAD IS IT?
THEY GOT CLEANED OUT AND ALL THE STORES ON THE BLOCK GOT BROKEN INTO. OUR PAWN SHOP GOT HIT TWICE THIS MONTH.
LOOKED LIKE THEY TRIED THE LOCK TO YOUR PLACE UPSTAIRS, BUT THE CATS MADE ENOUGH NOISE TO PUT THEM OFF.
CL JEWERLY
POLICE
RENT'S DUE IN A WEEK. LINDA'S BARELY KEEPING IT TOGETHER AND THE COPS WON'T DO SQUAT.
IT'S VILLA HERMOSA. EVERYONE KNOWS WHERE THE STOLEN CRAP ENDS UP IN THIS CITY.
WITH A CHINATOWN FENCE CALLED THE BROKER. AND NO COP'S EVER GOING TO TOUCH HIM. ≡SIGH≡
JEWERLY
POLICE
AND YOU? HOW'RE YOU HOLDING UP, CARLOS?
I'LL BE OKAY. THEY TOOK SOME STUFF I HAD STASHED BEHIND THE COUNTER, BUT... THERE WAS A BRACELET.
A BRACELET?
EXPENSIVE, TOO. I SAVED UP FOR A YEAR.
I WAS GONNA GIVE IT TO AMAR AND ASK IF HE WANTED TO GO STEADY.
NO ONE SAYS "GO STEADY" ANYMORE, CARLITO.
I...I GUESS NOT.

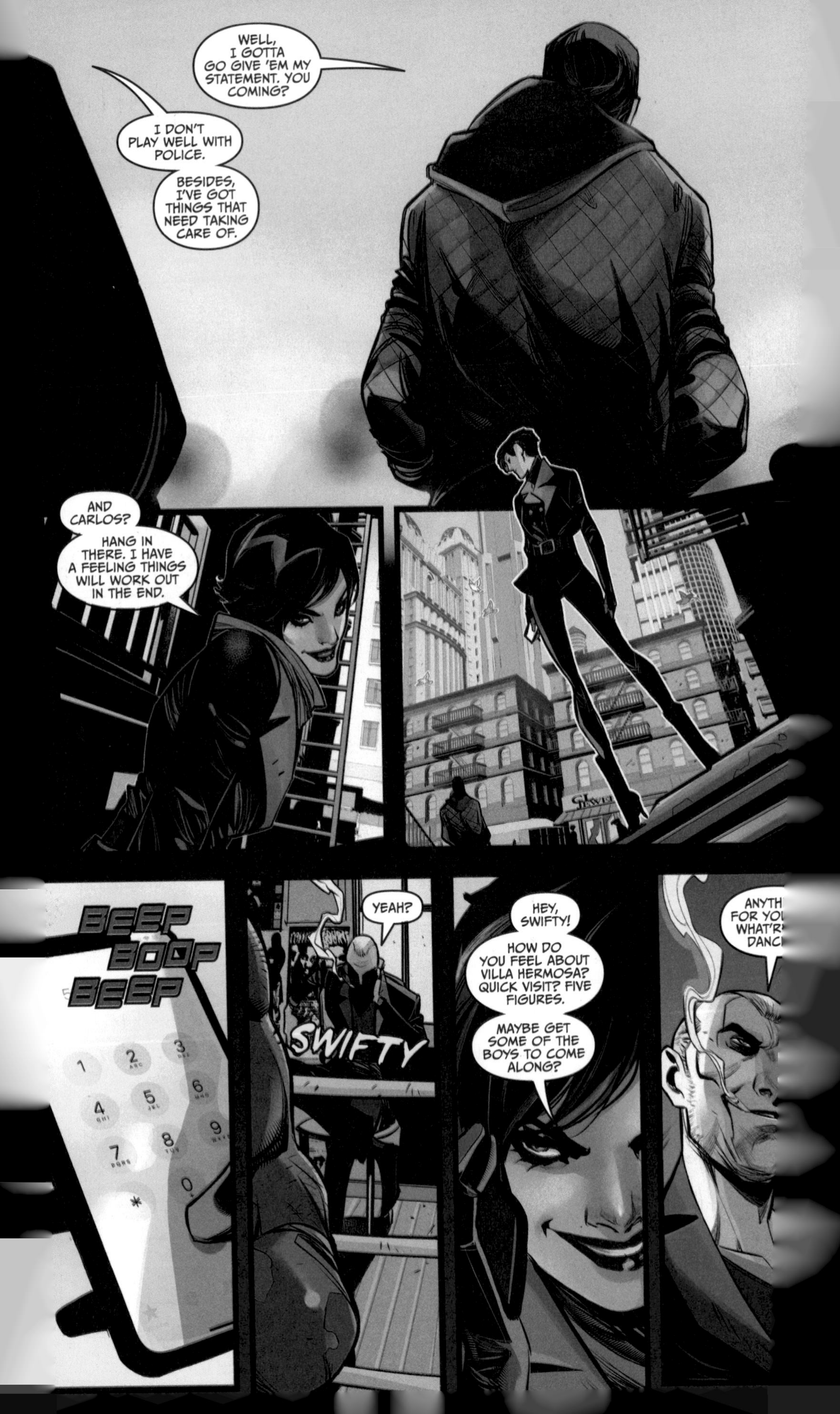
WELL, I GOTTA GO GIVE 'EM MY STATEMENT. YOU COMING?
I DON'T PLAY WELL WITH POLICE.
BESIDES, I'VE GOT THINGS THAT NEED TAKING CARE OF.
AND CARLOS?
HANG IN THERE. I HAVE A FEELING THINGS WILL WORK OUT IN THE END.
BEEP BOOP BEEP
YEAH?
SWIFTY
HEY, SWIFTY!
HOW DO YOU FEEL ABOUT VILLA HERMOSA? QUICK VISIT? FIVE FIGURES.
MAYBE GET SOME OF THE BOYS TO COME ALONG?
ANYTH
FOR YOU
WHAT'R
DANC

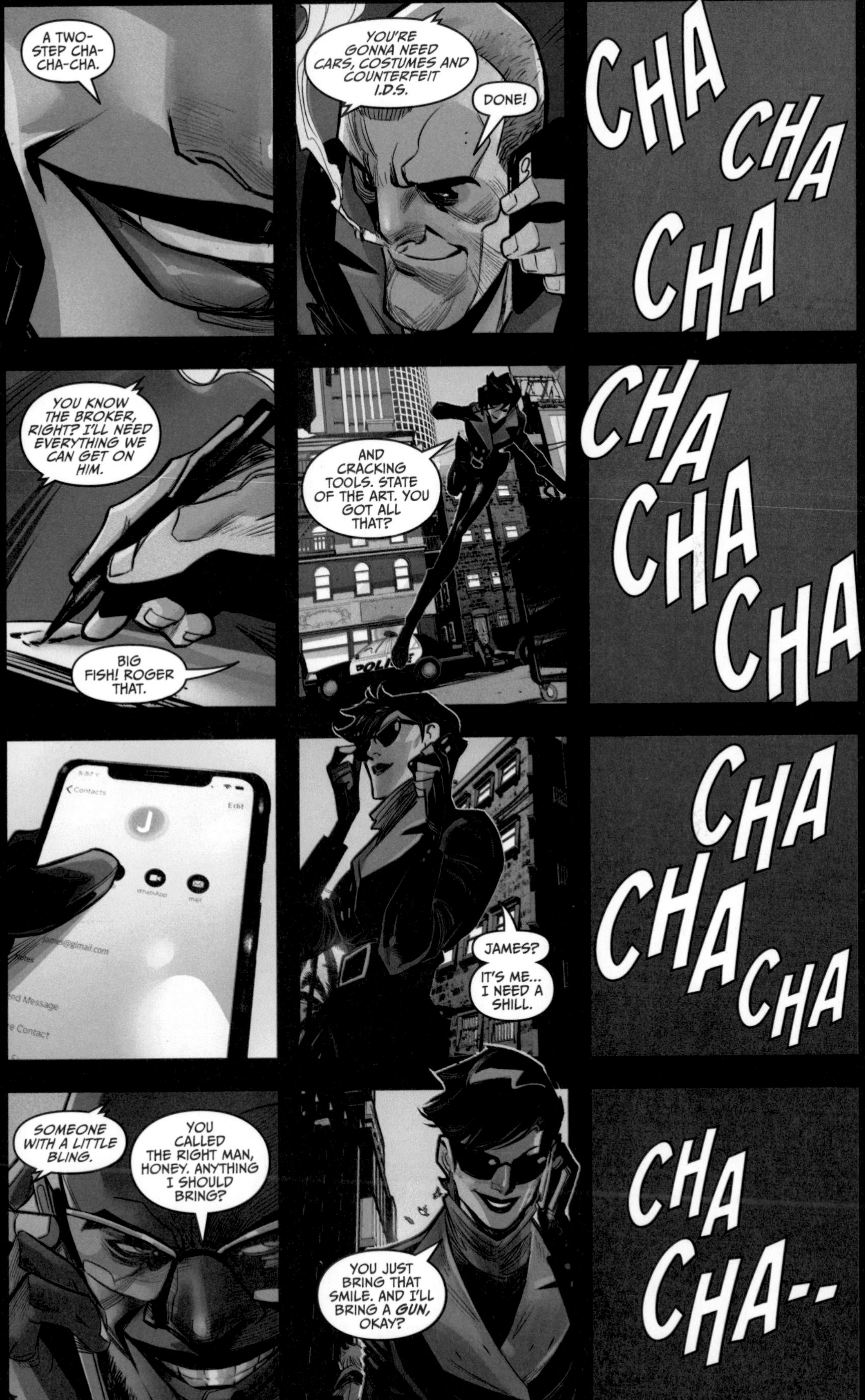
A TWO-STEP CHA-CHA-CHA.
YOU'RE GONNA NEED CARS, COSTUMES AND COUNTERFEIT I.D.S.
DONE!
CHA CHA CHA
YOU KNOW THE BROKER, RIGHT? I'LL NEED EVERYTHING WE CAN GET ON HIM.
BIG FISH! ROGER THAT.
AND CRACKING TOOLS. STATE OF THE ART. YOU GOT ALL THAT?
CHA CHA CHA
JAMES?
IT'S ME... I NEED A SHILL.
CHA CHA CHA
SOMEONE WITH A LITTLE BLING.
YOU CALLED THE RIGHT MAN, HONEY. ANYTHING I SHOULD BRING?
YOU JUST BRING THAT SMILE. AND I'LL BRING A GUN, OKAY?
CHA CHA--

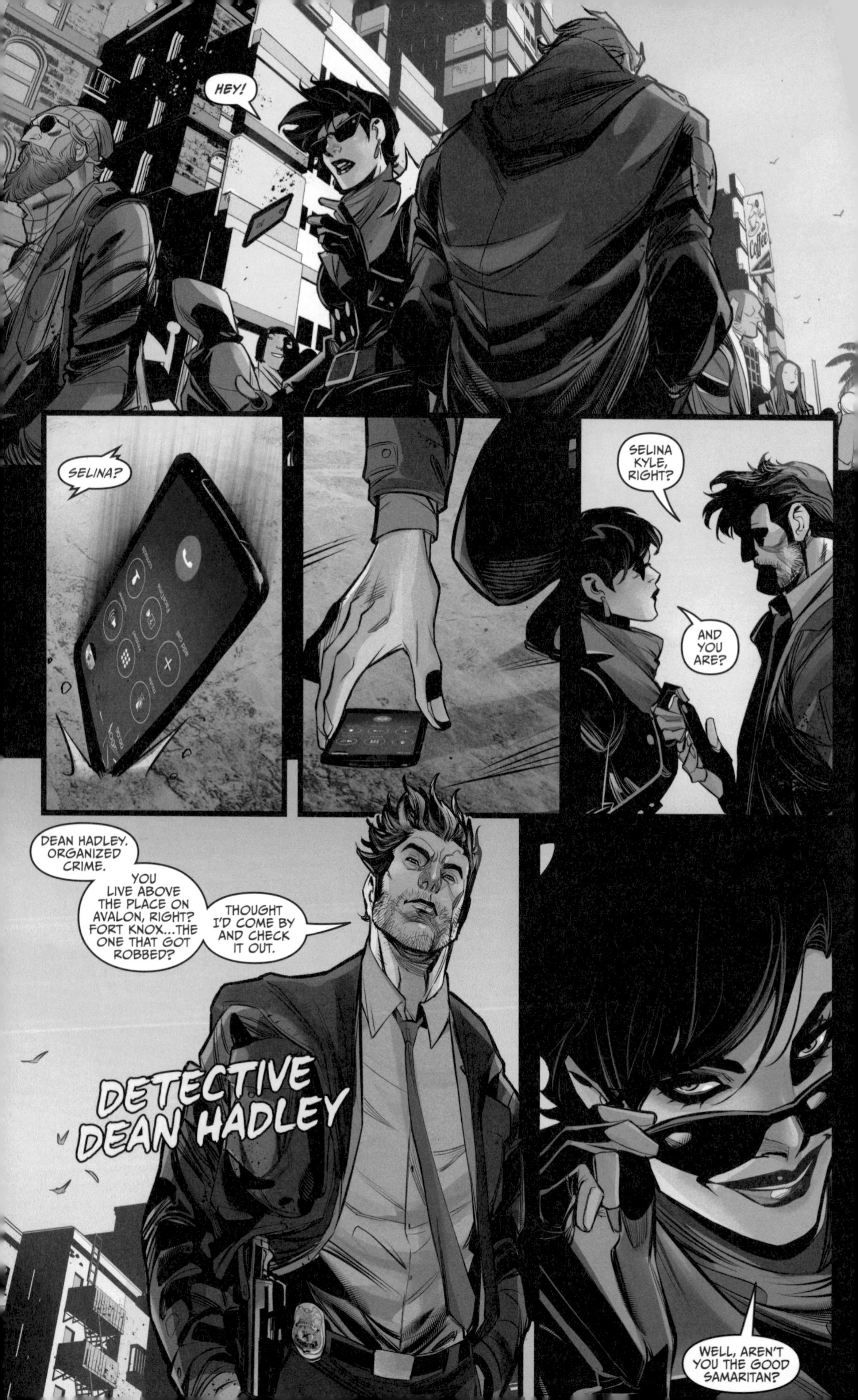
HEY!
SELINA?
SELINA KYLE, RIGHT?
AND YOU ARE?
DEAN HADLEY. ORGANIZED CRIME.
YOU LIVE ABOVE THE PLACE ON AVALON, RIGHT? FORT KNOX...THE ONE THAT GOT ROBBED?
THOUGHT I'D COME BY AND CHECK IT OUT.
DETECTIVE DEAN HADLEY
WELL, AREN'T YOU THE GOOD SAMARITAN?

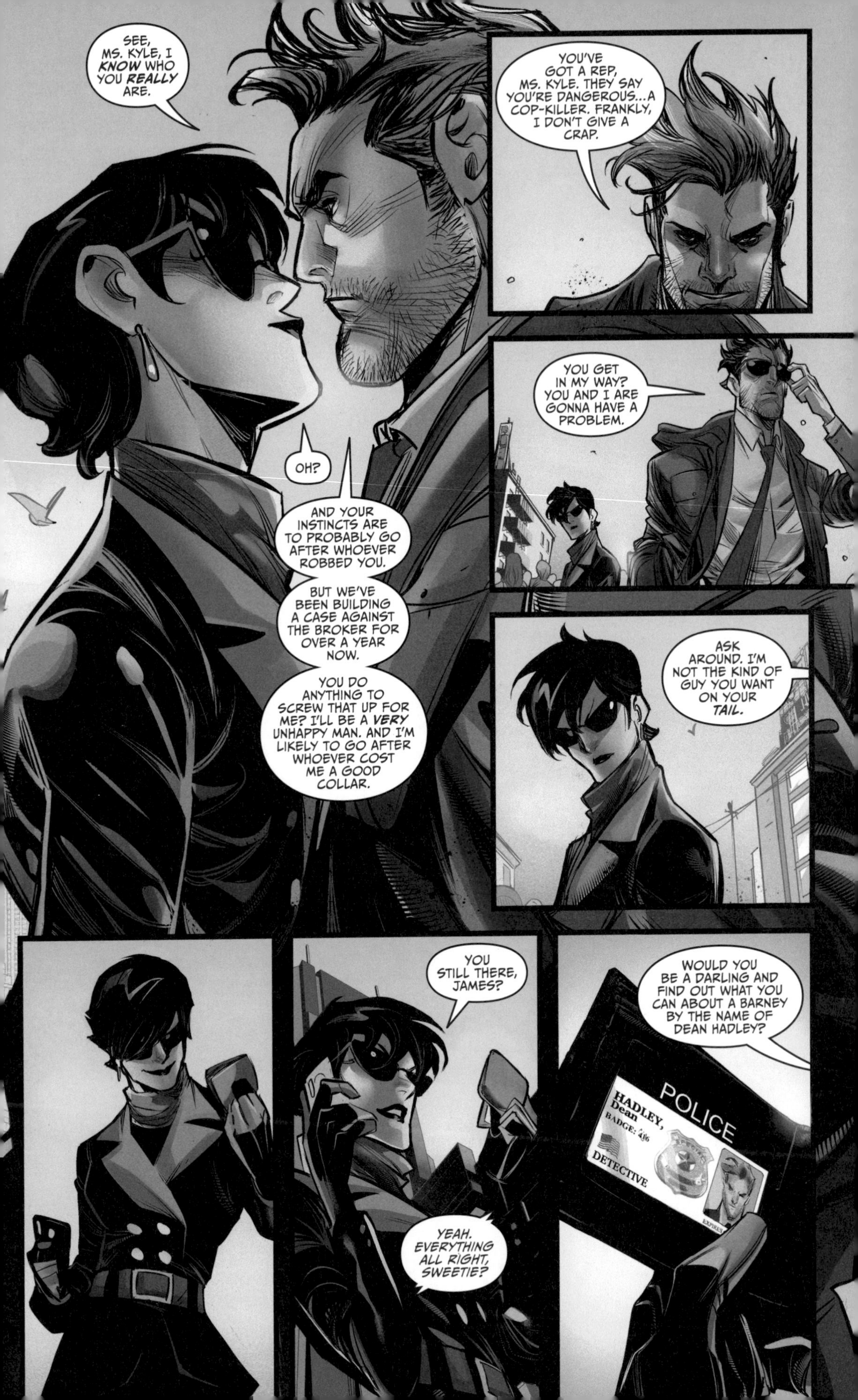
SEE, MS. KYLE, I KNOW WHO YOU REALLY ARE.
OH?
AND YOUR INSTINCTS ARE TO PROBABLY GO AFTER WHOEVER ROBBED YOU.
BUT WE'VE BEEN BUILDING A CASE AGAINST THE BROKER FOR OVER A YEAR NOW.
YOU DO ANYTHING TO SCREW THAT UP FOR ME? I'LL BE A VERY UNHAPPY MAN. AND I'M LIKELY TO GO AFTER WHOEVER COST ME A GOOD COLLAR.
YOU'VE GOT A REP, MS. KYLE. THEY SAY YOU'RE DANGEROUS...A COP-KILLER. FRANKLY, I DON'T GIVE A CRAP.
YOU GET IN MY WAY? YOU AND I ARE GONNA HAVE A PROBLEM.
ASK AROUND. I'M NOT THE KIND OF GUY YOU WANT ON YOUR TAIL.
YOU STILL THERE, JAMES?
YEAH. EVERYTHING ALL RIGHT, SWEETIE?
WOULD YOU BE A DARLING AND FIND OUT WHAT YOU CAN ABOUT A BARNEY BY THE NAME OF DEAN HADLEY?
POLICE
HADLEY, Dean
BADGE: 416
DETECTIVE
EXPIRES

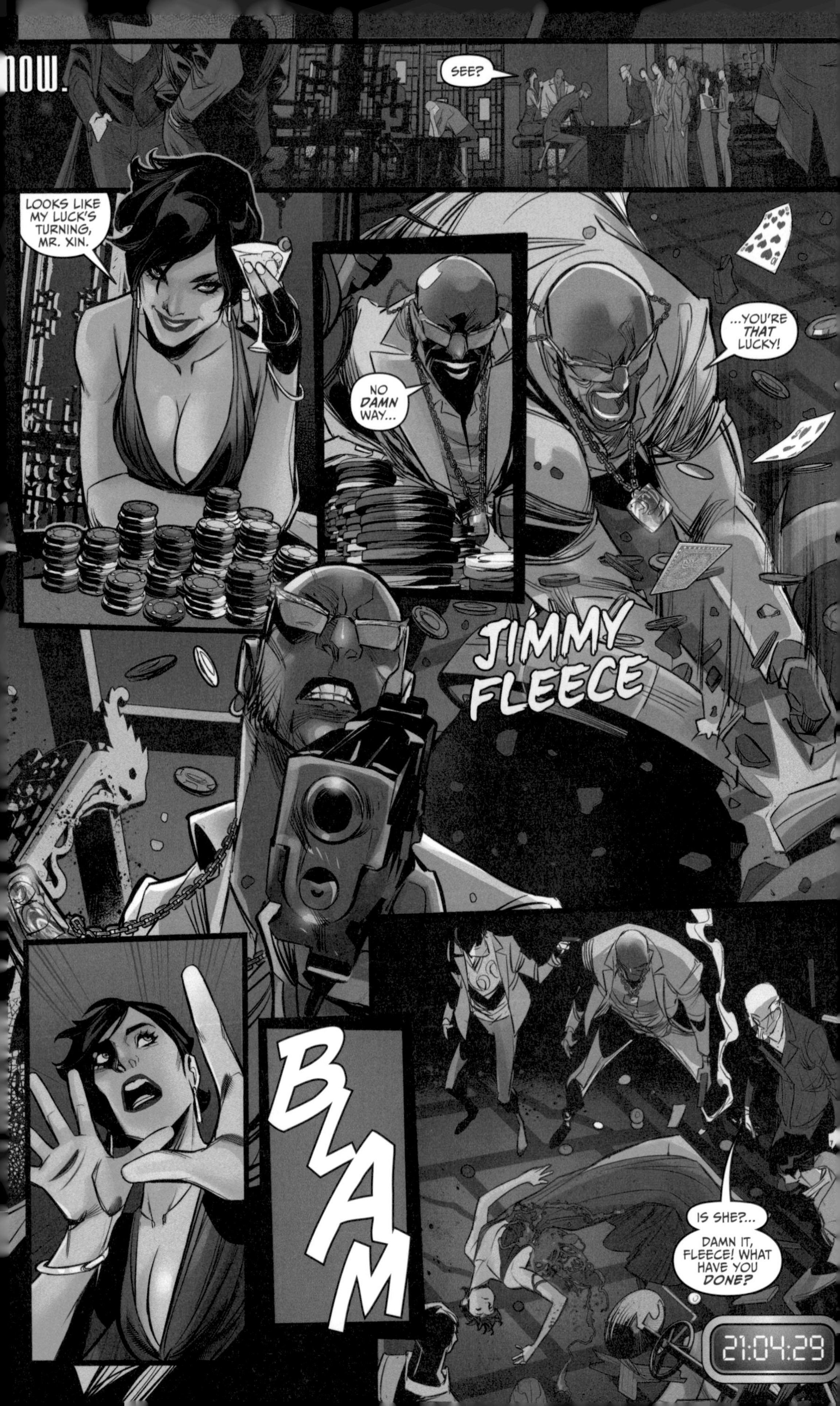
NOW.
SEE?
LOOKS LIKE MY LUCK'S TURNING, MR. XIN.
NO DAMN WAY...
...YOU'RE THAT LUCKY!
JIMMY FLEECE
BLAM
IS SHE?...
DAMN IT, FLEECE! WHAT HAVE YOU DONE?
21:04:29

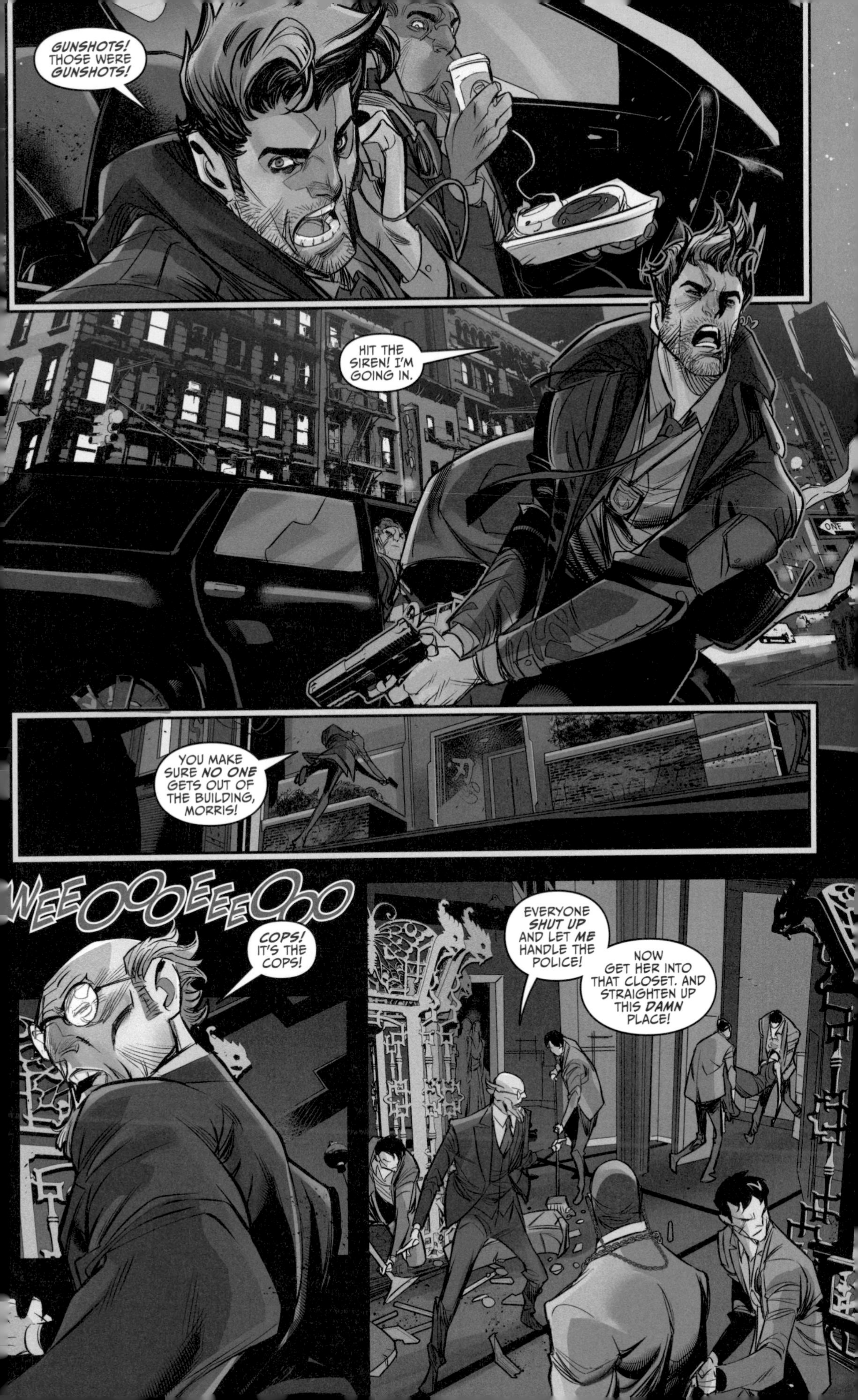
GUNSHOTS! THOSE WERE GUNSHOTS!
HIT THE SIREN! I'M GOING IN.
ONE
YOU MAKE SURE NO ONE GETS OUT OF THE BUILDING, MORRIS!
WEEOOOEEEOOO
COPS! IT'S THE COPS!
EVERYONE SHUT UP AND LET ME HANDLE THE POLICE!
NOW GET HER INTO THAT CLOSET. AND STRAIGHTEN UP THIS DAMN PLACE!

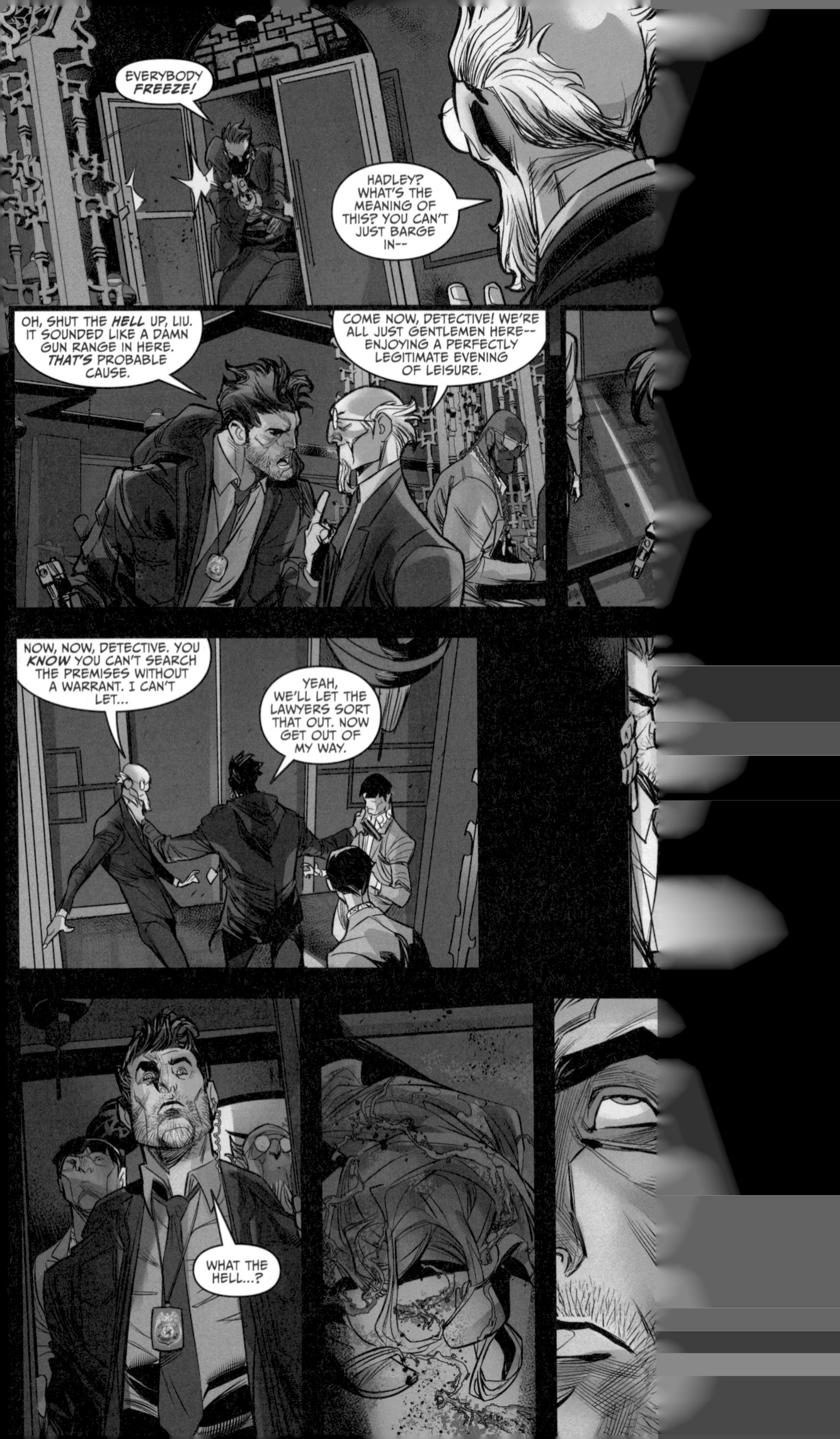
EVERYBODY FREEZE!
HADLEY? WHAT'S THE MEANING OF THIS? YOU CAN'T JUST BARGE IN--
OH, SHUT THE HELL UP, LIU. IT SOUNDED LIKE A DAMN GUN RANGE IN HERE. THAT'S PROBABLE CAUSE.
COME NOW, DETECTIVE! WE'RE ALL JUST GENTLEMEN HERE--ENJOYING A PERFECTLY LEGITIMATE EVENING OF LEISURE.
NOW, NOW, DETECTIVE. YOU KNOW YOU CAN'T SEARCH THE PREMISES WITHOUT A WARRANT. I CAN'T LET...
YEAH, WE'LL LET THE LAWYERS SORT THAT OUT. NOW GET OUT OF MY WAY.
WHAT THE HELL...?

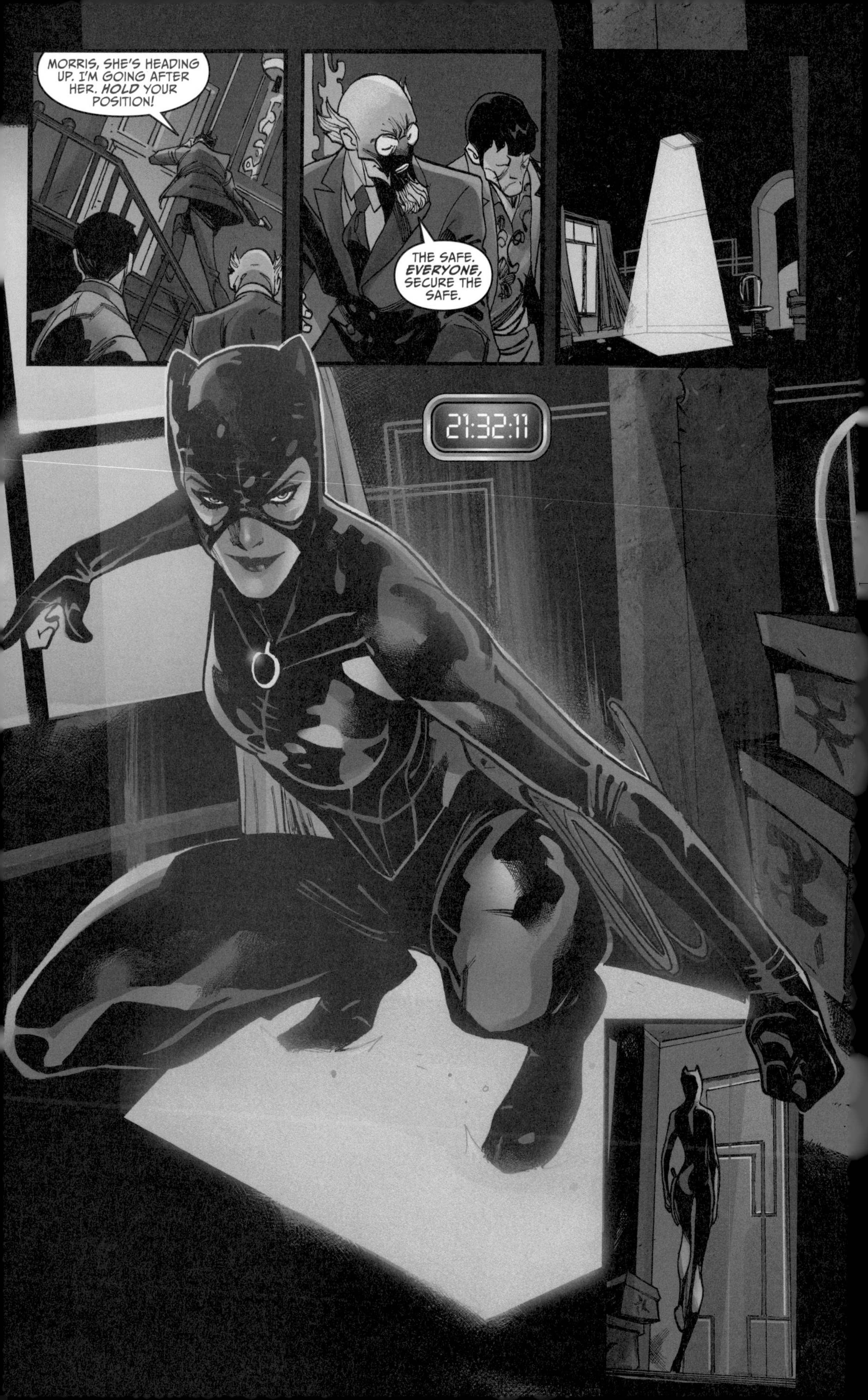
MORRIS, SHE'S HEADING UP. I'M GOING AFTER HER. *HOLD* YOUR POSITION!
THE SAFE. *EVERYONE,* SECURE THE SAFE.
21:32:11

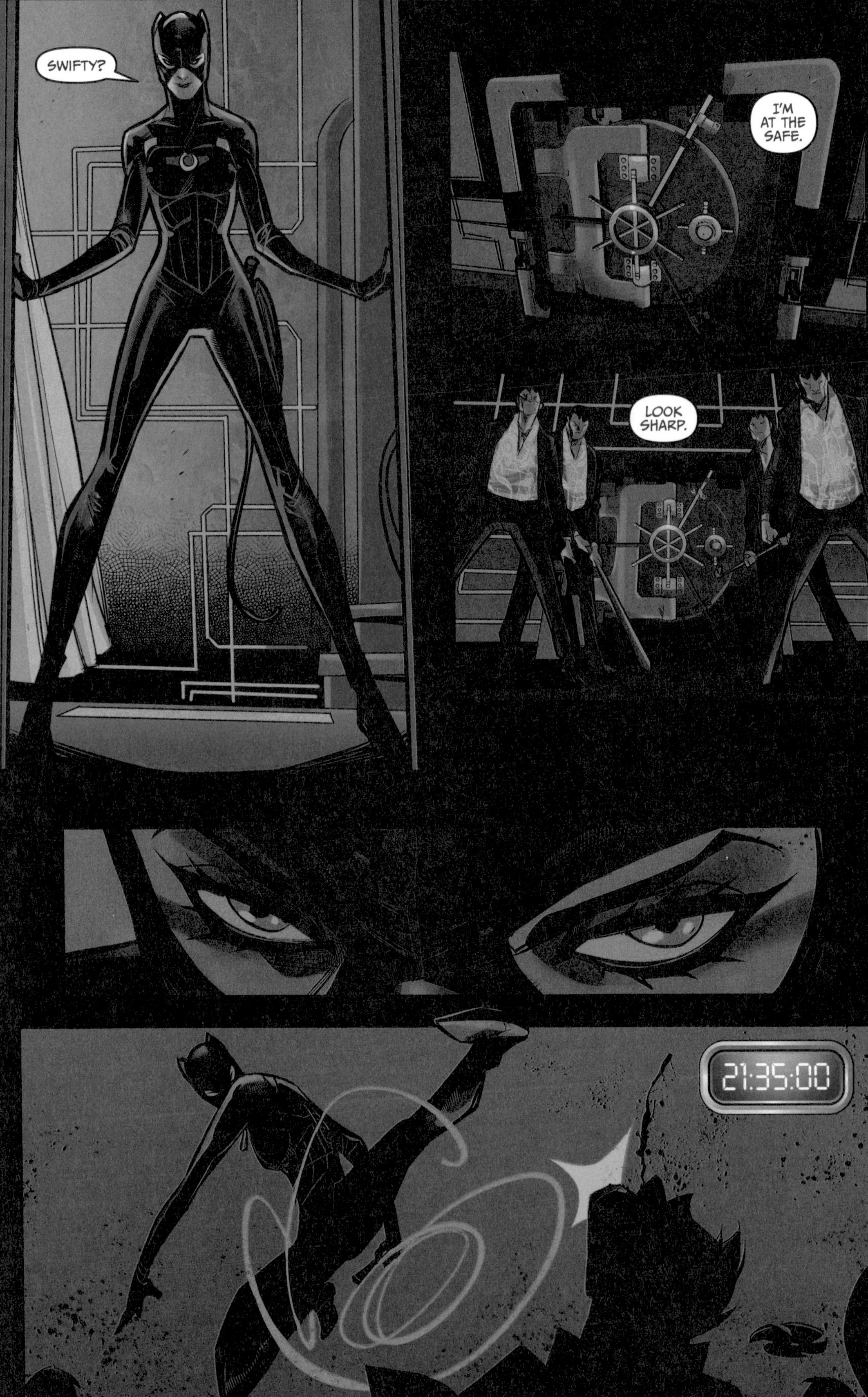
SWIFTY?
I'M AT THE SAFE.
LOOK SHARP.
21:35:00

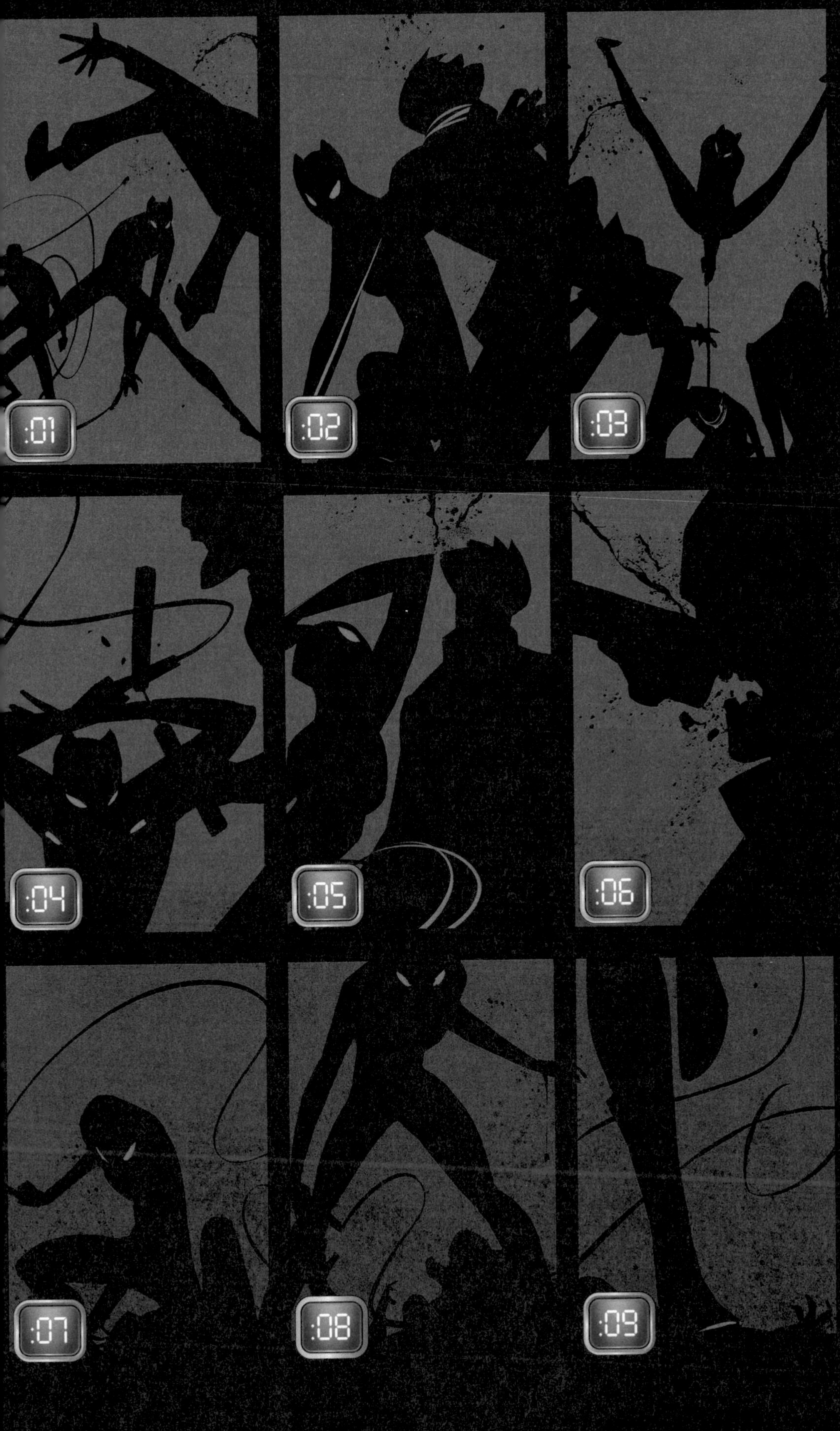
:01
:02
:03
:04
:05
:06
:07
:08
:09

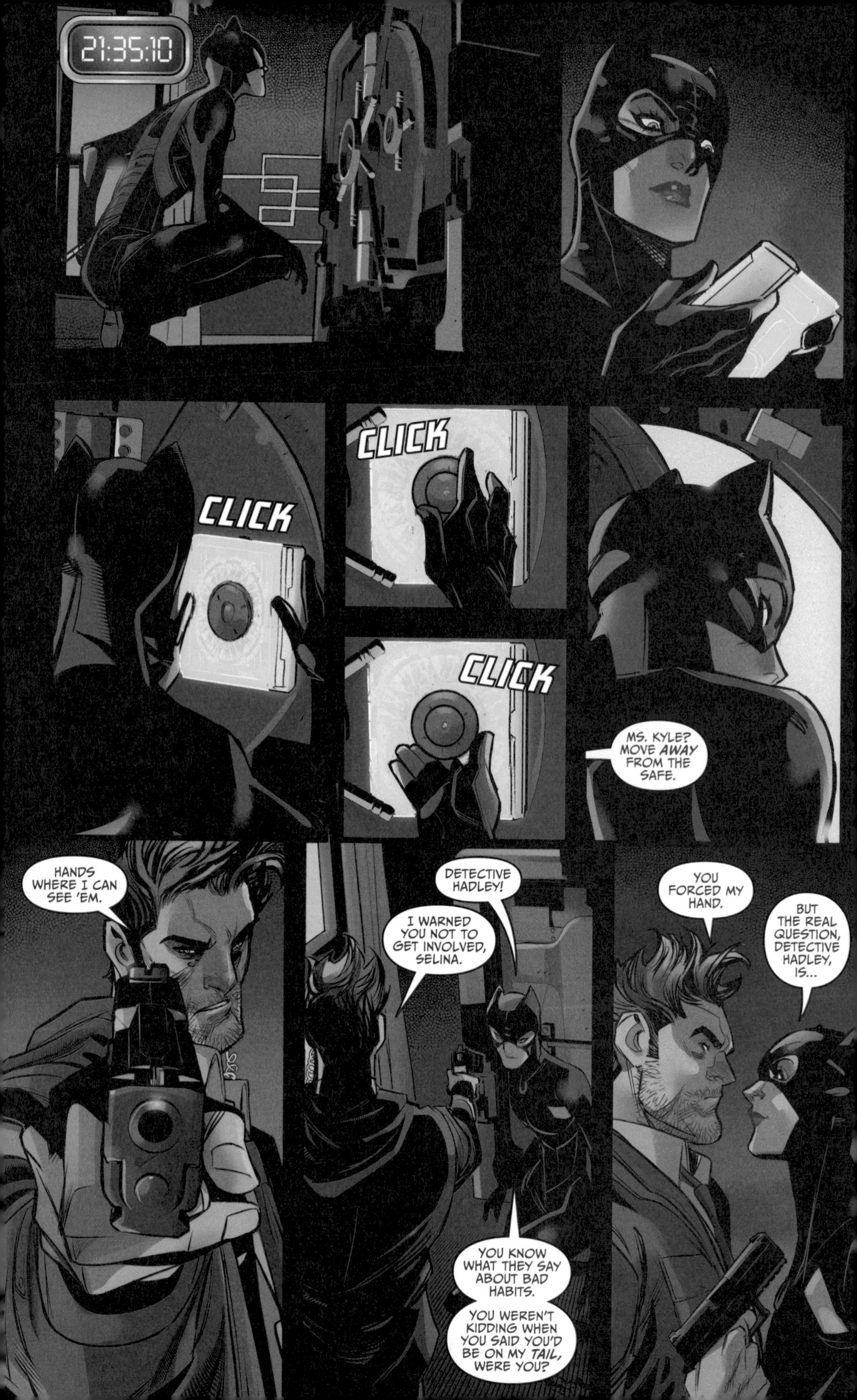
21:35:10
CLICK
CLICK
CLICK
MS. KYLE? MOVE AWAY FROM THE SAFE.
HANDS WHERE I CAN SEE 'EM.
DETECTIVE HADLEY!
I WARNED YOU NOT TO GET INVOLVED, SELINA.
YOU KNOW WHAT THEY SAY ABOUT BAD HABITS.
YOU WEREN'T KIDDING WHEN YOU SAID YOU'D BE ON MY TAIL, WERE YOU?
YOU FORCED MY HAND.
BUT THE REAL QUESTION, DETECTIVE HADLEY, IS...

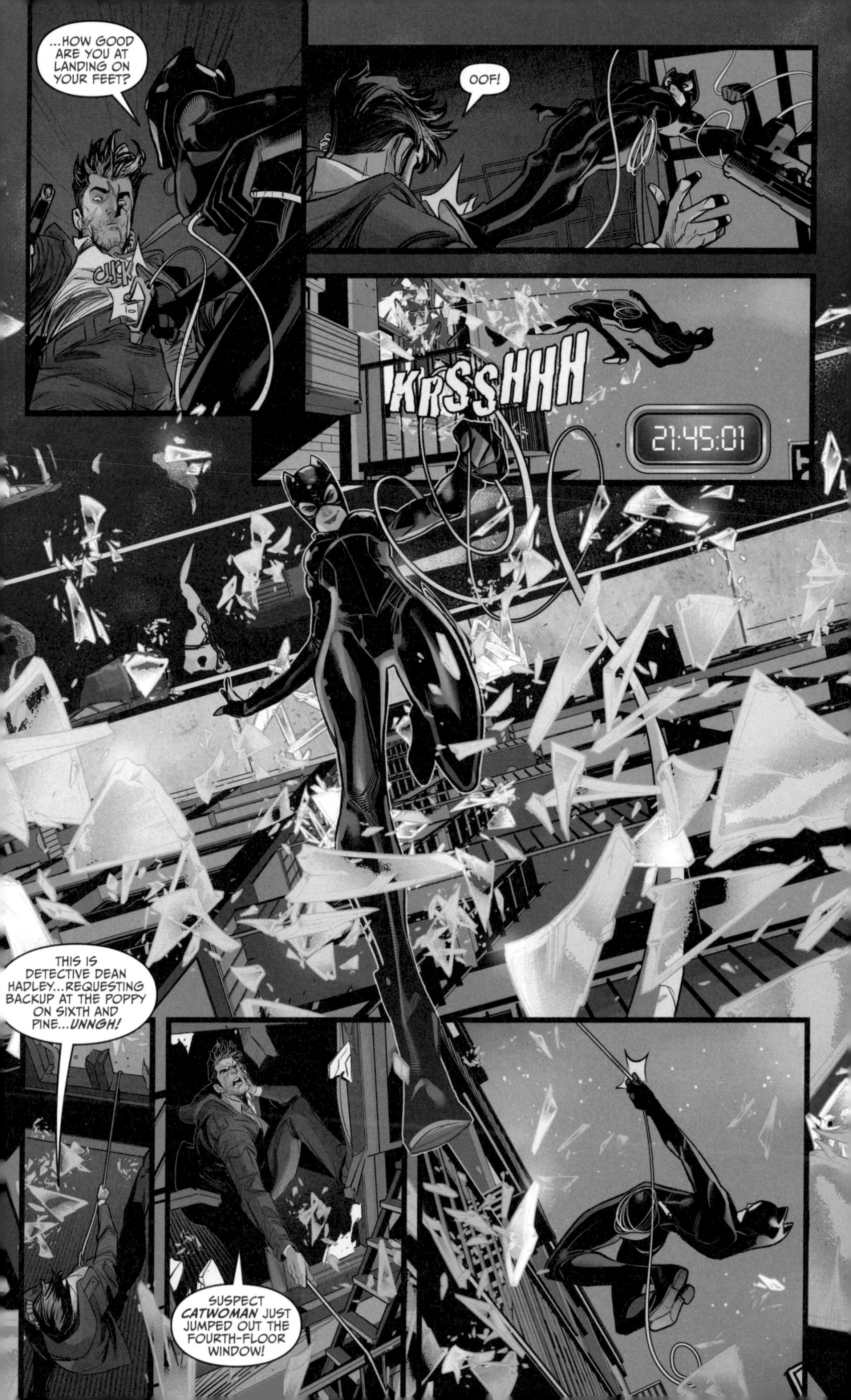
...HOW GOOD ARE YOU AT LANDING ON YOUR FEET?
CLICK
OOF!
KRSSHHH
21:45:01
THIS IS DETECTIVE DEAN HADLEY...REQUESTING BACKUP AT THE POPPY ON SIXTH AND PINE...UNNGH!
SUSPECT CATWOMAN JUST JUMPED OUT THE FOURTH-FLOOR WINDOW!

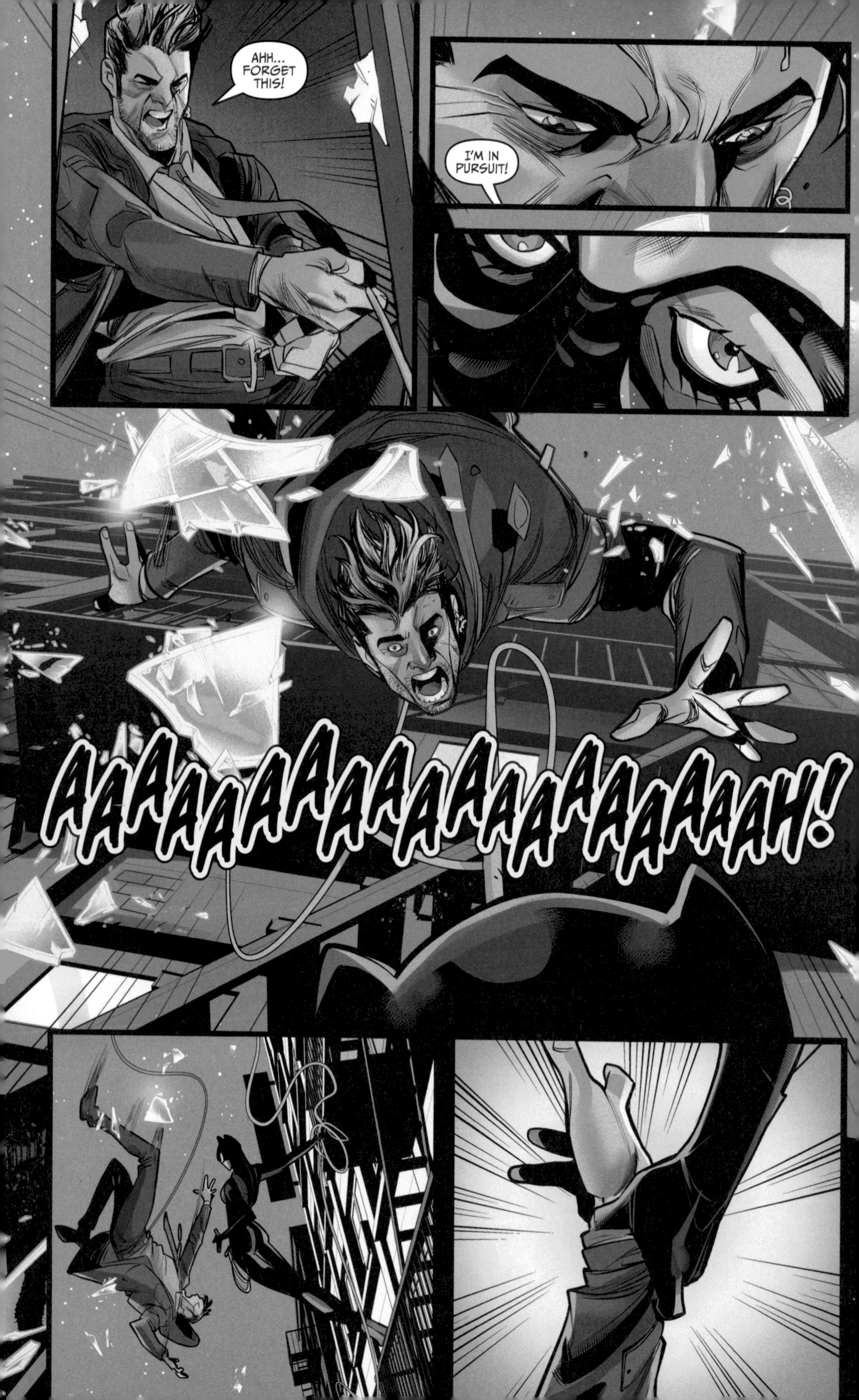
AHH... FORGET THIS!
I'M IN PURSUIT!
AAAAAAAAAAAAAAAAAAAAAH!

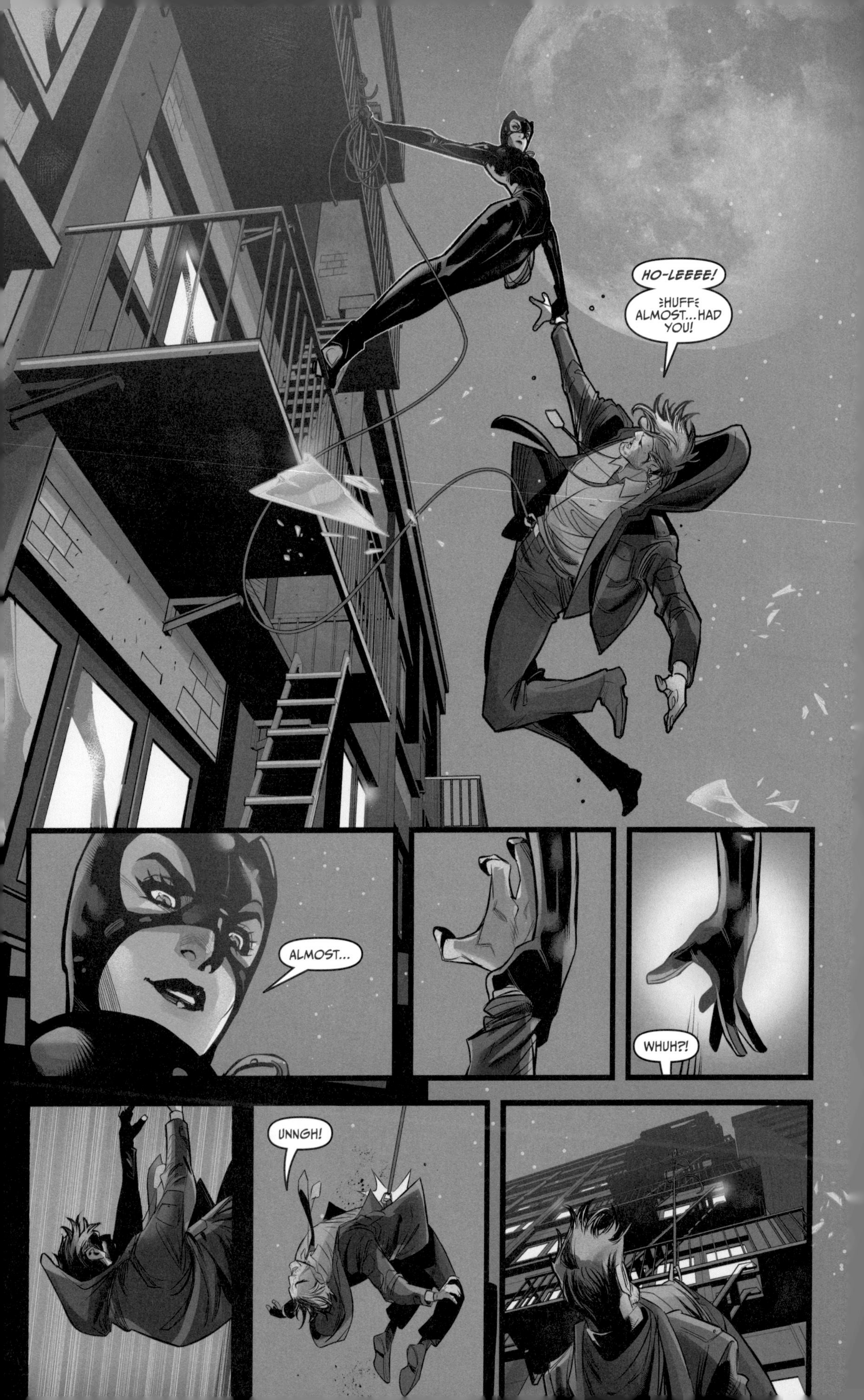
HO-LEEEE!
HUFF
ALMOST...HAD YOU!
ALMOST...
WHUH?!
UNNGH!

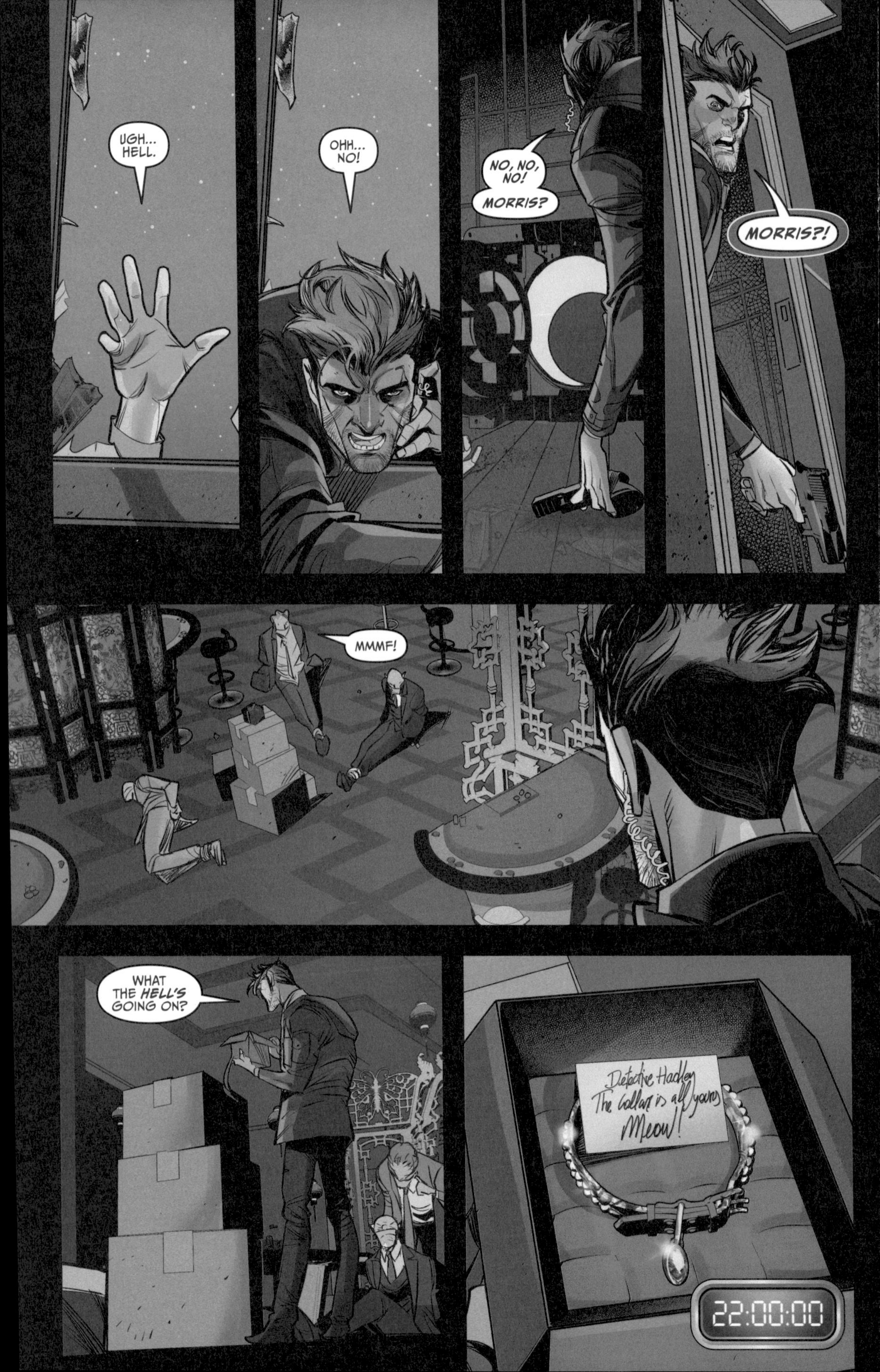
UGH... HELL.
OHH... NO!
NO, NO, NO!
MORRIS?
MORRIS?!
MMMF!
WHAT THE HELL'S GOING ON?
Detective Hadley
The Collar is all yours
Meow!
22:00:00

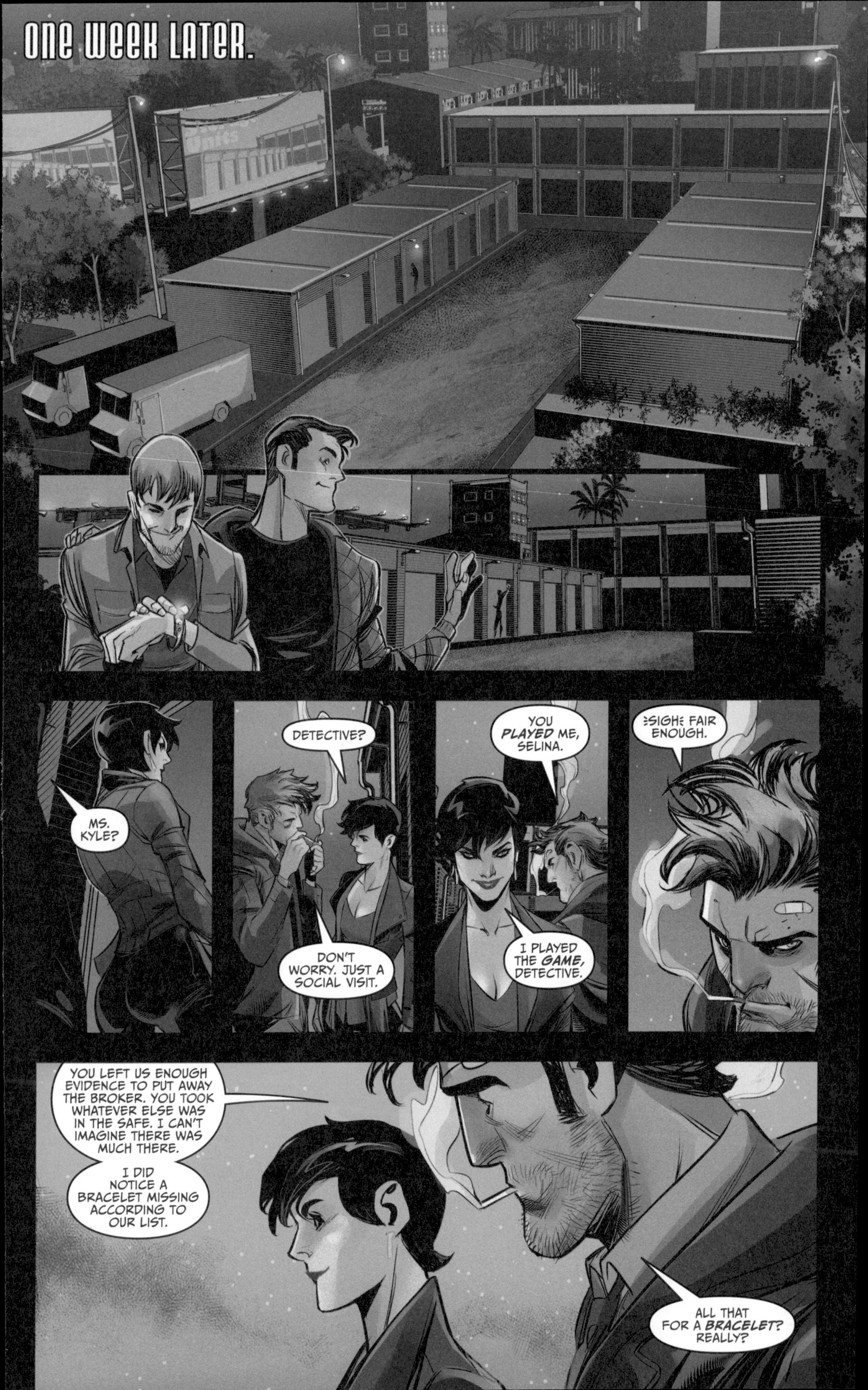

ONE WEEK LATER.
MS. KYLE?
DETECTIVE?
DON'T WORRY. JUST A SOCIAL VISIT.
YOU PLAYED ME, SELINA.
I PLAYED THE GAME, DETECTIVE.
SIGH FAIR ENOUGH.
YOU LEFT US ENOUGH EVIDENCE TO PUT AWAY THE BROKER. YOU TOOK WHATEVER ELSE WAS IN THE SAFE. I CAN'T IMAGINE THERE WAS MUCH THERE.
I DID NOTICE A BRACELET MISSING ACCORDING TO OUR LIST.
ALL THAT FOR A BRACELET? REALLY?

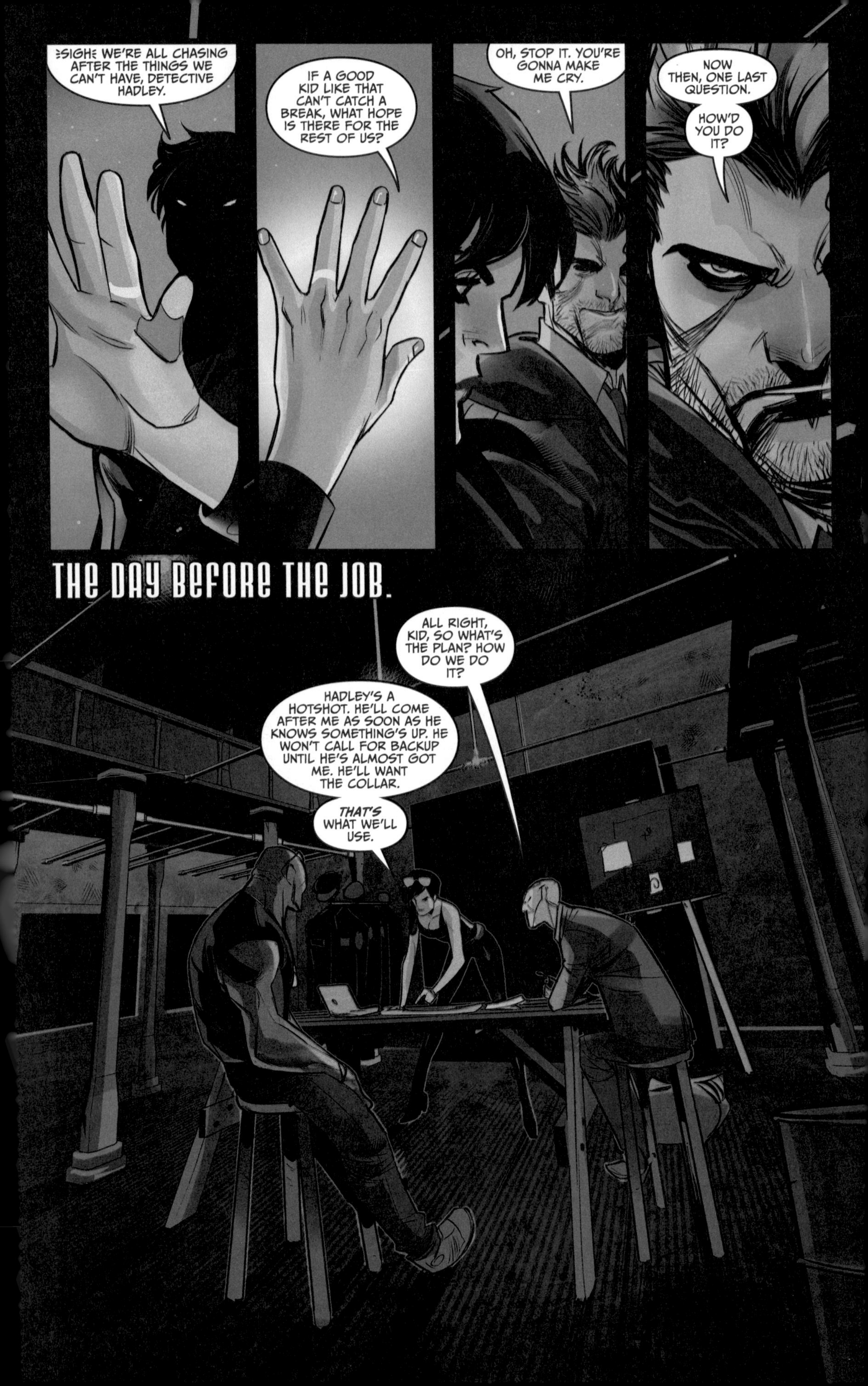

≡SIGH≡ WE'RE ALL CHASING AFTER THE THINGS WE CAN'T HAVE, DETECTIVE HADLEY.
IF A GOOD KID LIKE THAT CAN'T CATCH A BREAK, WHAT HOPE IS THERE FOR THE REST OF US?
OH, STOP IT. YOU'RE GONNA MAKE ME CRY.
NOW THEN, ONE LAST QUESTION.
HOW'D YOU DO IT?
THE DAY BEFORE THE JOB.
ALL RIGHT, KID, SO WHAT'S THE PLAN? HOW DO WE DO IT?
HADLEY'S A HOTSHOT. HE'LL COME AFTER ME AS SOON AS HE KNOWS SOMETHING'S UP. HE WON'T CALL FOR BACKUP UNTIL HE'S ALMOST GOT ME. HE'LL WANT THE COLLAR.
THAT'S WHAT WE'LL USE.

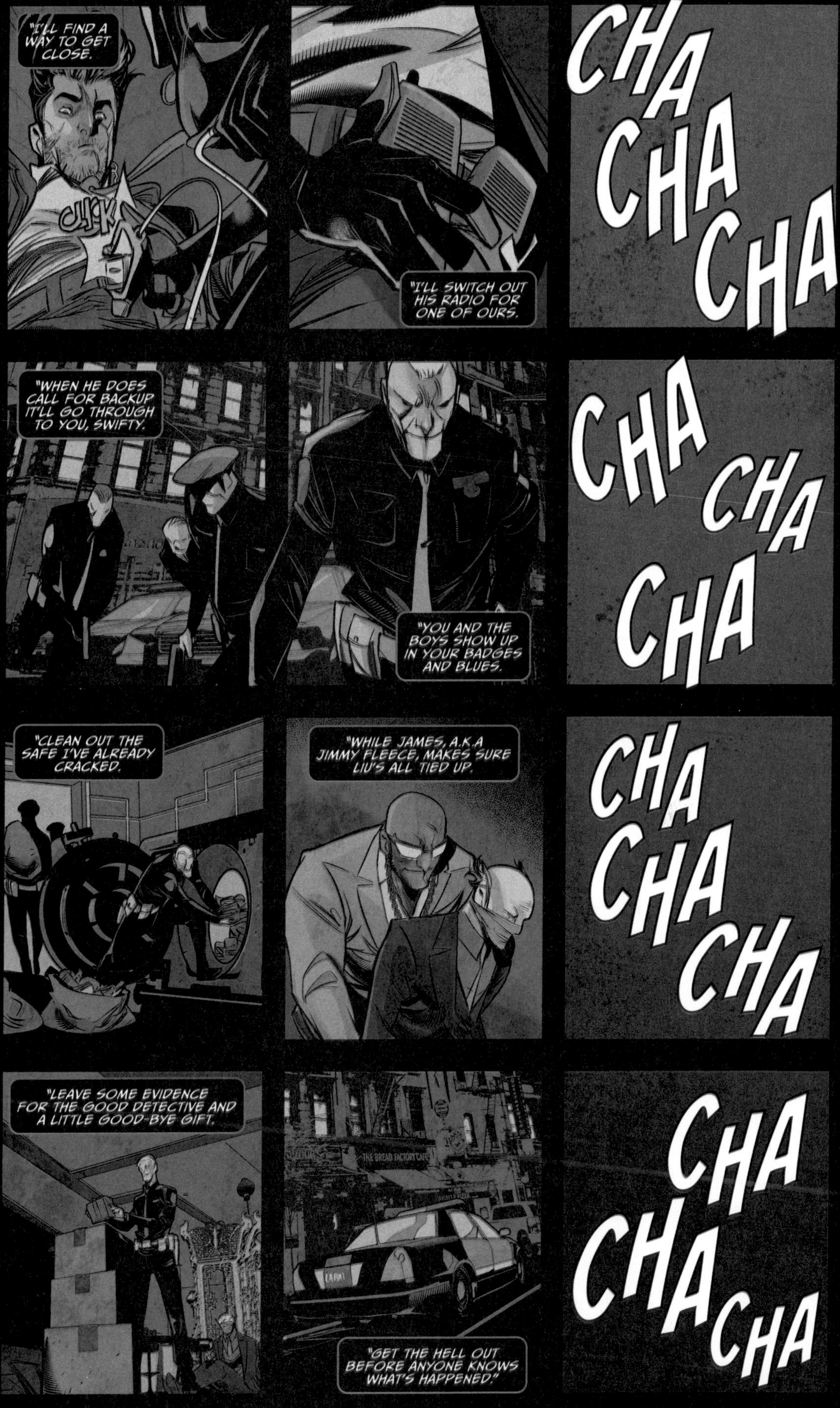
"I'LL FIND A WAY TO GET CLOSE.
CLICK
"I'LL SWITCH OUT HIS RADIO FOR ONE OF OURS.
CHA CHA CHA CHA
"WHEN HE DOES CALL FOR BACKUP IT'LL GO THROUGH TO YOU, SWIFTY.
"YOU AND THE BOYS SHOW UP IN YOUR BADGES AND BLUES.
CHA CHA CHA
"CLEAN OUT THE SAFE I'VE ALREADY CRACKED.
"WHILE JAMES, A.K.A JIMMY FLEECE, MAKES SURE LIU'S ALL TIED UP.
CHA CHA CHA
"LEAVE SOME EVIDENCE FOR THE GOOD DETECTIVE AND A LITTLE GOOD-BYE GIFT.
THE BREAD FACTORY CAFE
"GET THE HELL OUT BEFORE ANYONE KNOWS WHAT'S HAPPENED."
CHA CHA CHA

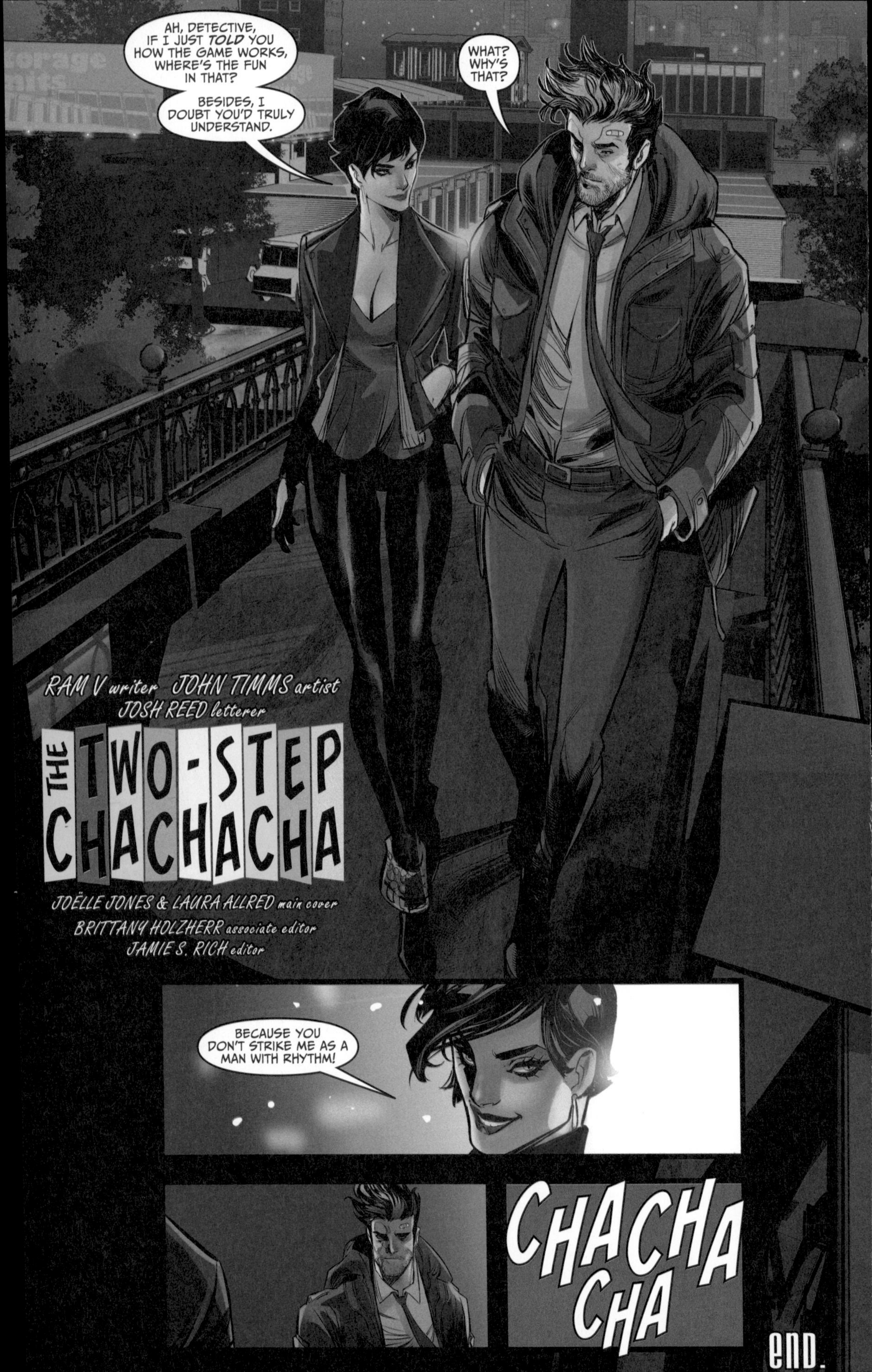

AH, DETECTIVE, IF I JUST TOLD YOU HOW THE GAME WORKS, WHERE'S THE FUN IN THAT?
BESIDES, I DOUBT YOU'D TRULY UNDERSTAND.
WHAT? WHY'S THAT?
RAM V writer JOHN TIMMS artist
JOSH REED letterer
THE TWO-STEP CHACHACHA
JOËLLE JONES & LAURA ALLRED main cover
BRITTANY HOLZHERR associate editor
JAMIE S. RICH editor
BECAUSE YOU DON'T STRIKE ME AS A MAN WITH RHYTHM!
CHACHA CHA
end.

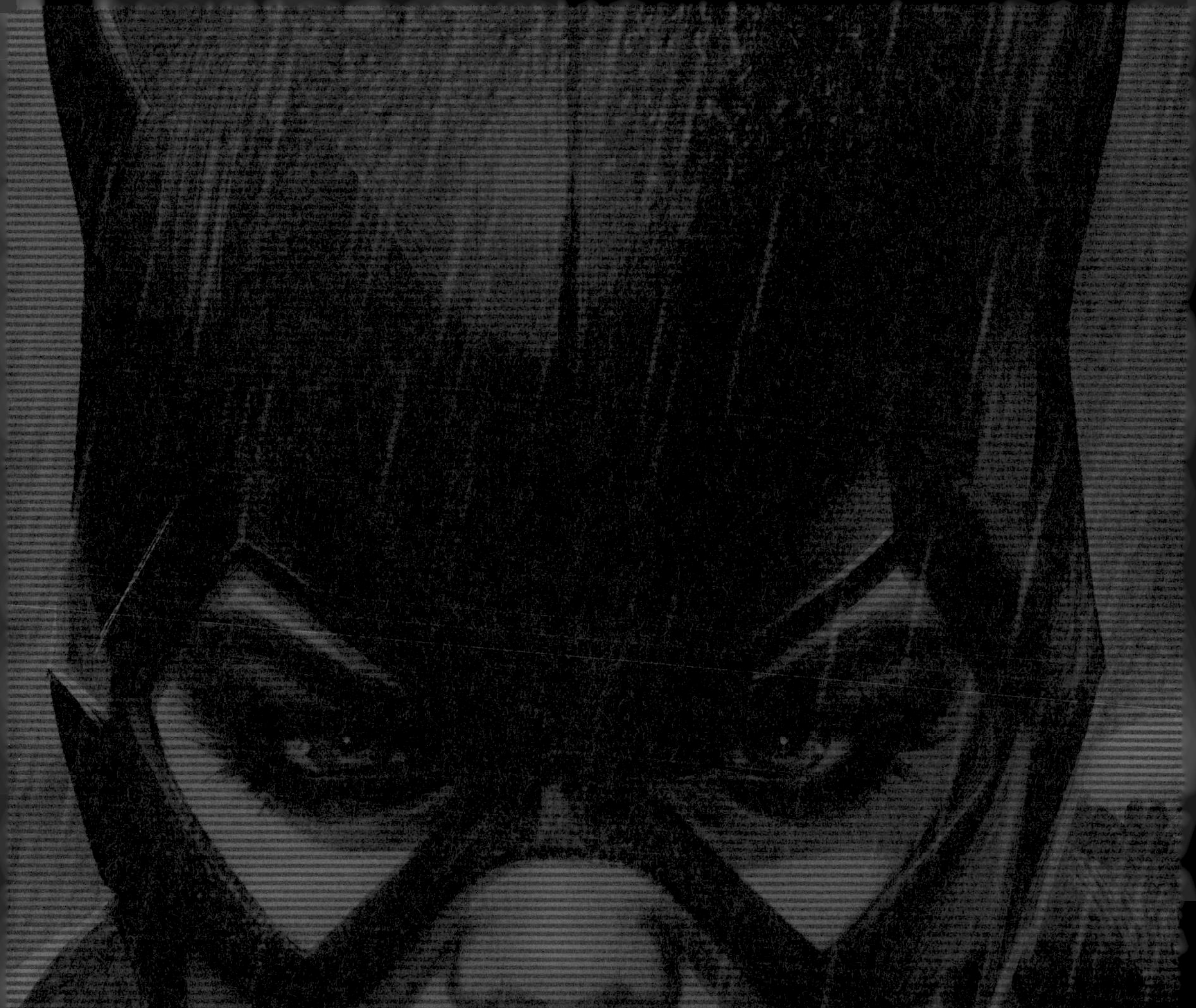

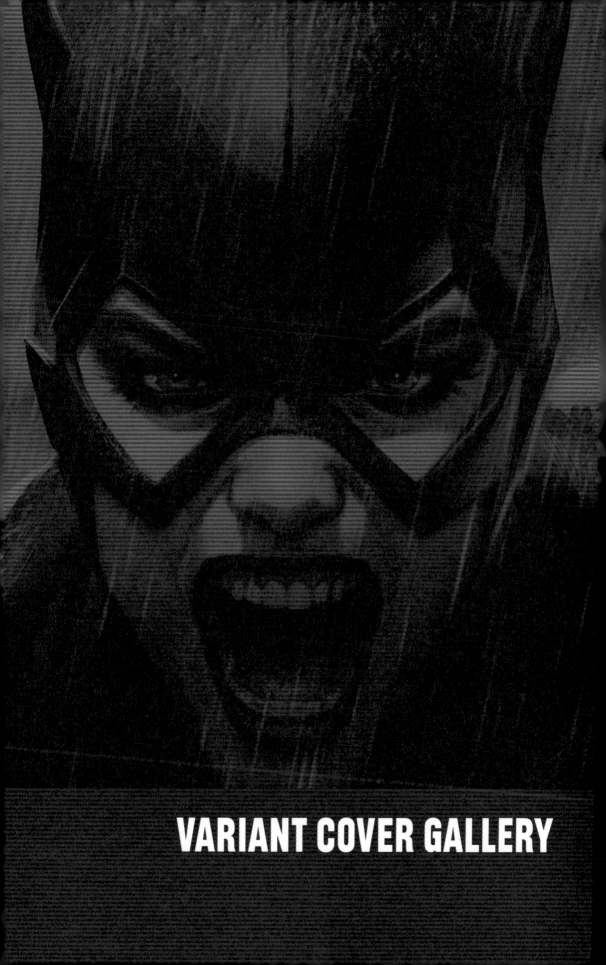

# VARIANT COVER GALLERY

**CATWOMAN #7** variant cover
by BEN OLIVER

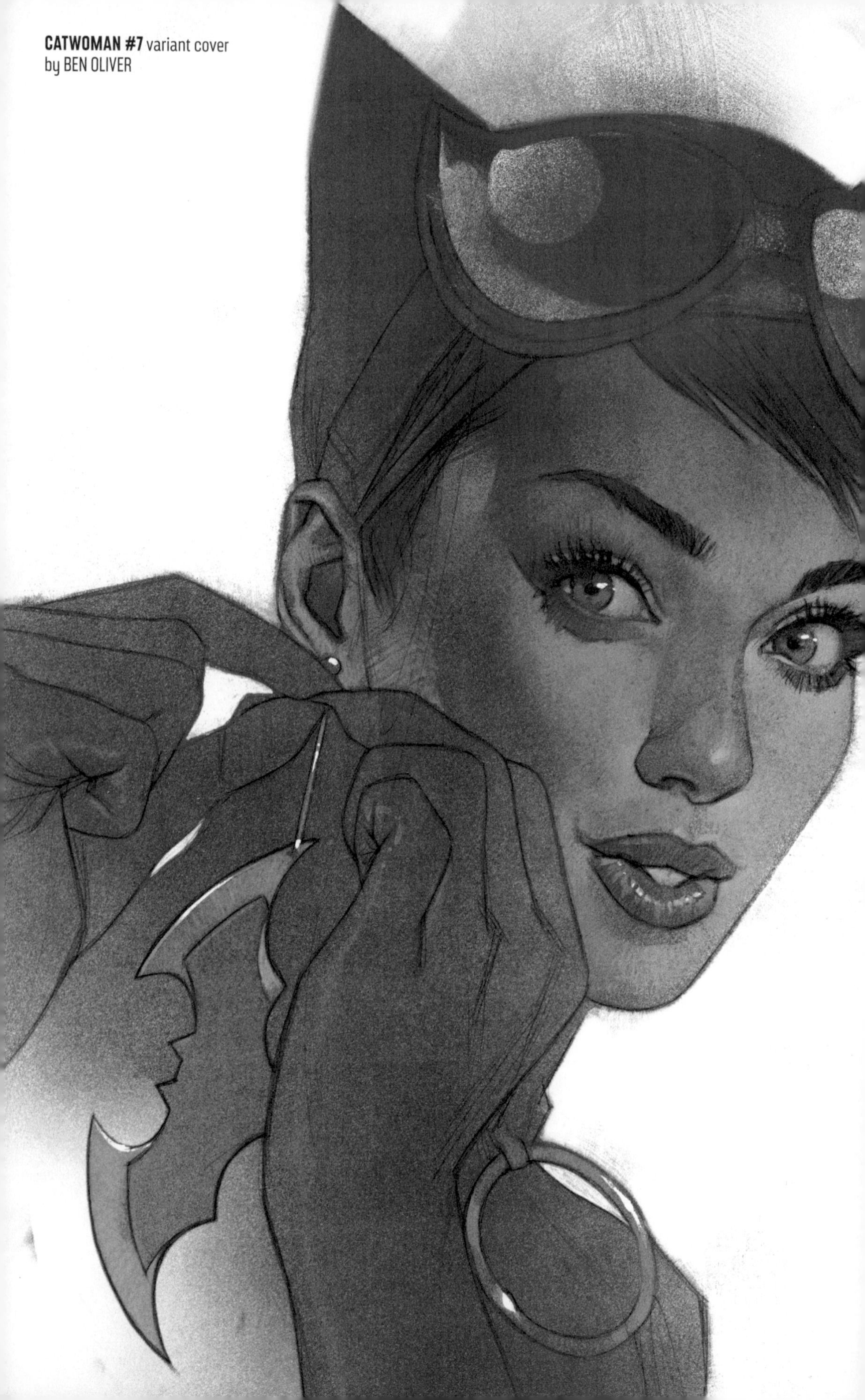

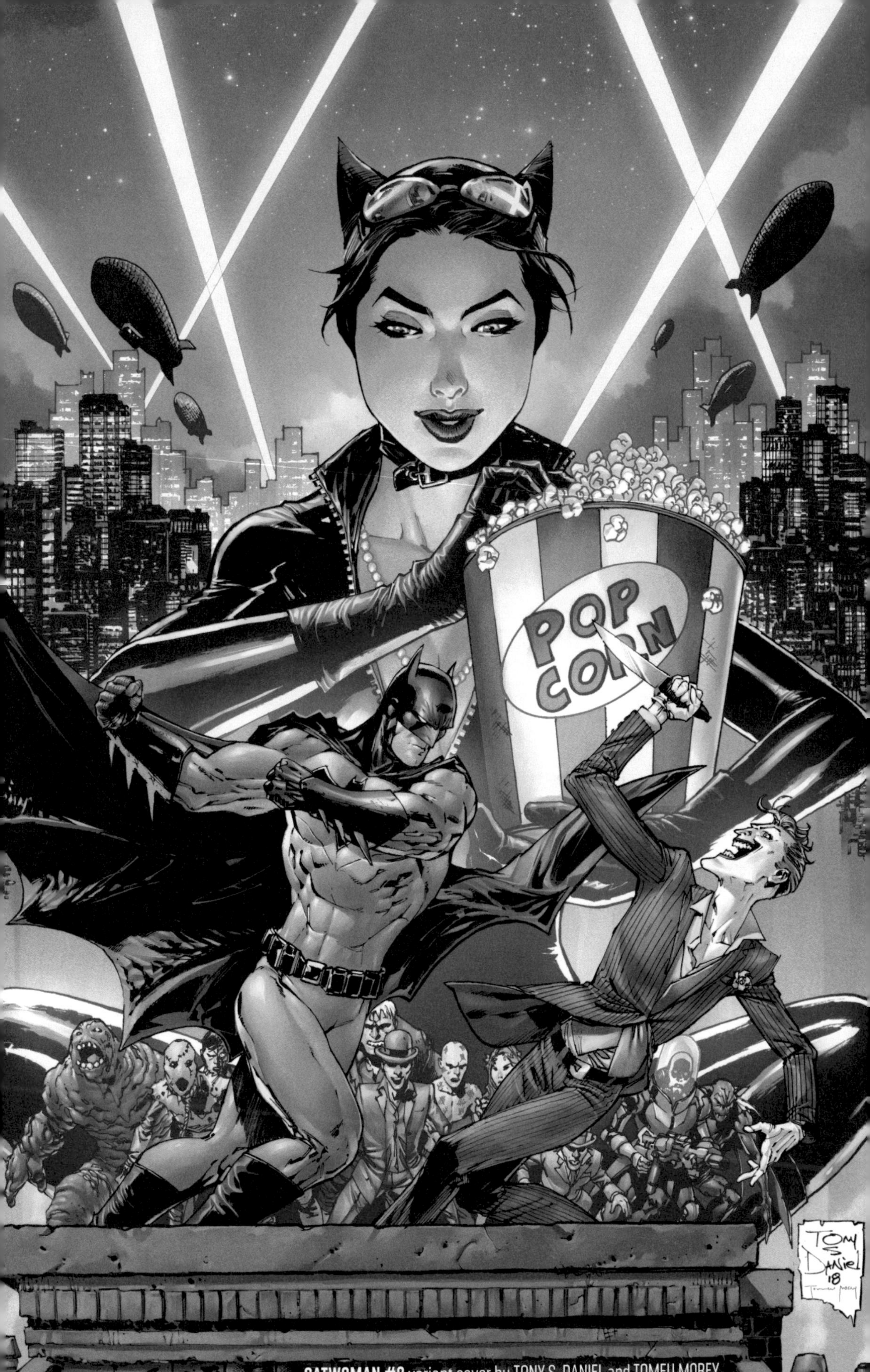
POP
CORN

**CATWOMAN #8** variant cover by TONY S. DANIEL and TOMEU MOREY

**CATWOMAN #9** variant cover
by STANLEY "ARTGERM" LAU

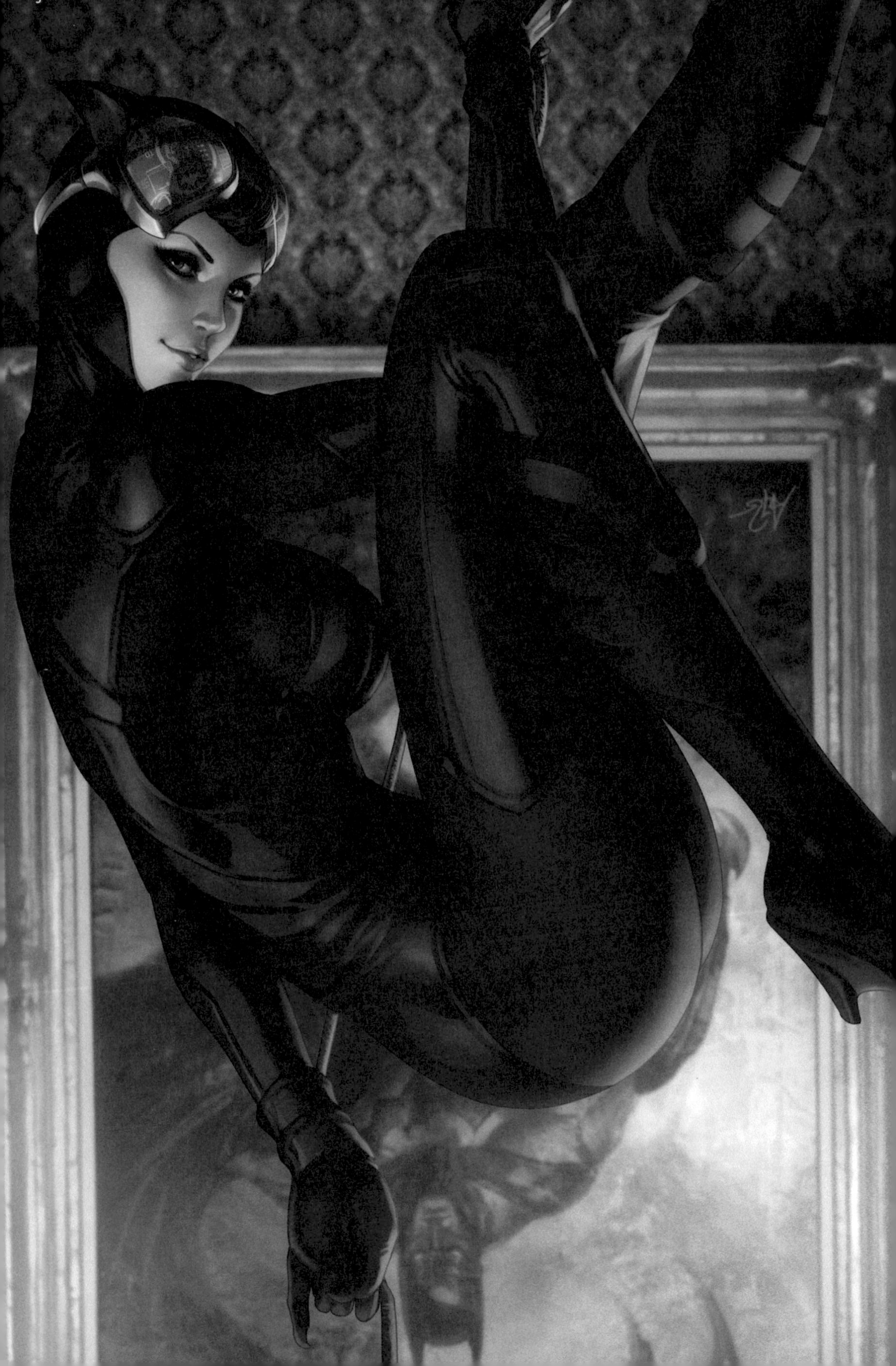

ARTG

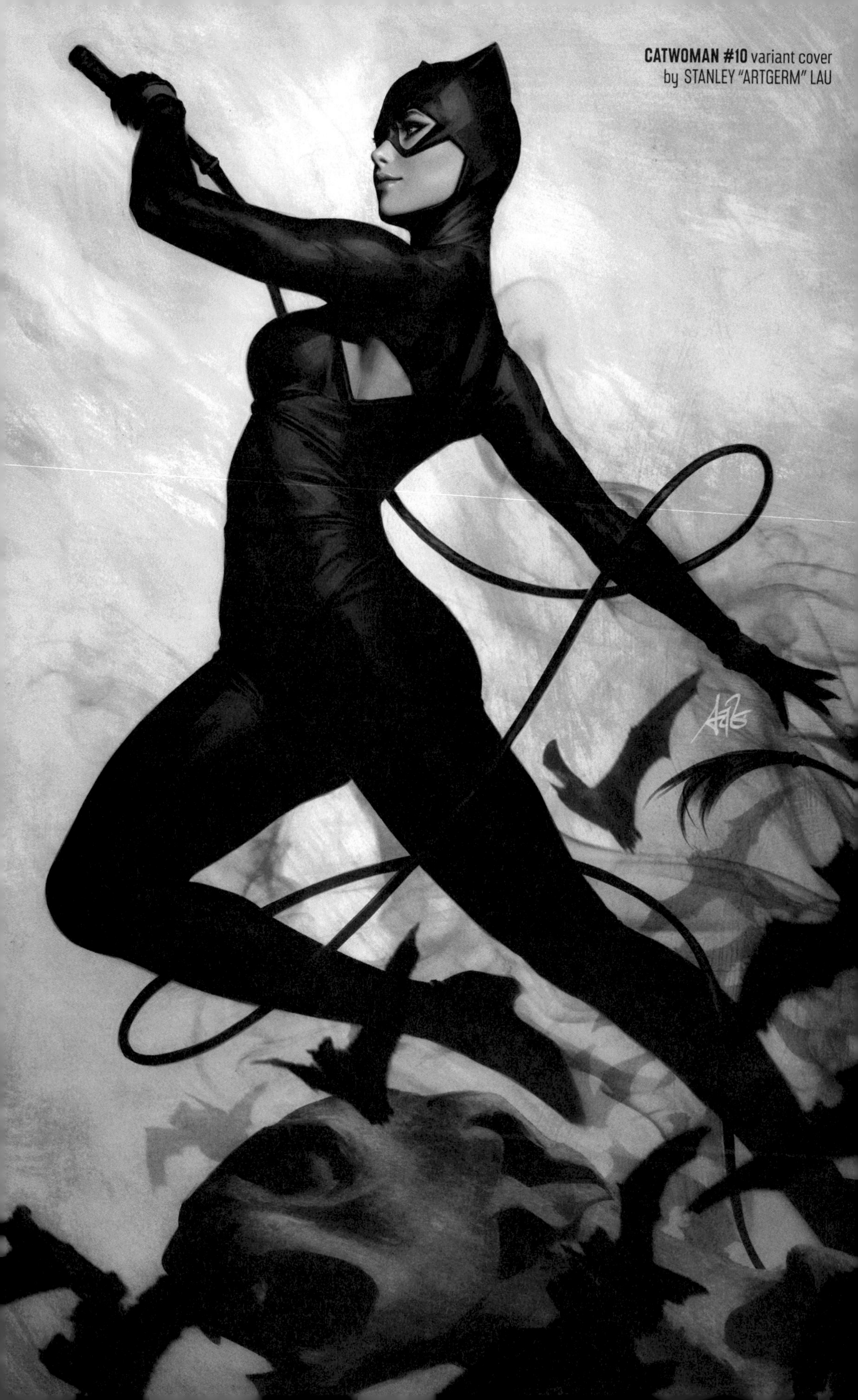

**CATWOMAN #10** variant cover
by STANLEY "ARTGERM" LAU

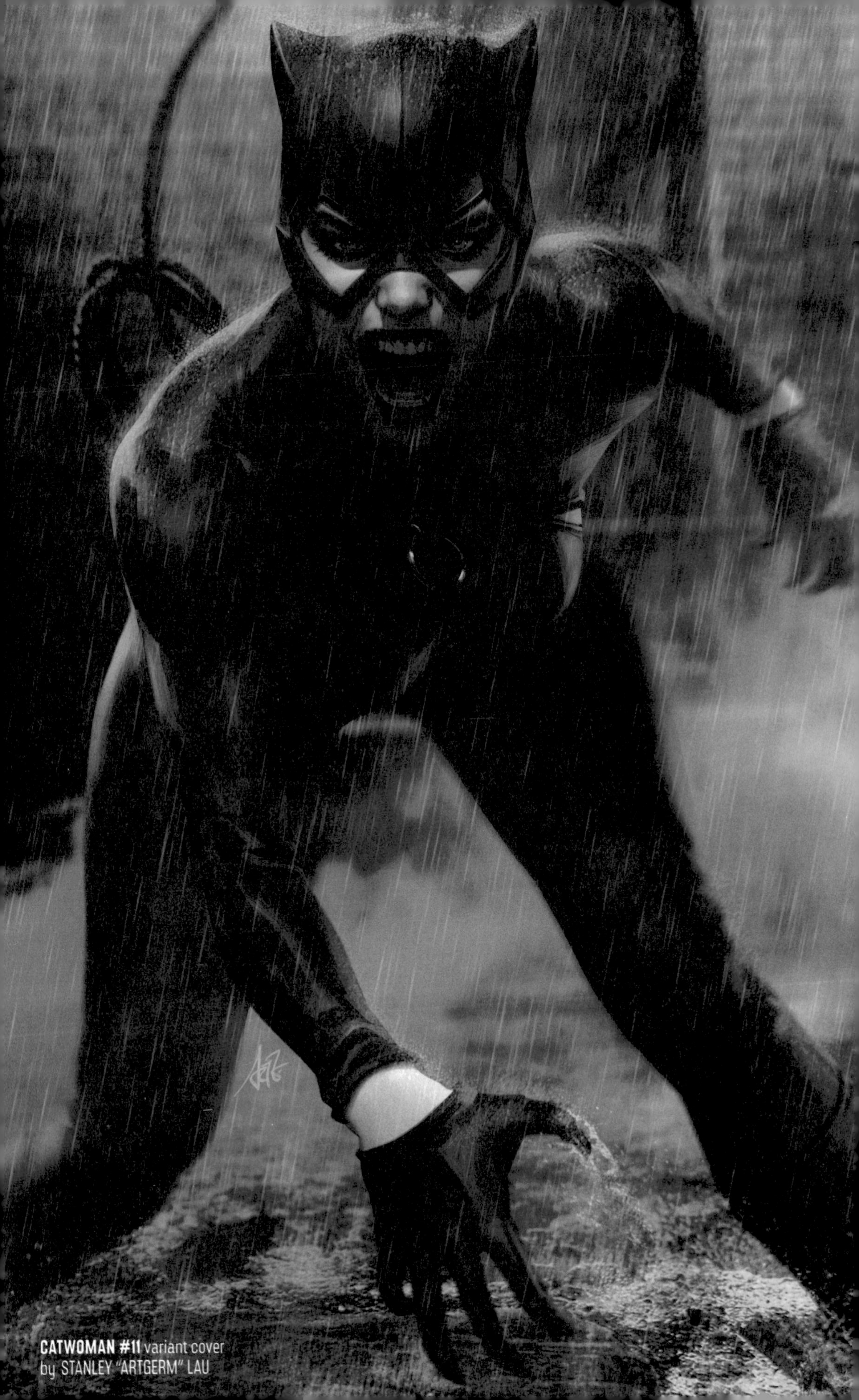

**CATWOMAN #11** variant cover
by STANLEY "ARTGERM" LAU

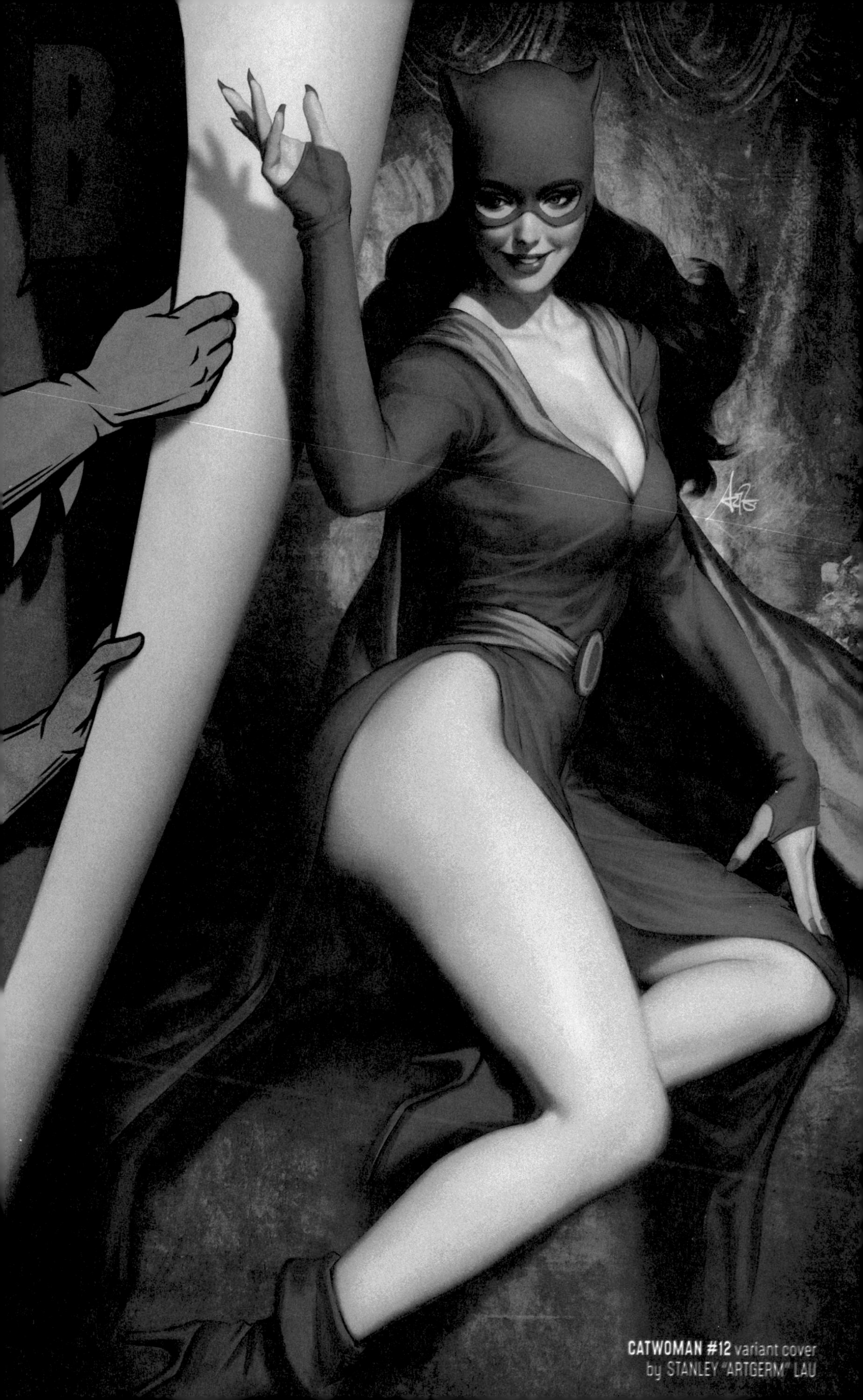

**CATWOMAN #12** variant cover
by STANLEY "ARTGERM" LAU

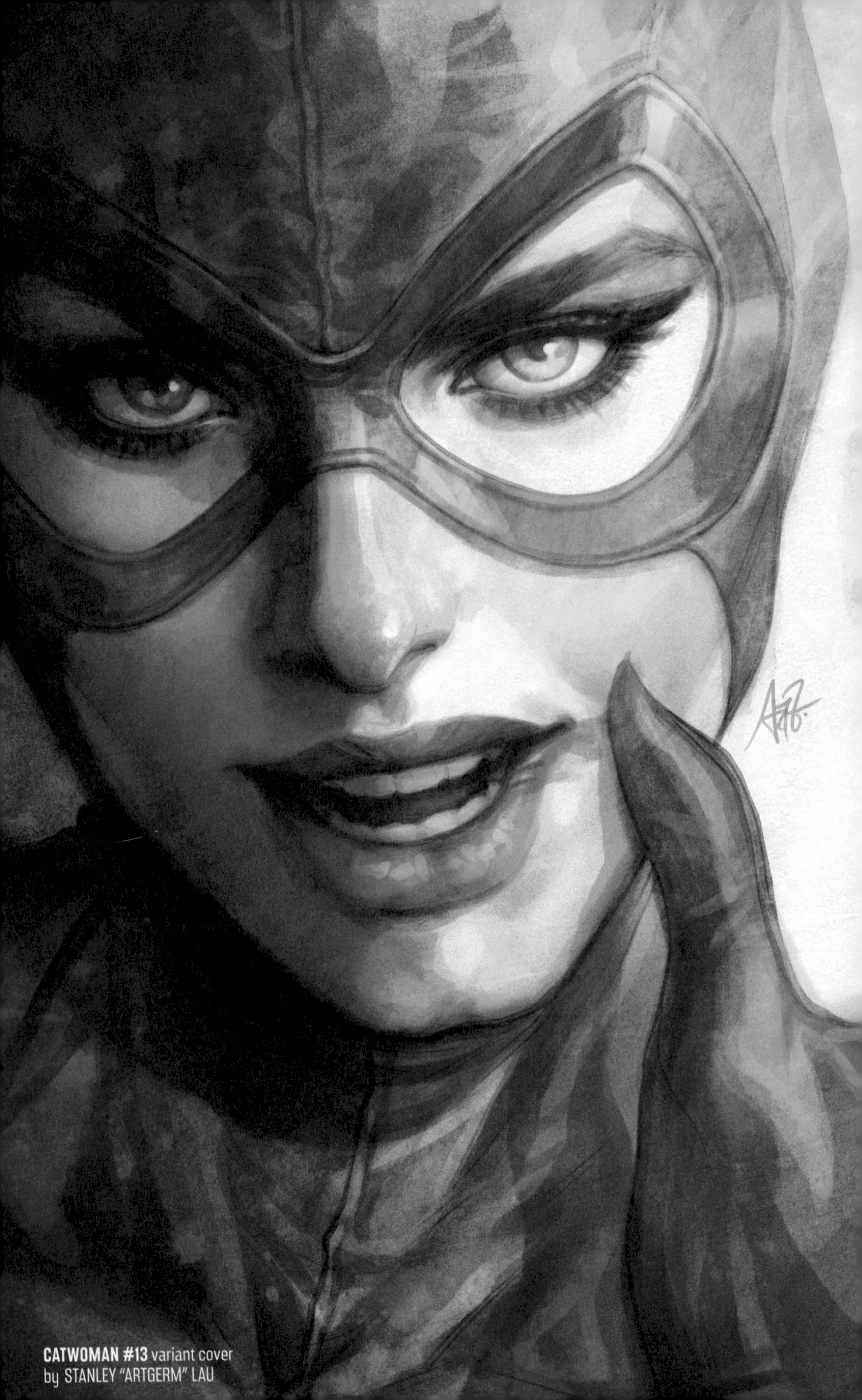

**CATWOMAN #13** variant cover
by STANLEY "ARTGERM" LAU

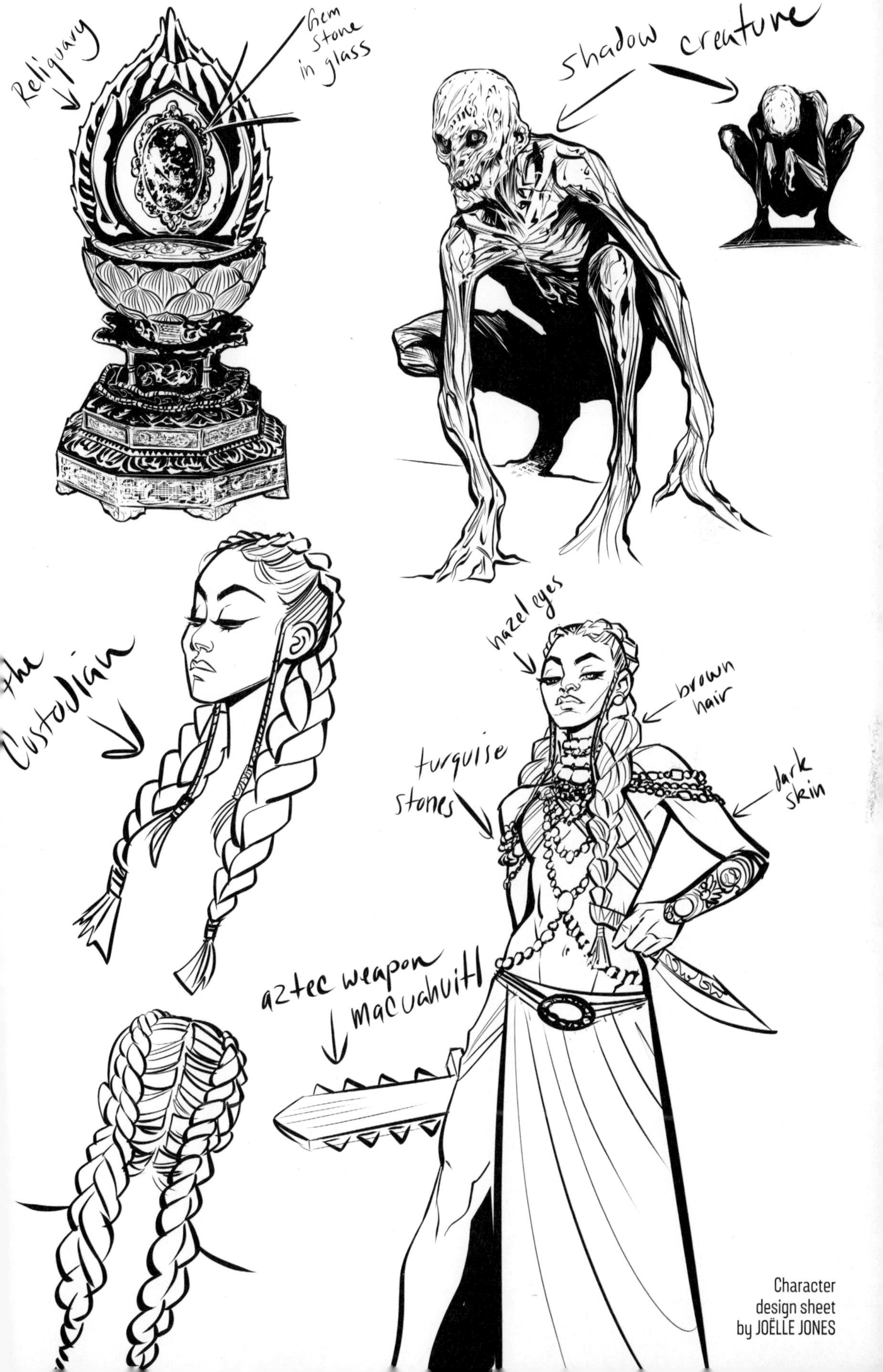
Religuary
Gem stone in glass
shadow creature
the Custodian
hazel eyes
brown hair
turquise stones
dark skin
aztec weapon macuahuitl

Character
design sheet
by JOËLLE JONES

**CATWOMAN #10** cover line art by JOËLLE JONES

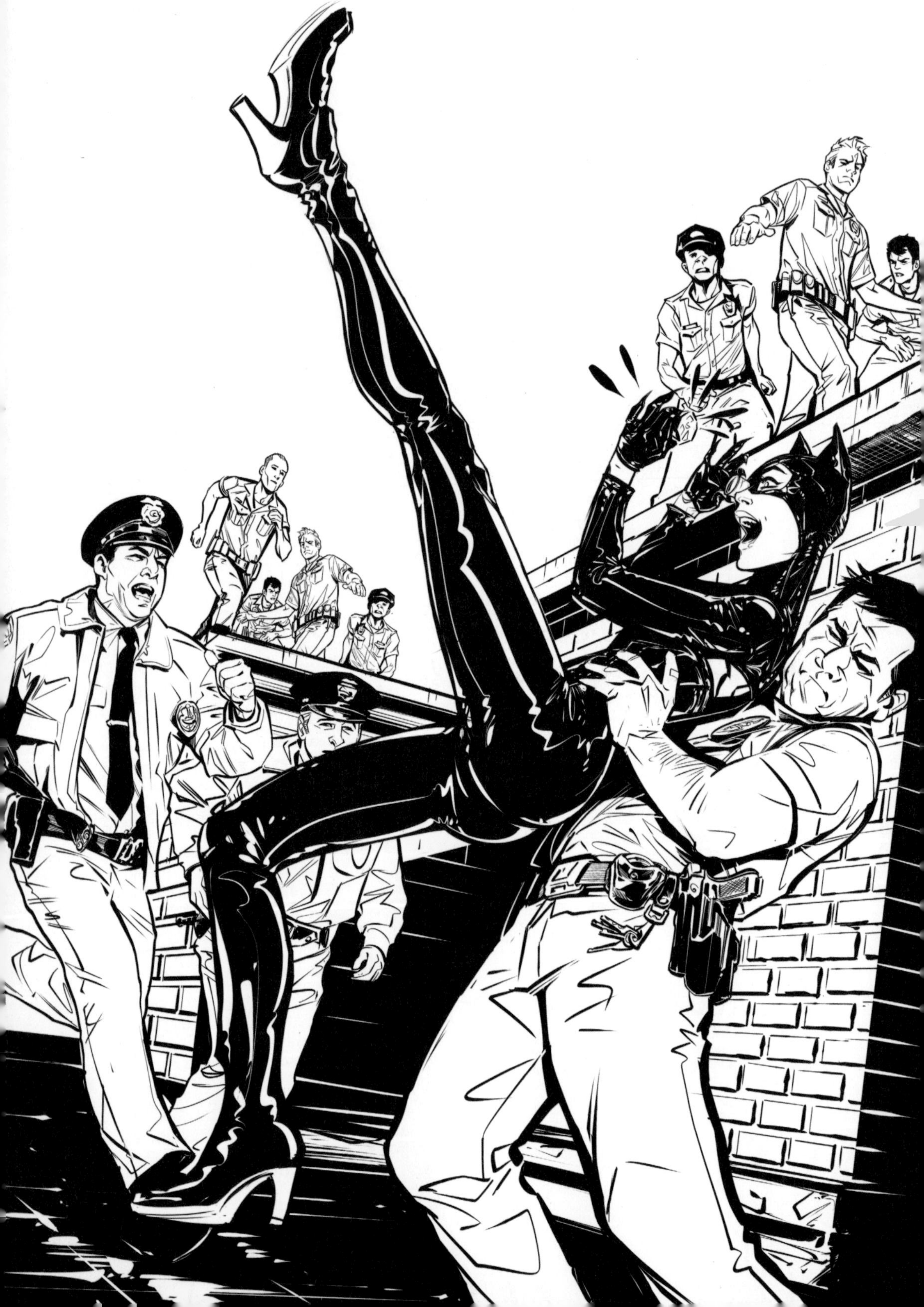

**CATWOMAN #11** cover line art by JOËLLE JONES

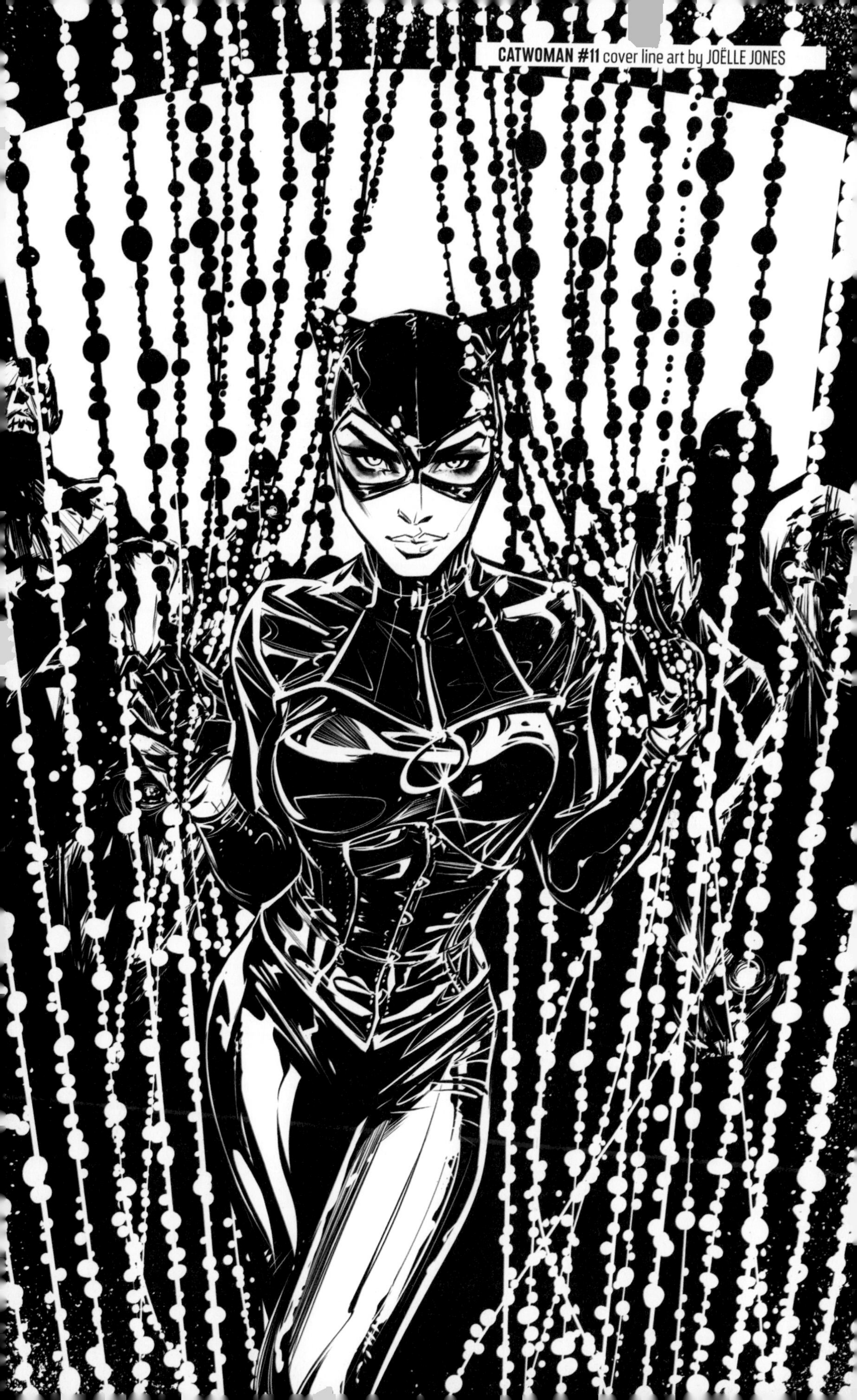